T0270645

THE
ELEPHANT
MOVES

THE ELEPHANT MOVES

*India's New Place
in the World*

AMITABH KANT

AMIT KAPOOR

PENGUIN
BUSINESS

An imprint of Penguin Random House

PENGUIN BUSINESS

USA | Canada | UK | Ireland | Australia
New Zealand | India | South Africa | China | Singapore

Penguin Business is part of the Penguin Random House group of companies
whose addresses can be found at global.penguinrandomhouse.com

Published by Penguin Random House India Pvt. Ltd
4th Floor, Capital Tower 1, MG Road,
Gurugram 122 002, Haryana, India

First published in Penguin Business by Penguin Random House India 2024

Copyright © Amitabh Kant and Amit Kapoor 2024

All rights reserved

10 9 8 7 6 5 4 3 2

The views and opinions expressed in this book are the authors' own and the facts are as
reported by them which have been verified to the extent possible, and the publishers are
not in any way liable for the same.

ISBN 9780670097449

Typeset in Adobe Garamond Pro by Manipal Technologies Limited, Manipal
Printed at Thomson Press India Ltd, New Delhi

This book is sold subject to the condition that it shall not, by way of trade
or otherwise, be lent, resold, hired out, or otherwise circulated without the
publisher's prior consent in any form of binding or cover other than that in
which it is published and without a similar condition including this condition
being imposed on the subsequent purchaser.

www.penguin.co.in

To the maestros of competitiveness,

Professor Michael E. Porter

&

Professor Christian H.M. Ketels

Contents

List of Figures

1

Of Elephants and Tigers

Development economics parlance has seen the usage of metaphors comparing economies with different animals, drawing parallels based on certain characteristic features. It was about three decades ago when China and India came to be pitted against one another while policymakers and soothsayers made forecasts about where each would land and how. The metaphors used—India being termed an elephant; China, the dragon; and East Asian economies, tigers—were visible across media. India was named so due to its supposed slow pace. It was, however, said that when the economy does move, it prompts the world to sit up and take notice, as would an elephant's move. This was also a time when the popular belief projected one development path to be the only gateway to all things prosperous. Looking back at the time only reinforces the idea that the future can seldom be predicted. The Indian economy has indeed witnessed robust growth over the years. The International Monetary Fund (IMF) forecasts suggest that growth in the Asia-Pacific region is set to increase from 3.9 per cent in 2022 to 4.6 per cent in the current year, in line with the projection made in April. This growth is primarily attributed to China's post-reopening recovery and the stronger-than-expected economic performance in Japan and India during the first half of the year.[1] However, certain fundamental drawbacks have held India back from attaining its maximum potential. In recent years, the focus has been narrowed down to taking comprehensive and concrete actions through major policy reforms, aimed at addressing these foundational issues. This resolve to act and work towards betterment has been a major factor in helping India overcome the pandemic and its aftereffects. It reinforced the fact that an economy that is strong within can stand tall in the face of unprecedented headwinds.

An Expedition through the Ages

Economics, as a discipline, has for the longest time garnered significant clout. Its practitioners, more so. The field has a reputation of coming across as rather esoteric, an indication of which is the subject frequently being called the 'physics of social sciences'. While the complexity of the discipline is true to a large extent, economics can essentially be boiled down to a set of primary questions. Throughout history, across time and continents with the ebbs and flows of empires and leaders, these questions can be seen to form the focal point of economic thought. They broadly deal with which goods and services should be produced in the country, how they should be produced and how they should be distributed among people. As simplistic as the questions may seem to be, the answers are multifaceted and different for different scenarios. What is to be emphasized in particular is that the degree of complexity only amplifies for a country that forms one-sixth of humanity and the most diverse population imaginable. India is *the* case in point. While every country has its own circumstances, India stands out given its sheer size, complexity and internal heterogeneity. This has made it hard to fit India into the traditional categories used to group countries by their stage of economic development or their growth model. Its unique characteristics have made the country a subject of extensive thought. Writers and historians have put pen to paper to voice out their understanding of a nation that is daunting, bemusing, impactful and incredible, all at once. Guha (2007) quotes a range of writers who offered forecasts on the Indian future—from it becoming an autocracy, being Balkanized or descending into anarchy.[2] There is a mention of India as an 'unnatural nation,' one that is home to states that can be seen as countries in all respects. When it made its tryst with destiny, it must have been an unlikely thought that the nation, fantastically coloured with a splash of cultures and geographies and largely backward in development, would go on to be the world's largest democracy.

Many countries in Asia and other parts of the world witnessed decolonization, the birth pangs of nations that fulfilled their destinies becoming nation states in the aftermath of World War II. The responsibility of choosing a path that will structurally change all realms—political, social and economic—and shape generations to come, was placed on the shoulders of multiple newborn nation states. To outline the socio-economic character of the economy at the time of independence is no less than a colossal task. Our nascent nation was predominantly agricultural and rural. Productivity in agriculture was low despite it being the economy's mainstay back then. Social parameters such as literacy, schooling and health were at low levels of development. Breathing the life of a newly independent nation, after nearly two centuries of British colonial rule in 1947, India had to now shape its being. From that significant crossroads, India has traversed remarkably over seventy-six years. With its centennial year approaching in the next two decades and half, there is immense gusto and fervour in the policy circles over what's the path ahead.

So, how does one look forward to chart out a roadmap for India? Understanding how India is unique and why it is shaped the way it is, is more than a theoretical exercise. It is a critical part of getting at the root causes of India's current level of competitiveness, and it is a key aspect that needs to be taken into account when designing policy actions to improve the country's competitiveness. This section gives a historical perspective of the Indian economy in different phases of time since India's independence, setting the backdrop for a better understanding of the country's achievements and challenges today. There is a strong need to go much beyond didactic policy prescriptions. To understand why India is where it is, its history is key, especially as we intend to diagnose India's competitiveness fundamentals and chart out a forward-looking roadmap. Where India should go in the future must stand on the bedrock of an understanding of its past. From an inward-looking economy that relied on import substitution, characterized by a massive inefficient state that largely controlled private enterprise, to India jumping six positions over the last decade and standing tall as the fifth-largest economy in the world in terms of size, India's story calls for telling and retelling from different vantage points.

Figure 1: Growth of the Indian GDP

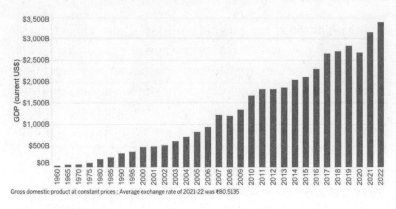

Gross domestic product at constant prices ; Average exchange rate of 2021-22 was ₹80.5135

Source: DBI—RBI

Does the graph above depict a triumphant rise of the Indian GDP from the 1960s till date? Prima facie, it does. While the story of Indian economic growth has undoubtedly been broadly one of accelerated growth and development, the graceful serpentine curve in the picture hides a million stories of economic reforms. Scholarly work on the subject of Indian economic reforms has divided the timeline as a pre-reform era before 1991 and a post-reform period that follows. However, the lines are not as distinct as they are made out to be. While such divisions help comprehend events and turns better, there needs to be a change in how we study our history. Reality hardly pans out in defined lines. Before we delve into an overview of India's economic journey so far, it is crucial to keep in mind that each reform was a product of its time.

The Planning Commences: The State and the Nehruvian Era

A crucial phase in the planning years of India coincides with the leadership of India's first prime minister Jawaharlal Nehru. This is where the oft-repeated term 'Nehruvian era' comes from whenever one reminisces or dissects the period post-independence up until the 1960s. This chunk of Indian economic history is associated with a few terms such as 'statism,' 'import substitution,' 'Soviet-inspired model,' among a range of others. However, it is planning that forms an umbrella word encompassing all the other adjectives utilized to assess this time period. From a colonial enclave, India had the vision of becoming an economy capable of sustained growth. This period is often criticized for its excessive reliance on the state and is labelled as the period where it all went wrong. However, to recall the note we began on, *reality does not pan out in defined lines.* A contextual reading is not to cushion criticism of certain time periods, but it is for the reader's holistic comprehension.

The 1950s was indeed a decisive decade. India had just embarked on the vision of a spectacular transformation. The point of transformation was one of immense gravity. It was the transition of a territory hitherto under an authoritarian colonial state, characterized by a traditional agrarian order, into an open democratic society functioning as a single economy. As Khilnani (2007) remarks, it was the 1950s when law was established as a basic tool for India's self-transformation.[3] He points to what he terms as an 'unusual interpretation' of the law as a tool of change rather than stability, the latter being the usual meaning derived. India focused on law not just for protecting and promoting rights but also for pursuing social goals. In tandem with law, it was this era that saw a strong will to create institutions, from the Atomic

Energy and Planning Commissions to the Election Commission. These new institutions breathed new life into India's public landscape. Such was the basis of the development path charted in the forthcoming decades.

Key Elements of India's Foremost Development Path: The Planning Years

The context in which the transformation of the nation was set out, from critical stagnation to planned economic growth, was ridden with challenges. In addition to the period witnessing the aftermath of World War II, the Partition throes, multiple famines and wars in the coming decades, and an oil crisis in the early 1970s and 1980s, India was building from the ground up an administrative and political apparatus in an unpredictable environment. These factors were critical in defining the nature and the impact of the development path chosen.

Why was planning the choice? History is replete with works pondering this question and investigating the reigning newly independent Indian mindset then. One of the recurrent themes discussed in this context is the primacy of a certain line of thought in those times. Newly decolonized countries had the reins of the nation in their control for the first time. Ambitions and hopes soaring high, the nation looked at the moment as a beginning of the end of its sorrows. Many of these countries considered redistribution of wealth and incomes as an important means to uplift backward and poor nations. To be able to do so was a mammoth task that called for systematic planning and guided execution.[4] This line of thought paved the way for powerful states assuming immense control of the socio-economic levers. Planning versus market was a debate that marked the 1930s and 1940s policy discourse across the world.[5] Those in favour of planning were essentially pointing to the inability of the market forces to deliver results that were the best for society in an efficient manner. Left to their own devices, the markets would not be up to the task to attain set societal goals. As opposed to this school of thought, the fraction that vouched for markets to take the charge shed light on the limitations of planning. The argument spoke to the limited extent to which planners could factor in the constantly evolving consumer needs and preferences and allocate resources accordingly and efficiently. The downside was clearly highlighted by the naysayers of planning—waste and inefficiency in comparison to a scenario where markets are given more of a free hand. [6] In the Indian context, there was a belief among the government and industry leadership that the socio-economic ills of society stemmed from laissez faire policies and market-driven functioning of the British Raj. They saw supporters of a free market attach great importance to self-interest and profiteering and little to building roads, power and much-needed infrastructure for the broader masses. The latter was seen as the desired goal of development. It is pertinent to call to mind the influence during that period of Keynesian economics. The Keynesian approach held government intervention crucial, especially to revive an ailing economy. It was a prevailing approach mainly in Western policymaking up until the 1970s. India's choice of taking the planning route can said to be influenced in some part by this framework, which was the contemporary stronghold.

A young graduate in India studying Indian economic history most definitely gets familiarized with the phrase 'Bombay plan.' It is often used as a keyword representing India's initial economic policy phase after independence. The plan is considered one of the watershed documents from the days of early independence and justifiably so. In ways known and unknown, the document went on to shape industrial development for decades to come.

Leading capitalists, such as the likes of J.R.D. Tata, Purshotamdas Thakurdas, Lala Sri Ram and G.D. Birla, came together to formulate a vision of what modern and industrialized independent India should look like. One of the reasons why these industry leaders showed willingness and desire for greater state control of affairs could be because they benefited from the British Raj's interventions, including greater tariffs on imported goods. The plan put forth a vision for a state-led mixed economy and for rapid and self-reliant industrialization, and it outlined goals such as tripling India's GDP in fifteen years, increasing per capita income and improving the overall standard of living.[7] The two-part document delineated the roadmap for India's development through three five-year plans and a pronounced emphasis on state investment in basic capital goods industries, such as iron and steel, cement, coal, chemicals and heavy engineering. A little-known fact is that the plan made some path-breaking proposals for the social sector as well.[8] The plan clearly outlined a crucial role for the state in the social sector, facilitating provision of education and healthcare. The plan stood out as against earlier plan proposals also because it was not entirely qualitative; it proposed figures. The Nehruvian idea of the state at the 'commanding heights of the economy' can be traced back to the pages of this document. In the history of a nation, there are a few documents that constitute major landmarks. In addition to understanding the economic thinking back in the day, it goes to show that what is considered a fact today may not have been so a few decades back. Industry doyens argued for greater state intervention because of the contemporary circumstances in the 1940s and 1950s as opposed to the notions we hold about the private and the public spheres today. The plan offers important lessons for contextual historical reading. Part 2 of the plan consisted of issues related to employment and distribution in India. The plan set ambitious targets to enhance the quality of living in the country. The authors of the plan also put out details on financing the plan. The idea of a mixed economy, wherein the state/public sector would invest and build the basic industries, given the large-scale requirements of the sector, and the private sector would oversee areas where investments deliver quick returns, stood out in the document. While the plan never saw the light of day in terms of official implementation, India's era of planning was hugely influenced by the 'mixed economy' notions set forth in the plan.

By 1950, India had embarked on efforts at planning for accelerated growth with the objective of social justice. The five-year plans delineated the nature and extent of these efforts as well as the objectives. From 1951–56, the first plan played out. The Indian economy grew, in real terms, at 3.5 to 4 per cent per annum on the average, from 1950–60. There was a decline during the third five-year plan to an average rate of growth of about 2.5 per cent.[9] The five-year plans, based on the Harrod-Domar economic growth model, involved extensive planning, resource allocation, implementation and appraisal. Largely, the first five-year plan in 1951 emphasized on agriculture and irrigation to enhance output in the sector, while the second plan in 1956 had rapid industrialization and a focus on heavy industries and capital goods as its mainstay.

Established in 1950, the Planning Commission has a major role to play in India's economic development story. The body put forth five-year plans that, even while lacking the force of law, held considerable clout given that the prime minister assumed the chairmanship of the commission, becoming the planner as well as the leader. P.C. Mahalanobis, a man often regarded as the architect of Indian planning, brought to the Planning Commission an intellectual drive composed of rational enquiry and scientific temper. He assumed a central position in policymaking in those times. The First and the Second Plan were based on his ideas. The first-five-year plan, from 1951 to 1956, designed by Professor Mahalanobis, adopted a two-sector investment goods/ consumption goods model of Soviet planning. Focusing heavily on investment goods, the plan gave way to huge investments in heavy industry, which led to modest returns. Owing to private sector investment in consumption goods, the demand generated by the former was absorbed by the latter. Private industry reaped quick returns and more efficiently so due to a slew of protective tariffs that secured their position from external competition. The first-year plan was largely considered a success. In the second and a more ambitious plan, Professor Mahalanobis drew up a four-sector model, retaining the focus on investments goods and heavy industry but dividing the other sector intro three arenas viz., industrial, agriculture and cottage industry and services, education, health, etc. Cottage industry was also given a level of importance, recognizing the labour-intensive nature of the arena. The sector was also considered as a crucial source of consumption goods by planners (Rothermund, 199). In real terms, Planning was initiated with the second five-year plan. The rapid industrialization that the plan aimed towards was in the context of a very limited export capacity and stagnant economy. Developing our own capital goods sector was considered a priority. Heavily influenced by the Soviet strategy of heavy-industry emphasis, P.C. Mahalanobis designed an inward-looking industrialization strategy for India's second five-year plan that was led by the development and expansion of the capital goods industries.[10] At the time, there did exist a crucial critique of the Mahalanobis heavy-industry-development strategy ascertained by Professors Vakil and Brahmanand of Bombay University. Their outlook was based on a wage-goods model of development, wherein wage-goods industries were accorded greater emphasis in the development strategy.[11] However,

Mahalanobis's ideas held greater sway at the time. Such was the influence of the heavy-industry focus and state-ownership that the Industrial Policy Resolution of 1956 reserved seventeen industries for the public sector, allowing private entry but with excessive state controls. This decision went on to determine the trajectory of the forthcoming decades. The growth in this period was hinged upon the establishment of large industrial and infrastructural projects. The intent underlying the planning process shone vividly in Nehru's words when dedicating the Bhakra-Nangal dam to the people of India—'This dam has been built with the unrelenting toil of man for the benefit of mankind and therefore is worthy of worship. May you call it a Temple or a Gurdwara or a Mosque, it inspires our admiration and reverence'.[12] Going forward to the third five-year plan (1961–66), investment was ramped up substantially, with a new added element of emphasis: transport and communications. The emphasis on heavy industry was a common thread throughout the foremost planning years. A strong hold on industry was seen as the very symbol of India's independence and its promising potential of uplifting its economy and people. The planning phase has been criticized for neglecting agriculture. Dantwala (1976) aptly pointed out that this criticism, more often than not, is associated with inadequate budgetary allocation in the plans for agriculture.[13] The author brought to attention the general appreciation that prevailed then about agriculture being given a 'pride of place' in India's first five-year plan (1951–56). The share of agriculture and community development in the Public Sector Outlay in the first five-year plan stood at 15.1 per cent, while that for industries and minerals was 6.3 per cent. The second five-year plan allocated 14.4 per cent to industries and 11.8 per cent to agriculture.[14] The discussion on India and its planning era right after independence brings forth debates on whether the path chosen was right or whether there could have been a better one. Was the emphasis on heavy industry extensive beyond reason and at the expense of other important factors, or was it the right path? The questions are endless. The continuation of debate is a healthy marker as it only enriches our thought for the path to be carved out ahead of us.

In the decade spanning 1960–70, India clocked in an economic growth rate averaged around 3.5 per cent per annum.[15] Multiple writers and historians state that the 1960s are considered a strenuous period of time for India. American academic John P. Lewis termed the 1960s' circumstances a 'quiet crisis.'[16] There had been an almost flattening of agricultural production trends since 1960, with a brief interregnum of respite in 1964, followed by two droughts in the decade. Additionally, expenditure on defence had spiked substantially in the context of the Indo-Sinese war. Growth in exports had also come to a slowdown. The situation led to a greater reliance on western aid, followed by a massive import of food and a drastic devaluation of the rupee from Rs 4.76 to Rs 7.5 to a dollar in 1966.[17] Food inflation raised its unpropitious head, leading to further exacerbation of circumstances. While the 1960s saw multiple crises, it was the arena of food production and consumption, which took a major hit and affected each and every household. In this regard, it is apt and revealing of the times to quote author Mihir Bose from a piece for *India Today* in 2007. Bose writes on the changed eating habits of the Indians in the 1960s.

> Parliament in the 1960s spent much time debating over famine-stalked parts of the land. At our dining tables we were told that we should eat less rice and have more wheat: so cut out the plate of rice for dinner, have chapattis instead. In West Bengal, the Congress chief minister tried to engineer a more radical change in food habits. Following a tremendous

milk shortage, he had the brilliant idea of telling his fellow
Bengalis that they should cut down on sweets, most of which
were made from milk. The Bengalis were outraged and it made
many middle-class Bengalis distrust the Congress and turn to
the communists. Whatever else Marx may advocate, he would
never target the beloved Bengali rosogolla.*

In a decade where the country faced severe droughts and consequent
food shortages, overhauling agriculture became the need of the
hour. What is famously known as the green revolution can be
traced back to this time. The green revolution is considered to be
synonymous with mechanization, greater usage of fertilizers, high-
yield varieties of seeds, irrigation—an all-in-all modernization
of agricultural practices and systems. The aim was to increase
agricultural output to attain self-sufficiency and overcome severe
food shortages on the basis of new technologies, knowledge and
expansion of credit to farmers for increasing their capacity to
adapt to the newly introduced methods. The green revolution
today either gets immense appreciation and applause for bringing
the country to a secure position in terms of food self-sufficiency or
it gets criticized for adverse and unintentional consequences. This
time period calls for a contextual reading. It is crucial to bring
to mind that the era was one of war experiences: the Cold War,
and newly born states emerging from devastating conflicts and
multiple famines. In this context, being able to provide for one's
people was of the essence for a nation. India was well aware of the
fact that political and domestic stability is tied to food stability.
India's shift from a community-development-measures approach
to a technology-driven approach for revolutionizing agriculture

* https://www.indiatoday.in/magazine/india-today-archives/story/
20070702-indian-decade-of-dos-and-donts-1960s-748418-1999-11-29

was indeed a paradigm shift, marking an important time in 1960s' India, which came to shape our future in a major way.

While there is a wide consensus on the Indian economy seeing near stagnation in real GDP growth till the late 1970s, some studies offer a different view. If each decade after independence is studied, one can see the GDP growth increasing decade on decade, with the exception of the 1970s.[18] One of the major follies of this period is its neglect of education or general investment in human capital. From a bird's eye view, over a period through the 1950s, the 1960s and the 1970s, the economy had increasingly become more controlled. Private entrepreneurship and export performance were constrained. The development strategy based on the cornerstones of heavy-industry investment and import substitution held greater relevance in the 1950s and the 1960s. However, times had substantially evolved and the need for reforms was felt across the board.

The Maruti: Driving Early Winds of Change

In the early 1980s, India's first indigenous, efficient and affordable 'people's car,' the Maruti 800, was launched. When Harpal Singh, an Indian Airlines employee, was handed the keys to India's first Maruti 800 car, little did he know that he stood at the point of the onset of a new age of reforms, a full decade prior to the 1991 watershed. This was the initial stirring up of middle-class aspirations, and symbolic of the reforms that tip-toed in, in the 1980s. It is recognized that growth in the 1980s was relatively higher than in the preceding decades. However, it was rather fragile exhibiting significant variance. The decade registers a high growth rate particularly because of the 7.6 per cent rate clocked in the 1988 to 1991 period. Being initiated, the 1980s' liberalization reforms were implemented tacitly, getting them associated with the phrase 'reforms by stealth.'[19] Almost all industrial areas were touched by the reforms in this period. They form a significant move as they lay the foundation for the 1991 reforms. Industrial growth increased to 9.2 per cent during the high growth period of 1988–91. The import penetration ratio in the capital goods sector saw a jump from 11 per cent in 1976–77 to 18 per cent in 1985–86. Another notable trend highlighting growth in the 1980s was an increase in the productivity of investment, especially in private manufacturing. However, growth during this time was also driven by fiscal expansion funded through external borrowing, constituting one of the major reasons underlying the crisis of 1991. [20] In addition to these major trends, it is crucial to state that the 1980s were also a time when India saw consumerism sprout and consumerist aspirations began to grow. The symbols of this shone through in the form of the people's car Maruti 800 and the television. Interestingly, ownership of TVs expanded to a great degree in the decade. Of the numerous standard accounts chronicling and explaining India's growth in the 1980s, Subramaniam & Rodrik (2004) stand out.[21] They emphasize that India's growth transition kickstarted in the early 1980s, as opposed to popular accounts that trace it to the crisis of 1991. This growth can be associated with what they call an attitudinal shift in the government towards private business. This period witnessed the removal of licensing of twenty-five categories of industries, extending delicensing to large companies in twenty-two industries previously restricted by the Monopolies and Trade Restrictive Practices Act (MRTP) and Foreign Exchange Regulation Act (FERA), allowing companies that had reached 80 per cent capacity utilization to expand their capacity up to 133 per cent of that reached in any of the previous years. [22] To facilitate a better understanding of this period, the authors distinguish between a pro-market and a pro-business orientation. While a pro-market approach emphasizes removal of barriers to markets and benefiting entrants, a pro-business approach focuses on easing the functioning of existing industries and businesses. What played out in terms of liberalization in India in the 1980s was closer to a pro-business outlook. The reforms in the 1990s were of a more systematic and systemic nature. The narrative in the next section puts forth the idea that liberalization was not a first-time one-strike event of 1991. The groundwork had been laid in the earlier decades through various means. While the 1980s were a much better decade in terms of economic performance than the preceding ones, the structure and policies were inadequate to address challenges of the day and sustain accelerated growth.

Towards a New India—The 1991 Reforms

The year 1991 is etched in Indian history and is regarded as the beginning of a new India. The 1980s' reforms did lay the groundwork for 1991; however, the latter reforms were more sweeping and deeper. Panagariya (2004) points out the fundamental change in approach. [23] The norm shifted: from restrictions being the norm until 1991 to their absence assuming the position. Prior to 1991, regulations were the norm, and changes involved the selective removal of these regulations through a 'positive list' approach. However, with the introduction of the July 1991 package, the standard shifted, making the absence of restrictions the norm, and regulations were retained based on a 'negative list' approach. Contrary to popular perception, India did not open up all at once in 1991. The shift was gradual; as highlighted previously, it went back to certain reforms ushered in in the 1980s. However, the paradigm shift in philosophy took root in 1991.

In the late 1980s, fiscal deficit climbed to dangerous levels, threatening economic stability. The current account deficit rose to a point where it peaked at 3.2 per cent of GDP in 1991. With high levels of commercial borrowing in the years preceding 1991 since 1985, India found itself in a precarious situation when the Gulf crisis triggered a rise in oil prices. Additionally, India's foreign-exchange reserves had dried up to a low of $2.2 billion, with less than fifteen days' cover against annual imports. The nation found itself on the brink of defaulting.[24] While this balance of payment crisis triggered a systematic shift in India's economic orientation, the need for a policy shift was evidently felt by multiple scholars and policymakers. Additionally, around that time, many countries in east Asia had exhibited remarkable growth and poverty reduction on the back of policies that were export oriented and encouraging for the private sector. In 1991, the then Prime Minister Narasimha Rao said that the government intended to 'sweep the cobwebs of the past and usher in change'.[25]

Initiated with the rupee devaluation, the 1991 reforms encompassed a range of measures, including a removal of import licensing on all intermediate inputs and capital goods. There has been a substantial liberalization of trade in services as well. Key sectors such as insurance, banking and telecommunications had been in the ambit of the public sector previously. The reforms flung open the doors to participation from the private sector and foreign investors. Along with other sectors, the industrial sector underwent some major policy changes including the elimination of entry barriers, liberalization of the foreign investment policy and the import policy with regard to intermediate and capital goods, reduction in the items falling under industrial licensing, reduction in the number of industries reserved for the public sector and a range of measures to promote foreign investment, etc. Power, road and airways—all saw manifold reforms being brought in.

A major policy shift was ushered in the area of the exchange rate in 1993 when India moved from a dual exchange-rate regime to a single, market-determined exchange-rate system. The switch to the new system implied the absence of an officially fixed exchange rate. Instead, the new system let demand and supply conditions in the foreign exchange market determine the exchange rate. Additionally, efforts were undertaken to move towards a simpler and rationalized tax structure. Both direct and indirect taxes were rationalized, and efforts were taken to create a wider base as well as make enforcement better. Corporate income tax rate and tax on foreign companies saw a significant reduction. Similarly, import duties were also brought down substantially.[26]

It is commonplace to discuss the liberalization reforms in India earmarking 1991. In the vein of this chapter's emphasis on reforms' gradualism in phasing out, it is to be noted that there was a second phase wherein economic reforms witnessed a substantial expansion from 1998 to 2004. Various sectors in the industrial arena and a slew of import items were delicensed. Trade between SAARC countries and India was facilitated through different measures including removal of quantitative restrictions on imports. India also entered into a Free Trade Agreement (FTA) with Sri Lanka in 1998, thus marking a major point in India's trade history. To boost the knowledge economy, measures such as lowering custom duties in multiple IT and telecom items were brought in. India's transport ecosystem strengthened with the development of highways connecting major cities such as Delhi, Mumbai, Chennai and Kolkata. In continuation with tax reforms initiated earlier, service tax coverage was further expanded and custom duties were rationalized, among a range of other reforms.[27]

In the post-reform period, acceleration of growth was a hugely encouraging trend. There was a significant jump in GDP growth, with the real GDP growth averaging 5.7 per cent per annum in the 1990s to 7.3 per cent per annum in the 2000s.[28] One notable characteristic of this period was the increase in the growth rate of industry and services and a simultaneous decrease in that of agriculture. Studies associate this with an absence of a technological push in the agricultural sector after the 'green revolution.' The average growth rate registered from 1992 to 2002 was 6.0 per cent, making India one of the fastest growing developing countries in the 1990s. Ahluwalia (2002) suggests that growth in the 1990s was strong despite the East-Asian crisis. Moreover, poverty also declined significantly in the post-reform period.[29]

There are studies galore on the impact of the 1991 reforms. The aftereffects of the reforms varied for different parameters. In addition to a higher rate of growth, the secondary and tertiary sectors registered greater growth; there was a sustained increase in exports and imports and an improvement in the Balance of Payments (BoP), an inflow of foreign capital and foreign exchange reserves, a more expansive range of options for consumers available at affordable prices, among other effects. There was also a rise in the value of the rupee and lower dependence on foreign borrowing. Over the years, the 1991 reforms have been analysed thoroughly and from multiple vantage points. Studies point out the adverse impact of the reforms that led to a lacklustre impact in terms of employment generation, rural development, expansion of public services, etc.

Broadly, one can remark with a level of certainty that they did rectify key barriers that had inhibited the Indian economy in the preceding decades. There is a considerable downward trend in poverty. Without a doubt, the 1991 reforms are a paradigm shift. However, they did fall short in bringing the same degree of shift in terms of the profile of India's economy. There could have been a greater alignment with India's inherent advantages in labour-intensive activities and less of its unintended consequences in terms of exacerbated inequality and environmental degradation. The reforms brought down the regulatory burden on companies to a large extent and opened doors to the global economy. Both factors drove overall growth. Two crucial features of the reforms stand out distinctly. Firstly, market reforms were aimed at the removal of barriers in product and service markets and less on factor markets (labour, land, capital). Secondly, there was less of a focus on investing in factor input conditions. Once markets are opened up, those that are capable of competing can benefit and enhance their growth and productivity from the newly available incentives. But if there are insufficient investments in making factor inputs ready for competing in the modern economy, they will not be able to make the most of the reforms.

Post-Reform India

Often when a sweeping transformation occurs, the implications of it are felt by individuals only in hindsight. When the shift is in play, the enormity of the situation rarely occurs to an individual. The same is the case with the liberalization reforms. The gradualism undertaken by India in rolling out the reforms is one reason why it took time for the gravity of the reforms to dawn on the people of the nation. The shift was most evident through certain goods, which now feature in day-to-day conversations, drawing comparisons between an earlier India and the India of today. From Goldspot to Coca-Cola, Doordarshan to cable TV, Maruti to an array of automobiles to pick from, the Indian palate began to see a variety of choices hitherto unseen that evoked a desire for taste. With the number of 'super rich' having risen from 98,000 in 1994 to 1.8 million in 2020–21 and with the share of the middle class in the total population growing from 15 per cent two decades ago to 31 per cent in 2020–21, as per People Research on India's Consumer Economy (PRICE)'s report 'The Rise of India's Middle Class,' people started harbouring the means to acquire the options that flooded their gradually changing markets.

Figure 2: GDP Growth at Market Prices

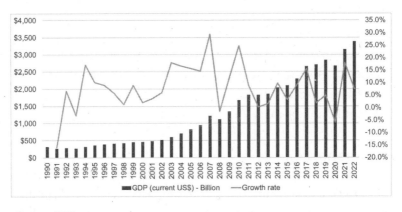

Source: RBI

As is evident from the graph above, GDP at market prices has steadily increased since 1991. This is not to suggest an absence of slumps or variations. The aftermath of the reforms has seen positive as well negative ramifications. As compared to the decades prior to reforms, gross domestic saving as a percentage of GDP exceeded the 22 per cent mark in all the post-reform years. Additionally, the gross domestic investment as a percentage of GDP also climbed to 26 per cent. While inflation was relatively on the higher side, hovering around 8.9 per cent during the 1990s, the late 1990s saw it remain subdued. An encouraging trend in these times was the almost halving of external debt to GDP ratio from 1991 to 1999.

A greater control on the Current Account Deficit (CAD) front can be observed with it remaining below 2 per cent of the GDP in this decade.[30] However, an economic crisis was looming right in our neighbourhood. This decade ended with an unstable East Asia. A balance of payment and exchange rate crisis that started in 1997 in Thailand spread to countries including Malaysia, Indonesia and South Korea. Some impact of the crisis was felt in India as our foreign exchange reserves dwindled to some extent in 1998. However, as Gupta (2000) notes, the foreign exchange reserves did make a comeback in the same year.[31] The increase on this front could be attributed to a recovery in exports, particularly because of an increase in the sale of software. The import bill saw a reduction owing to a fall in the price of crude oil back then. Moreover, inflows from non-resident Indians (NRIs) also saw a spike. This was an event where liberalized India saw, for the first time, the shockwaves of a major external economic crisis. The Asian crisis was the first major externally originating crisis that impacted India, even if we stood far more resilient than other Asian countries.

The early 2000s, once again, came with their own set of jolts. The dot-com collapse and two subsequent droughts marked the early years in the turn of the century as the average GDP growth slowed to 5.7 per cent in the period between 1997 and 2003. However, the years that followed were springtime for the Indian economy. Studies have regarded this period as a dream run as well. India grew at a 9 per cent average annual growth rate between 2003 and 2004 and 2007 and 2008, emerging as one of the world's highest in this period. The era post 2000 also saw a significant rise in exports.

Figure 3: Indian Export Growth

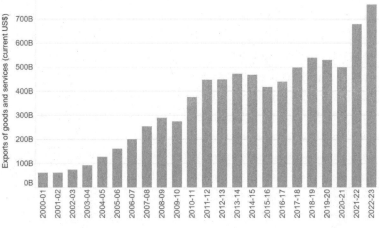

Source: DGCIS

Economists argue over the drivers of the dream run. It is said that it was driven by private borrowing and investment, funded through domestic savings. This was considered unlike the conventional consumption-led economic ebbs and flows. By 2008, the gap in investment and savings was at 2.3 per cent of GDP as compared to below 1 per cent in five years preceding the boom. Additionally, there was also a remarkable increase in private capital inflows.[32] The dream run was not just restricted to India. It was bumped up, in fact, by strong global tailwinds of growth. The world witnessed magic as GDP growth unravelled with low inflation and low interest rates. There is a consensus among policymakers on the euphoria felt during this period about the economic prospects of the world at large. However, when everything seems hunky-dory, it is good to have extra caution on your side.

The 2008 crisis hit the world like a tonne of falling bricks. As the Lehman Brothers collapsed in September 2008, major financial institutions started suffering major losses. As financial markets stopped in their tracks and growing uncertainties were cast on balance sheets, a domino effect engulfed various segments of markets and economic activity. By this time, subsequent waves of globalization had ensured significant integration of economies across the north and the south. Given this level of integration, the contagion spread from advanced economies to emerging markets. Despite Indian banks' limited exposure to subprime assets, the crisis dealt a blow to the economy.

Figure 4: GDP Growth, India and the World

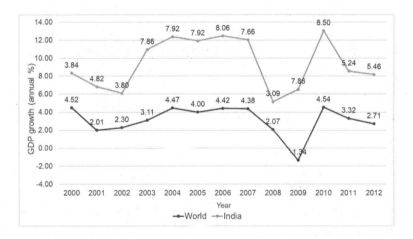

Source: World Bank

The trends above are that of GDP growth (annual per cent) from the World Bank database, mapped for India and the world. The slump in 2009 during the global recession is evident. It led to a drop from 7.66 per cent to 3.09 per cent GDP growth for India and from 2.07 per cent to −1.34 per cent for the world. India experienced large capital outflows and a sharp drop in domestic stock markets as Foreign Institutional Investors (FIIs) fled and a major depreciation of the rupee against the US dollar. The crisis highlighted vulnerabilities posed in the face of an increasingly globalized world. It is only timely and significant that discussions on the 'resilience' of economies have grown in depth and importance. The globalized IT hub of the nation, Bengaluru, Karnataka, registered a sharp drop in growth during the crisis. Similarly, Andhra Pradesh, Maharashtra, Gujarat and Tamil Nadu were some states that witnessed a decline in growth as an effect of the crisis. In the Indian context, the years after 2010–2011 were unfortunately a period that came to be regarded as one of 'policy paralysis.' It was hard to fathom a period of this nature especially after India had experienced the boom of 2003–2008. The policy paralysis stemmed from a variety of reasons. The time was marked by colossal corruption scandals, a fragmented public–private relationship, divided government leadership at the helm and multiple challenges in capital-intensive projects.

Throughout these ebbs and flows, the Indian economy broadly registered positive growth on the macro aggregates. It is well understood that macro aggregates speak of the realities of the nation of a people only to a limited extent. However, they are necessary to gauge the growth of a country at a broader level. As is distinctly clear in the graph below, the Gross Value Added (GVA) in services has leapt to greater heights in the post-reform period, engulfing a larger share of the total GVA pie. While the numbers remain relatively flattened in the agriculture arena, manufacturing does show growth. There is, however, a greater need to push manufacturing further. A point to be taken note of is that the trend growth in per capita income in the two decades after the 1991 reforms leapfrogged doubly as compared to the preceding four decades. However, the gap between the rich and the poor has widened substantially, exacerbating existing inequalities and creating new ones. While India's dwindling absolute poverty figures are indeed a positive sign, there are serious concerns to be pondered and worked on, given the rising inequality.

Figure 5: Sectoral Gross Value Added (GVA) for India

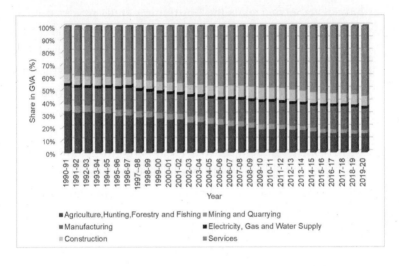

Source: KLEMS Database

A Shift in Perspective and Policy Reform Since 2014

Assessing economic reforms cannot be an exercise removed from political influences around them. Generally, economists and policymakers use the 2014 peg in terms of a political shift. The year 2014 is undoubtedly a milestone; however, it is not just one because of the political regime change. It can be seen as a drastic change in policy and governance approach. The year 2014 marked a transformative period in the landscape of policy development and implementation, ushering in a significant paradigm shift.

Our approach to policy-making underwent a comprehensive reevaluation, setting the stage for a monumental transformation that has reshaped the fabric of India over the past decade. The India of today stands as a testament to the profound impact of this shift, presenting a stark contrast to the nation of a decade ago. Across various socio-economic parameters, the country now exhibits robust performance, showcasing resilience and adaptability. The effects of these policy changes have not only been felt domestically but have reverberated globally, positioning India as a nation of increasing influence on the world stage.

The political mandate delivered by the masses led to the ruling dispensation's thumping majority win. The government in 2014 took over the reins of an economy and society that had immense aspirations. It was a massive responsibility to be able to deliver on the faith instilled by the people of the nation and not just push reforms but implement them in a guided and steady manner. According to World Bank estimates, the economy was showing signs of recovery since 2013. Economic activity started to stabilize in 2017 after a short-term fragility over 2016 to 2018. One of the key sweeping reforms of this time is the Goods and Services Tax (GST). Coming into effect in 2017, it has included 1.3 million taxpayers into a unified indirect taxation system. While there is a debate on whether 2014 can be considered a watershed in terms of change in policy approach, what is extremely hard to deny is that reforms since 2014 have been undergirded by a new set of principles. The aim of creating public goods, trust-based governance, greater collaboration with the private sector for accelerating development efforts, enhancing agricultural productivity, and considering social and economic progress as two sides of the same coin are what constitute the key set of principles underlying the wide-sweeping structural and governance reforms initiated in the last eight years (Economic Survey, 2022–23).

Strengthening physical infrastructure has been a crucial paradigm of the range of reforms initiated. Improving road connectivity, electrification and railways and operationalizing new airports have been some major activities that the economy has been witnessing. Programmes such as Bharatmala and Sagarmala have spearheaded a huge push towards infrastructure betterment. According to the Economic Survey 2022, there has been a significant increase in the construction of national highways and roads, with 10,457 km of roads constructed in FY22 as compared to 6061 km in FY16. In terms of enhancing electricity connectivity, the total installed power capacity of utilities and captive power plants has increased by 4.7 per cent between 2021 and 2022. A huge portion of this increase in electricity generation between FY21 and FY22 came from renewable energy resources for utilities and for captive plants. India has targeted 50 per cent installed capacity for electric power to be generated from non-fossil fuel-based energy resources by 2030. India is undertaking concerted efforts towards the attainment of this goal.[33] Additionally, the National Infrastructure Pipeline (NIP) is contributing immensely to create a robust baseline for infrastructure development. As of January 2023, the NIP has about 8964 projects with a total investment of over Rs 108 lakh crore.[34] India's capital expenditure by the central government as a per cent of GDP has seen a significant rise from 2014 to 2023.

Figure 6: Capital Expenditure by Central Government as a Percentage of GDP

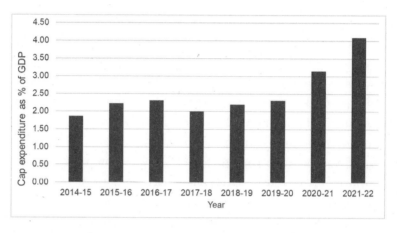

Source: RBI and MoSPI

As per Economic Survey 2022–23, between 2014 and 2019, India's core digital economy has grown at 2.4 times the overall economic growth. Digitalization holds the potential to support and act as a catalyst for achieving all the seventeen sustainable development goals, including reduction of maternal and infant mortality, promoting sustainable agriculture and decent work, attaining universal literacy, expanding quality healthcare and enhancing access to basic amenities, among others. Advancements in digital sectors have promising positive spillovers in non-digital sectors, accelerating transformation in multiple arenas. India's digital revolution stands on robust pillars: digital identity Aadhar, linking bank accounts with Pradhan Mantri Jan Dhan Yojana and the penetration of mobile phones (JAM Trinity). Financial inclusion had been a major problem for many years. However, a substantial improvement in financial inclusion was seen in the country, owing to greater digitalization. The overall population with bank accounts increased from 53 per cent in 2015–2016 to 78 per cent in 2019–2021. In addition to the aforementioned initiatives, digital verification (e-KYC), digital signature, digital repositories (DigiLocker) and digital payments (UPI) have expanded the breadth of the digital world in India. The total number of digital payment transactions has risen from 2071 crore transactions in FY 2017–18 to 8840 crore transactions in FY 2021–22.[35] In 2022, the value of instant digital transactions in India stood more than that in the United States, Britain, Germany and France. The Pradhan Mantri Jan Dhan Yojana has led to the opening of over 46 crore bank accounts. Its coverage has expanded to 67 per cent rural or semi-urban areas as well as 56 per cent of Jan Dhan accounts held by women. The policy emphasis has shifted from 'every household' to 'every adult.'

Figure 7: Percentage of Women Having a Bank or Savings Account, Owning a House and/or Land

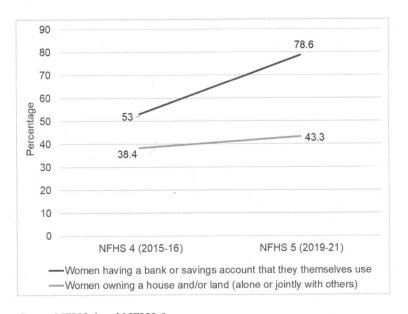

One of the main areas of improvement for digitalization in India is its formalization. India has struggled with strategies to formalize an expansive informal economy. Various reforms have been tried and tested to attain this goal. However, none had the impact that was desired. In recent years, digital identities such as Aadhar, registration of unorganized workers on various portals such as e-Shram, SVANidhi and registration of MSMEs on the Udyam portal have contributed to including workers and organizations in the formal economy umbrella. As the Economic Survey 2022-23 states, it is now possible to oversee about 1.27 crore enterprises registered on the Udyam Portal, over 93,000 micro-enterprises that have grown to small enterprises and 10,000 small enterprises that have transformed to medium enterprises in the last two years.

Yet another notable trend in this period has been an increased emphasis on social action through widespread reform targeting poverty alleviation. The shift of focus from subsidies on prices of goods and services to provision of direct financial transfers to households is a reflection of the shift in thought. Governance is being perceived from the ground up. States and districts are now the focal point of development as they are recognized as essential building blocks of the nation. The 100 Smart Cities Mission facilitated competitive co-financing for urban development and the Aspirational Districts initiative launched in 2018 to buttress growth in some of India's most challenged districts are essential cases in point to grasp the breadth of the reforms initiated. The Government of India attempted to go to the very roots of long-standing issues prevalent in the system, such as low school-enrolment rates among girls, poor sanitation facilities and lack of financial literacy, etc. It is important to understand that social issues can be dealt with comprehensively only when addressed from the ground-up. We see this thinking reflected in reforms such as the Swachh Bharat Abhiyan. Every household, across the length and breadth of the nation, became familiar with the programme's call to action. The mission focused on behaviour change among masses. This led to a transformational change in the way the habit of washing hands with soap and using toilets was instilled. Additionally, the installation of water taps and functional toilets were prerequisites that the mission brought about. Health and education form the building blocks of society. There has been a positive trend in reforms recognizing the importance of the two interconnected aspects. The Samagra Shiksha scheme has focused on establishing smart classrooms, ICT labs in schools and e-content for teaching, along with the required educational software. The pandemic made us realize the importance of e-learning. Digitalized education has the potential to encompass a wider base of learners, in terms of different learning capacities and accommodating learners coming from different backgrounds. Harnessing this potential has been a focus area in recent years. There has been an improvement in Gross Enrolment Ratios (GER) in the secondary level of education in schools, with the GER increasing from 73.8 to 79.6 from 2013 to 2022. The pupil–teacher ratio has also improved at all levels from 2013 to 2022, from 34.0 to 26.2 at primary level and 30.0 to 17.6 at the secondary level and 39.0 to 27.1 at the higher secondary level[36] (PIB, 2023). As seen in the graph below, the drop-out rate of girls has reduced at an all-India level, from 2014 to 2022. To push modern infrastructure in schools and provide world-class education to our students, the government launched the PM Schools for Rising India (PM SHRI) in 2022. Equipped with modern infrastructure, these schools are to implement the NEP and be showcased as schools par excellence. The scheme aims to establish over 4500 PM SHRI Schools from 2023 to 2027.

Figure 8: Girls' Drop-Out Rate

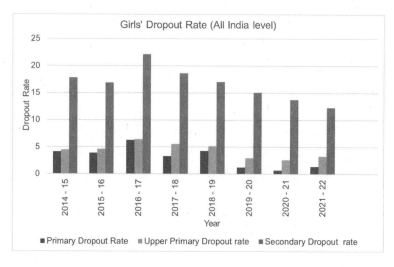

Source: UDISE +

The dawn of 2020 brought with it an unprecedented crisis so widespread that not a single region of the world escaped unscathed. The COVID-19 pandemic hit the Indian economy in ways much more than statistical trends can capture. There was a pre-pandemic slowdown in the economy from 2017–18, leading to the lowest growth in 2019–20 since the global financial crisis (GFC). This was further exacerbated due to COVID-19 induced tremors in the socioeconomic sphere. India witnessed one of the steepest contractions in GDP in the first quarter of 2020–21. Despite this fact and the prolonged nature of the crisis, 2022 saw estimates that indicated that the economy surpassed its pre-COVID level in 2021–22, owing mainly to extensive and robust policy support from monetary and fiscal authorities.[37] We demonstrated to the world our unique strength in creating opportunities in every crisis. India ramped up its pharmaceutical endeavours and health infrastructure during the pandemic. Embarking on a unique initiative—Vaccine Maitri—India exported over 235 million supplies of COVID-19 vaccines to 98 countries of the world. In addition to ramping up our physical health infrastructure, India successfully rolled out a digital platform, the Co-WIN platform, for health management during the pandemic. Aadhar played a crucial role in making the utilization of Co-WIN successful. Yet another milestone reached was in surpassing the $400-billion mark in exports of merchandise goods. With all the positive developments the nation has witnessed even in the aftermath of an unprecedented pandemic, India has emerged more confident about its capabilities to attain greater heights.

Figure 9: Middle Income and Beyond

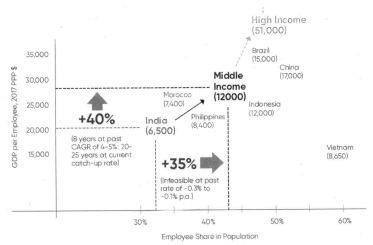

Source: Competitiveness Roadmap for India @100*

---

* Data from World Bank

Currently, we are a lower middle-income country with prosperity levels at around $2200 ($7200 at purchasing power parity). We have had an interesting journey, marked with significant gains and challenges over the years. The country aims to attain upper middle-income status, moving eventually to being a high-income nation. Measured at PPP terms, becoming an upper middle-income nation would mean 80 per cent high prosperity as compared to the current levels. As a high-income nation, we would be a $60 trillion economy and twenty times the size of today.

In the next twenty-five years of 'Amrit Kaal' or a 'golden period,' India has set this goal for itself. IMF forecasts India to grow at 6.3 per cent in 2024. In the World Economic Outlook, IMF projects a pronounced growth slowdown particularly among advanced economies, from 2.6 per cent in 2022 to 1.4 per cent in 2024. Considering this outlook, India is indeed showing promising potential to deliver even in a rocky global terrain. While the reforms explored here speak volumes about the changes brought about in the last decade, India continues to face major challenges. It is hard to encapsulate decades of economic reforms of a behemoth of a nation. We move forth to first explore what are the external challenges that a dynamic global landscape brings along, what drives growth in nations, competitiveness fundamentals and India's performance in terms of the same. Further, the discussion moves closer to pondering and building future pathways and a renewed approach to strategizing.

2

Sailing Ahead: Keeping Abreast with the Global Winds

If there were ever a period of rapid global changes, it would be now. The world and the global economy are going through extraordinary circumstances and a constantly evolving external context. Ongoing geopolitical conflicts are leading to adverse effects on global supply chains, soaring energy costs and food shortages in developed and developing countries alike. It also acts as a hindrance to an already gradual and uneven recovery from the COVID-19 pandemic. The IMF projected that global growth will fall from 3.5 per cent in 2022 to 3 per cent in 2023 and 2.9 per cent in 2024.[1] Additionally, climate change and the threat of ecological collapse have brought about the need for urgent action and global coordination. The number of climate-related disasters has been on the rise. In order to maintain the habitability of our planet, experts anticipate that the increase in global temperature should be limited to 1.5 degrees Celsius above pre-industrial levels. Unfortunately, the situation is critical, and the planet has already warmed by 1.1 degrees Celsius. On the other hand, a digital wave is sweeping across the world and also radically transforming lives in different ways. Digitalization has made massive changes to global value chains, enabled new products and services, and boosted innovative business models. It has created a demand for skilled labour and digital infrastructure. Be it the adverse effects of climate change and geopolitical conflicts, or the impact of digitalization on the world—these are potent factors shaping our ever-evolving external circumstances.

In this evolving context, the growing role of developing and emerging economies, especially those in Asia, in driving global growth is undeniable. These changing dynamics reflect in certain key trends. For instance, the demand side is undergoing a restructuring with a market growth shift from North America and Europe to Asia. The Asian Development Bank posits that if Asia continues on its current trajectory, its share of the global GDP can double to 52 per cent by 2050, allowing it to regain the previous dominant economic position it held some 300 years ago, before the Industrial Revolution.* Within Asia, India's performance and prospects call for greater attention. Despite the bleak predictions of an economic slowdown globally, the IMF and the World Bank have identified India as a 'bright spot' in the global economy that is better positioned to tackle the global headwinds than other emerging markets, owing to the country's robust macroeconomic fundamentals, healthy domestic demand and relative insulation from international trade flows.[2] The World Bank finds that a 1 per cent point decline in the United States' growth rate prompts a 0.4 per cent point decrease in India's growth rate while the

---

* https://www.adb.org/sites/default/files/publication/28608/asia2050-executive-summary.pdf

impact on other emerging economies is 1.5 times greater. Similar results were obtained in the analysis of growth spillover from the EU and China.[3] Global circumstances provide a fertile ground for India's growth story, but it needs to be supplemented with a conducive environment that can strengthen the country's competitive advantages. So, while opportunities abound for the nation, there are no simple gains. This chapter delves deeper into these external headwinds and how they continue to change our world.

Connecting the Dots: Globalization and Global Value Chain Transformations

Global value chains (GVCs) have undergone profound transformation over time. More than simply trading products, participation in global value chains enables a knowledge and technology transfer that can transform economies and enhance national competitiveness. Industrialization in the eighteenth and nineteenth centuries led to the formation of more complex trading chains, wherein specialization of labour and increased efficiency of production generated prosperity for many nations. Colonialism in the nineteenth and early twentieth century accelerated this process of construction of global commodity networks and subsequent technological advances, such as the Internet and digitalization and containerization facilitated rapid movement of goods, capital and knowledge across borders.

Since the 1990s, international trade underwent a significant boost owing to the emergence of GVCs, even causing remarkable poverty reductions as developing nations began to catch up with their richer counterparts. Between 2003 and 2007, growth in emerging markets and developing economies grew from the long-term average of 4.4 per cent to 7.6 per cent. Advanced economies actually grew slower at 2.7 per cent compared to 2.8 per cent in the preceding quarter century.[4] Between 1990 and 2017, the share of low and middle-income countries in global exports went up from 16 per cent to 30 per cent, and the proportion of the world's population living in extreme poverty fell from 36 per cent to 9 per cent.[5] Bangladesh, China and Vietnam, countries that speak to this growth phenomenon, became critical parts of GVCs and experienced a surge in productivity and income. In fact, the greatest poverty declines have occurred precisely in those countries. China and Eastern Europe were integrated into the global economy and landmark trade agreements took place during this period, such as the Uruguay Round and the North American Free Trade Agreement (NAFTA).[6] However, this period of trade liberalization has been slowing down and growth has been sluggish since the 2008 global financial crisis. Political support underpinning market liberalization is waning, and protectionist trading policies are taking hold globally. Today, GVCs have gone far beyond mere manufacturing to services and intangible assets. The concentration of production sites in certain regions of the world is now being upended, with remote work emerging as a viable option after the pandemic and hence not limiting labour to any physical boundary. Increasingly, there is also a focus on sustainability and climate change, which has led to a new-found vigour in minimizing waste and reducing emissions across the global value chains. Thus, economic, political and technological factors have left us with complex, integrated and dynamic value chains.

A related phenomenon, reinforcing and in turn reinforced by the dynamism of global value chains, is the changing nature of globalization. There is a growing role of emerging economies, such as China, India, Brazil and Russia, as they become important decision makers in the global economy and significant players in the demand and supply markets. According to the IMF, China and India will account for nearly half the global growth in 2023.[7] The Asia Pacific region as a whole will contribute to over 70 per cent of global growth, with a growth rate of 4.6 per cent this year over the 3.8 per cent last year.[8] There is also the emergence of a services-oriented globalization, where outsourcing of services allows companies to reduce costs and increase efficiency. The world is more connected than ever before, but the pace of interlinking is slowing down. The COVID-19 pandemic and the ongoing war in Ukraine are thought to have reversed decades of global economic integration. The United Nations Department of Economic and Social Affairs states the following on the economic consequences of the war:

> Estimates of the cost of economic fragmentation vary widely. According to IMF scenarios, the longer-term cost of trade fragmentation alone could range from 0.2 per cent to almost 7 per cent of global GDP. Factors influencing these estimates include reduced global trade flows, technological decoupling, sectoral misallocation, lower diffusion of innovations and slower productivity growth. Alternative payment systems, if developed to mitigate the risk of potential economic sanctions, would increase transaction costs for businesses. Fragmentation would also undermine diversification of production and export bases, reducing economic efficiencies and potentially reducing resilience.[9]

So, decades of trading in specialized expertise and leveraging comparative advantage are being jeopardized. In addition to the disruptions in supply chains, there are increasing geopolitical tensions and decoupling of major economies, such as the United States and China, which threaten the pace of globalization.

While globalization created unprecedented national prosperity, especially for developing economies, it is also thought to effect inequalities within nations. What was termed as 'slowbalisation'[10] after the 2008 crisis is thought by many to now have turned into de-globalization. According to research by Barclays Corporate and Investment Bank, 4 per cent of corporate transcripts mentioned onshoring in 2022, as compared to less than 1 per cent prior to the pandemic. Additionally, increased onshoring of jobs is taking place chiefly in Asia, while trends in the United States and Europe still point towards globalization.[11]

Pandemic Fallout: Unravelling the Complexities of Global Value Chains

The COVID-19 pandemic has left an indelible mark on the world, causing widespread disruption across nearly all facets of life. One area that has been particularly affected is the intricate networks that connect economies and businesses around the globe through production and distribution channels. The impact of these disruptions has been felt in various ways, ranging from supply chain interruptions and labour shortages to trade restrictions. The pandemic has also exposed the intricacies and fragilities of our interconnected world. The year 2020 saw a decline of 8 per cent in global trade, which is comparable to the contraction experienced during the Great Recession of 2008–2009.[12] The lack of digital infrastructure to mitigate the negative effects of reduced labour mobility also makes the recovery process slower and more complex for developing economies. Some of the key lessons from the pandemic on global trade have been along the following themes:

Diversification of supply chains: Global division of labour helps nations to benefit from the natural endowments and competitive advantage of other countries while increasing the efficiency of their own resources, but it also increases dependency. If this dependency is not spread across different regions, it breeds an overreliance on a single supplier. This was seen during the pandemic with essential items, such as protective gear, masks and medical equipment. The global trade flows were disproportionately influenced by China's strict pandemic policies and revealed vulnerabilities, especially as a significant supplier of active pharmaceutical ingredients (APIs) globally.

Digitalization of trade: Digital technologies for trades, such as e-commerce and electronic payments, shot up during the pandemic, along with the understanding that digitalization can contribute extensively to enhancing productivity. Digitalization reduces transaction costs while providing access to larger and faraway markets. In fact, the resilience and stability of several economies pivoted around their abilities to integrate digitalization in daily operations during the pandemic.

Global cooperation and coordination: Despite the cleavages revealed in international value chains, the need for collaboration during a global calamity, such as a pandemic, remains undisputed. Collaborative research and innovation enabled vaccine rollout at unprecedented rates. There were donation and awareness campaigns at all levels as well as several national initiatives to ease the adverse effects of the virus.

Inclusive and resilient global governance: Global institutions like the World Health Organization (WHO) coordinated and guided international efforts in the fight against the virus. The COVID-19 Solidarity Response Fund was set up by the WHO to provide support to countries with inadequate health systems, and alongside that, the WHO launched the Access to COVID-19 Tools (ACT) Accelerator, a worldwide partnership aimed at expediting the development, manufacturing and fair distribution of COVID-19 tests, treatments and vaccines.* There were other bodies at the regional level too that worked to coordinate emergency responses. The pandemic brought to the fore the need for reliable global institutions that governments and citizens can trust to take just decisions and regulate fair international exchanges in emergency situations.

On the whole, the COVID-19 pandemic has underscored the necessity of resilient, diversified and cooperative global trade systems that can withstand future shocks and crises.

From Local to Global: India's Integration with the Global Value Chains

When it comes to globalization, it has indubitably led to unprecedented growth and prosperity for developing nations. However, the pandemic has revealed the vulnerabilities in global value chains and coupled with rising geopolitical tensions, it propelled nations to secure their national interests first. Long-term resilience from external shocks is prized more by some nations than the benefits of participation in global value chains. This tug between self-reliance and open collaboration to tackle the global challenges of our times, such as climate change, requires to be balanced delicately to enhance long-term competitiveness and resilience. Complete disregard for an external orientation and open economy will not do any good, neither will compromising on national priorities and citizen welfare. One thing that is clear is that globalization and integration with global value chains do

---

* https://www.who.int/initiatives/act-accelerator

not lead to shared prosperity by itself. Policy acts as a viable route to reconcile the two. For instance, to improve the resilience of GVCs in low-income countries, it will be crucial to safeguard them against export restrictions on essential goods and services. To avoid sudden contract cancellation, governments could implement policies that address market information failures, weak contracts and limited access to trade finance. This will help foster durable and stronger relationships with foreign buyers and sellers and be particularly beneficial for smaller exporters that are yet to be fully embedded in the trading networks.[13]

India has a window to integrate more beneficially and fully with global value chains and become a global leader, all the while maintaining a stronghold on self-reliance. The idea is to reduce external dependency while building domestic capacity. Amidst the geopolitical strains and post-pandemic lessons, 'trust' will come into the picture as an important element that will determine international partnerships. India, as a historically non-aligned and democratic country, thus emerges as a desirable trading partner. The president of the Asian Development Bank (ADB), Masatsugu Asakawa, posited that India has an opportunity to embed itself in the global value chains more meaningfully as more foreign investment is being directed to the country against the background of tensions between the United States and China.[*] In August 2020, nearly twenty-four electronic goods companies, including Samsung and Apple, expressed interest in moving out of China to India.[†]

---

[*] https://economictimes.indiatimes.com/news/economy/finance/window-for-india-to-be-linked-to-global-value-chains-deeply-adb/articleshow/98160749.cms?from=mdr
[†] https://www.eos-intelligence.com/perspectives/supply-chain/covid-19-unmasks-global-supply-chains-reliance-on-china-is-there-a-way-out/

The global context is changing, and India needs to take steps to ensure that it enhances the value of its existing assets and capabilities to leverage this opportunity. For certain sectors like pharmaceuticals, India is already a leading second competitor to China. In 'strategic' sectors like renewable energy and semiconductors, India's markets and manufacturing capabilities are steadily evolving, reflecting the positive momentum for growth and development in these crucial areas.[14] With the current budget's impetus to infrastructure and capacity building, India already has a robust domestic market to leverage. India's position in South Asia puts it in an advantageous position to serve the emerging markets, which by all predictions are going to be significant contributors and fast-growing economies in the global economic system. Increased investment in human capital can assist the nation in reaping its demographic dividend and consolidating its position in the world. A delicate balancing act is required between utilizing India's current competitive strengths, such as enhancing the skills of its vast young population and boosting export competitiveness, while also increasing fiscal and policy support for previously neglected areas like green development.[15] Digitalization and climate change present themselves as two sectors that will determine the country's growth trajectory in the years to come. Going forward, the discussion explores digitalization's potential in driving competitiveness, evolution of the digital world and digitalization from the perspective of the developing world.

Digitalization: Driver of Innovation, Economic Growth and Competitiveness

Digitalization—the process of incorporating digital technologies into our daily lives—and new production technologies as a global trend are termed by many as the Fourth Industrial Revolution, where automation and hyperconnectivity transform the way society behaves and industries evolve. Industry 4.0 incorporates artificial intelligence, machine learning, the Internet of Things (IoT) and big data into our manufacturing and production chains. Digitalization has vast implications for innovation, economic growth and competitiveness. Digital globalization has shifted greater parts of our business and interactions online— from streaming to e-commerce to remote jobs to social media; a vast majority of our expression of globalization and global interconnection is now in the virtual space. Even the threats and risks have evolved, with cybercrime, online security and data protection taking centre stage.

Nowadays, infrastructural investments need to focus on not only enabling physical connectivity but also digital connectivity. Digitalization has the potential to drastically alter several parameters that have a bearing on competitiveness; digitalization can lower the transaction costs associated with accessing remote markets. It can increase efficiency through automation and error reduction. As vast amounts of data are optimized and technology transfer is facilitated, companies can innovate faster. This agility allows for quicker adaptation to changing market trends and customer needs, thereby fostering healthy competition. 'Data is the new oil,' and wielding it effectively is a major driver of economic growth. At the beginning of 2023, close to 64 per cent of the global population were users of the Internet, and more than two-thirds used a mobile phone.[*] Half the world is connected through social media.[†] These numbers are only expected to grow in the near future. The Global Innovation Index 2022 released by World Intellectual Property Organization (WIPO) has predicted

---

[*] https://datareportal.com/global-digital-overview
[†] https://www.un.org/en/un75/impact-digital-technologies

that two waves have the potential to transform productivity radically—the digital age and deep science.[16] Economic expansion is intrinsically related to labour productivity, which can see valuable gains through the penetration of information and communication technologies. Asia, especially India, has emerged as an important player in the consumer market of digital technologies and a prospective ground for scaling up digital infrastructure and digital labour.

Figure 10: Share of the Population using the Internet

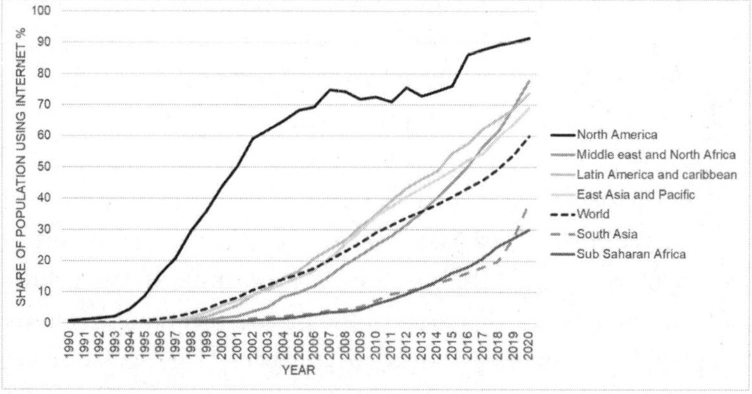

Source: Our World in Data

The Evolutionary Tale: Digital Information Flows

The history of the Internet dates back several decades, with email and file sharing being introduced as early as the 1960s and 1970s, respectively. In 1982, the standardization of TCP/IP also played a significant role in the Internet's development. However, it was the creation of the World Wide Web in 1989, by British scientist Tim Berners-Lee, that changed the game of the history of communication. Berners-Lee developed a system that allowed for the sharing of information through a network of computers, leading to a revolution in the way we communicate and access information.* The concept of the 'digital economy' emerged around 1995 against the backdrop of inventive production of equipment for information technology. The Internet too was a new source for a plethora of 'free' content. It was leading up to the formation of the 'information society,' where information becomes an inexhaustible, renewable resource with open access and the ability to boost competitiveness.[17] The boom was unprecedented, and the very nature of technological innovation implied that it grew multifold. It took the Internet twelve years to accumulate its first billion users and only five years to gain its third billion. The uptake also shot up in the context of the COVID-19 pandemic. From 4.19 billion people in 2019— approximately 53.6 per cent of the global population—the number of Internet users increased to 4.7 billion in 2020, around 60 per cent of the population.[18] In recent years, the trends that have dominated the digitalization space are a sizable uptick in the adoption of Artificial Intelligence (AI) and Machine Learning (ML), with diverse implications in finance, marketing and healthcare. The number of Internet of Things (IoT) devices has increased substantially, and cloud computing has emerged as a popular tool to facilitate remote storage, management and data and software applications access. Further, the adoption of 5G networks is on the rise, enhancing the dependability of connectivity that benefits consumers and businesses. Blockchain technology promises secure solutions for data management and transactions across a range of sectors.

A decade ago, our world looked very different from what it is today. Trade and information flows have layers

---

* https://ourworldindata.org/internet#licence3

of added meanings owing to digitalization. The swift pace of digitalization is impacting various aspects of our lives, such as our means of communication, shopping, employment and service delivery. Moreover, it is transforming how value is generated and exchanged. Global data flow then becomes an element of great significance in understanding globalization in today's world. The COVID-19 pandemic also played a role in accelerating the adoption of digital technologies. They ensured the continuation of our societal functions across education, health, leisure and communication in the absence of in-person interactions. Evidence from advanced economies shows that strong levels of digitalization played a crucial role in protecting productivity and employment during the economic disruption. The industries that had higher levels of digitalization suffered considerably fewer losses in terms of labour productivity and working hours compared to the less digitalized sectors.[19] Not only that, but the virus also itself was confronted and battled through digital technologies; genome sequencing to track virus mutations and the development of the vaccine all employed sophisticated digital tools. Nonetheless, digital technologies can also have unintended negative externalities, such as an increased carbon footprint, sustainability concerns due to their usage of rare resources and associated waste, as well as their potential to adversely affect labour demand and exacerbate the digital divide. How the global society wields this powerful revolution will decide the future prospects of the planet and its inhabitants.

Digital Leapfrogging: How Developing Economies are Harnessing Technology for Growth

The remarkable capabilities and cutting-edge efficiency of emerging technologies allow for a significant reduction in functional costs across a range of operations, making it a potential enabler of wealth creation. Their incorporation can become a means to reduce the gap between developing and developed economies. Humanity has never had a more accessible opportunity to reduce inequalities radically, but enabling the process involves more than mere lip service and actionable plans on the part of all stakeholders—private and public, local and global. Furthermore, digitalization brings with it the adverse possibility of exacerbating existing chasms between the haves and the have-nots. For instance, women are 16 per cent less likely to use the mobile Internet than men and 7 per cent less likely to own a mobile phone. At the end of 2021, Internet users in urban areas were double the number in rural areas, and 71 per cent of the global population aged fifteen to twenty-four were using the Internet, while this percentage was only 57 per cent for all other age groups. Around 2.6 billion people still remain offline.[20] In the post-pandemic recovery phase, those without access to digital technologies are more likely to be left behind and face damaging outcomes over this period. A study by the McKinsey Global Institute suggests that 400-800 million jobs could be lost to automation and AI by 2030.[21] Generative AI can have biased algorithms and lead to the propagation of harmful stereotypes and further fragmentation of opinions. Thus, the digital realm is no longer limited to inside our screens and has noteworthy implications for our social, political and cultural well-being. It can be used to fulfil the 2030 sustainable development goals or, on the flip side, intentionally or unintentionally weaken the welfare of the disenfranchised. Below are some ways in which developing economies are harnessing technology—using them to power the SDGs, the digital market potential of the Asian market and the curious comparative advantage of developing economies over developed ones in digitalization.

o *Powering the Global Goals: Digitalization's Role in Achieving the SDGs*

Financial inclusion, access to bank accounts and online financial services has been proven to help alleviate poverty (SDG 1). Incorporating ICT tools in agricultural practices helps farmers increase yields more effectively while reducing the usage of harmful chemicals and excess energy (SDG 2). Digital interventions in the medical space improve health informatics and enhance access to medical facilities, including remote access (SDG 3). By augmenting imaging and ecological monitoring of life below water and life on land, GIS-based technologies provide better ways to protect our flora and fauna and understand their needs. RFID chips and sensor networks can help track the behaviour and migration of endangered species (SDG 14 and 15). The provision of tools and global platforms can empower individuals and communities to articulate their needs, form collectives and safe spaces, voice their opinions and participate in decision-making processes, thereby contributing to the realization of various goals, including but not limited to gender equality, reduced inequalities and the establishment of just and peaceful institutions (SDG 5, 10 and 16). Electrifying transport, setting up smart grids and smart cities all enhance the ease of living, expand channels of governance and increase social well-being. Digitalization has also led to digital globalization, forging new international and intra-national partnerships that previously had no legs. Television, the Internet and telecommunications bring the world to us in a palatable and readily available form. Such a digital society relies less and less on physical borders and more on a network of information and communication. It also requires the creation of a new sphere of digital rights and digital diplomacy, where political functions and alliances are enacted

(SDG 17). In all these ways, digital technologies contribute towards sustainable development goals through increased efficiency, monitoring, improved access to information and innovation fostering. All of these directly or indirectly also feed into economic growth and national prosperity, while ensuring that this prosperity is equitable and shared.

o *Digital Adoption and Market Potential in Asian Economies*

The growing digital economy has led the pandemic recovery in South and Southeast Asia and helped them overcome the hurdles of conventional trade. In 2021, digital sales in the retail e-commerce sector reached almost $2.992 trillion, making the Asia-Pacific region the biggest market by a significant margin. China is the world's largest e-commerce market, fuelled by its massive number of digital buyers and their growing purchasing power.[22] Market research company eMarketer predicts a period of massive e-commerce growth for India from 2021 to 2025 due to an influx of retailers joining the online space and opening online stores. It is a largely untapped market that has the potential to see demand and supply hikes. China, Japan, South Korea and India all ranked among the top ten countries with the largest retail e-commerce sales globally. Through comprehensive digital inclusion policies, Bangladesh has improved its ranks in the Inclusive Development Index (IDI) and GDP growth rate. The country is capitalizing on the convenience of online labour and is expected to become the twenty-fourth-largest economy in the world by 2030.* McKinsey and Company estimate that Asia will have digital payments comprise a 65 per cent proportion by 2024

---

* https://www.weforum.org/agenda/2019/06/how-the-digital-economy-is-shaping-a-new-bangladesh/

against an average of 52 per cent globally.[*] All these facts and figures go on to say that digitalization has transformed and has the potential to accelerate progress in developing economies further. However, there are areas that need to be fortified before that can happen—digital inclusion, digital infrastructure and regional cooperation and skilling for the future.

Digital Inclusion: To ensure the continued effectiveness of digitalization, digital inclusion is important. Most of the non-users of the Internet are concentrated in the least developed countries (LDCs), landlocked developing countries (LLDCs) and small island developing states (SIDS). Those without Internet access or limited access in the pandemic lost out on opportunities for education and employment. Beyond the population and varying socio-economic groups, access to technologies is uneven across firms. The World Economic Forum posits that the digitalization wave favours individual consumers, not small- and medium-sized enterprises (SMEs). There is a mismatch between the input and share of SMEs to their eventual output. For instance, SMEs are crucial to the economy of the Philippines, employing 63 per cent of the workforce and a whopping 99.5 per cent of all businesses. However, they account for a mere 36 per cent of value added to the economy.[†] One possible solution could be financial inclusion and enabling digital financial products that can address the specific needs of the SMEs. Another option to reduce the digital divide at the individual and community levels is to supplement the digital revolution with physical infrastructure. In Bangladesh, over

---

[*] https://www.weforum.org/agenda/2022/02/digitalization-south-southeast-asia/

[†] https://www.weforum.org/agenda/2022/01/south-east-asia-sme-digitization-financial-services

5.000 digital centres have been established to provide 'last-mile' connectivity to the range of digital services, ensuring that they reach all citizens in all areas.* Even when there are no cost or access barriers to being 'online,' there is a need to take additional steps to welcome disenfranchised and vulnerable groups there. One way to do this and to enable larger benefits is to allow for checks and balances for abuses and fraud online, strengthen cybersecurity and protect personal data online. Secure and reliable digital systems are paramount to ensuring trust and continued use.

Digital Infrastructure and Regional Cooperation: The digital economy can be said to have four main drivers: demand, supply, institutions and innovation.[23] Demand refers to Internet usage and consumer income and demographics; supply is the sophistication of infrastructural support for supporting digital commerce; institutions refer to the policy and trade set-up and innovation reflects the overall competitive landscape. Digital infrastructure is the backbone that supports all these segments. While Internet and mobile penetration is high, it is not 100 per cent. There are vast disparities across and within regions. A favourable policy and regulatory framework can boost investment in the digital sphere, including private businesses, social enterprises, international organizations and civil society at large. Innovative financial models can help distribute the costs of incorporating digital infrastructure, such as public-private partnerships, crowdfunding and regional cooperation. High-quality digital infrastructure can have positive externalities beyond its own regional boundaries and hence provides fertile grounds to advance international cooperation and diplomacy, often having further positive effects on political, cultural and economic outcomes.

---

* https://www.weforum.org/agenda/2020/02/digital-inclusion-made-bangladesh-stand-out

The collaboration across regions enables governments and stakeholders to synchronize policies, jointly bear the expenses of infrastructure development and upkeep and extend markets to propel the growth of the digital economy. Furthermore, the mechanisms of regional cooperation foster the establishment of trust and standardization, which are vital for digital development across countries. As a result, progress in the digital domain stimulates regional cooperation in various sectors, such as trade, finance, transport and energy, among others.[24] A good example of such a multi-nation strategy plan is the Digital Strategy 2030 endorsed by the Central Asia Regional Economic Cooperation (CAREC) member countries.

Skilling for the Future: There is a need to build upon digital skills and sectoral resilience so that economies can provide labour for the work of the future and sectors can stay afloat with new developments and an ever-evolving context, thereby standing as competitive players in the game. Education and training, especially vocational training, proves extremely crucial to achieve this. Many developing countries, most notably India, are experiencing a demographic dividend, and the burgeoning younger population can be the key to activating a golden era of economic growth. This requires, and what is often found lacking, academic education and curriculum to be aligned to industry and stay abreast with rapid technological advancements. Solidifying and promoting industry-academia relations can prove helpful in this scenario. In a virtuous cycle, digital facilities themselves can be used to augment digital skills through the use of online courses and professional degrees. A digital medium already reduces the cost of providing such amenities, and government support and investment can further boost the process. This process of digital literacy should be made accessible and attract all sections of the digital population—those who are extremely tech-savvy and fast adapters, those who are gradual with the uptake of new technologies and the minority that is technology averse. There is a need to reduce the digital divide in digital literacy. Another important aspect of preparing labour and various industries to be forward facing and future ready is the provision of safety nets to support these transitions and reduce the risk of failure.

o   *Harnessing the Comparative Advantage of Developing Economies*

While developed economies have comparative advantages over developing economies in terms of access to more resources, cutting-edge technology, and higher capital to invest, developing economies too have some tools to boost competitiveness in the context of digitalization. Developing countries oftentimes have more flexible regulatory frameworks, which can help them become agile adopters of newer technologies and business models. There are lower legacy costs in the absence of established infrastructure, and newer models can be taken up with more ease. They can leapfrog over older and inefficient technologies in the cycle and directly adopt new ones. This late-mover advantage can significantly reduce costs and risks associated with research and experimentation and accelerate the uptake of new technology that advanced economies go through more gradually.[25] Crises breed innovation, and emerging economies have more of an appetite and need for innovating. Frugal innovations are more sustainable and can make use of available digital technologies to scale up operations. Many developing countries are also laden with larger populations that are often younger in age than the average age of the populations in developed economies. This makes them a lucrative market as both consumers and producers of digital products and services. Developing economies can tap into their comparative advantage and accelerate digital adoption by focusing on digital inclusion, digital skilling, ramping up digital infrastructure and fostering regional cooperation. The next section explores India's digital story, its unique aspects, and its example-setting legacy in the world.

India's Digital Revolution: Pioneering a New Frontier for Global Innovation

'I dream of a Digital India where the world looks to India for the next big idea.'

Prime Minister Narendra Modi,
1 July 2015, Digital India Week Inauguration

India's march towards digitalization has been nothing short of remarkable. In a world where most technological innovations have originated and still originate from developed economies, India's progress and innovation in the sphere is a model example for other developing economies on the potential of digitalization to improve all aspects of societal well-being. The country has become a strong voice for emerging economies in international forums on digitalization. What began as a gradual process of proliferation of digital alternatives to supplement the existing amenities was accelerated in the pandemic and has now become a digital revolution. Digital India, the government of India's flagship programme, was launched in 2015 with the vision to empower India to become a digitally empowered and knowledge economy. * The three key areas of attention in the initiative are improved digital infrastructure, e-governance and digital empowerment. At

---

* https://csc.gov.in/digitalIndia

the beginning of 2023, there were 692 million Internet users and Internet penetration was at 48.7 per cent. Close to 33 per cent of the population are social media users and 1.1 billion cellular mobile connections were found active at the beginning of the year.[26] India also has one of the highest data consumptions in the world, with the lowest cost of data globally; it has an average cost of Rs 50 per GB and an average per-user consumption of 14.1 GB.* There has been a prominent shift in the FDI inflows composition towards digital services, which now make up over 50 per cent of the total inflow. India currently ranks third as the largest recipient of FDI for technology transactions worldwide. As a result of this shift, the growth rate of India's service exports has outpaced that of goods exports.[27] India benefits immensely from free data flows, and states in India with a significant information technology industry tend to exhibit high living standards and are more likely to entice foreign direct investment. A greater number of patents filed and start-ups initiated are linked with higher exports of digital services.[28] India has adopted a domestic development-oriented approach to cross-border data flows. In addition, the Government of India has taken steps to bring over 63 million MSMEs into the formal economy through the implementation of GST in 2019. This move towards formalization has incentivized businesses to adopt technology for tasks such as tax filing, which has further driven the growth of Internet adoption in India.† Some prominent digital payment methods that have grown over the last few years are NEFT/RTGS, credit cards, mobile banking, debit cards and e-wallets, etc.

At the centre of this digital transformation has been India's digital achievements in terms of its inventive payments system,

---

* https://www.ibef.org/blogs/investing-in-india-s-digital-revolution
† Ibid.

Unified Payments Interface (UPI), part of a larger umbrella of digital public goods and fintech innovations called the India Stack. The idea behind UPI is that every citizen can link their bank account and create a Virtual Payment Address (VPA or UPI ID) and make payments through their mobile phones, and the ultimate aim was to make India a cashless economy. India records eleven times more digital payments than the United States and Europe, and four times more than China.* The transactions completed using UPI soared from 179 lakh in 2017 to 782 crore in December 2022, equalling Rs 12.8 lakh crore. Previously, the Indian economy was heavily reliant on cash, so much so that the currency in circulation has floated around 11 per cent of GDP for decades. The value of the currency in circulation was Rs 32.42 lakh crore on 23 December 2022. The share of digital transactions has also been rising, from 11.26 per cent in 2015 to 2016 to 80.4 per cent in 2021 to 2022, with an estimated rise to 88 per cent in 2026 to 2027.† The usage of cash, while habitual, brings along hidden costs to the economy in terms of costs of printing and distribution and leakages. Monetary policy devised to alter economic activities is less than effective if cash circulation occurs outside the formal financial system. For all these reasons, digital payment methods help to keep track of the money in the economy as well as reduce transaction costs. The Jan Dhan-Aadhaar-Mobile (JAM) trinity pertains to an endeavour by the Indian government to connect the Jan Dhan accounts, mobile phone numbers and Aadhaar cards of Indian citizens. This initiative is aimed at preventing the leakages of government subsidies, which is a significant proportion of

---

* https://www.indiatoday.in/business/story/india-today-conclave-2023-amitabh-kant-digitisation-model-future-world-2348055-2023-03-17
† https://www.ndtv.com/india-news/demonetisation-cash-circulation-in-public-nearly-doubled-in-6-years-since-notes-ban-3658916

the GDP, and ensuring direct benefits to the poor who need it most. This was especially useful during the COVID-19 pandemic and allowed the government to provide immediate monetary assistance. It was accompanied by the Pradhan Mantri Jan Dhan Yojana (PMJDY), which aimed to ensure inclusive access to a range of financial services at affordable costs.

o   *Dismantling Data Colonialism: Financial Inclusion and Social Progress at the Domestic Level*

The biggest contribution of these digital advancements has been their positive effect on social progress and economic empowerment. India's expanding digital capacities are shielding it from 'data colonialism,' a scenario where rich and advanced countries benefit from cross-border data flows at the cost of domestic interests and welfare. The JAM trinity helped bring banking facilities and financial services directly to the people. Through mobile phones, the last of the trinity, all information about government schemes and benefits was sent to the citizens, even in their own regional languages.[*] A varied set of subsidies could be collated into one medium, thereby reducing transaction costs, making awareness raising more targeted and, hence, effective. The Global Financial Index (GFI) released by the World Bank shows how the gap between the rich and the poor in terms of formal banking reduced from 16 per cent to 5 per cent from 2014 till 2017. The number of women making digital payments also doubled from 11 per cent to 22 per cent during the same period.

---

[*] https://economictimes.indiatimes.com/news/economy/policy/jam-trinity-proved-to-be-game-changer-helped-reach-out-to-people-during-pandemic-fm-nirmala-sitharaman/articleshow/86259816.cms

UPI provided a seamless and enhanced transaction experience for merchants and consumers. Merchants could be assured of reliable and convenient receipt of payments directly to their bank account and small-business owners could stress less about money theft. The mode of payment is also compatible with online and offline merchants, and there is no tedious process of collecting or storing customers' bank details.* For the customers, the benefit was that they were not obligated to share any sensitive data. There was enhanced convenience in the form of round-the-clock availability and no or low costs. The system is interoperable with a range of applications and services and multiple payment options increase the product's reliability. It also helps individuals create a digital financial footprint that can further assist in obtaining credit and other financial services. This increased formalization and the availability of a conducive business space spurs economic growth. It increases economic activity, makes it accessible to all rungs of society, improves user experience and allows for quicker adaption to external events (such as the JAM-trinity facilitation during the pandemic) and, thus, improves national competitiveness. Financial independence is a key aspect of economic empowerment, and digitalization acts as a force multiplier on the back of which disparities are tackled and governance is improved. A conducive policy environment and the impetus towards digital infrastructure have also allowed India to house the third-highest number of unicorns in the world. There are more than 58,000 homegrown start-ups, and digitalization has aided many entrepreneurial dreams in the country.[29] Not only economic advancement but also the digital revolution in India has led to the increased resilience of its people

---

* https://static.pib.gov.in/WriteReadData/specificdocs/documents/2021/oct/doc2021101211.pdf

and society at large due to its positive spillover in the areas of health, education and ease of living. E-governance measures do not simply digitize government functions but improve them. They augment transparency and trust and put citizens at the centre of discourse. Increased control over finances encourages women to participate in the economy and make more informed choices. With easier ways of banking, households can increase their savings and plan better for external shocks. More than Rs 23 lakh crore has been transferred to beneficiaries through Direct Benefit Transfers (DBT) since 2014.* Through these strides in the digital space, India is gaining prominence as a powerful player in the digital field, countering any data colonialism threats, which refer to the dominance of digital information by influential entities.

o   *Digital Diplomacy and India's Example Setting in the Global Context*

While India's digitalization strategy has been focused on domestic progress, it has set an inspiring example in the sphere for the rest of the world. India's vaccination campaign is considered to be one of the biggest digital-vaccination drives globally, with billions of registrations made through the CoWIN app. The CoWIN app—COVID-19 Vaccine Intelligence Network—was the digital backbone of India's fight against the virus. It allowed for registration for vaccination and facilitated the certificate process. It also helped in monitoring the supply of vaccines, tracking the distribution of vaccines to various vaccination centres and keeping records of vaccinations administered. India, as a leader in building population-scale digital public goods, offered the tech

---

* https://theprint.in/india/india-has-performed-well-in-digital-public-infrastructure-sector-cowin-chief/1026588/

platform to the world as a digital public good. This shows the nation's commitment to collaboration in times of crisis, as was also evidenced by its Vaccine Maitri scheme. The India Stack too is an ambitious initiative aimed at establishing a distinctive digital infrastructure that can tackle problems at a population scale by creating a range of open Application Programming Interfaces (APIs). Through this project, various services such as Aadhaar for presence-less verification, e-KYC and e-Sign for paperless documentation, Digilocker for digital document storage and UPI for cashless transactions have been made available for healthcare and urban governance purposes.[30] During India's G20 presidency, the RBI facilitated and extended UPI-based payments for travellers from G20 countries where they were able to make use of UPI to make payments during their time in India without having an Indian bank account.* Digital payment systems from India are currently accessible in multiple countries, including Singapore, UAE, Oman, Saudi Arabia, Malaysia, France and the BENELUX markets, such as Belgium, the Netherlands, Luxembourg and Switzerland. Additionally, it has been reported that India has signed a Memorandum of Understanding with thirteen countries that aim to adopt the UPI interface for facilitating digital payments.†

This digital diplomacy and innovation in public infrastructure positions India as an important global player, something that other nations can rely on and trust. With a booming IT services sector, a long history of scientific and technological prowess

---

* https://economictimes.indiatimes.com/industry/banking/finance/banking/g20-india-to-provide-hands-on-upi-experience-to-visiting-delegates/articleshow/103432606.cms.

† https://www.india-briefing.com/news/global-acceptance-of-indias-digital-payment-systems-europe-latest-to-join-26183.html/

and a good spirit reflecting multilateral alliance, India enhances its competitiveness, proving that increasing competitiveness is not a zero-sum game where one nation's progress inhibits another's. Financial and social inclusion through digitalization was an important theme identified in the G20 Global Agenda, and India's opportune presidency allowed the nation to solidify its position in the world as a digital leader while providing a strong voice for other developing countries. While there may be varying approaches needed to incorporate India's strategy and public goods in one's own economy depending on the context, for example, the lack of as large a population or domestic market, India's global efforts can help middle-income economies address similar barriers, such as digital inclusion, access and literacy, faced by the nation itself.

Like digitalization, another pertinent factor that determines the growth trajectory of nations and will continue to dictate the terms of development in the years to come is climate change. Climate change mitigation and policies are one of the most important aspects of securing the future prosperity of nations.

A Planet in Peril: Climate Change and Policies for Carbon Neutrality

Never in the history of humanity has the world faced such unprecedented and unpredictable environmental threats. Hidden in the long shadows of the pandemic has been a dark year; a world battling with the triple planetary crisis of climate change, biodiversity and pollution. The planetary pressures pose a major challenge to long-term-development objectives, especially reduction of poverty and other multi-dimensional vulnerabilities exacerbating disparities in a world already beset by inequalities.

The COVID-19 pandemic was a wake-up call for the world, underscoring that nothing reigns supreme over individual and collective health. After three years of uncertainty, tackling wave after wave, the global society is finally in the recovery stage of this relentless pandemic. At the same time, it is a race against time to avoid further suffering and loss of life from environmental catastrophes. The world's first climate treaty was signed three decades ago in 1992 and, yet, we are standing at irreversible tipping points, including largescale biodiversity loss and extreme weather events. Climate-related disasters have increased significantly in the past fifty years and caused two million deaths and losses of $3.64 trillion.[*] The exacerbation of resource bottlenecks, the potential collapse of biodiversity, the harmful effects of air pollution on human lifespan, the proliferation of plastics and the acidification of oceans are all contributing to significant imbalances in natural systems. These environmental crises are the cascading challenges of our time and can potentially cause much greater social and economic harm than we have experienced due to COVID-19. To ensure the liveability of planet Earth, experts predict that the global temperature needs to be restricted to 1.5 degrees Celsius over our pre-industrial levels. The current situation is dire, and the planet is already 1.1 degree Celsius warmer. Though the rate of greenhouse gas (GHG) emissions have slowed in recent years, the combined emissions reductions achieved by some countries have been outweighed by rapid emissions growth elsewhere, particularly among developing countries that have grown from a much lower base of per-capita emissions. This adds a new dimension of unpredictability and complexity to the challenges that are growing exponentially. To achieve our climate goals, the

---

[*] https://sdgs.un.org/topics/climate-action-synergies

United Nations Environment Programme (UNEP) posits that global emissions would need to be reduced by 45 per cent by 2030 and attain net zero by 2050.* Currently, the progress and commitments made by national governments fall short of the mark, and gradual or incremental changes will not suffice. There is a need to reimagine our society and lives radically. Our long-standing assurance with respect to having enough for everyone is waning, and fast. Accelerating economic growth while fulfilling our environment and climate targets is the transformative shift that will be instrumental in delivering a breakthrough for people and the planet. The upcoming section delves into the interlinkages between climate and development, highlighting crucial aspects to bear in mind while working towards the attainment of net-zero objectives. These include climate justice, the imperative of individual and systemic behaviour change, the facilitation of sustainable choices, the promotion of a circular economy, the potential and existing challenges of Green Budgeting, India's climate goals and endeavors, as well as policy recommendations aimed at shaping a more environmentally sustainable future.

Climate-Development Nexus

Climate change has a direct adverse impact on factors pertaining to human life and dignity. The phenomenon not only limits itself to themes of environmental degradation but has the ability to undermine economic and social progress severely. As climate change affects agriculture and water quality, food and water shortages abound in many regions and contribute to malnutrition, hunger and conflict over resources. Air pollution can cause respiratory illnesses and reduce the quality of life.

---

* https://www.un.org/en/climatechange/net-zero-coalition

Ecological collapse, rising sea levels and extreme weather lead to displacement and loss of life and property. Not only that, but displacement can also further cause a loss and disruption of local culture. This has grave consequences for people's identities and dignity. Such degradation also weakens economic stability and prosperity, leading to diminished standards of living. Equitable adaption and mitigation measures to address climate change are crucial to achieving lasting development. The interwoven relationships and potential conflicts between Sustainable Development Goals (SDGs) and climate undertakings can vary, and these trade-offs can be effectively addressed through policy design. This process of enhancing synergies and reducing trade-offs is particularly challenging for developing nations with limited institutional, financial and technological capacities, and the focus needs to be on strengthening governance and intra- and inter-sectoral collaboration.

The good news is that this is not a zero-sum game. The COVID-19 pandemic illustrated the fragility of territorial borders. Keeping this in mind, if we treat a healthy planet as a global public good, it can also help secure the collective well-being of the people and the global economy, The two agendas of climate and development is therefore mutually reinforcing and not competing. Recent reports have clearly drawn out the co-benefits of the climate-development agenda, making a strong case for deepening synergies between the two. For instance, agroforestry has the potential to facilitate enhanced employment and local livelihoods. The table illustrates one such example of the complementarity between the two agendas.

Table 1: Climate Resilient Development – Synergies – Trade-Offs

Theme	Action	Synergies	Trade-Offs
Sustainable Urban Planning	Designs incorporating green roofs and facades, interconnected parks and open spaces, strategies for managing urban forests and wetlands, urban agriculture practices and water-sensitive features	Mitigates the risks of flooding, alleviates stress on urban sewage systems, counteracts urban heat island effects and provides health advantages through decreased air pollution.	Raising urban density as a means of curbing travel demand may result in increased susceptibility to heat waves and flooding.

Climate-Resilient Development

In the past, significant progress has been made at the expense of climate preservation. The Industrial Revolution transformed our way of working, but the factories, mills and industrial units that emerged subsequently released large amounts of pollutants and caused deforestation and habitat loss. Unprecedented levels of urbanization and population growth have contributed to unprecedented energy consumption. We have reached a stage of overdrawing where development, it seems, cannot be sustained and sustainable unless it is climate resilient. There is a need for alternate growth models where decarbonization and growth can co-exist. To advance climate-resilient development, it is critical to address the particular causes and effects of the triple planetary crisis—climate change, pollution and biodiversity loss—without picking and choosing. Another urgent and interrelated goal is achieving carbon neutrality, i.e., realizing the balance of greenhouse gases emitted into the atmosphere to the greenhouse gases removed from it. This calls for reducing emissions as much as possible and offsetting the remaining amount through carbon sequestration and carbon credits. Carbon neutrality has found a prominent place in most national policies around the world. What would a climate-sensitive and growth-oriented economy look like? The following key elements need to be considered while moving towards net-zero goals.

Social Floors and Ceilings—Minimum Requirements for Human Dignity and Well-Being

Climate change and its reversal are inherently moral issues. The actions, at the individual and collective levels, require consideration for people and communities beyond our own. The repercussions too are not just and well-balanced; vulnerable groups affected most by climate change are rarely the ones chiefly responsible for it. This situation mimics a prisoner's dilemma, where every nation has the incentive to prioritize its own economic development over committing to collective climate goals. However, everyone is worse off in the long run if environmental degradation worsens. Additionally, if some nations decide to not reduce their emissions, the economies that do act ethically and take on the short-term losses while implementing climate-friendly policies suffer more. In 2009 at COP15, developed nations had jointly committed to mobilizing USD 100 billion per year by 2020 to support developing countries in tackling the ill effects of climate change, which they have yet to deliver on. A developing economy like India is then faced with the challenge of transforming into an industrialized economy without harming the environment. Climate justice is thus an important conversation in the discourse, and fair social floors and ceilings need to be enacted to ensure human dignity and well-being for all.

Fair Consumption Space

Changes in traditional lifestyles are required to meet climate goals, and high-consuming societies need to be at the forefront of this transition. Hot or Cool Institute, a public interest think tank that works at the intersection of society and sustainability, introduced the concept of a 'fair consumption space' in their report titled '*1.5-Degree Lifestyles: Towards A Fair Consumption Space for All.*' They defined it as follows:

> An ecologically healthy perimeter that supports within it an equitable distribution of resources and opportunities for individuals and societies to fulfil their needs and achieve wellbeing. Within this space, there are a range of regenerative options, but there are also clear demarcating limits to over- and underconsumption: with a cap in emissions, overconsumption by one person affects the prospects of another, and encroaches into another's consumption space, requiring collectively working toward a more equitable distribution of limited carbon budgets.[31]

A contracted carbon budget, growing inequities and an urgent timeline underscore the urgency of moving towards such a fair consumption space. It would require both systemic and individual behaviour change; there should be absolute reductions in consumption in tandem with a shift towards more sustainable and efficient options. The onus of change has to be borne not only by individuals but by governments, businesses and communities at large. India has a lower carbon footprint than most upper-middle and high-income economies. According to the '*1.5 Degree Lifestyles*' report, India can achieve the 1.5-degree target by adopting sustainable practices at the rate of 30 per cent in both system-focused and consumption-focused scenarios. Transport forms a significant portion of India's ecological footprint, and reducing demand and moving towards lower-intensity modes would be beneficial in the long run. A low-carbon lifestyle can be fostered by targeting system-focused options, such as encouraging renewable energy transitions, which are locked in in the given infrastructure and are not within the purview of consumer choice.

India's vast and growing population makes it an important global player in achieving climate goals through the adoption of a low-carbon lifestyle. The country has a rich history of organic and sustainable practices. Nonetheless, growing urbanization and rapid economic growth are putting massive pressure on the environment. India was positioned as one of the top seven emitters in the world in 2020, alongside China, EU27, Brazil, Indonesia, the US and the Russian Federation. However, the nation's per capita emissions are well below the global average; the world average GHG emissions were 6.3 tons of CO_2 equivalent[*] (tCO2e) in 2020, and India's per capita emissions were 2.4 tCO2e. In contrast, the per-capita level stood at 14 tCO2e for the United States of America, 13 tCO2e for the Russian Federation, 9.7 tCO2e in China, and above 7 tCO2e for Brazil, Indonesia and the European Union. On average, least developed economies emit 2.3 tCO2e per capita annually, evidencing that there are unfair gaps between the consumption and burden of change levied on emerging and high-income economies.[†] The issue requires more efficient multilateralism—in diplomacy, policy and financing—to enact climate justice and ensure that developing nations are able to meet their full growth and development potential without compromising on climate goals.

---

[*] CO2e (e for equivalent) refers to the number of metric tons of CO2 emissions with the same global warming potential as one metric ton of another greenhouse gas.

[†] https://www.unep.org/resources/emissions-gap-report-2022

Figure 11: Current Annual Lifestyle Carbon Footprint Per Capita in India (rounded values)

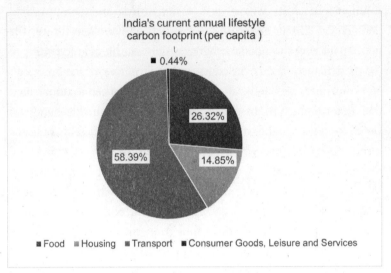

India's current annual lifestyle carbon footprint (per capita)

■ 0.44%

26.32%

58.39%   14.85%

■ Food ■ Housing ■ Transport ■ Consumer Goods, Leisure and Services

Source: Hot or Cool Institute

Aspirational Lifestyles—Opening Room to Improve Human Well-being

Since climate change threatens human dignity and well-being, the goal of transitioning to a greener economy is also to provide better educational, skilling and income opportunities to people. However, there is a need to decouple well-being from its traditional association with higher consumption and resource use. In this spirit, PM Modi envisioned 'LiFE'—'Lifestyle for Environment' as a global movement where individual lifestyles and sustainable consumption propel climate action with the support of all key stakeholders. The environmental consequences of lifestyles are not deliberate but rather the result of people aspiring to improve their lives. LiFE is a forward-looking approach that blends traditional knowledge and practices with sustainable technology and innovations. The PM envisioned three major transitions that will drive the global LiFE movement: a shift in demand, a shift in supply and a shift in policies. These simultaneous shifts will empower individuals and communities, democratize climate action and help us achieve a resilient future. The policy paradigm should incentivize a sustainable lifestyle according to the particular context of the country. The incentives of the producers and consumers need to be aligned, and countries need to understand that there is no one-size-fits-all measure for sustainable living. In India, for instance, the transport sector bears the highest share of the carbon footprint, two-wheelers in particular. In Iceland, where 100 per cent of the electricity grid is produced from renewable sources, it would be a good idea to transition to electric vehicles.* However, in India, electricity is chiefly generated from coal. What makes for a stronger case for our nation is thus strengthening and promoting the use of public transport systems and perhaps the electrification of last-mile connectivity options.

Figure 12: India's Carbon Footprint per Capita, Transport Sector

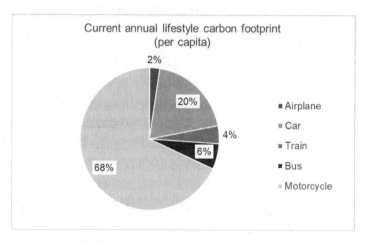

Source: Hot or Cool Institute

---

* https://hotorcool.org/1-5-degree-lifestyles-report/

We should work towards enabling systemic shifts to create a new 'choice set.' Beyond individual choices, an ecosystem must exist that fosters a low carbon footprint and presents sustainability as the easier choice to make.[32] This can be achieved by decarbonizing high-impact sectors of the economy, agriculture, energy, mobility and buildings and construction among others, through a mix of technological innovation, behaviour changes and government policies. Increasing energy efficiency, upgrading supply chains, transitioning to renewable energy sources and implementing low-carbon technologies, such as carbon capture and storage, all help realize this goal.

Circular Economy: Waste to Wealth

Close to 35 per cent of India's population lives in urban areas that produce fifty-five million tonnes of municipal solid waste (MSW) every year. This number is expected to soar up to 125 million tonnes annually by 2031.* With rapid urbanization and a looming climate catastrophe, there is no room to underutilize the limited resources we have left. That is where the concept of circularity comes in; a malleable term that has varying understandings, circularity and the circular economy moves away from a linear form of consumption and production to multi-cycle value chains where the waste at the end of the chain is used again at the beginning, thereby advancing directives of 'zero waste.' It reimagines the material flow of the manufacturing process in a comprehensive manner and may as well be the key to India championing a green transition without conceding its growth potential. Estimates show that India could

---

* https://www.ibef.org/blogs/circular-economy-for-sustainable-development-in-india#:~:text=Circular%20Economy%20in%20India&text=It%20is%20a%20restorative%20approach,materials%20to%20reduce%20environmental%20impacts.

reap yearly benefits of $624 billion or 40 lakh crore by 2050 by reducing negative externalities.[*] The circular economy can potentially generate 1.4 crore jobs. India's G20 presidency comes at an opportune time to endorse circularity at a national and multilateral level. The global stage provides an opportunity to advance the concerns and development of other emerging economies. The Federation of Indian Chambers of Commerce & Industry (FICCI), NITI Aayog and the European Union, along with other industry partners, are working to develop a Unified National Circularity Measurement Framework for standardized benchmarking and reporting, which can potentially extend and be adopted by other developing nations. The system solutions framework can only be effective if all parts of society cooperate and participate in the transition. By the very nature of circularity, cross-sectoral collaboration is key to achieving the optimization of the supply chains and enhance the competitiveness of the economy. Sustained growth cannot be attained by chasing the low hanging fruits of environmental degradation, labour exploitation and devaluing exchange rates. Instead, public and private players need to work together to increase the underlying productivity of resources and, thereby, secure a healthy ecology for the future.

Table 2: UNIDO's Nine Rs

Guiding Principle	Reduce-by-Design
User-to-User Perspective	Refuse, Reuse, Reduce
User-to-Business Perspective	Repair, Refurbish, Remanufacture
Business-to-Business Perspective	Repurpose, Recycle

Source: https://buildingcircularity.org/

---

[*] Ibef.org _Circular-economy-for-sustainable-development-in-india.

The Government of India has enacted several recycling and waste-management policies towards this goal. Eleven focus-area committees were established with leadership from the corresponding line ministries and officials from the Ministry of Environment, Forest and Climate Change of India (MoEFCC) and NITI Aayog, in addition to experts, academics and industry representatives. The purpose of the committees is to create all-inclusive action plans for moving from a linear to a circular economy in the particular focus areas and implement the procedures required to guarantee the efficient execution of their conclusions and suggestions.

S. No.	Focus Area	Concerned Line Ministry
1	Municipal Solid Waste and Liquid Waste	Ministry of Housing and Urban Affairs
2	Scrap Metal (Ferrous and Non-Ferrous)	Ministry of Steel
3	Electronic Waste	Ministry of Electronics and Information Technology
4	Lithium Ion (Li-ion) Batteries	NITI Aayog
5	Solar Panels	MNRE
6	Gypsum	Department for Promotion of Industry and Internal Trade
7	Toxic and Hazardous Industrial Waste	Department of Chemicals and Petrochemicals
8	Used Oil Waste	Ministry of Petroleum and Natural Gas
9	Agriculture Waste	Ministry of Agriculture and Farmers' Welfare
10	Tyre and Rubber Recycling	Department for Promotion of Industry and Internal Trade
11	End-of-Life Vehicles (ELVs)	Ministry of Road Transport and Highways

Source: https://pib.gov.in/PressReleasePage.aspx?PRID=1705772

Green Budget and Green Finance

Green budget tagging initiatives have been proposed and implemented in several nations to help policymakers and observers better understand and act in support of climate-positive objectives. Some existing tagging initiatives have ostensibly been effective in meeting this purpose[*] and spurred other nations to follow suit. There is also potential for those that perform highly on green budget tracking to use the system to demonstrate progress to donors and the private sector. Yet, it is arguable whether green tagging efforts have any impact on decision making, in part because the two-point Likert scale (green or not green) for measuring climate impact provides rather limited new information. Further, in many developing nations where these efforts take place, there is no systematic approach to making impact-based trade-off decisions, so it is unclear where the green budgeting information filters in. A 2021 World Bank report[†] provides a helpful review of national approaches to green budget tagging, considering eighteen national and subnational governments. Additional budget-tagging guides have been developed by the OECD (2021),[33] the IMF (2021),[34] the IADB (Pizarro et al., 2021)[35] and the European Commission (2022).[36] The World Bank report delineates two approaches to the definition of climate-relevant activities in green budget tagging: objective-based definitions and policy-based definitions. Objective-based definitions identify climate-positive activities based on their intended impact (often using the Rio markers), while policy-based ones consider the activities directly 'referenced in national climate change policy documents'[37] and usually consider ten to twenty policy types.

---

[*] https://openknowledge.worldbank.org/handle/10986/35174
[†] Ibid.

The Paris agreement adopted at the 21st Conference of Parties (COP21) in December 2015 is the first legally binding universal treaty on climate change. The primary goal of the Paris agreement is to limit global warming to well below 2 degrees Celsius above pre-industrial levels while pursuing efforts to limit the increase to 1.5 degrees Celsius. Under the treaty, nations need to submit nationally determined contributions (NDCs) where they submit their goals and targets for reducing greenhouse gas emission. India updated its NDCs submission to the UNFCCC in August 2022 and, amongst other things, proposed a reduction of emissions intensity of its GDP by 45 per cent by 2030 from its 2005 level, achieving 50 per cent cumulative electric-power-installed capacity from non-fossil fuel-based energy sources by 2030 through technology transfer and low-cost international finance including the Green Climate Fund (GCF) as well as creating an additional carbon sink of 2.5 to 3 billion tonnes of CO_2 equivalent through an increased forest and tree cover by 2030. Further, India promises to 'put forward and further propagate a healthy and sustainable way of living based on traditions and values of conservation and moderation, including through a mass movement for 'LiFE' as a key to combating climate change.'* The traditional way of living in India has always incorporated elements of recycling, reusing and judicious use. Mission LiFE emphasizes the merits of such a living and mobilizes individuals and communities to be at the center of conservation efforts. A target, to be achieved by 2028, has been set to make at least 80 per cent of all villages and urban local bodies in India environmentally friendly. Finance, education and technology are key enablers for climate and development action.

---

* India's Updated First Nationally Determined Contribution Under Paris Agreement (2021–30)

Policy Recommendations for a Greener Future

The climate change phenomenon is uninsured, and its consequences are spread evenly across the developed and developing economies. The developed economies have already used up 70 per cent of the world's carbon budget and the rest of the world has very little space for consumption-driven growth. Current models of growth are extractive and exploitative, and unless we begin the transition to alternative models, it is impossible to enhance competitiveness in the long term. This requires investments in resilience building and capacity building, without which the whole planet will suffer the consequences of hitting the planetary limits. Climate action and sustainable development are intrinsically interlinked because both aim to address the challenges of environmental degradation, social inequality and economic development, which are all interconnected and interdependent. Hence, there is an urgency of climate resilient development, which requires multi-level, multi-stakeholder collaboration across key areas including finance, technology and sustainable consumption and production. This also requires a systemic transformation across sectors including energy, agriculture and finance. The efforts towards these transitions often create friction and to maximize synergies, it is crucial to create an international enabling environment for smoother and swifter transitions for developing countries, which includes access to low-cost technologies and financing. The way forward for a climate-resilient development is to identify key policy areas that require urgent international attention.

Strengthening International Cooperation and Partnerships: International cooperation on climate change has a long history both within and outside the UN climate regime. Recently, the climate and environment agenda are also being actively discussed in a growing number of international agreements operating at sectoral levels, as well as within the practices of many multilateral fora including the G20 and G7. The Indian G20 presidency in 2023, for instance, prioritized the LiFE initiative to mainstream sustainable lifestyles by focusing on sustainable patterns of consumption and production. It mainstreamed certain key components including technology, innovation and financing as crucial to create an international enabling environment. The Global Infrastructure Facility is another G20 initiative led by Australia to fund sustainable infrastructure projects. The facility has identified certain key sectors for action including energy, transport, social infrastructure and ICT to promote mitigation, adaptation and resilience building. International cooperation therefore helps countries achieve long-term targets when it supports development and diffusion of low-carbon technologies, often at the level of individual sectors, which can simultaneously lead to significant benefits in the areas of sustainable development and equitable access. Now, it is also the time to bring a chronological and substantive sequencing to international climate negotiations. A continuity in the discussion will strengthen the legitimacy of claims and accelerate progress towards achieving the goals laid out in various COPs. It is also important to rebuild the trust in multilateral processes through inclusion, accountability and active participation of key stakeholders at all levels. International cooperation and strengthened partnerships will lay the foundation for paving climate-resilient development pathways. It also necessitates the world to acknowledge the special needs of developing countries and emerging economies that are striving to enhance economic competitiveness while preserving the environment at the same time. These countries need a larger share of the carbon budget to grow while also investing in infrastructure for a just and green transition. From this foundational block flows the next critical element—financing for green growth.

Transforming International Financial Architecture: It is impossible to reimagine development and build climate-proof ecosystems for the future without significant investments. The world is already falling backwards on the hard-fought progress on SDGs. Developing countries, battered by the pandemic, geopolitical conflicts, rising inequalities, natural disasters and impacts of climate change, have limited policy and fiscal space to help their people deal with these challenges. Further, lack of access to technology, finance and limited capacity is inhibiting their efforts to grow sustainably. All these are adding to their woes created by non-transparent financing models and pushing the countries on the brink of debt crisis. Most of the world's poorest countries are at risk of insolvency and default. Further, an SDG financing gap of $500 billion per year is crippling the developing countries to fulfil their three-fold priority of mitigating and adapting to climate change, industrializing without carbonizing and lifting millions out of poverty, all at the same time. There is an urgent need for developing countries to be provided with adequate liquidity, concessional financing, effective mechanisms of debt relief and restructuring and accelerating private financing. Even as we do not have clarity on how developed countries will double adaptation finance to at least $40 billion in 2025, as agreed in Glasgow, there is still the question of delivery of the $100 billion a year promise to support climate action in developing countries, which remains unfulfilled. The scale of resources required to meet current and future global challenges necessitates exploring innovative ways to mobilize financial resources through a mix of concessional and non-concessional loans, equity participation, guarantees, dedicated trust funds, as well as other blended financing and de-risking mechanisms. If the current cascading crises and the failure of countries and multilateral institutions to urgently respond to the crises present a key learning to us today, it is that business as usual models and discussions will not work in coming years and there is an urgent need to revamp international financial architecture.

Actions	Pathways
Tap into synergistic opportunities to achieve sustainable development and address climate change.	• Enhance integrated planning by leveraging existing instruments such as NDC, Voluntary National Reviews (VNR), National Biodiversity Strategy and Action Plans (NBSAPs). • Invest in climate resilient-development models. • Maximize co-benefits.
Transform financing instruments.	• Reform Multilateral Development Banks (MDBs) • Ensure countries have access to low-interest loans for the long term to finance green transition. • Reduce the cost of capital in developing countries.
Reimagine policy and regulatory frameworks.	• Leverage the potential of data for efficient policymakers. • Create an international enabling-policy space for easy transfer of technology. • Overcome technical, financial, planning, organizational and behavioural barriers. • Affirm the need for evidence-based policies.
Transform the relationship between humanity and nature.	• See value in initiatives such a LiFE – for demand-side mitigation.
Climate justice is to be at the core of all actions.	• Prioritize the needs of marginalized, poor and vulnerable communities, most impacted by transformational pathways. • Strengthen national and local development and climate strategies including NDCs.

Climate action and sustainable development are intrinsically interlinked and interdependent. There is a need for climate-resilient development with a focus on adaptation and mitigation and the future sustainable world should take into account the need to transform human interface with nature. This slowdown has been widespread. Effects of climate change on GDP in developing countries can amount to close to 12 per cent. GDP losses can make much stronger impacts—increased poverty rate, disproportionate and additional hardships for children. While several developed nations got away with progressing at the cost of the environment, developing nations in this day and age hardly have the same allowance. Vulnerable and marginalized countries that contribute minimally to the climate crisis bear a disproportionate burden of its costs, and a balance of responsibilities is required to ensure climate justice.

After a comprehensive examination of the significant trends that are currently shaping the global landscape, impacting nations and their citizens, and, by extension, our collective future, we go on to explore the dynamics of countries within this dynamic global backdrop. Our focus now shifts to understanding the factors contributing to a nation's growth and the drivers of prosperity.

3

What Makes Nations Tick?

Evolving global value chains, geo-political conflicts, digitalization and climate change all become important aspects that define the world we live in. This brings to attention the importance of taking into account the drift of the winds while the nation steers forward or understanding the dynamic changes unfolding in our external context. Embedded in this external global context are nations whose growth rate and strategy vary greatly from one another. Individual countries across the globe have followed different growth trajectories depending on their conditions, locations and what is suitable for their economy. For instance, as per a study by Kim and Lau (1994),[1] a comparison of the sources of economic growth in the Four East Asian Tigers compared to Germany, France, the United Kingdom and the United States revealed a significant difference. Capital accumulation emerged as the primary driver of economic growth in the Four Tigers, contributing 48 to 72 per cent, while in the other group of industrialized countries, technical progress played a larger role, accounting for 46 to 71 per cent of their economic growth.

To be specific, every country needs to leverage its current contemporary context and chart their own growth strategy to create national prosperity Industrialization and International Trade have historically served as significant drivers of growth for many nations.[2] Governments have often prioritized industrial development for rapid economic expansion, sometimes at the expense of sectors like agriculture. Additionally, international trade is widely recognized as a crucial component of growth, particularly in the case of East Asian countries that have experienced exceptional economic progress, influencing trade policies in many developing nations. In an era of globalization, a nation's competitiveness relies on its capacity for innovation and advancement. Companies often thrive when they are confronted by strong domestic rivals, responsive suppliers and demanding local customers. As a result, competition increasingly becomes centered on assimilating knowledge and the role of the nation becomes exceedingly important. Competitive advantage is a localized process shaped by national values, culture, economic structures, institutions and historical factors.[3] Different countries exhibit varying patterns of competitiveness, excelling in specific industries when their environment fosters growth and competition. Whatever growth strategy a nation may choose depending on its priorities and competitive advantage, the national policy and business environment has a crucial role to play in the success or failure of the adopted strategy. Therefore, countries prosper in some industries because their domestic environment is progressive and dynamic in nature.

A nation's prosperity is significantly influenced by the pursuit of economic growth, which is driven by factors such as capital accumulation, technological advancement, human capital development, entrepreneurial innovation, favourable institutions and government interventions. The phenomenon of economic growth elicits a question about its driving forces and whether they will remain consistent for this growth to happen. Historically, classical economists tied growth to investments and improved productivity, with an emphasis on the role of capital accumulation. Neoclassical economists in the early twentieth century identified land, capital and labour along with technological progress as key growth factors in capitalist nations, where increased utilization of these elements correlated with economic growth.[4] The growth models can broadly be classified into two categories—exogenous and endogenous models. The former adopts the neoclassical production function and assumes that the productivity of production factors decreases over time, while the latter argues that the productivity of production factors remains relatively constant.[5] Neoclassical models estimate a concept called convergence, where less affluent economies are expected to grow at a faster rate compared to wealthier ones due to diminishing returns on factors of production. In contrast to neoclassical models, endogenous models do not anticipate convergence. They contend that a country's level of human capital, among other factors, plays a crucial role in long-term development. Nations with a significant stock of human capital are expected to grow faster than those lacking in this regard. There are various models that explain drivers of economic growth. What makes nations tick? – is an age-old question that the discipline of economics has been addressing.

Economic growth can be viewed as a dynamic process in which each economy creates interactions between the various productive factors that, in conjunction with economic policies, enable the production of a greater quantity of goods and services, thereby enhancing the well-being of the population. Based on exogenous and endogenous growth theories, different models have been proposed to explain economic growth, including the human factor, capital accumulation and technological change, among other factors of production.[6] Robert Lucas's paper, 'On the Mechanics of Economic Development' provides a detailed analysis of economic development mechanisms, presenting three key models that serve as fundamental frameworks for understanding the drivers and dynamics driving economic growth and prosperity.[7] The first model strongly emphasizes the aggregation of human capital and technological advancement as drivers of economic growth, wherein the rate of technological progress is exogenous and determines the paths that per capita consumption and the stock of capital should take to maximize utility over time. The second model assumes that technological progress is endogenous. The aim is to determine the trajectories that the variables of state, level of knowledge and stock of capital, as well as the variables of control, per capita consumption and effort directed towards production, must take to maximize the function of intertemporal utility. According to this, capital growth must correspond to the expansion of the population plus the increase in technological stocks. The third model highlights international trade between nations and the aggregation of human capital through practical learning as the main forces behind economic growth.

There is a long-term relationship between institutional structures, economic growth and policy settings in most countries. In particular, the focus is twofold: first, the potential impact of human capital, research and development activity, macroeconomic and structural policy settings, trade policy and financial market conditions on economic efficiency; second, the impact of many of the same factors on the accumulation of physical capital.* Conforming to Bassanini and Scarpetta (2011), one of the key determinants of actual output per capita is the accumulation rate

---

* https://www.oecd.org/economy/growth/18450995.pdf

of physical capital, albeit its impact may be more or less lasting depending on how much technical innovation is integrated into new capital.[8] Cross-country variations in production per capita may be influenced by significant variations in investment rates, with business-sector investment rates typically averaging 10-20 per cent of GDP. Moreover, major changes in investment rates between nations are not very uncommon.

Availability and quality of human capital is yet another key driver of economic growth. One of the main drivers of growth in most developed countries has been the improvement of human capital. Numerous empirical scholarly studies on economic development and growth also assume that the formal skills and experience incorporated into the labour force serve as a kind of human capital. On the one hand, human capital may experience diminishing returns, which means higher education and ability-driven workforces may eventually achieve better income levels but not always achieve higher income-growth rates. On the other hand, investing in human capital may have a more lasting effect on the growth process if high levels of training and skills are combined with more intensive Research and Development (R&D) and a faster rate of technological advancement or if a highly skilled workforce aids the adoption of new technologies. Simultaneously, spending on R&D can be seen as an investment in knowledge that produces new technologies along with more efficient uses of the physical and human capital that is already in place. There seems to be a stronger consensus about R&D's potential to have a long-lasting impact on growth, implying that higher R&D spending would be connected to consistently higher growth rates. Government intervention may impact the resources allocated to R&D. Spillover effects, in particular, suggest that innovators may not fully capture the potential rewards from new ideas. As a result, without government involvement, the private sector would probably conduct less R&D than what could be socially optimal. This justifies certain government involvement in R&D, including direct funding and provision as well as indirect actions like tax incentives and the protection of intellectual property rights to promote private-sector R&D. Since the 1980s, total expenditure on research and development (R&D) as a share of GDP has increased, notably in OECD nations like Sweden, Japan and others. This rise is mostly attributable to an increased R&D activity in the business sector, representing most of this expenditure.

In the context of growth studies, three issues have generally been considered with respect to macroeconomic policy settings: the benefits of establishing and maintaining low inflation, the impact of government deficits on private investment and the possibility of negative impacts on growth stemming from a too-large government sector.[*] Common explanations for lower and more steady inflation rates include decreased economic uncertainty and improved price mechanism effectiveness. In situations where there are tax distortions or where investment decisions are made with a long-term perspective, a decrease in inflation may have an overall impact on the rate of capital accumulation. Additionally, the uncertainty brought on by increased inflation volatility may deter businesses from engaging in initiatives that provide high rewards and higher levels of inherent risk.

The fiscal policy setting can also have an impact on output and growth throughout the business cycle. It has been asserted that taxes required to pay for government spending may also skew incentives, which would have a negative impact on the effective use of resources and, in turn, on the level or rate of increase of the output. It can be concluded there is a possibility of a 'size'

---

[*] https://www.oecd.org/economy/growth/18450995.pdf

effect of government intervention as well as effects resulting from the financing and structure of public expenditures. The productive effects of public expenditure are likely to be greater than the social costs of generating money at a low level. However, government spending and necessary taxes could rise to a point where they start to dominate growth at the expense of efficiency. These detrimental impacts might be particularly pronounced in situations where public spending is primarily dependent on 'unproductive' activities, and the financing is heavily dependent on more 'distortionary' levies (like direct taxes).

Financial systems support capital accumulation and the dissemination of new technology, both of which contribute to economic growth. By directing small individual savings into successful large-scale investments and providing savers with a high level of liquidity, a well-developed financial system has the potential to mobilize funds. Additionally, diversification protects individual savers from idiosyncratic risk and lowers the cost of gathering and analysing information about potential initiatives, for instance, through professional financial advising services. These services will certainly enable the economy to flourish. Theories have proposed that trade can also result in profits via economies of scale, exposure to competition and the dissemination of information. These might lead to increased overall efficiency as well as a potential increase in investment. Certain large nations (especially the OECD countries) that have made progress by lowering tariff barriers and removing non-tariff barriers suggest there have been positive outcomes from trade. Additionally, trade can also be endogenous in the growth process. The relative openness of the trade policies in countries implies that the volume of trade reflects growth patterns as much as it restricts in the form of tariff and non-tariff barriers. Over the years, institutional and policy settings have undergone tremendous transformation. Thus, multiple aspects including trade, human resources, investment, government intervention, private sector participation, monetary and fiscal measures, have been studied through the lens of understanding their impact on a nation's economic growth. Each of the aforementioned aspects get thoroughly investigated across the world by various scholars to draw insights on what makes nations tick. The next section of the chapter will showcase a few case studies and shed light on the drivers of growth that led their economies to prosper. The following cases will emphasize specific strategies that have worked for each of them based on their unique circumstances and locations. Rather than offering a one-size-fits-all theory of what spurs growth, the goal is to identify specific variables that have proven effective in certain economies and consider how well they may apply in different contexts.

The East-Asian Miracle

The economies of East Asia witnessed exponential growth after the 1990s; their economies have been termed the 'East Asian miracle,' starting with Japan and followed by the Four Asian Tigers, namely South Korea, Singapore, Taiwan (China) and Hong Kong, and further continuing with Malaysia, Indonesia and Thailand. These countries, driven by exports and rapid industrialization, technological advancement and government interventions, have maintained an increasing economic growth rate since the 1960s, joining the world's wealthiest nations. Most economists and policymakers concur that openness to international trade most likely promotes development and growth. The experience of East Asian tigers has helped to create this consensus in certain aspects. Scholars have put forth different theories explaining the rise of the East Asian tigers. In agreement with Masahiko Aoki (1998),[9] the 'market friendly' view suggests that this exceptional economic growth in these East Asian countries resulted from long-term macroeconomic stability that led to large-scale capital accumulation and that state intervention had little to no impact on the economy. On the other hand, the 'market-failure' approach says that market failures in the various processes (resource allocation, capital mobilization, technology upgradation etc.) of the development of the economy require the state to intervene to maintain equilibrium.

Trade Strategy and Industrialization as Growth Engines in East Asia

The achievements of East Asia appear to demonstrate the benefits of pursuing an outward-looking trade strategy, the openness strategies that were adopted and close coordination between the government, private entities and the market. In Hong Kong and Singapore (after the end of its experimentation with import substitution in the early 1960s), openness was accomplished by ending all import restrictions and allowing free rein to the export sector. While export credit was made available by both economies, it was not subsidized, and Singapore concentrated its efforts on attracting in foreign investment for exporting companies.[10] Certainly, Japan, South Korea and Taiwan took a distinctive approach during their periods of rapid economic growth by maintaining substantial trade barriers. In the case of South Korea, their net tariff rates varied from approximately 40 per cent in the mid-1960s decreasing to around 21 per cent at the beginning of the 1980s, and further dropping to approximately 12 per cent in the early 1990s. Taiwan, on the other hand, had tariff levels of 35 per cent, 31 per cent and 10 per cent during similar time frames.[11] In addition, these countries also retained significant non-tariff barriers, although they eventually reduced them. To illustrate,

South Korea imposed restrictions or prohibitions on 40 per cent of its imports in 1973, a figure that decreased to 25 per cent by 1981 but remained substantial. The proportion of restricted imports decreased even more in the 1980s, reaching 3 per cent by 1991. In the case of Taiwan, the percentage of goods subject to various import limitations decreased from about 50 per cent in the mid-1960s to less than one per cent in the early 1980s.

To elaborate more on the concept of openness, the East Asian economies' accelerated growth is intrinsically linked to international trade and outward-oriented policies. According to Coe and Helpman's study (1995), international trade can support economic growth by providing a pathway for the diffusion of managerial and technological expertise.[12] Regarding imports, producers in less-developed nations may benefit from the education provided by more developed foreign suppliers and the innovations included in imported products. On the export front, producers might pick up tips from foreign buyers about using more cutting-edge technology to satisfy global market standards. In contemporary development models, the diffusion of technology through such channels is a major source of growth. Domestic firms are encouraged by outward-looking policies to compete in international markets rather than make goods for a niche domestic market. Without the protection of trade barriers, domestic firms are encouraged to develop and improve efficiency, which supports growth. Access to bigger markets, which had been made possible by international trade, may also encourage growth. A nation's capacity to develop may depend on its capacity to sell to a large market in economies with competitive markets and increasing returns to scale in production. Suppose, a leading sector, such as the export sector, generates a sufficiently large market. In that case, growth can be achieved even if the domestic market is so small that a single sector cannot benefit from investing.

Subsidies or exemptions permitting duty-free entry offset or eliminate import barriers for certain capital goods or inputs used in the export industry.[13] Furthermore, East Asian countries assisted exporters by ensuring that credit was rationed, offering tax breaks and implementing several other preferential measures to boost export development. These measures were typically applied uniformly across sectors and to all potential exporters to avoid discrimination between different export activities. Therefore, it appears that policymakers in these nations were more focused on growing exports than on the product exported. This combination of policies had the overall impact of making the effective tariff protection rates in several manufacturing sectors 'moderate' and, occasionally, negative, which reflected the incentive for businesses to focus on domestic rather than international markets. Policies in East Asia tended to support a close integration with international markets. In the end, their trade and growth performance mirrored this.

The second element of the development strategies used by East Asian countries, again with some variation, was an industrial policy meant to support industries or select winners through non-neutral subsidies and other measures. South Korea is a good example of how these policies were implemented, and at the same time, the general approach to industrial policies differed by nation. In order to promote particular emerging industries, the Korean government encouraged the establishment of large companies that received temporary monopolies in the late 1960s and early 1970s.[14] Examples from the early 1960s include cement, fertilizer and petroleum processing; from the late 1960s and early 1970s, steel and petrochemicals; and from the mid-to-late 1970s, shipbuilding, other chemicals, capital goods and high-end consumer goods. More medium- and small-sized businesses have recently received preferential treatment, notably in the electronics industry. These sectors benefited from preferential loan access, lower taxes and, most importantly, protection from foreign rivalry. Taiwan and Singapore used industrial policies to some degree. For instance, since the early 1980s, Taiwan has given preferential loans, technological assistance and management support to certain 'strategic' industries as it has steadily lost its comparative advantage in labour-intensive manufacturing. Although it hasn't made a conscious effort to identify specific 'winners,' the Singaporean government has invested in state-owned enterprises and offered incentives to draw private capital into several important industries since the late 1960s. Singapore also attempted to direct output toward more skill-intensive industries by increasing wages through administrative guidance from the middle of the 1970s to the middle of the 1980s.

It is important to note a few general characteristics of East Asian industrial- and export-promotion strategies. Firstly, government assistance was typically provided to businesses based on their market performance, especially in global markets. East Asian policymakers managed to resist the urge to allocate the majority of resources to rent seekers with access or to subsidize businesses operating at a loss. Secondly, with different degrees of import barriers, all East Asian exporters had reasonably uniform incentives for exporting across almost all industries and activities. The purpose of these export subsidies was to counteract the incentives given by current tariffs and non-tariff import barriers to producing for domestic-protected sectors. Thirdly, despite trade barriers, free entry for imports that supply inputs to the export sector was sufficient to open the import sector significantly. A portion of the trend towards liberalization mentioned above can be assigned to the fact that, as the export sector diversified, the variety of imported products also expanded. For instance, the quantity of automatically approved import items in South Korea grew from 800 in the late 1960s to 5600 in the early 1980s and nearly 10,000 in the early 1990s. This partially mirrored the effects of the exemptions for products intended for export. Additionally, the number of imported inputs increased along with the export sector's growth. Governments that attempted to encourage rather than 'pick' individual winners to fight in global markets appeared to have the most success with industrial policy, with the market serving as the final arbiter of whether ongoing support of industry was warranted.[15] It was anticipated that East Asian governments would support emerging industries, and when they did so, it was expected of them to become competitive exporters. The fact that the new industries, with few exceptions, could not export successfully clearly indicated to the South Korean government that the heavy chemical industry push was not producing the desired results. As a result, there weren't many economic pursuits within the domestic economy for which producers could expect constant protection from global competitive pressures. In this sense, the ability to export competitively became the 'market test' used by the authorities.[16]

Role of East Asian Governments in the Financial Markets

East Asian governments have undertaken extensive interventions in the functioning of their financial systems, which is one of the core reasons for their rapid economic growth. They significantly influenced financial institutions and markets by imposing regulations and directing credit towards specific industries, aiming to boost savings and control investment. However, their actions extended beyond capital markets, with limited credit incentives in exchange for robust export performance. Government interventions focused on two main objectives: enhancing the efficiency of financial markets and institutions, which enable firms to diversify investments beyond retained earnings, and reducing risk premiums by spreading risks more broadly. However, resource allocation may be ineffective if there are systematic disparities between private and societal returns. Therefore, the goal of government intervention in financial markets was also to rectify any subsequent misallocation of resources.

Government financial policies can be categorized into three types: creating markets and financial institutions; regulating them; and incentivizing companies through subsidies, credit, or foreign-exchange access, frequently on preferential conditions, to groups or industries that carry out important tasks or perform admirably.[17]

The East Asian economies were adept at channeling their savings into ventures that yielded substantial returns. This success owed much to government interventions in the financial sector, aimed at promoting savings and efficient capital allocation. Governments in East Asia employed various strategies to encourage national savings, such as creating financial institutions, overseeing their operations, maintaining minimal fiscal deficits or even achieving surpluses. Among the significant institutions established by governments to boost savings, the postal saving systems in Japan, Malaysia, Singapore and Taiwan (China) held a prominent place.[18] These systems attracted a large number of small savers by providing security and easy accessibility. Remarkably, in rural areas, the postal saving system provided convenient access through an extensive network of post offices. Through the implementation of income tax exemptions on interest accrued from postal deposits, Japan further promoted the utilization of postal savings. A parallel approach has been adopted by Taiwan (China) since 1965, and South Korea follows a similar policy for accounts falling below a predefined threshold. Postal savings institutions in Japan, Taiwan and Singapore have successfully mobilized substantial savings since the 1950s. They played an influential role during financial uncertainty, for instance, families shifted their savings from banks to postal savings. By 1930, demand deposits in banks were only twice as high as postal savings, a significant change from the sixfold difference seen in 1920. Governments also influenced national saving rates with three different kinds of regulations. Some regulations were designed to discourage consumption, some to enhance the safety and soundness of private financial intermediaries and some to transfer resources from households to corporations.[19] To begin with, many East Asian governments actively discouraged the expansion of the mortgage market and other types of consumer lending, which in turn deterred household consumption. Consumers had to rely on their savings to make significant purchases, such as buying houses or consumer goods, since access to consumer credit for housing and durable goods was severely limited. This limitation on borrowing led to a rapid increase in the proportion of income saved, and it's worth noting that constraints on liquidity and the development of consumer credit markets may explain regional variations in savings rates. Secondly, stringent banking regulations, including prudential measures, significantly reduced the risk of bank failures, thereby increasing dependence on the banking system. This further strengthened deposit growth due to enhanced security. Third, despite conventional knowledge suggesting that financial repression discourages saving, it can, in fact, lead to higher savings rates. Financial repression, also known as financial restraint, may improve savings when interest rates are lowered for income transfers from households to corporations, especially considering that the corporate sector typically has a higher propensity to save than households. This ultimately contributes to an overall increase in total savings. East Asian economies maintained relatively moderate levels of financial repression, with interest rates staying slightly below equilibrium levels. Moreover, policies associated with financial restraint encouraged savings by pitting companies against each other to achieve higher rates of exports and investment. Entry restrictions, combined with financial repression, enhanced the profitability and stability of financial institutions, thereby providing strong incentives for banks to make prudent investments.

East Asia stands out for its great stability in its macroeconomic policies as compared to many other developing regions, like Latin America. This stability has several benefits for savings. A key aspect is the impact on the variability of returns for savers, especially in a context where most countries do not offer fully indexed accounts. Macroeconomic stability, characterized by low inflation rates, translates to a more secure return on savings, which, in turn, encourages saving. High and extremely unpredictable inflation, which often results in significantly negative real interest rates, tends to deter savings. In contrast, real interest rates on deposits have generally remained positive and steady in East Asian economies, aligning with trends observed in the United States and other industrialized nations. The foundation of macroeconomic stability in East Asia is partly built on the government's practice of maintaining modest deficits or substantial surpluses, directly influencing high levels of national savings. Across the East Asian nations, a consistent commitment to both public and private savings has been maintained. Governments in the region have enacted various regulations aimed at enhancing the solvency of financial institutions, which has a positive ripple effect on savings rates and the efficient allocation of resources. Security is vital for preserving savings, and even if individuals lack confidence in financial institutions, they might save, albeit with lower returns compared to a stable financial system.[20] Furthermore, well-functioning financial institutions are indispensable for efficient financial intermediation, directing funds to their most productive purposes in the economy.

Simultaneously, there is substantial evidence indicating that financial crises occur quite frequently in the absence of government intervention. Relying solely on private entities is inadequate to prevent such crises, as financial institutions tend to take on excessive debt without sufficient precautions. These issues are exacerbated by the presence of negative externalities resulting from information gaps, where individuals may struggle to distinguish between sound and unsound banks due to limited information. In addition, interbank credit dynamics and moral hazard concerns contribute to the problem, as undercapitalized financial institutions are more inclined to take substantial risks, knowing that they would incur lower losses in the event of a debt default compared to well-capitalized institutions.

Prudential regulations, also known as safety regulations, were reinforced in several stages across several East Asian countries, beginning with Japan, Hong Kong and Singapore in the 1970s, followed by Malaysia, Taiwan (China) and Thailand in the 1980s, and Indonesia in the 1990s.[21] The adoption of these strict regulations was driven by three main factors. Firstly, in countries like Singapore, the early recognition of the significance of solid prudential regulations for domestic and global trade has greatly benefited its financial services sector, which constitutes a substantial portion of its GDP, supported by the confidence of foreign financial and business communities. Secondly, in some countries, governments initially held direct control over banks and financial institutions as part of their development strategy, but as these nations advanced and deregulated in areas like interest rates and market entry, the necessity for more strong indirect prudential regulations emerged due to the reduction in direct control of the government. Thirdly, in specific countries, prudential regulations were introduced solely in reaction to financial crises, exemplified by Hong Kong's reinforcement of regulations in 1965 and 1985, prompted by financial turmoil linked to real estate speculation. According to Stiglitz and Uy (1996),[22] prudential regulations come in various forms, each requiring different levels of regulatory oversight. The simplest regulations involve monitoring aspects like capital, net worth and collateral, with some discretion involved, especially in collateral valuation. On the other hand, assessing the riskiness of specific transactions necessitates more active involvement from bank examiners. Capital adequacy requirements stand out as a instrumental tool for governments to ensure the solvency of financial institutions. These requirements reduce the risk of liabilities surpassing assets and encourage banks to take calculated risks.

To lessen the danger of defaults, East Asian regulators have encouraged banks to enforce substantial collateral requirements, resulting in the characterization of banks in the region as 'pawnshop' banks.[23] Despite the fact that collateral requirements won't keep banks afloat, regulators have adopted this conservative method to reduce the amount of risk banks can take. Many East Asian banks have predominantly used real estate as collateral, inadvertently tying their fate to the real estate market. During the period of high real estate inflation, they extended their lending aggressively, leaving their portfolios vulnerable to declining asset values. For example, in Japan, banks that engaged in speculative real estate lending in the 1980s faced challenges when real estate prices sharply dropped in the early 1990s. To address this issue, East Asian policymakers aimed to discourage speculative lending, which had been a major cause of financial crises in countries like Hong Kong, Malaysia, Thailand and Japan. Speculative lending was aggravated by loans to related parties seeking to profit from speculation. In response, regulatory authorities imposed tighter restrictions on real estate lending, lending to related parties and concentrated lending to a small number of borrowers. However, enforcing restrictions on related-party lending proved difficult due to weak disclosure regulations and interconnected ownership among banks and companies in Indonesia, Japan and Thailand. Central banks in East Asia, with the exception of Indonesia, have been fairly effective in monitoring the loan portfolios of commercial banks, resulting in a lower proportion of nonperforming loans compared to many other developing countries. They've also maintained considerable supervision over bank management to prevent dishonest or unqualified lenders from entering the market. Singapore, in particular, takes pride in its regulatory authorities, who have denied admission to institutions like the Bank of Credit and Commerce International (BCCI) due to issues that were overlooked by supposedly more capable regulators in the United States and the United Kingdom. However, there have been noticeable exceptions to this generally positive perception of bank supervision. In the 1980s, weak supervision contributed to financial difficulties in banks in Hong Kong, Indonesia, Korea and Malaysia. Subsequently, Indonesia tightened its bank supervision when it opened up entry for private banks, revealing the issue of nonperforming loans more prominently. These details provide a more in-depth understanding of the regulatory landscape in East Asia, highlighting both successful instances and challenges that have been encountered in the region, and the importance of effective monitoring in mitigating financial risks.

In contrast to the more rigid regulatory frameworks of industrialized nations, East Asian countries have adopted a regulatory approach characterized by regulatory discretion and continuous dialogue between regulators and banks. This method enables regulators to provide banks with feedback on the risk levels in their portfolios. In several East Asian nations like Japan, Malaysia and Thailand, modern supervision practices blend contemporary prudential regulations with traditional interactive monitoring, encouraging cooperation through the government's influence over branch licensing, rediscounts and various regulations. Government-owned banks in South Korea followed a similar approach until their privatization in 1983, and a comparable pattern was observed in Singapore and Taiwan. This contrasts with the behavior of government-owned banks in numerous other developing countries. In various countries, political factors frequently lead to the distortion of lending decisions by government-owned banks, resulting in loans aimed at compensating for the deficiencies of underperforming public enterprises. Moreover, because governments frequently introduce funds into publicly owned banks when they encounter financial troubles, these banks may prioritize solvency less than their private counterparts. To mitigate these issues, East Asian governments implemented various measures. Taiwan enforced rigorous security requirements and incentivized responsible behavior among public bank employees, even penalizing those whose loans defaulted. Meanwhile, South Korea established strict performance standards to guide the lending decisions of its banks. Broadly, East Asian governments have employed proactive measures to address the challenges associated with government-owned banks, eventually promoting responsible lending practices and reducing the influence of political factors.

Regulators in East Asia and other emerging economies have expressed concerns about effectively overseeing nonbank financial entities like cooperatives, merchant banks and leasing firms. These institutions have multiplied since the early 1980s but they have faced less stringent supervision compared to commercial banks, leading to considerable instances of insolvency. For instance, Thailand and Malaysia experienced bankruptcies among finance firms and deposit-taking cooperatives in the early 1980s, which jeopardized the solvency of commercial banks as they often used nonbank financial subsidiaries to avoid regulatory scrutiny. Consequently, regulators have intensified their supervision of nonbank financial institutions in response to these insolvency issues.

Growth in East Asian countries has been successful after their governments embraced new economic strategies in land reform, financial measures to encourage investment, mechanisms to hold down inflation, incentives for labour-intensive, outward-looking industries, government intervention to correct distortions in free market operations and heavy investment in education.[24] The East Asian experience makes it abundantly evident that economies that have adopted consistent outward-oriented trade strategies have outperformed on a drastic level. This indicates that other emerging markets should adopt a development strategy that depends on global economic integration rather than isolation. In East Asia, governments aimed to harness and guide market forces rather than replace them. Their government lending initiatives worked alongside private lending, rather than removing it. While governments regulated lending priorities and discouraged real estate and consumer goods lending, they still adhered to commercial standards. Effective macroeconomic management, characterized by low inflation and modest fiscal deficits, encouraged long-term planning and investment, contributing to significant savings rates. These economies promoted a business-friendly environment, supported by legal and regulatory frameworks conducive to private investment. They also emphasized improved communication between businesses and government. A critical aspect was the government's allocation of rewards, such as access to credit and foreign exchange, based on performance, monitored by both the government and competing firms.[25]

The Japanese Economic Miracle: Tremendous Economic Growth after World War II

Japan exhibited rapid and consistent economic growth between the years 1945 and 1991, particularly after the World War II till the end of the Cold War; this extraordinary growth is termed as the Japanese Economic Miracle. Despite having nearly nothing left, Japan's economy recovered very quickly. In a span of less than ten years, the country's economy reached a high growth, which surpassed the pre-war average every year after 1955 at a rate that was last seen in 1939. Japan's remarkable rapid economic growth can be attributed to four key factors: technological advancement, capital accumulation, an increase in the quantity and quality of labour and a boost in international trade. The country managed these elements through strategic planning, encouraging collaboration among businesses, individuals and the government. This collaborative effort propelled Japan to become the world's third-largest economy.

After suffering significant industrial losses during World War II, the country was left with a surplus of devalued capital assets. This adversity prompted Japan to embark on a path of renewal and innovation. The country acquired cutting-edge technology without waiting for their assets to fully depreciate that was complemented by government policies favouring technological progress. An expansionary monetary policy made low-cost capital accessible to new companies, while strict regulation kept interest rates low. Growing businesses enjoyed substantial tax deductions and depreciation benefits, promoting their expansion. Personal income taxation was also slowed through partial exemption of interest and dividend incomes from taxation. Personal income taxation was eased, partially exempting interest and dividend income from taxes.* The Japanese effectively expanded their economy by taking advantage of their unique characteristics, particularly their ability to adapt and utilize foreign technologies. They were skilled at integrating imported technologies. Foreign nations influenced and inspired much of Japan's new technology, prompting substantial imports. For example, imported robots and tools were widely used in the automobile industry, while imported generators were enhanced to improve their effectiveness. Japanese ingenuity refined these technologies, boosting their efficiency by 20 per cent. In order to import and use the application of these new technologies, Japan invested in growing industrial and manufacturing firms. This led to accumulating substantial returns due to the high marginal productivity of capital. As a result, the country was able to maintain a reasonable level of inflation. Japan's average personal saving to disposable income ratio between 1959 and 1970 stood at 18.3 per cent, in stark contrast to Germany's 12 per cent and the United States' 7 per cent.† It's crucial to understand that Japan's success in adopting foreign technology was only possible because they combined it with domestic innovation, thereby turning it into industrial strength.

Improving labour quantity and quality was a major factor in Japan's prosperity. Since there was a significant increase in labour after the war, wages increased at a slower rate than labour productivity in the 1950s. Productivity increased alongside wages in the 1960s, enabling businesses to operate effectively and expand. Additionally, labour shifted from low-productivity activities, such as agriculture and forestry, to high-productivity industries, such as automotive, electronics and aviation. The *Keiretsu*, large corporate organizations affiliated by shareholdings, played a significant

_____

* https://econreview.berkeley.edu/the-japanese-economic-miracle/
† Ibid.

role in boosting the Japanese economy. They connected banks, trade firms and industrialists through ownership of stock or other assets. Because of their sheer size, they had the resources and contacts to surpass domestic and foreign competitors, aggressively capturing market share in industries with rapid development and long-term potential. Additionally, the government promoted the *Keiretsu* by implementing regulations that would reduce rivalry between firms. Supporting industries of Japan were vital in two specific areas. Firstly, the Japanese trading companies, which were enormous firms, had established global networks and aided many Japanese companies in entering foreign markets. They continue to be crucial for marketing to less developed and smaller nations, and they serve as valuable information sources for Japanese companies with limited staff abroad or less established worldwide operations. Secondly, the media was a crucial supporting industry. As a result, mass media and mass advertising are well-developed in Japan, and the country also ranks second to the United States in terms of daily television advertising minutes. This was a significant advantage for Japanese durable consumer goods companies looking to enter competitive overseas markets, such as the United States and United Kingdom that required mass marketing knowledge.

While the Japanese people played an instrumental role in driving rapid economic growth, it is also important to acknowledge the significant influence of economic policies and planning in this process. These policies and strategies have been carefully devised and put in place by policymakers to sustain this growth signifying the incredible role of the Japanese political system in its development. Two major initiatives were significant in driving Japan's rapid economic expansion—the Yoshida Doctrine and the role of the Ministry of International Trade and Industry (MITI).[26] The Yoshida Doctrine supported in shaping Japan's postwar economic recovery. This doctrine prioritized economic reconstruction and development as immediate national objectives, while entrusting defense responsibilities to the US military, which resulted in considerable reductions in military expenditure. This strategic allocation of resources allowed Japan to channel its full resources and efforts toward rebuilding its economy, serving as a foundation for the nation's swift recovery following defeat in World War II. Shigeru Yoshida held a position of great authority within the government and was primarily responsible for driving industrial growth in the country, during the period of rapid expansion. MITI adopted an approach that involved providing guidance and incentives to private enterprises, creating a level playing field that favored industries identified by the government as having long-term growth potential. In particular, MITI focused on enhancing the output of a few distinct industries such as steel, shipbuilding, chemicals and machinery, as they had potential in the global market. By expanding these sectors, MITI facilitated Japan's entry into international markets and accelerated the overall economic growth. Lastly, in the post-war period, Japan's exports grew rapidly, stimulating the economy. The government was able to cut export prices, making them significantly less expensive than those of other nations, by offering tax exemptions for expenses related to international sales and preferential loans. Additionally, they primarily supported anticompetitive behaviour and mergers in industries with export-oriented businesses. However, the capacity of Japan to switch up its exports every few years was the single most significant aspect of global trade that helped it stay ahead of its rivals. Between 1950 and 1965, Japan's exports shifted from textiles and other general merchandise to machinery and metals.

Since it is clear that favourable government policies were necessary for Japan's economic recovery, post-conflict nations today should adopt similar measures. Additionally, improved international cooperation is crucial for the development of post-conflict nations' economies. While increased exports and knowledge exchange with other nations were significant factors in Japan's prosperity, current developing economies can benefit from international agreements. Some economists have recommended establishing global 'commodity stabilization agreements' to shield vulnerable but expanding sectors because commodities are prone to substantial price changes. Concentrating on industries with rapid and sustained growth is a crucial objective that is useful and relevant for rebuilding economies. Governments and other nations must work together on this by negotiating and enforcing tax laws that benefit vulnerable but expanding businesses. A nation can grow and recover rapidly by determining its comparative advantage and maximizing that industry's potential.

While the East Asian Tigers' case studies and Japan's economic trajectory offered valuable insights as to what worked for their economies, innovation as a driver of growth stands out strongly in the Danish economic system.

The Danish Innovation System

The Danish economy rests on the four pillars of high wages, narrow income disparities, investments in skills and education and high levels of taxation to fund an advanced welfare state.[27] Denmark's hybrid institutional approach to economic governance offers an interesting case study for understanding how to balance market-based and plan-based regulation. A constructive connection between the state and civil society at the core of this adaptability can be seen. This goes beyond only a specific history of tripartite interaction between the state, social partners and labour market regulation.

With only a few huge companies, the Danish innovation system is characterized by many SMEs. Danish businesses are innovative in general, but these innovations typically take the shape of incremental changes. Even if the percentage of share is declining, a significant portion of Denmark's manufacturing value-added employment and exports are in low-tech (defined as industries with low R&D intensity) enterprises. There are several exceptions to the low- and medium-tech industries' conventional dominance, with pharmaceuticals and other companies with a focus on healthcare being the most significant. However, low or medium R&D intensity does not equate to low knowledge-intensive production. In reality, the production of many of the so-called low- and medium-tech industries that define Denmark is based on extensive knowledge inputs related to a significant rate of change and flexibility in firms' resource use, which includes rapid diffusion of new innovations and frequent incremental product innovation, which combines a high level of expertise in industrial design with advanced organizational techniques and marketing techniques. The interactions between skilled labour, engineers and marketing people are frequently reflected in innovations.

Denmark as a Welfare State

Denmark has achieved social and economic objectives while creating a comprehensive welfare state. This is in contrast with the pro-market attitude of conventional economics, as shown in the policy recommendations made by global organizations like the Organization for Economic Co-operation and Development (OECD) and the World Bank. Large public expenditure, high and progressive tax rates and extensive public social programmes have all been identified as growth inhibitors. The threat posed by globalization has been used to reinforce this overarching argument.

Thus, globalization has been regarded as a danger to the welfare state. However, studies show that the effects of globalization on welfare states are not uniform, and the Scandinavian welfare model appears to be functioning rather well in this environment. For instance, the large investments in R&D and the fast-growing ICT sectors may contribute to Finland and Sweden's success. However, in Denmark, where low-technology industries such as food, textiles and furniture still significantly contribute to exports, this change has not occurred to the same extent. Another structural shortcoming of the Danish economy has been noted to be the absence of significant multinational companies. In the context of the increasingly globalized learning economy, where the ability and opportunity to acquire new knowledge is critical for the success of individuals, organizations and regions, certain perceived 'weaknesses' often reveal themselves as strengths. These so-called weaknesses are integral components of an innovation system that relies on learning through direct experience.[28] Simultaneously, it is vital for economic performance that a substantial portion of the public actively engages in the processes of transformation, collaborating in the conception, implementation and utilization of novel ideas.

In Denmark and other Nordic nations, compromises between centralized employers' organizations and centralized trade unions create the most significant framework for the labour market. This is contrary to systems where regulations are established through state-enacted laws. A complicated set of legislative laws forms the basis for the relative autonomy of the relevant organizations. The state's mediation programme, which can be used when disputes arise, is the most significant. Galenson, the American labor market expert who first proposed the idea of 'the Danish Model' in the early 1950s, mostly discusses this method of regulation and the harmonious interactions between capital and labour.[29]

Several mechanisms contribute to the dynamic performance of the Danish economy concerning the modern 'learning economy.' This includes the self-regulatory labour market; however, other aspects of the 'national system of innovation and competence-building'[30] must be considered. Over time, 'adaptability' can be viewed as the most important requirement for sustained economic expansion. The adaptability of the Danish system has a macro-political and microeconomic dimension.[31] Firstly, the interaction among the state, civil society and interest groups during times of crisis leads to the creation of new regulatory and reformative frameworks, which most likely illustrate the macro-political dimension. Secondly, one important factor underlying excellent economic performance is the microeconomic dimension of adaptability, which is represented in interactive learning and incremental innovation.

Origin of Denmark's Adaptive-Governance Mode

Some significant historical events have impacted Denmark's current socioeconomic system and the patterns of interaction between the state and civil society.[32] The events played a significant role in integrating and accommodating farmers and workers as citizens economically, politically and socially; this process further led to social cohesion in the Danish society. The year 1868 was significant for developing a strategy focused on consensus by the decision makers. The ruling class was forced to abandon its colonial aspirations. The event acquired a symbolic significance and prompted a change to a more reserved national policy with a social component.

The competition in the corn export market between the United States and Russia in the 1870s led to a crucial time of turmoil and transformation. Danish agriculture had to undergo major change because its exports to the United Kingdom had drastically decreased. After more than ten years of difficult adaptation—during which the establishment of farmers' cooperatives was vital—the result was a drastically transformed agricultural economy marked by the export of animal-based goods like butter and bacon, with the United Kingdom still serving as a major market. The proliferation of farmers' cooperatives manufacturing milk and meat products was a major factor in the transition. An important requirement for this transformation was a key social innovation—the establishment and the rapid expansion of 'people's high schools'[33] was founded on the philosophy of Grundtvig, a social philosopher. These new institutions' main goal was to educate farmers and instill confidence in them as citizens and producers. Self-organization among the farmers had a significant role in driving the transformation process, which was also encouraged and made legal by the state. A new law promoting the establishment of high schools was passed, and the constitution safeguarded the formation of free associations. At this point, civil society and the state were already interacting in public policy in a way that supported one another, particularly during times of economic and social crisis. This system was developed through significant social concessions, which further resulted in the enactment of laws, particularly in 1899 and 1933, that recognized the rights of organized workers.

This corporatist institutional structure, where centralized trade unions and employers' organizations took on significant responsibilities in close association with governmental authorities, was reinforced in the post-war era by the development of the welfare state and the continued growth of labour market institutions governed by tripartite bodies. The fact that in the post-war period (until 2001), neither the left- nor the right-wing governments had a solid majority in Parliament contributed to a climate of consensus-seeking.[34] This type of governance, in which the state and civil society work together, is analogous to a specific kind of economic dynamics in which social equality and economic productivity go hand in hand.

Macroeconomic Performance and the Development of Denmark

Denmark's strong macroeconomic performance and high standard of living are a result of its unique combination of a free market system and a strong social security. A proactive economic policy was formed after the war, combining Keynesian active finance theory with income and wage policy, in response to widespread fears of the onset of a new depression. According to Lundvall (2009), 'International competitiveness' was outlined as a key goal in the modest and increasingly open economy.[35] The strong, highly centralized labour unions agreed on wage restraint in return for social reforms that improved social security and job development, reflected in various 'economic policy packages' created as social compromises. One long-term result was an ambitious unemployment support system in terms of income coverage and duration of coverage. At the same time, the resources devoted to the 'active labour market' policy were very constrained until the 1970s–1980s. Additionally, the establishment of public care for children and the elderly was another crucial component of the reforms. As a result, all women, even those with young children, were free to enter the labour market, and jobs that catered primarily to women were also created.

The economy was still heavily reliant on agriculture and agro-food just after the war. Because of the limited industrial basis, most private services and products were either related to private consumption, the public sector or agro-food, construction and trading. The 1950s were a time of transition when there was a major change in the allocation of manpower from agricultural to manufacturing and services. Growth rates were high, as well as unemployment rates. Public sector initiatives for elderly care, childcare, education and health saw substantial growth in the 1960s. While unemployment rates were low, inflation rates increased a little bit. The growth in labour productivity was rapid. Full employment and inflation control were the goals of this economic strategy, but it ran into difficulties by the end of the 1960s as the public debt and balance of payments deficits started to rise. The approach was discontinued in the mid-1970s following a period of stagflation and excessive inflation.

In 1973, during the first oil crisis, the unemployment rate was remarkably low, at less than 1 per cent, while inflation surged. It took approximately two decades of restrictive economic policies for high unemployment rates to emerge, and it wasn't until 1990 that the unemployment rate dropped below 10 per cent. Since then, there has been consistent economic stability with annual reductions in unemployment. Over two decades, the economic strategy evolved to address weaknesses in the Danish Model. The public sector faced pressure to modernize for improved productivity and service orientation. Labour market policies became more active, limiting access to unemployment benefits for young workers. Currency rate policies were abandoned upon joining the European Monetary System. Wage constraints were imposed through high unemployment rates rather than explicit wage policies. The focus shifted towards long-term global competitiveness, emphasizing innovation and non-price factors. These changes reflect a comprehensive effort to adapt the economic strategy, seeking to enhance productivity, competitiveness and sustainability within the Danish economy.

Fundamentals of the Danish Model

o *Examining Self-Regulation of the Labour Market*

Flexibility in the labour market combined with job security has gained recognition as a key component of European labour market reforms, particularly in Denmark. Flexibility in managing the labour force is crucial for companies in the current dynamic market conditions and rapid advancement of technology. Security is key to achieving this flexibility without putting workers in an unsustainable situation.[36] In the Danish Model, adjustments between the centralized trade unions and employers' organizations serve as the primary foundation for labour-market regulations. These regulations establish a framework that leaves flexibility for additional sector-level specificity and even for tailoring the regulations to a particular firm or worker. In contrast, state laws are not used to establish rules in this system. Intricate governmental regulations support the autonomy of the pertinent organizations. The state's ability to mediate disagreements is the factor that is considered to be most significant. The state has the right to end strikes; in this case, the mediation authority has the power to compel a settlement between the parties.

The Danish labour model has evolved with changes in how wages and working conditions are determined at different levels, including central, sectoral, regional and individual levels. However, certain core aspects have remained unchanged. In the 1990s, negotiations became decentralized to individual firms, but they still operate within the framework set by sector and national agreements. This self-regulatory approach in labour markets continues to play a key role in the dynamic performance of the Danish economy.

o   *The Educational Model of Denmark*

In Denmark, central and local governments mostly provide primary and secondary education. Most of the educators and teachers at school agree that one of the main responsibilities of the educational system is to help students develop their 'social competence,'[37] which includes cooperative, collective and communication abilities. Even when they are not acknowledged officially, the educational system provides informal structures that facilitate interactive learning and economic innovation.

A country's culture and its educational system are closely intertwined, with the latter playing a significant role in the development of modern nation states. Denmark's educational history is distinctive, marked by a blend of official funding and educational standards, alongside significant freedom in structuring education to align with cultural values and pedagogical approaches. The influence of figures like Grundtvig, who emphasized public high schools for adult learners without formal diplomas, continues to shape the discourse on education.[38] In Denmark, students complete homework faster compared to other countries, often opting to work during their free time to earn money for personal consumption. This early engagement in wage-earning positions while still in school encourages financial independence from their parents. It highlights Denmark's unique educational landscape, emphasizing both academic and practical life skills, as well as individual financial responsibility among its young population.

Compared to larger European nations like France, Germany and the United Kingdom, the atmosphere at the primary and secondary schools of Denmark is more democratic and casual. At an early age, students develop the habit of challenging their instructors and other authorities and communicating and working with them in groups. Together, these components of youth education foster a variety of personal qualities, including the capacity for taking on responsibility as well as for interacting and cooperating with others.

o *Labour Market as a Foundation for Learning and Knowledge Creation*

Similar to its educational system, Denmark's labour market has unique characteristics that set it apart globally. These are essential in explaining the existence of a particular Danish mode of learning and innovation.[39] Some of the most significant institutional features of the Danish labour market include high participation rates, high job mobility, publicly organized and comparatively generous unemployment support, broad discretion in hiring and firing employees and fundamental social security provided by an advanced welfare state. Because of this, the labour market is characterized by high levels of flexibility when it comes to switching jobs between employers, similar to the US labour market.

However, as compared to the US model, the publicly organized system of unemployment assistance is more substantial than that of many other European countries. Globally, it has a high substitution rate and a lengthy period during which benefits can be obtained. This aspect is reflected in studies that indicate wage earners in Denmark report fewer concerns about job instability than wage earners in other European nations, despite frequent job changes and a lack of legally required employment security. As discussed, compared to the EU average, the labour-market participation rate among Danish people is considerably higher. At first glance, this appears counter-intuitive because a heavy tax burden combined with government subsidies ought to deter individuals from actively seeking employment. Economists have demonstrated that a sizable fraction of workers, particularly women, earn little from being engaged in the labour market as a result of the tax system. Danish employees, and women in particular, place a great deal of value on having an occupation and the individual liberty it offers, which could be one explanation for their continued activity.

The high labour-market mobility is also a reflection of the high proportion of small businesses and workplaces in the Danish industrial structure. Due to this high degree of mobility and the small size of firms, employers have little incentive to fund their own employees' education. Denmark has created an essentially unique publicly supported system of continuing education to make up for this. More adult workers than in other nations continue their education, and the public sector spends more of the Gross National Product (GNP) on higher education for adults than in any other country in the world. As a result, the public sector has assumed a role that small Danish businesses would find challenging to carry out on their own.

o *Relevance of the Learning and Innovation Approach*

A picture emerges in which competence in Danish business life develops primarily through recruitment and secondarily only through the establishment of internal education and further schooling under the auspices of the firm.[40] The high amount of mobility applies to technicians, professors and even top management in addition to just unskilled labourers. Danish businesses are operating in this environment in order to take part in the learning economy. High mobility has advantages and disadvantages, and it is comparable to the levels observed in high-tech areas like Silicon Valley.

On the bright side, companies can hire seasoned workers from other businesses. The relatively significant migration of skilled workers between companies causes the economy to quickly adopt new ideas. Given that employees frequently meet with co-workers from different companies, this also serves as a foundation for business interactions. These benefits are particularly reachable for business clusters situated in industrial districts, which are conglomerations of businesses with a similar industry or technological specialization. In these areas, specialized labour markets will emerge; they will include individuals who have a high degree of competence, and there will be a significant amount of knowledge transfer between companies through job changes. At the same time, firms might also become keen on investing resources in educating their own employees because they can anticipate an indirect return on their investment in the form of future employees who are educated by other firms. In such a setting, it is significant to emphasize that this is matched by labour-market policy, which incorporates representatives from unions and employee organizations and is primarily regionalized.

o   *Denmark's Learning-Based Economy in a Global Perspective*

Although Denmark's post-war history has been marked by uncertainties, long-term prosperity is demonstrated by a high GNP per capita, and the economy is currently doing quite well. Therefore, to get an understanding of the relative success of the Danish economy, it is essential to learn about its performance within the global context. The phrase 'learning economy' has been introduced with the intention of distinguishing this concept from that of the knowledge-based economy, which is more widely used. The 'learning economy' concept signals that the most important change is not the more intensive use of knowledge in the economy but rather that knowledge becomes obsolete more rapidly than before; therefore, it is imperative that firms engage in organizational learning and that workers constantly attain greater competence and new skills.[41]

Utilizing information technology extensively has turned into an imperative for competitiveness. The use of scientific knowledge presents new prospects for businesses in all areas of the economy, including the low-technology sectors. Codified knowledge is becoming increasingly important than it once was, particularly in high-income nations. However, these modifications accelerate change and transformation because they work in tandem with global competition. As a result, individuals as well as companies are increasingly faced with issues that can only be resolved by throwing out the old approaches and learning new ones. The accelerated rate of change is a sign of increased competitiveness, which has led to a selection of companies and individuals who can adapt quickly, thus speeding up the rate of change.

New issues arise as a result of the shift to a learning economy for individuals, businesses and national institutions. Over the course of one's lifecycle, it becomes vital for the individual to be able to acquire new abilities or to update existing ones. It might become even more important than the initial high wage to find a location of employment where there are opportunities to pick up new abilities. The promotion of what is occasionally referred to as 'personal skills' or 'social skills' needs to be accompanied by a significant emphasis on teaching fundamental disciplines like language and mathematics in the educational system.[42]

In the learning economy, an increasing emphasis on innovative organizational forms that support functional flexibility and networking at the level of the firm can be observed. Operating a hierarchical organization with multiple vertical layers and various divisions and roles within the company is inefficient in a continuously changing environment. It also takes time to respond because whenever information is obtained from the bottom level, it has to be communicated to the top level and vice-versa. Large, vertically integrated companies are frequently less productive than smaller ones that participate in relational networking and contracting. The way a company attracts talent is a crucial aspect of competition, and this will be demonstrated by the learning opportunities it provides to its employees. The level of participation and autonomy provided to employees is related to this. Combining a solid scientific foundation with national structures that support individual, organizational and inter-organizational learning is a challenge for national economies. Labour markets can include high mobility with substantial public training spending or low mobility with strong training investments.

The robust functioning of the Danish economy is a reflection of the system's micro-relationships, which are facilitated by institutions like the welfare state, gender dynamics, educational systems and labour markets. The effectiveness of the system in terms of Doing, Using and Interacting (DUI) learning is reflected in the performance of the economy. The success has been largely attributed to the consequent incremental innovation processes and adaptive capacity in the global setting where the rate of change is high.

The European Social Survey indicates that in Denmark, trust levels among agents appear to be consistently greater than elsewhere, and this along with the system's relatively small size leads to a high level of interaction between agents both within and between organizations. This results in low transaction costs but, more crucially, low-cost interactive-learning processes that quickly disseminate new knowledge on organizational best practices and technological advancements. The Danish innovation system has been quite successful in terms of learning by doing, learning by using and learning by interacting, despite being somewhat weak in terms of producing codified knowledge through its R&D activities.[42] The high level of frequency in terms of interaction is seen in the industrial networking and patterns of organizations.

Learnings from the Case Studies

Every nation has its own set of resources which drives growth for the economies. Deriving inspiration from the East Asian tigers, the Japanese economic miracle and the Danish innovation ecosystem, we draw invaluable lessons that highlight the inadequacy of a one-size-fits-all policy approach within the intricate landscape of economic development. All case studies show how countries have managed to synchronize their innate abilities and limitations with their external environment and prevailing conditions, enabling them to achieve high progress. Many countries took similar actions, but often with adverse rather than favourable results. For instance, some countries established development banks, only to discover that the funds were diverted to initiatives that tended to enrich politicians at the expense of the nation's welfare and low-return projects. The case studies highlight what worked best for the given countries in boosting their economies. The same factors may not work for other countries. The effectiveness of best practices is also limited by the external global context during a country's growth period. The core focus of this analysis are the valuable insights to be drawn from the way these countries addressed challenges and leveraged opportunities. It is important to learn from their process of strategy formulation. On analyzing the growth strategy of the case studies, one finds that economic growth was accompanied by the maintenance of macroeconomic and political stability. Cooperative behaviours and political stability within the private sector were encouraged by policies that supported a fairer income distribution and basic education for men and women. The outcome was a better business environment for investment and a more efficient utilization of human resources. At the same time, government policies changed rather than remained static in response to the economy, such as in the case of the East Asian economies. These economies, prominently represented by the Four Asian Tigers (Hong Kong, Singapore, South Korea and Taiwan), serve as a striking expression of the 'East Asian Miracle'. Their rapid industrialization and export-driven growth trajectories, despite divergent political and cultural backgrounds, emphasizes the importance of adaptable policies to distinct circumstances. On the other hand, Japan's economy was different compared to the other East Asian economies; the country's external context played a crucial role in its growth and development at an incredible rate. Governments actively contributed to the development of market institutions, such as long-term development banks and capital markets for trading bonds and stocks as well as the establishment of an institutional framework that made it possible for markets to function more efficiently. These markets and institutions aided in ensuring that a significant amount of savings was invested effectively. Governments also took advantage of their authority over the financial system to assist in allocating funds in ways that boosted economic growth. Japan's triumph underlines that a policy combination centered on technological advancement and human capital can promote sustained growth, even in resource-constrained nations. It is observed in the case studies covered that state-led interventions played a major role in enhancing and promoting economic growth. Simultaneously, for Denmark, the emancipation of women and young people and the integration of farmers and workers through self-organization, education and state-guaranteed civil rights are historical factors that laid the groundwork for the current success. In a society that values individualism as well as high levels of trust and low levels of corruption, participatory organizational learning is supported by social cohesion and an egalitarian work environment. The country's labour markets and its dedication to social welfare represent the adaptability of Nordic models in effectively confronting contemporary economic challenges. Denmark presents an alternative approach to the traditional neoliberal model of economic growth due to their unique approach to development which prioritizes social welfare, sustainable development and government intervention. Numerous neoliberal policies support reducing government intervention in the economy and encouraging free market ideals like privatization, deregulation and trade liberalization. The notion is predicated on the idea that the market allocates resources most effectively and that government intervention in the economy slows down economic growth. These policies have been criticized for aggravating income inequality by reducing social welfare programmes and deregulating the labour markets. According to a report by the Centre for Economic Policy Research (CEPR), a comparison of the period between 1960 and 1980, when most nations were restricted and inward-looking economies, and the period between 1980 and 2000, during the time of neoliberalism, showed contrasting results. The study found that before the 1980s, more progress had been made in the economic and social domains. Additionally, the East Asian countries and Denmark were able to leverage their population base to achieve economies of scale, which helped them to compete in global markets. This is because, in every nation, government and industry are primarily concerned with the concept of competitiveness. To build and maintain a competitive advantage in the global market, an industry must identify what characteristics of its home country are most important. The amount and rate of productivity development that can be achieved heavily depends on how the home country influences the pursuit of competitive advantage in specific industries.

These global lessons serve as noteworthy case studies for India, grappling with their distinctive array of challenges and advantages. All these lessons from around the globe may or may not apply to India, which deals with its unique set of problems and advantages. The focus of this chapter has been on understanding how different nations have dealt with their specific set of circumstances and carved out growth strategies. India must focus on a development and growth strategy that takes into account the country's unique make-up and maximizes the productivity of its available resources. Mapping out the country's growth trajectory requires a deep dive into the particularities of India's competitiveness fundamentals as they relate to and influence its long-term prosperity.

4

Competitiveness Fundamentals

'The only meaningful concept of competitiveness at a
national level is productivity'

The above statement was articulated by Michael Porter in his
book *Competitive Advantage of Nations*[1] which underscores
the central importance of productivity when assessing nation's
competitiveness.

Michael Porter's work on competitiveness[2] posits that the
prosperity levels of a nation depend on productivity, which, in turn,
determines the competitiveness of the region. With this approach,
Porter ties firmly the notion of competitiveness with productivity.
A region is competitive if its firms compete in the global market and
the region prospers with improved income and living standards.
The fiscal and monetary policies help in bringing in the money,
but innovation brings in ideas bolstering the capacity and growth
of the economy through new technologies, services and products.
Innovation takes place at the grassroots, at the regional level.

There are clusters of interrelated groups of industries in a region, specialized in a certain industry, indicating their innovation and successful competitive standing in the global market. This break away from other conceptions of competitiveness emphasized that it is not about what a location possesses but how productively the firm or the nation uses available resources. The importance of productivity was also evident from the East Asian miracles studied in the previous chapter. It is clear that while the pathway to increasing competitiveness would vary from region to region, the centrality of productivity remains undisputed. After taking a broad view of India's economic trajectory, the significance of the external global context for countries and factors that make nations tick, we now dive deep into the competitiveness framework and examine India's competitiveness fundamentals.

A country must decide what actions to prioritize based on what a decomposition analysis of prosperity reveals, i.e., changes in labour productivity and labour mobilization. Decomposition essentially provides insights into underlying dynamics, needs and opportunities. It helps us assess what drives or hinders prosperity levels in a certain region. For instance, since productivity growth is a key driver of economic growth, we can implement policies that support research and development, promote innovation and enhance education and training. Similarly, if we observe that labour or capital inputs are propelling growth, we may prioritize policies that promote investment or improve the capabilities of our labour force. This aids policymakers not only in obtaining a complete understanding of the forces that drive prosperity levels but also for determining the most effective policy intervention to sustain it.

In this chapter, the competitiveness framework that Michael Porter has developed and applied across the world over the last several decades will be extensively discussed. This framework focuses on productivity as the key driver of long-term prosperity. Overall, it offers a strategic perspective on how to translate diagnostics on a country's competitiveness fundamentals into actionable insights that drive change. A comprehensive economic strategy goes beyond individual policy improvements. It describes a location's value proposition in the global economy, signalling where and how it intends to compete. Therefore, it is important to understand the location-specific patterns of India's existing competitiveness fundamentals and the challenges that they face relative to peer economies.

Further in this chapter, we will first explore India's performance relative to peer countries on prosperity levels, which can be measured by key parameters, such as GDP per capita, poverty, inequality and, finally, performance on non-economic indicators, i.e., the social progress index. Then, we explore what drives these prosperity levels, so we turn to understanding India's performance on the key fundamentals of competitiveness, i.e., labour productivity, labour mobilization and sectoral transformation over the last three decades. And finally, we gauge the role of trade, investment and innovation in the current and past competitiveness of the country.

Introduction: Debates around the Term 'Competitiveness'

Throughout history, the term 'competitiveness' has been used to refer to various parameters. Some definitions use the term to express the ability to achieve specific economic outcomes such as a higher market share, Foreign Direct Investment (FDI) inflows, a balanced budget, a competitive exchange rate, etc. The term also gets associated with advantageous locational attributes that drive economic growth. None of these definitions offers a satisfactory explanation of the term competitiveness. The sheer variety of ways that the term competitiveness gets used has hindered the development of a well-defined comprehensive concept.

Specific periods in history shaped the definition of competitiveness. In the 1980s, the United States faced concerns about Japan's expanding market share and general economic rise This was when competitiveness got associated with the idea of gaining more global market share and low labour costs. Competitiveness was viewed as a zero-sum game, wherein one nation could be competitive only at some other country's expense. Another view on the term links it with industrial competitiveness, which emphasizes on gaining market share in specific industries Competitiveness, seen as gaining more market share in certain industries, is a limiting definition as gaining industrial leadership cannot be the ultimate objective of economic policy. Another line of thought associates the term with cheap and abundant labour. This view also doesn't capture the essence of the term competitiveness. Countries like Germany and Switzerland prove that higher prosperity levels can be achieved even with high wages and labour shortages. Yet, another explanation that ties competitiveness to having abundant natural resources falls inadequate in its explanation as many prosperous countries, like South Korea and Italy, have achieved greater prosperity despite a lack of natural resources. A school of thought stresses upon government policy intervention—targeting, protection, subsidies, import protection—as a driver of competitiveness. However, the role of government intervention appears to be modest in prosperous economies and their industries. Another definition focuses on macroeconomic indicators, such as interest rates, low government deficits and stable currencies as drivers of competitiveness. Yet again, this parameter in isolation does not show the breadth of the concept of competitiveness. Countries like South Korea and Italy have attained higher living standards despite budget deficits. Germany and Switzerland are also examples of countries that have risen despite appreciating currencies. Thus, by itself, none of these definitions offers a satisfactory explanation of the term competitiveness. These definitions offer a partial explanation of the term. The sheer variety of ways that the term competitiveness gets used hindered the development of a well-defined comprehensive concept. In an attempt to define competitiveness in a comprehensive manner, Michael Porter set out a broad framework in 1990.

Competitiveness as Productivity: Producing More with Less

In response to the diversity of definitions, Porter, together with organizations like the Council on Competitiveness, defined competitiveness as the foundation of wealth creation and economic performance. The new definition was proposed taking into account three factors—the definition had to be directly linked to prosperity, be comprehensive in its coverage of the underlying drivers, and be focused on factors that could be shaped through policy.

> Thus foundational competitiveness came to be defined as the expected level of output per working-age individual given the overall quality of a country as a place to do business. Mercedes Delgado et.al (2012)[3]

The definition highlights the productivity-focused approach taken. The output level per worker indicates how productively the available inputs are being used. An important point to be considered is that this definition takes the output per potential worker as opposed to the output per current worker. It was understood that prosperity is influenced by the productivity of employed workers and the ability to mobilize the available labour force. The economic plan's bigger challenge is getting people who want to participate in the workforce into the workforce and employed productively. The output per potential worker captures this aspect well.

To build an integrated framework, it needed to include a wide range of factors that affected foundational competitiveness. The included factors are classified into two areas: macroeconomic and microeconomic. Social infrastructure and political institutions form one of the two sub-components included in the macroeconomic area. It broadly involves determinants such as education, healthcare, the strength of the rule of law and security. The other aspect included in this category is monetary and fiscal policy. While these factors set the context for the general economy, the components in the microeconomic area are those that influence company productivity and the labour force directly. The microeconomic determinants of competitiveness included in the framework are factor conditions, demand conditions, the presence of related and supporting industries and the sophistication of company strategies. Factor conditions reveal the quality and quantity of labour available, access to capital, quality of administrative practices and physical infrastructure. Demand conditions show the sophistication of consumers' demand and consumer expenditure. Clusters, geographical agglomerations of firms, institutions, suppliers and other related elements interlinked with complementarities, bring higher productivity. The fourth factor considers the managerial influences at a firm level, an aspect that has received less attention in the literature. In addition to this wide range of factors that the framework covers, it also addresses concerns regarding endowments.

Endowments are factors inherent in a country. The mere presence of endowments, such as natural resource deposits, country size and locational attributes, does not guarantee competitiveness. While they can add to prosperity, their presence can negatively affect the economy as well. It can do so by corrupting political institutions and distorting economic policy choices. Because of this, the framework controls the effect of these endowments when estimating the role of competitiveness in economic performance. This theoretical framework helps to analyse differences in the economic performances of countries. Because of the numerous determinants of competitiveness it covers, policymakers can get detailed insights on the strengths and weaknesses of the country. While each aspect of the framework is equally important, there are some that stand out, bringing out the uniqueness of the approach. With competitiveness defined in the manner described by Porter and the fundamental components of the competitiveness framework introduced, we will now proceed to explore the framework in greater detail.

Understanding the Competitiveness Framework

In his book *The Competitive Advantage of Nations* (1990), Porter focused on explaining the importance of a suitable business environment to find the competitive industry in a nation and how to boost its productivity through a cluster-based approach. In that sense, industries are the unit of analysis that ultimately positions the nation as competitive in its global market. He further explains in the book that the natural endowments, currency value, interest rates cannot be the sole determinants of a country's prosperity. It is its ability to keep innovating and upgrading its competitive areas.

In the paper titled 'Michael Porter's Competitiveness Framework—Recent Learnings and New Research Priorities,'

Christian Ketels (2006)[4] also noted that productivity is the foundation of Porter's definition of competitiveness, as it is the main gauge of a location's long-term prosperity. Recent applications have highlighted two ramifications of this emphasis on productivity: a fundamental distinction between created and inherited prosperity and a crucial distinction between individual and economic productivity. The prosperity of a country is dependent on its economy-wide productivity, which is the amount of GDP produced for each unit of factor input available for economic activity at market prices. If there are distortions, individual productivity represented by various indicators will exaggerate the potential for affluence.

The competitiveness framework prepared by Michael Porter,[5] consists of how endowments, macroeconomic and microeconomic factors impact the foundational competitiveness of a nation. Endowments influence the prosperity of nations directly; however, they don't guarantee sustainable competitive advantage. They are affected by the policies made by the nations, which further determine whether the value of the endowments is realized and they are utilized judiciously, affecting the business environment positively. Natural resources in a country are an important endowment to boost exports and trade for raw materials. Geographical location plays an important role as an endowment. A longer coastline aids easy trade and connectivity between destinations. These factors can only influence productivity so much unless they are exhausted economically through sound macroeconomic and microeconomic policies. How endowments are utilized shapes the contours of inherited and created prosperity in nation.

As explained earlier, Porter's framework consists of two main pillars—macroeconomic and microeconomic. The macroeconomic factors are circumstances creating higher productivity but unrelated to the firms and labour productivity. Microeconomic competitiveness is different in the sense that it is focused on specific local competitive advantages of a region that enable its firms to compete successfully in the domestic as well as the global markets.

Figure 13: Porter's Competitiveness Framework

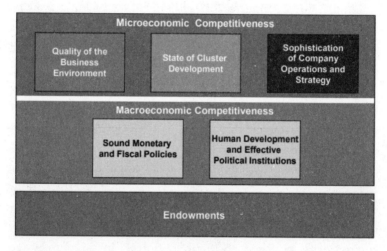

Source: Delgado, Ketels, Porter, & Stern, 2012

Macroeconomic Competitiveness

Competitiveness, as discussed in the previous section, is influenced by the circumstances in the global landscape. It is equally influenced by the condition of the nation in its macroeconomic sectors. The two dimensions of macroeconomic competitiveness are social infrastructure and political institutions (SIPI) and monetary and fiscal policy (MFP). The former includes basic health and education facilities, the rule of law and quality of political institutions in the country. The latter includes policies for fiscal sustainability, and debt inflation and the ability to manage short- and long-term fluctuations in the economy. Healthcare, education and safety are basic factors for a solid foundation to achieve competitiveness through workforce development. These facilities enhance human resources. A lower prevalence of diseases in the workforce translates to a healthier and more productive workforce. The presence of constant civil unrest or war robs the population of opportunities to learn and develop, venture forth and produce goods and services. These factors shape the social infrastructure of a nation.[6] An emphasis on strong social infrastructures is essential to produce a highly skilled workforce and attract investments for the economy, which is supplementary to a well-developed business environment. The influence of monetary and fiscal policy in the long run depends on different institutional qualities.[7] The identification of a 'good' monetary or fiscal policy is another challenge.[8] The policies need to fit all the regions' peculiarities and their requirements to achieve productivity, control inflation, structure local institutions and plan government spendings. Hence, the context for productivity to develop throughout an economy is established by macroeconomic competitiveness. However, it alone isn't sufficient to guarantee productivity.

Microeconomic Competitiveness

The microeconomic factors focus on the attributes of the national business environment, economic growth through cluster development, business management, operations and strategy. It is important to develop microeconomic capabilities within the domestic business landscape where companies compete for success. Without these capabilities, the overarching macro-framework would fail to yield desirable results.[9] The case of hyperinflation in Zimbabwe is an example of the failure of implementing strong microeconomic policies. In the late 1990s, macroeconomic reforms of land redistribution and price controls were introduced to stabilize inflation. No steps were taken to enhance microeconomic activities to promote productivity and exports. The policies disrupted agricultural productivity with a loss of exports and foreign currency, increase in corruption and black-market sales. The failure of microeconomic policies to promote sustainable economic growth and development contributed to the failure of macroeconomic reforms in Zimbabwe.[10] Endowments, the third factor in the framework, are introduced as a control since they merely act as an advantage for prosperity and do not influence productivity or get influenced by policies. The natural resources, land, labour and location of a region are what contribute to prosperity, but to increase it and the region's competitiveness, it must be utilized efficiently.

Microeconomic factors directly affect the productivity of a region and labour mobilization. They connect the inputs, incentives, strategy and operations of firms, and the quality of domestic demand and presence of related and supporting industries into one model to assess the competitive advantages of different regions. Using the diamond model as a tool to measure national competitiveness, Porter has proposed a competitiveness gauge to assess the business environment of a nation or a firm. The diamond model is, thus, an integral aspect of the microeconomic pillar of the competitiveness framework. The framework prepared by Porter and his colleagues has helped nations assess their foundational competitiveness and their attractiveness to investments. These factors must be looked at together as, without microeconomic development, the macroeconomic reforms may not result in increased prosperity.[11]

The Diamond Model

Porter proposed the diamond model as an approach to assess the quality of the business environment in a particular location. Since then, working with the diamond in a variety of locations has yielded numerous new insights into its constitution and many of its components.

Michael Porter's diamond model is the framework that points out the four forces, which if found favourable, force the firms and nations to continuously innovate and upgrade. The diamond model as a system helps answer the questions Professor Porter mentions in his book *The Competitive Advantage of Nations*:

> Why are certain companies based in certain nations capable of consistent innovation? Why do they ruthlessly pursue improvements, seeking an ever more sophisticated source of competitive advantage? Why are they able to overcome the substantial barriers to changes and innovation that so often accompany success? (Porter, 1990)

The value of an enabling business environment has been underscored time and again. Governments strive to attract investments and capital by driving efforts towards building an efficient business environment. The term captures such a wide range of factors that it can be difficult to delineate exactly what a business environment entails and what makes it conducive to growth. Porter's diamond model offers conceptual clarity here. He presents us with defined, interdependent and mutually reinforcing attributes that go on to form a dynamic system. The capacity of an industry to innovate and keep up with upgrades determines the competitiveness of firms and a nation. To keep up a nation's competitiveness, it is essential to align its changes in the drivers of competitiveness with the current circumstances in the region and the world through innovation. Nations with a competitive advantage, such as natural endowments, are not enough to sustain a position of advantage. There is a need for constant development and innovation in efficiency and developing specialized human resources, along with a domestic market with sophisticated demand, domestic rivalries and domestic suppliers.

Classical theory in economics posits arguments that suggest competitiveness exists due to cheap and abundant labour resources, government policies, different managerial practices, etc. However, through the diamond model, Professor Porter conveys that the above-mentioned factors are not sufficient to understand the competitiveness of a firm and a nation. According to him, if the classical theory explains the success of nations due to advantages in labour, land, capital and natural resources, then a new theory to understand competitiveness must begin with the premise that competition is dynamic and evolving. It should consider the globalization of competition, the power of technology, competition in global trade as well as for foreign investments and favourable business conditions in the home base for firms to run.

Looking at the diamond model, one can easily understand the crux of the competitiveness approach. The model helps us see how different components in the business environment fit together and interact with one another. Examining the economy from this perspective enables us to see the potential for all stakeholders to develop a shared understanding of what drives long-term prosperity.

Figure 14: The Diamond Model

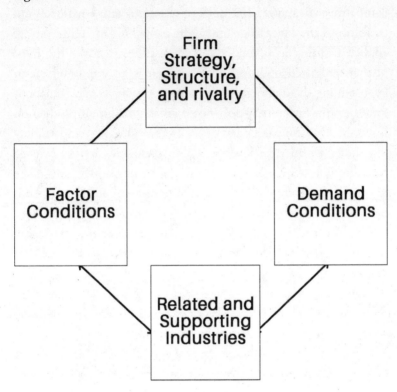

Source: Michael Porter, On Competition, 1990

1. Factor Conditions

The first dimension is factor conditions. According to Porter, the school of thought that labour, land, natural resources, capital and infrastructure are the determinants of what and how a nation trades is misleading and incomplete. He explains in his 1990 book that 'a nation is endowed with resources and it makes the most efficient and productive systems to use them for its advantage.' He asserts that the most essential resource today is the human resource, which has a knowledge base and skills to enhance these systems, increasing competitive advantage. The stock of resources with a nation is not useful until the knowledge and skills of its human resources are applied to bring in upgrades and innovations to make the most of their endowed resource. Specialization is an important factor in sustaining the competitive advantage. Having a massive labour force or heavy machinery does not translate to efficient production in industries. Companies can easily access technology and employ low-skilled workers for low wages, but their skills and knowledge base do not help bring innovation for competitive advantage in the modern international sphere of competition. To sustain a competitive advantage in the modern international competition, factors like machinery and labour force are required to be highly specialized in their respective areas. A specialized factor, such as a space scientist, has a deep knowledge to provide a set of solutions to build an uninterrupted connectivity bandwidth for the Internet. Such factors are rare and distinct, hence in the international competition, only the best nation will fare better.

The creation of specialized factors is an important determinant of a nation's ability to increase its competitiveness. Investing and developing institutions that provide education in highly niche areas of science, technology, social sciences, etc., and create a research environment for its students help bring in a specialized labour force as well as innovative equipment in the market. A nation's performance in competitiveness also depends upon how they use their selective disadvantages in their endowed resource field. Sometimes, a nation lacks correct management of its most abundant resource, assuming it already enjoys an advantage due to its existence. However, a nation that lacks resources, such as a labour force, raw materials, geographical constraints, etc., innovates to manage that scarce resource or find routes to acquire them or come up with a substitute. The disadvantage of scarce resource disguises as an important factor to induce innovation, which, in turn, makes them competitive. For example, Singapore is a small island nation with limited resources, but they emerged as a knowledge-based and a high-income level economy. The country went through decade-long transformations in different aspects, such as labour-intensive growth, skill intensive growth and knowledge- and innovation-focused growth. Their major investment was towards providing technical education and training to impart upgraded skill levels. Similarly, South Korea is another resource-constrained country that is a major player in the global competitive market, and it achieved this feat through innovation. The country set up public research institutes for advanced and applied research in the 1960s and 1970s. Government investments in R&D and incentives for private firms increased investments made by firms and even SMEs for R&D. South Korea became a highly skill-intensive country by the mid-1990s and companies like Hyundai, LG and Samsung became leading players in international competitiveness.[12]

2. Demand Conditions

The demand conditions are the second dimension. Porter, in his book *The Competitive Advantage of Nations*, talks about how the character of the home demand affects the domestic manufacturers more than the size of the home demand. The composition of home demand, made up of different age, income and cultural groups and their evolving needs, shapes a nation's demand conditions to either be favourable or unfavourable to its markets' competitiveness. The domestic buying patterns are an important indicator of emerging market-demand trends across the world. The evolving demands of the home market push the companies for constant innovation to capture the consumers, consequently helping the markets develop a sophisticated competitive advantage over their foreign rivals. The nature of the domestic buyers can help the nation gain competitive advantage if their demands are sophisticated and ever-changing. These demands lead markets to realize advanced customer needs and the standard of products and services they need to achieve. Addressing these demands keeps the markets up with innovating, upgrading and strategizing more and better, consequently meeting the demands and serving a larger demand group of international markets. If the home-demand trends represent those of another nation, the nation gets an opportunity to break into the market. The representation can sometimes be distorted due to the nation's internal political or economic conditions. Nonetheless, demand conditions push companies and nations to be more competitive by having them face such challenges. A great advantage also lies with the nations, whose tastes, preferences and values are exported along with and through their products and services.

3. Related and Supporting Industries

The third dimension, related and supporting industries, provide an advantage to the nation or a certain region with the presence of industries working closely with one another. If an industry is internationally competitive, then it can provide its related industries with efficient and cost-effective help through inputs and services to excel. Companies take advantage of the suppliers located in their domestic market with quick communication and constant exchange of knowledge and ideas, and, lastly, there is a competitive pressure on the companies and the suppliers to innovate and upgrade to keep up with each other's competitive ecosystem. The group of related industries produce complementary goods, such as for the automotive industry. The industries related are the steel industry, which makes the body of the car; the leather industry, which makes the seats and designs the interior of the car; the rubber industry, which makes the tyres of the car and the software industry, which provides navigation systems for the car, etc. The group of supporting industries provides inputs and services to other industries, such as the steel industry, and is the supporting industry for automotive companies, construction companies, etc.

The clusters of industries come into play here. The companies and suppliers are not only benefited through their related materials but also because of their proximity to each other. The presence of clusters of related industries generates a range of benefits for the local economy. Rui Baptista and Peter Swann (1998)[13] found that firms in a cluster tend to innovate more due to location externalities and knowledge spill overs. They found that a firm is more likely to innovate where the presence of firms related to their industries is stronger. In order to compete more effectively, firms also need to understand where the cluster strength of their region lies when compared with those of other similar firms.

Silicon Valley is an example for clusters that affected related industries through innovation and knowledge spill overs. Its competitive advantage lies in the natural resource 'silicon' found in the valleys of California, USA, which is used to make computer chips and transistors. The valley had a semiconductor revolution, making it a crucial place for computer hardware and software developers. The location is in proximity with institutes, Stanford and Berkeley, that provide access to world-class research programmes. A Stanford Industrial Park was created to give Stanford-owned start-up companies land on lease. The highly skilled researchers were near the suppliers of raw materials and had opportunities to set up start-ups. Hence, the educational institution aided the need for a talent pool in the Silicon Valley that brought on the research, knowledge base and investment and was in advantage due to its proximity with silicon suppliers. The Silicon Valley is home to the world's largest tech companies, Apple, Alphabet, etc.[14]

Industries also support other related domestic industries by competing. A competition within the nation speeds up the knowledge diffusion and technological changes. It fast-tracks innovation in a market within the country, which could have taken longer when competing with an international company. It creates a competitive pressure on firms to constantly improve their products and services. It also creates an opportunity for firms to collaborate in the process of knowledge sharing and encourages them to acquire workers with more specialized skills to keep up with its peers' pace of advancement. Suppliers cannot be dependent solely on the domestic companies to purchase materials from them and should participate in the international markets as well. However, companies do not need to depend on domestic suppliers for raw materials; they can source them from abroad, considering their needs, such as cost-effectiveness and quality, etc. Hence, the related and supporting industries in an economy are an important factor to encourage competitiveness through quick and easy access to specialized inputs, sharing of knowledge and information and an ecosystem for innovation.

4. Firm Strategy, Rivalry and Context

Finally, the fourth dimension is firm strategies, rivalry and context. These include approaches taken by a firm in an industry towards its area of requirement, such as cost efficiency, scaling the production, expanding the consumer base, etc. The structure of a firm refers to its organizational system and management techniques, while rivalry is the competition among firms in an industry, encouraging innovation and continuous improvement. A good strategy is crucial for a firm, as it helps identify market opportunities, understand consumer behaviour and discover new technologies, making the quality of its end products equally important.

In the process of formulating strategies, firms are able to differentiate themselves from their rivals with a unique approach to their production, which can either make or break their competitive stance in their respective industries. Countries have distinct goals that are targeted by their respective companies and individuals. As in, the companies work towards goals characteristic to their national capital markets. How companies hire talent and the quality of work and education received by these employees are important determinants of a company's success. The goals and values of the nation followed by individuals and companies determine the flow of capital and human resources in that country. This ultimately lays the trajectory of competitiveness of certain industries in that country.

A firm's structure is crucial to its efficiency and effectiveness in the market as it determines smooth operations systems. How companies are created, organized and managed depend largely on their respective national circumstances. In Italy, for example, successful international competitors are often small- or medium-sized companies that are privately owned and operated like extended families; in Germany, in contrast, companies tend to be strictly hierarchical in organization and management practices, and top managers usually have technical backgrounds.[15] There is a convergence of management structure and organization of firms that is reflective across the industry for that product. Firm rivalry helps firms by encouraging innovation and upgradation of their processes and products. Local rivals encourage constant creation and opportunities to achieve competitive advantage. This rivalry pushes every firm to produce new and better products, improving their profitability and growth, along with creating a competitive ecosystem. Porter deems domestic rivalry as the most important factor of all others in the diamond model. Domestic rivals not only want to have the greatest market share, but they also really fight for the people, technical advancement and 'bragging rights'.

A particularity about domestic rivalries is that one rival does not have an edge over another due to an advantage of classical resources. So, there is also no excuse for companies in competition to blame their domestic rival's success by calling it an unfair advantage like they do for the international competitive firms. The problem of complacent behaviour of firms towards factor costs, access to home markets, etc., due to their existence in a certain country is removed with the presence of domestic rivalries. Companies are forced to innovate and sustain their competitive advantages. Companies also collaborate to obtain government support, such as getting investments, opening the market to foreign trade, etc. Hence, domestic rivalries, a lot like domestic demand, challenges the firms to face competition within their nations. This strengthens the competitive-thinking strategy of firms to compete and excel in the international markets as well.

The Diamond as a System

The four points making up the diamond affect each other making it a system. Sophisticated buyers will not be able to move to more advanced products, for example, unless the quality of human resources permits companies to meet buyer needs. Selective disadvantages in factors of production will not motivate innovation unless rivalry is vigorous and company goals support sustained investment.[16] The elements of the diamond model are self-reinforcing. The systemic nature of the diamond requires the market to stay dynamic. According to Porter, domestic rivalry and geographic concentration are two important pieces of the diamond that transform it into a system. Domestic rivalry creates an ecosystem where specialized factors are employed or created, especially when they are in proximity. The model also shows how new entrants in a market are firms that would supply the industry with raw materials. Or vice-versa, a highly sophisticated firm enters its supplier market if it has the knowledge and expertise and finds the market attractive for profits. The diamond as a system also creates an environment for clusters of industries to flourish in a nation rather than one competitive industry. The competitive industries are interconnected through buyer-seller relationships, customers and knowledge and technology exchanges. They form a cluster concentrating geographically. The interconnectedness of industries, using the factor conditions, demand conditions, firm structure, rivalry and firm and related and supporting industries, mutually reinforces the process of competitiveness. The cluster induces the flow of benefits throughout the firms and industries in their relationships. Rivalry in one industry affects other industries in the cluster, through externalities, exercising bargaining power and diversification. New entrants in the cluster stimulate upgradation and introduction of new approaches to strategy and skills for the company. Information flows through customers and suppliers amongst the firms in the cluster leading to innovation.

These four elements engage in a mutually reinforcing process to form a dynamic system where the effects of one factor depend on the state of the others.[17] Looking at the diamond model, one can easily understand the crux of the competitiveness approach. The model helps to see how different components in the business environment fit together and interact with one another. Looking at the economy from this vantage point allows us to see the scope for all stakeholders to build a shared understanding of what drives prosperity in the long term.

With the macroeconomic and microeconomic aspects of the competitiveness framework encompassing the state of monetary and fiscal policies, quality of the business environment, the diamond model, cluster development, company strategy sophistication and endowments, there exists another essential dimension that adds to the framework's comprehensiveness. It is the social and political aspect of the framework.

India's Pursuit of Prosperity and Social Progress: A Closer Look

'The service of India means, the service of the millions who suffer. It means the ending of poverty and ignorance and poverty and disease and inequality of opportunity. The ambition of the greatest men of our generation has been to wipe every tear from every eye. That may be beyond us, but as long as there are tears and suffering, so long our work will not be over.'

—Indian Prime Minister Jawaharlal Nehru's Inaugural Address (A Tryst With Destiny)

India has been among the nations leading sustained, accelerating economic development since the 1980s. Prior to the 1980s, India's growth rate fluctuated between 3 and 4 per cent. Since the early 1990s reforms, average growth rates each decade have risen to between 5.5 per cent and 7.5 per cent. This places India, over the past three decades, among the global growth leaders; only China, Myanmar and Cambodia have experienced higher and more sustained growth. The trajectory of Vietnam was slightly lower but more stable than India's. However, it has accomplished remarkable long-term expansion. This expansion reflects major improvements in trend growth. Catch-up growth became a reality as a result of the low starting point and competitiveness changes brought about by policy reform beginning in 1991.

India achieved its highest annual growth rate of 9 per cent in 2016.* Since then, economic expansion has slowed to between five per cent and seven per cent before slowing dramatically in

---

* GDP growth (annual per cent) | Data (worldbank.org)

2020 as the pandemic took hold. Recent growth projections indicate a robust recovery after overcoming COVID-19 before growth reverts to its 6.5 per cent trend level. The causes of the pre-pandemic-development decline have been the subject of heated debate. The issues with the balance sheets of financial institutions and certain segments of the corporate sector have constrained investment. The credit-to-GDP ratio, which had experienced a decade of accelerated growth, remained stagnant since 2008. However, there have been countervailing factors at play over the years. Between 2008 and 2016, household consumption exhibited robust growth, while export expansion contributed significantly to the economic upswing up to 2013. Subsequently, from 2013 to 2018, government consumption added impetus to the economy. As a consequence of these contradictory forces, economic expansion declined in 2017 and again in 2019.[18]

India's prosperity level stands at 18 per cent of the global average, up from just over 6.5 per cent of the global average when economic reforms began in the early 1990s. India contains millions of people living below the poverty line. In addition, inequality is high and has increased over the years, with an increasing distribution of wealth and income among just a handful of people. The COVID-19 pandemic has further exacerbated these difficulties. It has also revealed and exacerbated existing inequalities, with women, children and older people disproportionately affected. The competitiveness of a country is dependent on a multitude of factors included in the competitiveness framework. So it is important to recall that a thorough investigation of what drives levels of prosperity, the elimination of poverty and inequalities in the country, is significant.

Bridging the Gap: Examining India's Performance

'The true wealth of a nation is measured by its capacity to deliver, in a sustainable way, high standards of living for all of its citizens.'

—Joseph E. Stiglitz (2019)

India is a lower-middle-income economy, with a GDP per capita of roughly $2047 (current prices) or $6609 (Purchasing Power Parity). This indicates that, on average, individuals in India earn less than those in high-income economies such as the United States, Japan and Europe. Nonetheless, even though India is a lower-middle-income economy, it has achieved substantial progress in terms of growth and prosperity over the past few decades.

Figure 15: Global Leaders in Sustained Prosperity Growth

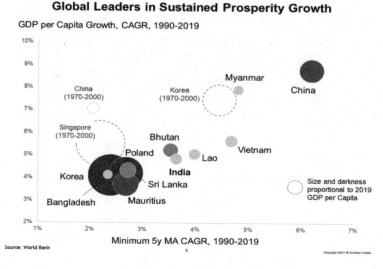

Source: Competitiveness Roadmap for India @100

---

* Data sourced from World Bank

India has been a worldwide leader in long-term prosperity and development. Over the last three decades, only China, Myanmar, Vietnam and Laos have experienced higher and more stable prosperity growth than India. In the three decades prior to the year 2000, only Korea had a higher performance than India. This indicates India's capability. This indicates that despite issues such as inequality, infrastructural deficits and governance issues, India has been able to sustain a robust economic growth trajectory.

India continues to confront significant poverty despite its robust economic growth. Around 20 per cent of the population lives in poverty; the exact figure depends on the definition of poverty used. This is a significant improvement from over 45 per cent at the start of the reforms in the early 1990s, and it brings India on par with an average for countries with middle incomes. After 1990, the poverty reduction was about three times faster than previously, as shown in the figure below.

Figure 16: Decline in Poverty since 1980s

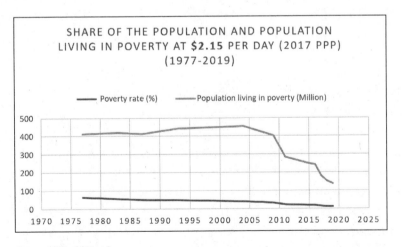

Source: World Bank

While poverty has reduced, inequality has risen significantly, particularly since 2000. This trend stands in contrast to the global and selected economies trend as seen in the figure below. Urban areas have experienced the most dramatic rise in inequality. Inequality in wealth and income is greater than in consumption. Rising incomes and wealth mainly at the highest levels of India's urban society have played a significant role in the rise of inequality.

Figure 17: Mind the Gap: Inequality Levels

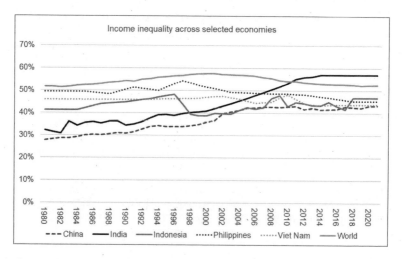

Source: Competitiveness Roadmap for India @100. Updated World Inequality Database for 2021

The India Human Development Survey (IHDS) offers an independent assessment of living conditions improvements across the country. Between 2004 and 2005, and 2011 and 2012, the highest 20 per cent of the distribution's consumption and income distribution exhibited disproportionate growth. The annual growth in consumption was 5.4 per cent for individuals in the top twentieth per centile and 1.8 per cent for those in the lowest twentieth per centile. However, according to IHDS-M data, this trend reversed in 2017. The bottom per centile saw a 3.6 per cent increase in consumption, while the top tenth per centile saw a rise of 1.9 per cent. A comparable pattern can be observed for income inequality. The Gini coefficient for inequality in consumption decreased from 0.359 in 2011–12 to 0.336 in 2017–18, while the coefficient for inequality in income decreased slightly from 0.510 to 0.494.[19]

Figure 18: India's Income and Consumption Dynamics (2004–17)

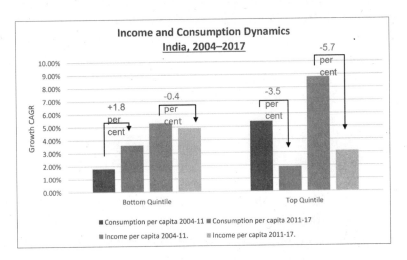

Source: India Human Development Survey

In their paper, Lucas Chancel and Thomas Piketty (2020)[20] concluded that India's income inequality is greater than it was before independence. Authors systematically tracked the income inequality trends in India from 1922 to 2015 by combining household surveys, national accounts and tax information. Their findings are based on extrapolated data from the Income Tax Act. According to their study and their benchmark estimates, the top one per cent of income share is at its highest point (22 per cent) since the creation of the income tax during the British Raj in 1922. In the late 1930s, the top 1 per cent of earners accounted for less than 21 per cent of total income before sliding to 6 per cent in the early 1980s and gaining to 22 per cent in recent years. During the period between 1951 and 1980, the bottom 50 per cent of the population captured 28 per cent of the country's overall growth, and their incomes grew faster than the average, whereas the top 0.1 per cent's incomes decreased. During the period of time between 1980 and 2015, the trend was reversed; the top 0.1 per cent of earners captured 12 per cent of overall growth, a greater share than the bottom 50 per cent, who accounted for 11 per cent. The top 1 per cent received a bigger share of overall growth, 29 per cent, than the middle 40 per cent did, i.e., 23 per cent.

A recent working paper of the World Bank[21] discovered that extreme poverty in India decreased by 12.3 percentage points between 2011 and 2019, but at a far slower pace than recorded between 2004 and 2011. Poverty reduction rates in rural regions are higher than in urban areas. Over 640 million people in India were living in multidimensional poverty in 2005 to 2006, but this figure has dropped dramatically to little more than 365.55 million by 2016 to 2017. In a decade, India has effectively moved 271 million people out of poverty. Real progress, however, is measured on a number of fronts, many of which are non-economic in nature. As highlighted earlier in the discussion on the competitiveness framework, attention to social aspects is equally important for the holistic development of a region. Lack of social progress hinders economic growth and stifles the real potential of a nation and its citizens.

Social Progress

'Economic growth without social progress lets the great majority of people remain in poverty, while a privileged few reap the benefits of rising abundance.'

—John F. Kennedy (1961)

The growing consensus that GDP alone cannot transform the lives of millions of individuals around the world has prompted a surge of efforts to address this concern and supplement the moving beyond GDP debate. It should be noted that GDP was not intended to measure the quality of life; therefore, excessive reliance on GDP and other economic measures can result in flawed policy decisions that fail to address the actual wants and necessities of citizens. With rising needs, expenditures and aspirations, the country must ensure that other aspects of life, such as access to food, shelter, and sanitation and reduction of inequalities are prioritized in addition to maximizing GDP. Likewise, it must provide access to economic opportunities with qualified human capital, enhanced financial inclusion and better transportation and connectivity, among others. This becomes exceedingly important as the COVID-19 pandemic has further highlighted our systems' structural weaknesses and inequities.

The Social Progress Imperative's Social Progress Index (SPI) is also a stride in the same direction.

The Social Progress Index rigorously measures country performance on many aspects of social and environmental performance which are relevant for countries at all levels of economic development. It enables an assessment of not just absolute country performance but also relative performance compared to a country's economic peers. The index gives governments and businesses the tools to track social and environmental performance rigorously, and make better public policy and investment choices. The Social Progress Index also allows us to assess a country's success in turning economic progress into improved social outcomes. Overall, the Social Progress Index provides the first concrete framework for benchmarking and prioritizing an action agenda advancing both social and economic performance.[22]

It is based on the premise that economic development without social progress will result in marginalization, environmental degradation and social distress. The index is the first comprehensive instrument designed to assess social advancement independent of GDP. By distinguishing the measurement of social progress and economic development, the Social Progress Index helps to provide an empirical relationship between the two concepts and consequently provides citizens with a clearer picture of how their country is progressing. It contributes to our comprehension of how economic growth influences social progress and vice versa, a long-debated topic. A deeper comprehension of this relationship can aid policymakers in making strategic decisions that promote inclusive growth.

India's Position on the Social Progress Index

The Social Progress Index (SPI) currently ranks India 110th in the world, with a score of 60.19. Currently, India is in the lower-middle tier, i.e., the tier on social progress represents countries that have attained moderate degrees of social progress but still confront substantial environmental and social issues. India's current SPI score is slightly below the global average of 65.24. However, the country's rate of improvement has slowed during the 2011–22 period. This is part of a larger global trend: the rate of growth for the whole world from 2017–22 is almost half of what it was from 2011–17. To comprehend what this entails for India, the SPI's twelve components must be broken down.

Access to information and communication has been the area in which India has made the largest gains (37.79 points). Since 2011, the number of mobile phone subscriptions has nearly doubled, reaching more than eighty per capita. In 2011, only 5.1 per cent of India's population had access to the Internet, whereas, now, 43 per cent do. In tandem, access to online government services has increased dramatically. Access to information has also experienced a decrease in its rate of progression. This reflects a broader global trend: the proliferation of mobile phone access has resulted in substantial social progress in this area. However, these advances are diminishing as we approach saturation.

Since 2011, India's score has increased by 8.49 points, the third-greatest improvement among the group of other major South Asian countries and other major African countries. This compares fairly when we look at global performance on social progress. During the period 2011–22, the SPI score for the world, which includes 169 countries, improved by 5.40 percentage points, i.e., from 59.84 in 2011 to 65.24 in 2022. This gain is substantial, but it is insufficient to meet sustainable-development-goal targets until the end of this century or the beginning of the next. The next largest improvement has been 20.99 points for Shelter. Since 2011, the percentage of households using renewable fuels has increased from 32 per cent to 64 per cent. Consequently, the adverse health effects of indoor air pollution have decreased significantly. The increase in the population having access to electricity from 75 per cent to 99 per cent supports the transition to better fuels. India has also witnessed a decline in housing-affordability discontent.

The water and sanitation component has also improved significantly since 2011 by 18.8 points. Access to sanitation has seen the greatest increase, from 44 per cent in 2011 to nearly 72 per cent of the population in 2022. Consequently, the health costs associated with inadequate sanitation have decreased by half during this time period. Access to clean drinking water has increased from 87 per cent to 92 per cent of the population since 2011, while satisfaction with water quality has risen from 66 per cent to 83 per cent in 2022.

Nutrition and basic medical care have gained 9.66 points. Since 2011, the infant mortality rate (IMR) in India has nearly halved, and maternal mortality has decreased by more than a third. During this time period, the prevalence of infectious illnesses has decreased by half. Child stunting has decreased from 33.5 per cent to 24.7 per cent, while child malnutrition has improved from 16 per cent to 15 per cent. In addition, health and wellness have improved significantly by 9.12 points since 2011. Life expectancy at age 60 has increased from 17.2 years to 19.0 years. The percentage of premature fatalities attributable to noncommunicable diseases has decreased by 6 per cent. These improvements are attributable to the increase from 43.1 per cent to 51.1 per cent in access to essential healthcare. From 47 per cent to 76 per cent, satisfaction with healthcare has gone up. Despite these encouraging trends, there are signs that access to healthcare has become less equitable since 2011.

Access to Advanced Education and Personal Freedom and Choice components have seen fewer improvements in India, i.e., 4.95 and 4.39 points, respectively. Overall, the level of tertiary education and women's access to higher education in the higher-education sector have witnessed an increase in quantity. In terms of international university rankings and citations, the quality of Indian universities has improved despite the reduction in academic freedom. In terms of personal freedom and choice, the rate of early marriage for girls between the ages of fifteen and nineteen has decreased from 21 per cent to 13.5 per cent, while the rate of demand for contraception has increased from 71 per cent to 72 per cent. Additionally, perceived levels of corruption component has improved by 4 points. A decline from 82.5 per cent to 73.9 per cent in vulnerable employment is partially offset by an increase of more than 2 percentage points among young people who are not in education, employment or training.

Access to basic knowledge and personal safety has made less progress, i.e., by 2.88 and 2.32 points, reflecting a global trend. The pattern in education suggests that enrolment in primary school and secondary-education attainment are declining slightly. This may be partly due to the effects of COVID-19 on education. Positively, the percentage of the population without formal education has decreased from 37.5 per cent in 2011 to 29.2 per cent in 2022. While gender equality in secondary education attainment has declined, access to education for all has increased. In terms of personal safety, transportation-related injuries have decreased by almost 19 per cent between 2011 and 2022. Additionally, interpersonal violence, political murders and torture have decreased. The issues of theft of money and domestic violence are still unchanged.

India has made the least progress in areas where the majority of other nations also struggle. Inclusiveness declined slightly by 0.29 points. Acceptance of homosexuals increased substantially, whereas political authority based on sexual orientation declined. Access to public services by social groups has decreased as have discrimination and violence against minorities. Environmental quality declined marginally by - 0.76 points from 2011 to 2022. The issues include deteriorating air quality and persistently high particle pollution. This arises from the adoption of inefficient cultivation methods and agricultural practices, including stubble burning, which deteriorates soil quality. Additionally, a largely carbon-based energy system and elevated levels of groundwater extraction have resulted in water shortages in certain districts of the country. In comparison to China, the oil-producing countries and OECD countries, India's CO_2 emissions have been relatively low to date. However, the country's rising energy demands coupled with the high carbon intensity of energy production and GDP foreshadow imminent challenges.

Lead exposure has risen, while species protection has remained unchanged. The personal rights component experienced the greatest decline, i.e., by 7.92, comparable to the decline observed in the global score for this component during the same time frame.[23]

It is noteworthy that India has made substantial improvements in social progress, but there is a lot more to be done to resolve the prevalent social issues that continue to affect many of its citizens. In addition to addressing the caste system, gender inequality and religious tensions, there are new challenges such as environmental degradation, technological disruption and urbanization that must be addressed. However, India's progress thus far is testimony to the tenacity of its citizens and their potential for future progress. This overview of India's performance on the twelve components of the SPI builds a strong foundation to assess India's social policy action.

Tracking Social Policy Action

'The difference between what we do and what we are capable of doing would suffice to solve most of the world's problems.'

—Mahatma Gandhi

India's social and political fabric is comprised of positive and negative characteristics. On the one hand, India is a strong democracy, which isn't always true of countries at the same stage of development. Freedom of the press, regular elections and a vibrant civil society that encourages dissent and debate are characteristics of India's democracy. This is a positive aspect of the social and political landscape in India. But India confronts significant social challenges as well. The caste system in India is a centuries-old social hierarchy that continues to divide society. Even though the Indian Constitution has officially abolished it, it nonetheless affects millions of people, especially those from lower socioeconomic groups who face discrimination and exclusion from opportunities. Gender inequality is also a significant issue. According to the World Economic Forum's Global Gender Gap Report 2021, India ranks 140 out of 156 countries in the world with a score of 0.625 out of 1.* This is because women face obstacles to education, employment and healthcare as well as high rates of violence and harassment. In addition, there are lingering tensions between religious groups as well. Overall, it is noted that the country has made significant strides in many areas of social

---

* Global Gender Gap Report

progress. It still faces significant challenges, and there is still much work to be done to resolve social inequalities and tensions. If India is to continue on its path towards sustainable development, it is necessary to recognize and resolve these social issues. While significant progress has been made, these issues continue to pose significant challenges to the country's social cohesion and economic development. To address these, every stakeholder, including the government, civil society and the private sector, must work together to develop an inclusive and equitable society for all of its people.

In recent years, the government has amended its policy blend to aid the impoverished, attempting to surmount the high fiscal costs and significant inefficiency of previous policies. Historically, there has been an emphasis on subsidized access to key consumption commodities such as food and energy, requirements to employ specific groups in the public sector (the reservation system) and regulations to shield small-scale firms in specific industries. These policies tended to be expensive in terms of the fiscal burden they placed on the government and the allocation inefficiencies they caused in the markets. Concerns were also raised regarding the ability of these policies to effectively target those in society who require assistance.

Recently, the government has begun to modify its policy mix to benefit the impoverished. The transition towards direct financial distributions to needy households as opposed to subsidizing the prices of the products and services they consume is a crucial element. In 2017, energy price reforms instituted such transfers to recompense low-income households for LPG market liberalization. Direct transfers utilize the Aadhaar number and the Pradhan Mantri Jan Dhan Yojana (PMJDY) scheme to increase financial inclusion by opening bank accounts for impoverished households.

Various initiatives to assist impoverished districts in augmenting the character of their governance and services constitute a second crucial element. In 2014, the Sansad Adarsh Gram Yojana (SAGY)* initiative was introduced to promote rural development through the establishment of 'model villages.' From 2014–15 and 2022–23, the members of Parliament (MPs) have adopted 3154 Gram Panchayats under the SAGY. SAGY has been highly effective in bringing about all-around development in the Gram Panchayats chosen by honourable MPs in accordance with the scheme's guidelines. Gram Panchayats prepare a Village Development Plan (VDP) in which the proposed activities are carried out through the convergence of various Government of India and state government initiatives. It seeks to initiate processes that result in the holistic development of the designated Gram Panchayats. As of 7 March 2023, 2625 SAGY Gram Panchayats have uploaded Village Development Plans containing a total of 2,34,404 projects, of which 1,63,633 have been completed. Under SAGY, the development of these Gram Panchayats (GPs) is ongoing.

Since 2015, the 100 Smart Cities Mission has provided urban development initiatives with competitive co-financing. In June 2015, the Pradhan Mantri Awas Yojana-Urban (PMAY-U) was introduced to provide an all-weather dwelling unit to eligible beneficiaries in every urban area. All homes constructed, acquired or purchased by the mission are equipped with a kitchen, water supply, electricity and a restroom. The mission has been extended until 31 December 2024 in order to finish the already-approved homes by 31 March 2022. More than 1.20 crore dwellings have been sanctioned under the mission as of November 2022, with over 64 lakh

---

* Gram Panchayats Adopted Under SAGY

completed and the remainder in varying phases of construction or grounding.[*] In 2018, the Aspirational Districts[†] initiative was introduced to assist some of India's most disadvantaged districts in improving their social performance. NITI Aayog identified 112 aspirational districts based upon composite indicators from health and nutrition, education, agriculture and water resources, financial inclusion and skill development and basic infrastructure, which have an impact on the Human Development Index (HDI). In addition, the government is addressing specific social issues such as improving cleanliness and sanitation; providing healthcare services and reducing malnutrition using initiatives such as the Swachh Bharat Abhiyan, POSHAN Abhiyan and AB-PMJAY.

The Swachh Bharat Mission[‡] is a nation-wide initiative of the Indian government aimed at the construction of household and community toilets, their usage and Solid and Liquid Waste Management (SLWM), thereby establishing a transparent mechanism for achieving an Open Defecation Free (ODF) India. In five years, 10.28 crore toilets have been built in thirty-six states and union territories, and 6,03,175 villages have been declared free of open defecation. The mission has helped India achieve Sustainable Development Goal (SDG) 6.2, which entails sanitation for all, an astounding eleven years before the UN's SDG target date of 31 December 2030 by achieving ODF status in record time. Over 55 crore individuals have altered their behaviour and begun using restrooms. This has resulted in rural households in India earning more than Rs 50,000 annually.

---

[*] Year End Review 2022: Ministry of Housing & Urban Affairs
[†] Aspirational Districts Baseline Ranking
[‡] Swachh Bharat Mission—Grameen—Ministry of Jal Shakti

The POSHAN Abhiyaan* was introduced in March 2018 to enhance the nutritional status of zero to six-year-old children, adolescent girls, pregnant women and lactating mothers. It's been implemented in all thirty-six states and union territories, including Tamil Nadu and Odisha. The initiative is a Centrally Sponsored Scheme (CSS) with state or union territory implementation. To guarantee that all Anganwadi Centres are outfitted with smart phones and growth monitoring devices (GMDs), the Ministry of Health & Family Welfare has issued revised guidelines for technical specifications and replacement of GMDs by the states. The ministry launched the Poshan Tracker application on 1 March 2021 via the National e-Governance Division (NeGD). Poshan Tracker leverages technology for dynamic identification of stunted and underweight prevalence children as well as last-mile nutrition service monitoring.

Ayushman Bharat Pradhan Mantri Jan Arogya Yojana (AB PM-JAY),† the world's largest health insurance scheme, seeks to minimize the out-of-pocket expenses (OOPE) of the target population resulting from healthcare expenditures. The scheme provides health coverage of Rs 5 lakh per family per year for secondary and tertiary care hospitalization to over 10.7 crore poor and vulnerable families or about 50 crore people. These families are in the bottom 40 per cent of the Indian population, which was determined by the deprivation and occupation criteria of the Socio-Economic Caste Census 2011 (SECC 2011) and other state schemes. The programme is intended to provide financial-risk protection against catastrophic health expenditures and is implemented through insurance, trust or mixed mode, as determined by the state or union territory. Over 21.9 crore

---

* POSHAN Abhiyaan
† AB-PMJAY—Ministry of Finance

beneficiaries have been verified under this scheme. The government also continues to administer the rural employment guarantee programme, the Mahatma Gandhi National Rural Employment Guarantee Scheme (MGNREGS).

However, there are still concerns regarding the fiscal resources employed to address issues of social development, particularly regarding healthcare. Here, India lags behind the rest of the world. Private spending has partially supplied the void left by government spending but not entirely. According to the World Bank's 2019 data, India spends 2.3 per cent less of its GDP than the average middle-income country on healthcare. This gap has grown by 0.5 percentage points since 2010. India's inadequate healthcare spending is a significant issue that results in inadequate access to health services for a large portion of the population. High out-of-pocket healthcare costs also place a financial strain on households.

Figure 19: Healthcare Spending

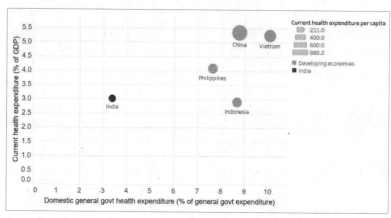

Source: Competitiveness Roadmap for India @100. Updated data World Bank

Low healthcare expenditures in India result in numerous problems. First, it restricts the accessibility and efficacy of healthcare services for people in general, especially in rural and remote locations with inadequate healthcare infrastructure. This results in considerable disparities in healthcare between urban and rural areas of the country. Low healthcare expenditures also reflect a shortage of investment in healthcare infrastructure, including hospitals, clinics and medical equipment. This causes lengthy wait periods for medical treatment and a paucity of medical personnel, which can result in a decline in the quality of treatment provided. It should be noted that economies that invest more in healthcare have improved health outcomes, increased life expectancy and decreased mortality rates. For instance, in China, life expectancy rose from sixty-four years in 1980 to seventy-eight years in 2019, whereas in India, it rose from fifty-four years in 1980 to seventy-one years in 2019.[*] This demonstrates that investing in healthcare can significantly enhance population health outcomes and ease of living.

In conclusion, despite the recent success of India's vaccination campaign, the country's low healthcare expenditure is a significant issue. To enhance better health outcomes and reduce healthcare disparities, India must invest significantly more in healthcare infrastructure and personnel. By doing so, the government can ensure that its citizens have access to high-quality healthcare services, resulting in improved health outcomes and a higher quality of life, thereby advancing social progress. After delving into the competitiveness framework, its constituent elements, and India's performance in relation to these elements, we proceed to explore three fundamental aspects of competitiveness—Labour Productivity, Labour Mobilization and Sectoral Transformation—and track India's trends in these domains.

---

[*] Life expectancy at birth, total (years)—China, India | Data (worldbank.org)

Labour Productivity

> 'Productivity isn't everything, but in the long run it is almost
> everything. A country's ability to improve its standard of living
> over time depends almost entirely on its ability to raise its
> output per worker.'

—Paul Krugman [24]

Krugman's emphasis on productivity has remained timeless.
This is simply because productivity has been regarded as a key
driver of economic growth and competitiveness, and, as such, it is
considered a key competitiveness fundamental and used for many
international comparisons and country-performance evaluations.
As previously defined in this chapter, Porter's competitiveness
concept places a strong emphasis on productivity.

Typically defined, productivity is the ratio between output
volume and input volume. In other words, it measures the
efficiency with which production inputs, such as labour and
capital, are used to produce a given level of output in an economy.
For instance, productivity data is used to examine the effect of
product and labour-market regulations on economic performance.
In addition, it enables analysts to determine capacity utilization,
which, in turn, enables one to assess the position of economies in
the business cycle and predict economic development. Moreover,
production capacity is utilized to evaluate demand and inflationary
pressures. There are various metrics of productivity, the selection
of which depends on the purpose of the measurement and/or
the availability of data. The per-hour-worked GDP is one of the
most widely used measures of productivity. This metric captures
the utilization of labour inputs more accurately than output
per employee.[25]

In comparison to other countries as presented below in the graph, India's labour productivity is relatively high, indicating that Indian employees produce a substantial quantity of output per hour worked. Despite achieving only 50 per cent of China's prosperity, India's labour productivity is 80 per cent of that of China. This is a positive indicator for India's economic development as it indicates that Indian labourers are extremely efficient and productive. Moreover, India's labour productivity is nearly 25 per cent higher than Vietnam's, despite Vietnam achieving 20 per cent. This suggests that India is utilizing its workforce more effectively, which may be attributable to a large population of educated and skilled employees, a favourable business environment and technological advances.

Figure 20: Labour Productivity over Years

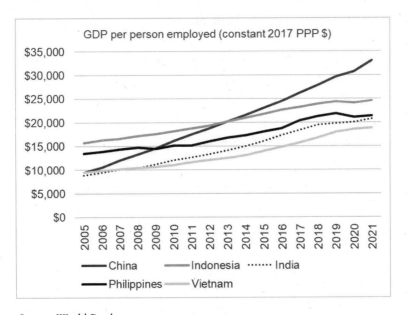

Source: World Bank

It must be noted that India's labour-productivity growth has accelerated over time. During the 1980s and 1990s, labour productivity increased by just over 3 per cent annually (CAGR). During the 2000s, growth surpassed 5 per cent and then exceeded 6 per cent in the subsequent decade. Until 1996, China's productivity grew by over 11 per cent annually; since then, it has declined by 9 per cent annually until 2005 and continued to grow by over 10 per cent annually until 2011. Since then, productivity growth has only declined in China.*

Various factors influence India's labour productivity, including capital intensity, human capital and total factor productivity growth, and that recent improvements in productivity could be attributed to technology advancements. India's labour productivity is boosted by its comparatively high capital intensity relative to other countries, which indicates that the country has a relatively high quantity of tangible capital per worker, such as machinery, tools and infrastructure. This can result in increased production-process efficiency and output. China and Indonesia are considered outliers in this comparison because their labour productivity and capital intensity are not necessarily correlated. This suggests that other variables may be influencing their labour productivity.

---

* GDP per person employed (constant 2017 PPP $) | Data (worldbank.org)

Figure 21: Drivers of Productivity

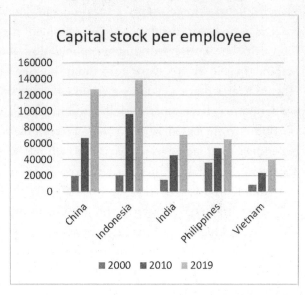

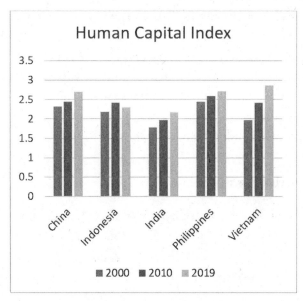

Source: (Feenstra, Inklaar, and Timmer, 2015)[26]

Second, India trails behind on the Human Capital Index (HCI), which refers to the workforce's skills, education and knowledge. However, it is noted that the HCI report considers the data, which represents the entire working-age population, but the human capital in the active work force may be significantly higher. This indicates that the younger, more educated segment of the population may have superior skills and knowledge, which could contribute to increased labour productivity. Finally, it is noted that India's total factor productivity growth has outpaced that of its rivals. Total factor productivity growth refers to the increase in labour productivity that cannot be explained solely by capital deepening or human capital enhancements but rather reflects technological and managerial advancements. This indicates that India may be using more efficient management practices and utilizing technology more effectively, resulting in increased labour productivity.

Overall, high labour productivity can have a number of positive effects on the economy, including increased competitiveness, higher compensation for workers and enhanced living standards. Consequently, India's high labour productivity is a significant advantage that could assist the nation in maintaining its economic growth trajectory. However, it is also important to look at another critical dimension, labour mobilization.

Labour Mobilization

Labour mobilization is India's greatest economic vulnerability. The percentage of the labour force that is of working age has decreased from approximately 70 per cent in 1990 to 56 per cent today. India now trails significantly behind its peers. The low and declining labour mobilization has profound effects on the economic value produced by its working-age population.

Lower labour mobilization is one of the primary reasons for the disparity in prosperity between India and China. Labour mobilization is the proportion of the working-age population that is either employed or actively pursuing employment. This factor alone accounts for 60 per cent of the difference in prosperity levels between the two countries. It means that a larger proportion of China's population is in the labour force, resulting in increased economic growth and prosperity levels. A larger labour force would mean that more people are contributing to the economy, which can result in increased output, higher wages and increased consumer expenditure.

Figure 22: Employees as Share of Working Age Population

Employment to population ratio, 15+, total (%)

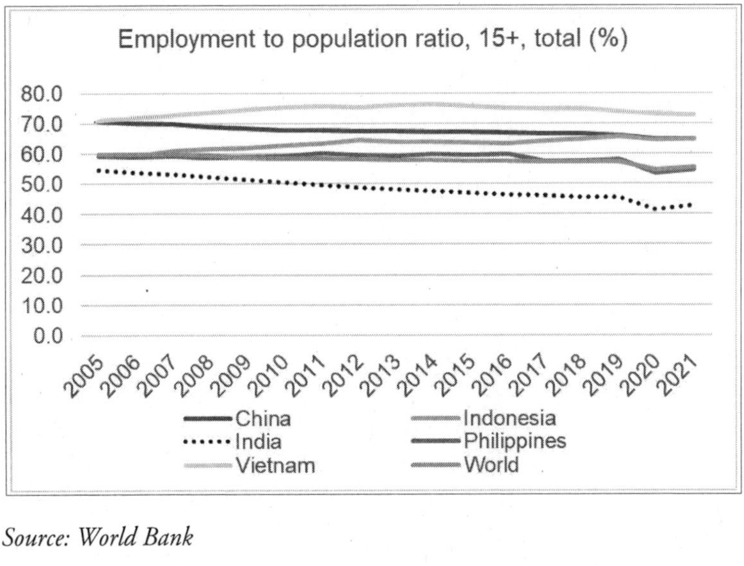

Source: *World Bank*

On comparing India to Vietnam, two distinct factors contributing to the gap in prosperity are observed. On the one hand, India generates 15 per cent less value per working-age citizen than Vietnam. This indicates that, on average, each Indian generates less economic value than each Vietnamese. In contrast, India's labour productivity per employee is 25 per cent higher than Vietnam's. This indicates that each labourer in India can produce more output per hour than their Vietnamese counterparts.

Figure 23: Unlocking the Link between Labour Force Participation (LFP) and Economic Prosperity

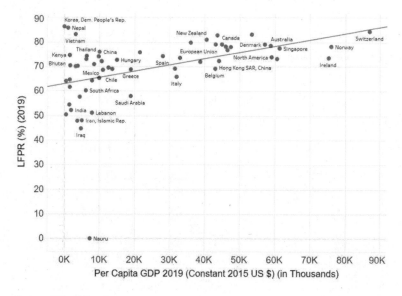

Source: World Bank

There is also the need to understand the link between GDP per capita and participation rate in the labour market across major economies. There are many economies like Nepal, Korea and China that have low prosperity levels but very high labour force participation rates. Many factors, such as changes in demographics, social and cultural norms, governmental initiatives and the availability of employment in different sectors of the economy, can influence labour force participation rates. Even though there is a correlation between GDP per capita and labour force participation rates, it is essential to consider these other factors when analysing labour-market trends. In terms of labour productivity, while India has been faring well, it is observed that the gap in GDP per capita between India and China has been growing over the past decade. In other words, while each labourer in India is becoming more productive, the GDP per capita is not increasing as rapidly as in China and Vietnam.

Another reason for lower mobilization is India's low labour force participation rate for women, i.e., 25 per cent of all employees are women, which is significantly low when compared to peer countries. In addition, women in India earn less than 50 per cent of the national average wage. However, there are significant differences in labour force participation and wages between industries and, to a lesser extent, among locations.

Figure 24: Labour Force Participation Rate (LFPR) (aged 15+)

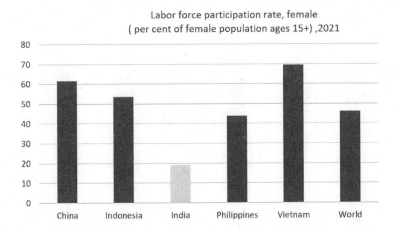

Source: Competitiveness Roadmap for India @100. Updated with World Bank Data for 2021

Significant numbers of women are employed in low-wage industries, such as the agricultural sector, textiles, apparel and tobacco, where they earn even less than the national average. These women face obstacles, including limited access to education, training and technology, which limit their earning potential and upward mobility. Many of these women are also employed in the informal sector, which is characterized by low pay, lengthy hours and limited legal protection Women employed in higher-paying industries, such as education, healthcare and advanced services, typically make earnings that approach or exceed the national average. They frequently possess superior levels of education, abilities and training, which makes them more competitive in the labour market. However, even within these higher-paying industries, wages and employment opportunities vary significantly across regions and industries. Therefore, it is important to investigate the factors which drive the LFPR of women.

Women's labour-force participation is influenced by a variety of economic and social factors, including educational attainment, childbearing rates, marriage age, economic growth and cyclical impacts and urbanization. In India, much of the discussion has centred on four important explanations: the increasing enrolment of young women in educational institutions, the paucity of employment opportunities, the impact of household income on participation and its measurement. According to the ILO(2014)[27] report, over the past decade or so, India has made significant progress in expanding access to secondary education for females. Despite this, the nature of economic growth in the country has prevented the creation of a lot of employment in sectors that could readily accommodate women, particularly in rural areas.

It further noted that despite inadequate employment creation, household incomes increased, which may have decreased women's participation, particularly in subsidiary activities (income effect), due to a change in preferences. It is important to understand that the majority of women in India work and contribute to the economy in some capacity; however, much of their work is not documented or accounted for in official statistics, and thus women's contributions to the economy are frequently underreported.

Regarding the accuracy of LFPR calculations for India, there is evidence that it may be underestimated. In India, a notably high proportion of women indicate that they are engaged in domestic work. In 2011–12, 35.3 per cent of all rural females and 46.1 per cent of all urban females performed domestic tasks, whereas in 1993–94, these percentages were 29 per cent and 42.2 per cent, respectively. Inaccurate measurement may have an impact on the level and trend of the participation rate. The ILO report[28] also noted that the low participation rates in South Asian countries like India may be attributed to a range of factors, such as the underreporting of women's employment and the increased enrolment of young women in school. However, it also suggests that there are substantial barriers to women's empowerment and opportunity costs associated with not utilizing the complete capabilities and skills of the workforce.

In April 2017, the National Statistical Office (NSO) initiated the Periodic Labour Force Survey (PLFS) to acknowledge the need for more frequent availability of data on the labour force. The primary purpose of the PLFS is twofold: the first is to estimate the main employment and unemployment indicators (i.e., worker population ratio, labour force participation rate and unemployment rate) within a three-month window for urban areas only in the Current Weekly Status (CWS). Another objective is to annually estimate employment and unemployment

indicators for Usual Status (PS+SS) * and CWS in rural and urban
areas. According to PLFS, the estimated LFPR for women aged
fifteen and older in the country has seen an upward trend. It has
increased from 30 per cent in 2019–20, 32.5 per cent in 2020–21,
32.8 per cent in 2021–22 and 37 per cent in 2022–23.[†]

Although India's overall unemployment rate remains
moderate, there is room for improvement in addressing the youth
unemployment rate, which warrants attention. Currently, youth
unemployment in India is 23.89 per cent. Youth unemployment
can contribute to a variety of social and economic issues, including
destitution, social unrest and inequality. One of the primary
causes of high youth unemployment in India is a mismatch
between the talents that young people have and the skills that are
in demand in the labour market. This disparity between talents
and job requirements can make it challenging for graduates to
obtain employment. This is particularly true for young women,
who confront extra obstacles as a result of societal and cultural
conventions as well as employment discrimination. Limited job
creation in specific sectors of the Indian economy is leading
to heightened competition for a limited number of positions.
This dynamic may result in some young people temporarily
disengaging from the labour market and exploring alternative
avenues for employment.

Sectoral Transformation

The structural transformation of the Indian economy from
agriculture to services and, to a lesser extent, manufacturing is

---

[*] *(ps+ss) = (principal activity status + subsidiary economic activity status)*
[†] Ministry of Labour & Employment: (LFPR) of women shows an
increasing trend as per the annual PLFS

a major factor in the aggregate changes in labour productivity and employment. Over the last few decades, the structural transformation of the Indian economy from agriculture to services and industry has been a significant driver of changes in labour productivity and employment. This transformation has resulted in a transition in the composition of value addition, with agriculture's share of gross value added (GVA) reducing and services and manufacturing's share increasing. The transformation has had a significant impact on labour productivity. As the Indian economy has transitioned from agriculture to services and industry, labour productivity has increased overall. This is because services and manufacturing are typically more capital intensive and utilize technology to a greater extent, which can result in greater levels of productivity. This rise in productivity has been a propelling force behind India's economic expansion. While the transition in the composition of output has benefited labour productivity, it has not had the same effect on employment.

As per the RBI KLEMS database, in the 1980s, the share of agriculture in GVA of India accounted for 41 per cent, and it employed more than 69 per cent of the working age population. Over the next three decades, this share has dramatically reduced to 15 per cent and it still employed more than 42 per cent of the population. On the other hand, the services share has increased from 32 per cent to 55 per cent of GVA and its share of employment has increased from 17 per cent to 34 per cent. High-skill services contribute about half of this GVA, but less than a third of employment and job creation. Capital-intensive manufacturing has increased its contribution to value-added without a corresponding increase in jobs. On the other hand, the construction sector has created more jobs without a proportional increase in value-added.

Figure 25: Share in Value Added by Industry

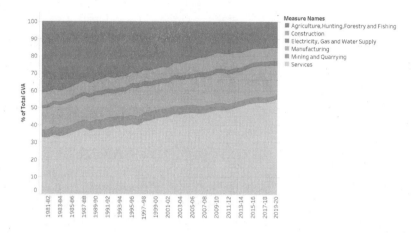

Source: *Competitiveness Roadmap for India @100. Updated with RBI KLEMS database for 2019-20*

India is often seen as a country with a huge service industry but a limited manufacturing industry. This is partially accurate, but the truth is more complex. Services constitute a substantial portion of the Indian economy's exports. In terms of value added and employment, however, the service sector's proportion is comparable to that of other lower middle-income countries and has fallen behind China. This indicates that India's service sector may not be as substantial as previously believed.

Labour-productivity growth in services and in agriculture, and the transition from agricultural employment to other sectors have been the largest individual contributors to labour-productivity growth in the economy as a whole. In the last four decades, these three factors have contributed to approximately 70 per cent of India's labour-productivity growth. This emphasizes the significance of labour-productivity growth in both services and agriculture as well as the employment transition from agriculture to other sectors.

Around two-thirds of all labour productivity growth was attributable to labour growth within sectors, while the remaining third was attributable to changes in the relative scale of individual sectors. These figures are comparable to those of India's counterparts. Nevertheless, what distinguishes India is the comparatively small role of the manufacturing sector, particularly labour-intensive manufacturing, and the high-labour productivity level in services relative to manufacturing. In order to attain sustainable economic growth and employment, India may need to place a greater emphasis on advancing its manufacturing sector.

The successful transition from employment in agriculture to other sectors of the economy is a key factor in labour mobilization across the economy as a whole. As employees transition into industries that utilize technology and capital more effectively, this shift may result in increased productivity. In India, however, this process has not met expectations. Even though the transition out of agriculture began in the early 2000s, labour productivity development in agriculture accelerated during this period. This has made the transition away from agriculture even more difficult. Other sectors need to generate sufficient job opportunities to accommodate individuals transitioning from agriculture sector every year. Between 2 and 4 million jobs have been created annually in India's service sector, which has been a vital factor in the country's economic growth. This is a substantial size, but it is still insufficient to provide sufficient job opportunities for those seeking employment. In addition, in the service sector, there is a bigger opportunity to enhance skill sets to foster greater potential for productivity growth.

Another significant source for potential job creation lies in the manufacturing sector. While job creation in manufacturing slowed after 2005 and faced challenges from 2005–12, the construction industry partially offset this decline. Despite the existing void in the labour market, there is a current thrust to revitalize the manufacturing sector in India. The objective is to position India as the global manufacturing hub, offering a substantial potential for economic development and job creation. In conclusion, the transition from employment in agriculture to other sectors of the economy is a key driver of economy-wide labour mobilization, and India has much to address on this front to enhance its labour mobilization levels.

Inefficient Allocation of Resources in India

Another significant factor that influences changes in labour productivity and employment is the way that economic activities are redistributed across different firms in an economy. In other words, changes in productivity and employment are largely driven by the shifting patterns of firm-level performance, such as changes in their market share, profitability and competitiveness. The inefficient allocation of resources across firms is a hindrance to India's economic performance.

Several studies have examined the role of firm-level heterogeneity and reallocation of resources in shaping productivity and employment dynamics in India. Many papers have stressed that misallocation of inputs across firms can reduce aggregate Total Factor Productivity (TFP) in a country. For instance, Chang-Tai T Hsieh and Peter J. Klenow (2002)[29] used micro data on manufacturing plants to investigate the possible role of such misallocation in China (1998–2005) and India (1987–94) compared to the United States (1977, 1987 and 1997).

One of the most significant findings of the paper is that there is substantial variation in productivity across firms in India, and this variation is significantly greater than in the United States. It further investigates the influence of reallocation of economic activities across firms on India's productivity. The paper argues that reallocating resources from less productive enterprises to more productive firms may play a significant role in increasing aggregate productivity and that policies that promote such reallocation can be an effective method of fostering productivity growth. To examine the role of reallocation in India, they developed a measure of resource misallocation that quantifies the extent to which firms allocate resources inefficiently. They also show that obstacles like regulation, financial frictions and infrastructure limitations obstruct the reallocation of resources across firms in India. They finally conclude that policies that address these constraints, such as improvements to the business environment, reform of the financial sector and investments in infrastructure, could promote a greater reallocation of resources and increase aggregate productivity. Ghani's paper also examined the role of reallocation of economic activities across firms in shaping productivity dynamics in India[30]. The paper provides empirical evidence on the importance of reallocation of economic activities across firms in shaping productivity and employment dynamics in India and highlights the need for policies that promote greater reallocation and reduce barriers to entry and exit. The authors argue that there is significant heterogeneity in the productivity of firms in India, and that reallocation of resources from less productive to more productive firms can be an important driver of aggregate productivity growth. They constructed a measure of within-industry reallocation and found that it is low and has remained stagnant over time due to regulatory barriers, financial constraints and labour market rigidities. Another paper argued that resource misallocation, which refers to the inefficient allocation of inputs such as capital and labour across firms, can be an important driver of differences in productivity levels across countries. The paper also finds that resource misallocation in India is high and has remained stable over time. It further argues that misallocation can lead to lower aggregate productivity and slower growth as resources are allocated to less productive firms instead of more productive ones. To reduce misallocation, the paper suggests that policies must address the various factors that contribute to it, such as regulatory barriers to entry and exit, financial constraints faced by firms and labour-market rigidities. Further, it argues that addressing this issue can lead to higher aggregate productivity and welfare, and that such gains can be shared broadly across the population. It must be noted that while the paper does not focus specifically on the role of reallocation of economic activities across firms in India, it does provide insights into the broader issue of resource misallocation and its implications for productivity and welfare in the country.

Thus, one of the key issues that India is faced with is that less productive firms continue to operate in the market, while more productive firms do not develop sufficiently to compensate for the inefficiencies of the less productive ones. In other words, 'dynamic allocative efficiency' is lacking in India's economy. Dynamic allocative efficiency refers to the capacity of the economy to progressively reallocate resources from less productive firms to more productive firms. India faces obstacles in its pursuit of dynamic allocative efficiency. The growth of more productive firms is inadequate, indicating that the gains made by more productive firms are insufficient to counterbalance the losses of less productive firms. Smaller, less productive enterprises continue to operate in the market, indicating a misallocation of resources.

For instance, 0.04 per cent, i.e., 350 large firms, constitute 55 per cent of the enterprise's overall income. Smaller enterprises account for only 1 per cent of the total income. However, even in the manufacturing sector, these enterprises with fewer than fifty employees account for close to 85 per cent of all employment, compared to 25 per cent in China. In addition, Indian firms do not experience significant growth over time, and even firms with poor performance do not leave the market. This leaves India with a huge number of low-performing and stagnant enterprises that provide limited prospects for employment generation and job upgrading. India falls short in the prevalence of medium-sized businesses, which in many countries serve as the backbone of the economy. These businesses in India have experienced the highest productivity growth in recent years. However, these are far too few.

The lack of growth momentum is linked to the problem of informality. Low-performance firms don't see much point in getting 'more formal,' and being informal keeps them in a low-performance, low-dynamism atmosphere. Formality is a progressive process, beginning with the payment of value-added tax on products and services, continuing with the payment of income taxes for employees and concluding with the observance of all government regulations. The dynamics of many Indian markets continue to favour informal competitors, allowing them to compete more effectively. Simultaneously, there exists a distinct picture of India with globally successful companies and an increasing number of tech-based start-ups vying for access to Indian and global equity markets. Furthermore, there are numerous demonstrations of successful Indian entrepreneurs who have established thriving (and formal) businesses outside of India.

It may be concluded that lack of dynamic allocative efficiency can have multiple repercussions on the economy, such as delayed growth, lower productivity and lower wages. To address this issue, India may need to implement policies that encourage a greater reallocation of resources across firms, reduce entry and departure barriers and address other factors that contribute to the inefficiency of resource allocation. Efficiency in resource allocation impacts labour mobilization, labour productivity and sectoral transformation. Going further, we will examine the role of trade, investment and innovation in increasing competitiveness.

Trade, Investment and Innovation

The ability of a country to develop, produce and market goods and services that can compete successfully in global marketplaces is an important indication of that country's competitiveness. Trade and investment serve as vital measures of a country's competitiveness in the international market as they indicate the strength and variety of the country's sectors, infrastructure and institutions. These factors matter for bringing in foreign investment, which, in turn, may boost growth and development in the economy. They are also signs of past and current competitiveness. However, past and present competitiveness cannot guarantee future success. A nation's emphasis on innovation, the ultimate source of continuous prosperity, is vital for the retention and improvement of the country's competitiveness through time. Innovation entails developing new goods, services and business models that deliver distinctive value to consumers and allow organizations to compete on distinction rather than cost.

For new ideas to flourish, businesses need support that encourages risk taking and provides resources for R&D and training employees. To foster innovation and new ideas, an ecosystem must be established in the country. Therefore, the level of competitiveness can be inferred from a country's trade, investment and innovation performance. A country can only maintain its competitive edge in the future if it continues to invest resources in its strengths, works to improve its weaknesses, and fosters an atmosphere that rewards innovation and efficiency.

Trade

Global economists and decision makers widely agree that export-led growth is a fundamental concept. While private consumption, investment and government spending are other drivers of economic growth as measured by GDP, export growth is crucial for a country like India, which is rich in human resources, production capabilities and, to some extent, natural resources. In this vein, the Indian government has been refining its policies and strategies to boost export growth.

Since 1991, India has made strides to integrate itself into the global economy. Export growth is essential to the country's overall economic growth. To transition from import substitution to export-oriented growth, India has been formulating outward-looking policies. The regions have become more competitive as a result of the national export-oriented policies. By devising policies based on regional strengths and valuable resources, they are incentivized to establish an export-centric approach within their states. The economic reforms of 1990–91 considerably enhanced the country's macroeconomic stability and revitalized the Indian economy. India is one of the world's fastest-expanding economies, with exports playing a vital part in its economic growth. Exports of products and services have grown their contribution to GDP from 7.05 per cent in 1990 to 21.34 per cent in 2021.* It should be noted that India's exports of goods surpassed $400 billion in the fiscal year 2021–22. This is significantly greater than the previous record of $330 billion set in 2018–19. However, there is still a lot of ground to cover. With an exports-to-GDP ratio of 21 per cent, India is less trade-oriented than many of the world's foremost exporting nations; it attained its highest level to date in 2011 at 24.5 per cent. Exports from China as a share of GDP peaked in 2006 at 36 per cent; in 2021, it stood at 20.03 per cent as the economy shifted its focus to the expanding domestic market.

Figure 26: Exports as Share of GDP, Leading Export Nations

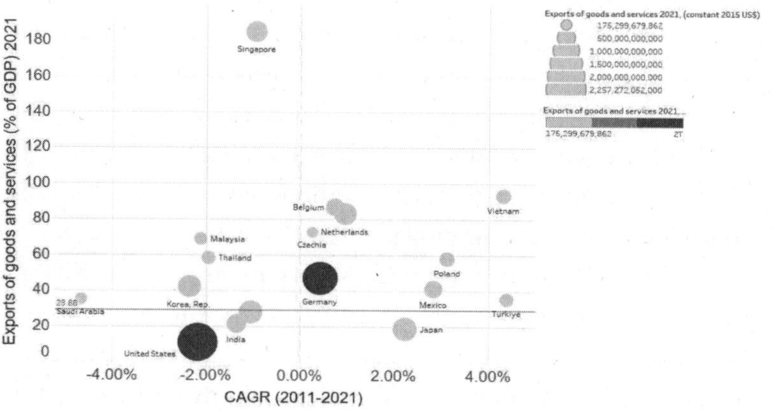

Source: World Bank

Small export-oriented countries achieve much greater values; Vietnam, whose exports now account for 93.29 per cent of GDP, and Poland, whose exports account for 57.91 per cent of GDP,

---

* Exports of goods and services (per cent of GDP) | Data (worldbank.org)

have experienced consistent growth in their export shares. From 2015–16 and 2018–19, India's merchandise exports exhibited an upward trend. This is largely due to the government's determined efforts to also improve the business environment. The government also took significant steps to enhance the ease of doing business in India, resulting in a rise in the ranking of 'Ease of Doing Business' from 142 in 2014 to sixty-three in 2020 and an increase in India's overall ranking.*

India's integration into global value chains continues to be restricted, particularly after a decline in the previous five years. The limited capacity of domestic suppliers limits India's export capacity. Foreign industries use only Indian IT service exports to contribute significantly to their exports. Aside from IT, the majority of Indian exports serve direct foreign demand rather than participating in complex global value chains.

Over the years, the export composition of India has shifted towards more skill-intensive industries, such as pharmaceuticals, machinery and transportation equipment. The growth of service exports is also indicative of a transition towards skill-intensive industries. Thus, India's export portfolio appears to diverge further from the nation's comparative advantages in terms of abundant low-skill labour. Smaller, technology-intensive industries, where India still has a modest presence on the global market, have experienced the most robust export growth. Following the European Union, China, the United Arab Emirates and the rest of Asia, the United States is India's largest export market. For the United States and the United Arab Emirates, jewellery is a key export item, whereas China exports commodity inputs and Europe exports textiles, machinery and pharmaceuticals. The top five importers of India in 2021–22

---

* Ease of Doing Business—Scaling New Heights

were China ($94,571 million), United Arab Emirates ($44,834) and United States ($43,314).[*]

Since 2014, the Indian government has launched a new Foreign Trade Policy (FTP), introduced export-promotion schemes, created a logistics division, implemented interest equalization and mentorship schemes, launched an Agriculture Export Policy, implemented duty remission and rebate schemes, identified Champion Services Sectors, promoted exports at the district level and supported domestic industries. Additionally, Indian missions abroad have actively promoted India's trade, tourism, technology and investment objectives.[†]

Investment

A lack of profitable investment opportunities, reflective of a business environment that renders such investments unfavourable for investors, is one possible explanation. for the recent decline in Gross Fixed Capital Formation as a percentage of GDP for India, as shown in the figure below. The corporate tax rate has been reduced from 30 per cent to 22 per cent in 2019. Most business-environment conditions have not deteriorated. However, lack of available investment capital is a factor that is more likely to explain the trends of the past few years. Here, financial-system problems in India are likely to play a significant role.

---

[*] Dashboard of Commerce
[†] Government takes several steps to boost Indian exports

Figure 27: Gross Fixed Capital Formation (GFCF) (Per Cent of GDP)

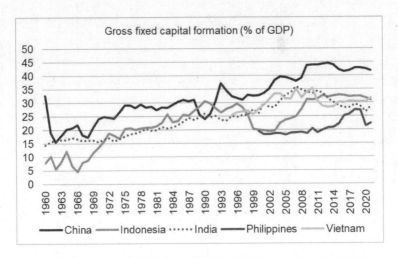

Gross fixed capital formation (% of GDP)

— China — Indonesia ·····India — Philippines — Vietnam

Source: Competitiveness Roadmap for India @100.[*]

India has historically been behind in terms of inward FDI stock relative to GDP, indicating that foreign entities invest less in India compared to other countries with comparable economies. Except for Vietnam, all countries have moderate FDI inflows as a percentage of GDP, within a 1–3 per cent range, as shown in the graph below.

---

[*] World Bank

Figure 28: Navigating Investment Landscape: 3y Moving Average, Per Cent of GDP

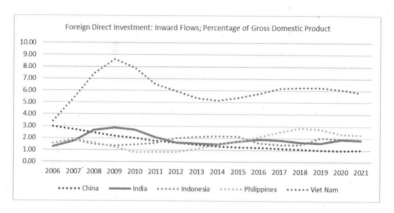

Source: UNCTAD 2021

India's FDI inflows have increased considerably over the past ten to fifteen years, and in 2019, the country ascended into the top ten recipients in terms of FDI globally. Despite this improvement, India's inward FDI per employee remains lower than that of its counterparts, even when the productivity level of Indian employees is taken into account. In other words, although India has made progress in attracting FDI, investment per employee remains relatively low. This suggests that infrastructure or regulatory barriers may be preventing foreign entities from investing in the nation. Additionally, a greater emphasis on acquisitions as opposed to greenfield investments has accompanied the recent increase in FDI inflows to India. Acquisitions involve purchasing an existing business, whereas greenfield investments involve launching a brand-new enterprise. The shift towards acquisitions suggests that foreign investors may be more interested in servicing the Indian market specifically rather than using India as a platform to service global demand.

Innovation

Innovation is crucial for economic development and competitiveness. From space technology and smart cities to healthcare and telecommunications, this decade belongs to India. It is going through significant transformations today, all of which is fuelled by innovative solutions. Indians accounted for one-third of all immigrant-founded engineering and technology companies founded in the Silicon Valley between 2006 and 2012 as well as a significant portion of the CEOs of the world's foremost technology companies. Moreover, the launch of the Aadhaar Digital Identification, the Chandrayaan 2 and 3 missions and the development of the indigenous vaccine Covaxin® during the pandemic are just a few stories of India's present innovative prowess across various sectors.

Over the last several years, India's position on the Global Innovation Index (GII) has consistently improved. GII is a rigorous measure designed to represent the success of national innovation ecosystems worldwide. It annually ranks 132 nations based on their innovation capabilities and outcomes. It has been published since 2007 by the World Intellectual Property Organization (WIPO). In the 2022 edition of the GII, India ranked 40 out of 132 economies, up from its 81st place in 2015.* This is India's highest position on the index ever. India has surpassed Vietnam as the leader of the lower middle-income category. It has also made strides in sectors such as ICT service exports and creative goods exports, which have emerged as important drivers of the country's economic growth. It continues to lead the world in the ICT services exports indicator (first), as well as other indicators

---

* India climbs to the 40th rank in the Global Innovation Index of WIPO; a huge leap of 41 places in 7 years (pib.gov.in)

such as the value of venture capital recipients (sixth), finance for startups and scaleups (eighth), science and engineering graduates (eleventh), labour productivity growth (twelfth) and domestic industry diversification (fourteenth). Except for infrastructure, India's innovation performance is above average for the upper middle-income group in practically every innovation pillar. This suggests that the country's innovation ecosystem is growing more supportive of innovation and entrepreneurship. (WIPO, 2022)

One of the key factors in India's fast-expanding innovation ecosystem is that it has made substantial investments in R&D, notably in the fields of Science, Technology, Engineering and Mathematics (STEM). It currently ranks eleventh in the world in terms of science and engineering graduates and third in terms of global corporate R&D investment. Therefore, there is a large pool of highly skilled and creative human capital readily available, which is critical for promoting innovation and entrepreneurship. It ranked twelfth in the world in terms of culture and creative goods exports, which include film, music and entertainment. This demonstrates the country's expanding ability to innovate in creative sectors, which are becoming more crucial drivers of growth in the economy.

With government efforts such as Startup India, Digital India and Aatmanirbhar Bharat Abhiyaan, India has been on pace to cultivate an innovation ecosystem. In 2016, NITI Aayog developed the Atal Innovation Mission (AIM)[*] to promote innovation and entrepreneurship in schools, institutions and society at large. India's emphasis on innovation is reflected in the number of start-ups founded annually, the number of unicorns that emerge from that group and its relative innovation capacity.

---

[*] Atal Innovation Mission (AIM) | Government of India's flagship initiative

On 16 January 2016, the Startup India initiative[*] was introduced with the goal of establishing a robust ecosystem for fostering innovation and businesses in the country, which would promote sustainable economic development and generate large-scale employment opportunities. Since the launch of Startup India in 2016, DPIIT has recognized 93,000 entities as start-ups, and the country is home to 108 unicorns.[†] It has assisted India in becoming the third-largest start-up ecosystem, boosting employability and fostering independence. According to the Economic Survey of India (2021–2022)[‡], India has surpassed the United Kingdom and is only behind the United States and China.

The Startup India programme has played a crucial role in fostering entrepreneurship outside of Tier-1 cities. While Tier-1 cities account for 55 per cent of the recognized start-ups, Tier-2 and Tier-3 cities account for 45 per cent of the total. It has also been revealed that the Indian startup ecosystem has a robust representation of women, with approximately 45 per cent of start-ups being led by women.[§]

India-based startups were able to successfully withstand the pandemic and even flourish during the crisis. During the year 2021–22, India registered over 26,542 start-ups.[¶] Technology startups contributed the most to India's list of unicorns. This was accomplished through widespread smartphone adoption, thriving digital payment platforms and digitally centric business models. In addition, the pandemic accelerated the digitization of commerce

---

[*] ABOUT US (startupindia.gov.in)
[†] Ministry of Science & Technology, 17 March 2023
[‡] Key Highlights of the Economic Survey 2021–22
[§] Year End Review—2021 for Department for Promotion of Industry & Internal Trade, Ministry of Commerce and Industry
[¶] Ministry of Commerce & Industry

and led to the rise of e-commerce, fintech and SaaS (software as a service) start-ups across the country.

With the Science, Technology and Innovation Policy (STIP), the government has prioritized taking the measures necessary to advance India towards a knowledge-based economy. STIP 2020 has taken steps to incorporate economic development, social inclusion and environmental sustainability into policy evaluation and dynamic policymaking. However, the scope of its activity is not limited to state research and development centres. The talent pool of a nation is comprised of its citizens who are skilled in the arts, athletics, law, business and scientific innovation. The government has since taken a holistic approach to attaining development, which includes social, economic and scientific planning and consultation.[31]

Figure 29: India's Share of GDP Spent on R&D Higher Relative to Peer Countries, Despite Decrease in Share over the Years

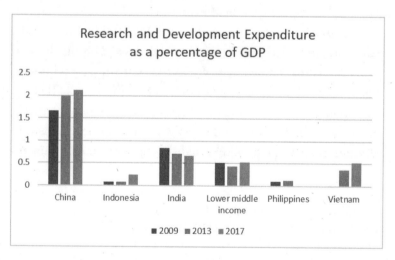

Source: World Bank

However, it must be noted that, in terms of investments in R&D, while India has made significant progress in this area, it still performs significantly lower than a country like China. As a percentage of GDP, India's R&D expenditure is modest. Other lower middle-income nations are catching up, including Vietnam, which has substantially increased its expenditure on R&D. India has a small proportion of researchers in comparison to its population. On this metric, it has already fallen behind its counterparts in terms of its peers as per GII; Vietnam has nearly three times the research intensity of India and ranks 60, whereas the latter ranks 82.

It is further noted that in India, as per DST statistics,[*] the government spends the most on R&D (more than 55 per cent). This needs to change. India needs to find that inflexion point after which the private sector can take over. One of the key factors contributing to this is the low R&D investment made by Indian firms. Companies account for less than 40 per cent of the modest Indian R&D spending, compared to more than 65 per cent in the most R&D-intensive economies. India has twenty-nine companies among the global top 1000 firms by R&D spending, which is slightly below its share in global GDP. These firms spend much less on R&D compared to their sales, their capex, and the country's GDP than their global peers.[32]

Although R&D by businesses rapidly rose from 2005–06, it wasn't fast enough to overtake R&D by the government. Theoretically, this is a positive trend as it indicates that R&D is increasingly being conducted by the same sector that can convert research output into commercial products and processes. But the curve for R&D by businesses needs to intersect the curve for government R&D and rise. Only then can India be at par with

---

[*] Research and Development Statistics 2019-20_0.pdf (dst.gov.in)

other developed countries. For this, it needs to ensure that the present increase in business spending on R&D becomes more systematic, as has been the case in countries such as China[33]. Moreover, it is important to note that it is not just important to spend enough on research and development but also important to look at its sectoral composition. More than one-third of the total national expenditure on R&D is spent on health and defence. While these two sectors are crucial, India also needs to focus on other sectors for all-encompassing growth.[34]

India still confronts obstacles in areas such as business sophistication, ICT infrastructure and ecological sustainability. Therefore, even though India's performance on the GII indicates that the nation has made significant advances in fostering its innovation ecosystem, there is still work to be done before the country can completely realize its potential as a rising global-innovation hub.

Marathon, Not a Sprint

Improving competitiveness is a marathon, not a sprint. As we have learned from global experiences, there are no shortcuts or straightforward solutions based on limited interventions. However, it is possible to accelerate progress through a defined strategy that enables action to concentrate on what is most important at a given moment. Understanding the fundamentals of India's competitiveness as they relate to and influence its long-term prosperity is essential for outlining the next steps towards shared prosperity.

This chapter's analysis of India's competitiveness fundamentals examines the underlying determinants of prosperity relative to the performance of peer economies over the past few years. Overall, it is recognized that India has vast potential to increase labour productivity, labour mobilization and enhance sectoral development. To address these challenges, a revision of our approach to development is necessary, one that takes into account the unique characteristics of the problems at hand as well as a granular perspective. The competitiveness approach is the key, especially for a diverse country like India. Geographical diversity suggests that different locations possess their own distinct characteristics and features. This diversity can be harnessed and turned into our forte. We will explore this idea in detail in the next chapter.

5

The Many Indias

The rapid emergence and evolution of new economic models have prompted countries to rethink their competitiveness and approach their economies from a different perspective. Before, the focus of states and nations was on the economy as a whole, and national economic policy was viewed as the key factor. However, understanding the link between competitiveness and a region's productivity has become a new viewpoint. It is essential to use a microeconomic, bottom-up strategy to comprehend how businesses compete and become competitive in particular areas. This is especially true for a country such as India, which is known for its boggling heterogeneity. A top-down national economic policy formulation approach may not help as much as a bottom-up approach that leverages our heterogeneity would. At the regional level, India's diversity can be truly tapped into for enhancing economic growth. The regional business environment in which a firm operates is a critical driver of productivity. It is at this level where specific locational attributes affect firms' operations. These attributes can be shaped to build an environment conducive to business growth and expansion.

Any regional business environment is represented by four granular factors forming a diamond: factor conditions, demand conditions, context for firm and strategy and related and supporting industries, as expounded on in the previous chapter. Of these four elements, clusters primarily constitute only one of the facets of the diamond, i.e., related and supporting industries; however, they are best seen as a manifestation of the interaction between all the diamond's elements.[1]

A cluster can be described as a group of interconnected firms, suppliers, service providers and associated institutions in a particular field, often linked by commonalities and complementarities, which compete as well as coordinate.[2] They tend to have unusual competitive success in particular business areas and are a striking feature of most economic regions and countries, especially those with advanced economies. Examples of a few such clusters are Wall Street in New York, Hollywood in Los Angeles, Bollywood in Mumbai, consumer electronics in Japan and information technology (IT) in Bangalore. Putting the theory of national, state and local competitiveness within the context of a global economy gives clusters a prominent role. Although they are only considered to be one aspect of the diamond model, they are widely regarded as a reflection of their interaction with other elements.

Despite the widespread recognition of clusters as an integral part of a country's economy, economic geography is still the main factor that determines their significance. They have played a significant role in shaping the competitive landscape in various countries around the world. Economists have attempted to explain the presence of firm agglomerations by developing theories that examine how these types of economies emerge. These were typically thought to be in either urban or industrial settings. One particular focus of such studies is on minimizing costs by being near inputs and markets. However, the rise of technology, the increasing number of supply sources, and the cost-effective transportation of goods and services have cast doubt on such arguments. The increase in globalization and liberalization has diminished the traditional role and importance of locations, though new roles within competition have emerged, changing the nature of these agglomerations.[3] These clusters are now spread across industries having strong linkages with each other rather than being confined to specific industries. Additionally, clusters in different types of economies have revealed important insights into the competitive advantage that location can provide. Due to the complexity of the competition environment, their contribution to the competitiveness of a country's economy has increased. The existence of clusters signifies that most of a company's competitive edge comes from its geographic location rather than being solely derived from within its industry.

The link between competition and economic geography has significant implications for every level of a region's economic geography, including cities, districts, states and nations. While the concept of clusters gives a framework for understanding the dynamics of economic activity within a certain region or industry, economic geography provides a framework for understanding the variables that lead to the establishment and success of clusters.[4] The numerous good economic effects of clustering are also generated and amplified by geographic proximity, boosting the firms' competitiveness. Clusters reflect and magnify competitive advantage mainly through three channels: first, by raising the productivity of the constituent firms or industries; second, by raising their capacity for innovation and, consequently, for productivity growth; and third, by encouraging the emergence of new businesses that foster innovation and broaden the existing cluster. A discussion on clusters and their effect on competitiveness must begin with an understanding of how the concept of clusters has evolved through the years.

Theoretical Aspect of Clusters

o *Historical Evolution of the Cluster: An Overview*

In the evolution of the cluster concept, many schools of thought have significantly contributed to its current understanding. All the theories were established against the backdrop of distinctive historical occurrences that profoundly changed the business environment and how organizations engage with their local environment. They are summarized in terms of their unique historical setting, fundamental assumptions and key claims regarding the competitive advantage of enterprises through clusters. The concept of geographical proximity was first established by Alfred Marshall during the nineteenth century. During this period, he witnessed a paradigm shift in the manufacturing process, which was later known as the industrial divide.[5] This divide became evident with the rise of large companies that had the ability to potentially replace smaller firms. They achieved this by capitalizing on internal economies of scale and focusing on producing standardized goods. These observations were based on the spatial pattern of economic activity in nineteenth-century England. He analysed the various factors that affect the competition between large and small enterprises in various regions, focusing his attention on the industries that were concentrated in certain areas. The two primary factors identified as contributing to this factor in these industrial districts were external economies of scale and the localized learning fostered by the industrial market environment.[6] As a result, the industrial districts represent an alternate kind of industrial organization during that time.

Marshall's idea of industrial districts was re-introduced by Italian academicians Becattini and Brusco in the 1970s as a framework to explain the economic success of central and north-eastern Italian regions, which were home to numerous SMEs mostly focused on labour-intensive sectors. While being modest in size, their product contributed around 28 per cent of the total manufacturing exports from Italy.[7]. It was noted that these businesses followed a common set of principles, standards and knowledge connections to maintain a balance between cooperation and rivalry. These New Marshallian Districts shared some similarities with the original model in terms of their main features. As a result of formal training and the presence of a supply-demand information network given their proximity, they supported a highly skilled worker force. Due to the interdependence of all the firms, this school of thinking made a significant addition to the literature by changing the emphasis from the individual firm to the community of firms. Their connection was the foundation for the district's success. Yet, this empirical investigation's extensive dependence on the Italian case made it difficult to generalize, which was a key flaw. As a result of this failure, we saw the emergence of the Californian School of thought, which made an effort to offer a general explanation of clusters.

The successful technological districts in southern and central California were examined by the Californian school of thought. These districts were geographically confined, made up of specialized and vertically disintegrating networks of businesses and institutions. The external transactions a firm engaged in grew quickly, according to their argument, as a result of the vertical breakdown of production. These transactions were more complex and less predictable, which raised the transaction cost even more. As a result, the firms frequently choose locations close to one another to better control them[8] (Šarić, 2012). They were then benefited by the agglomeration in a number of ways, including a decrease in transaction costs, an increase in flexibility and a reduction in risk. Based on the basic principle of transaction cost, their theory had wider applicability than the new Marshallian districts theory, as it can be applied to any region, industry or sectors of all sizes.

Central to Porter's competitiveness framework is his view that the sources of competitive advantage lie outside the firm. The firm is defined as a bundle of value activities, which determine its cost structure and ability to create value. A firm's performance is the result of how a firm utilizes its value activities to gain a favourable position within its industry compared to its competitors. Successful implementation of value activities, however, is costly and requires tangible and intangible assets such as capital, technologies and human resources as well as information, knowledge and skills. Because clusters 'enable any company in any industry to compete in the most sophisticated ways,' they represent an appealing chance to boost the productivity and inventive capacity of a firm's value activities.[9] He identifies that a country's competitiveness is primarily driven by clusters. Competition puts pressure on businesses and compels them to continuously improve their operations and invent new products in order to stay one step ahead of their competitors. Clusters have the potential to increase the competitiveness of the firms or to outperform their rivals economically. Accordingly, in his subsequent work, he repeatedly centres his arguments on the themes of competitiveness, productivity and upgrading.

o   *Porter's Idea of Clusters*

A cluster is defined as a geographically proximate group of interconnected companies and associated institutions in a particular field linked by commonalities and complementarities. A cluster's geographic breadth can encompass a single city or state, a whole nation, or even a network of neighbouring nations.[10] Depending on their complexity and depth, clusters can take a variety of forms, but they typically consist of businesses that provide the final product or a service as well as businesses that supply specialized inputs, components, machinery, services, financial institutions and businesses in related industries. Additionally, businesses in downstream industries (i.e., customers or channels); producers of complementary goods; providers of specialized infrastructure; governmental and other organizations that offer specialized instruction, information, research and technical support; (such as universities, think tanks and providers of vocational training), and organizations that set standards are frequently included in clusters. A cluster's constituent government organizations may be regarded as a component of it. Last but not least, a lot of clusters have trade associations and other groups from the private sector that work together to help cluster members.

As a result, clusters move one step ahead and present a unique way of organizing economic data and viewing the economies from a special lens rather than the more traditional approaches of companies, industries or sectors, such as manufacturing or services. The standard industrial classification methods rarely define cluster borders in a way that takes into account the connections between different industries and numerous significant players. Clusters also frequently involve traditional and high-tech businesses or have the potential to do so. These crucial linkages, complementarities and spillovers are fundamental in today's competition to improve the prosperity of the region. However, the narrow sectoral or industry perspective usually distorts competition. Due to the large number of participants in the market, there is a real threat that rivalry will diminish. Firms are reluctant to participate because they fear that they might help their direct competitors. In addition, viewing the world from the perspective of narrow industries or sectors can lead to lobbying over tax breaks and subsidies for certain companies, which can also distort markets.[11] On the other hand, placing a group of institutions and firms belonging to different but related industries and sectors together as a cluster provides an opportunity to improve the coordination and efficiency of their activities without undermining or threatening competition. This type of forum also facilitates dialogue between related parties and government, attracting various private and public investments.

Urban economics and regional science examine the different urban economies, including generalized urban agglomerations. These agglomerations are known for their diverse mix of industries and strong communication networks.. The importance of these economies, which are unaffected by the kinds of firms and clusters present, seems to be greatest in developing nations. However, the importance of urban agglomerations appears to be diminishing due to the rise of trade and the reduction in transportation and communication costs. As more countries develop similar infrastructures, the need for these types of economies is also decreasing. Regional science studies also look into the concentration of firms in certain fields, which can be referred to as clusters. In some industries, small- and medium-sized enterprises dominate the local economy. On the other hand, a mixture of foreign-owned and domestic firms is also commonly seen in specific fields. These theories only addressed certain aspects of clusters or clusters of a particular type; however, they contributed significantly to understanding the importance of clusters in the context of today's competition.[12]

A cluster's constituent parts can be identified by looking at the various firms and industries in its vertical and horizontal chain. The following step is to identify those that are complementary to the cluster's activities. Additional horizontal chains may be identified based on the utilization of similar technologies or inputs. Following the identification of a cluster's firms and industries, the next step is to isolate the entities that provide the organization with specialized expertise, capital, information and infrastructure. The next step is to find out which regulatory bodies influence the cluster's participants. Using the same approach, a cluster map for the automotive cluster in Maharashtra was created. It is presented below. The schematic diagram demonstrates the several chains of related industries involved in the Maharashtra automotive cluster. It consists of related technologies, shared inputs and complementary products. These industries also use common marketing media. Consequently, cluster boundaries encompass all firms, industries and institutions with strong linkages, whether vertical, horizontal or institutional. Such strong and numerous cross-firm links and synergies make the cluster significant as compared to other regions.

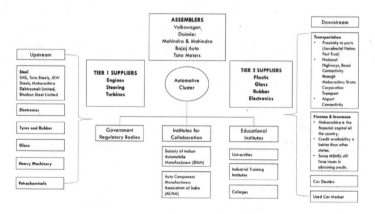

Source: Clusters: The Drivers of Competitiveness report, 2018

Clusters can be found in a wide range of sectors, including large and small fields and some locally owned establishments like eateries, auto dealers and antique shops. They even exist at various geographic levels: nations, states, metropolitan regions, cities and different types and sizes of economies in rural and urban settings. However, they significantly vary in terms of size, breadth and stage of development. Certain clusters are mainly made up of small- and medium-sized businesses. A few contain large and small firms. While some clusters have a focus on research institutions and other R&D organizations, others don't. These variations in clusters' nature highlight variations in the structures of their underlying industries. They are further affected by their geographical setting. A cluster with a deeper, more specialized and well-connected supplier base, with different sizes of firms and extensive supporting institutions, will be strong and well-developed.

The role that clusters play in the contemporary knowledge-based economy is far more nuanced, and its broader role in competition is only now becoming widely recognized. Unlike other theories, the cluster theory by Porter promotes capitalizing on emerging agglomeration and fostering the growth of those firms that have the strongest connections to other clusters or spillover effects from other clusters. These agglomeration economies are now known for their dynamic nature and focus on innovation and learning. Thus, compared to what has previously been acknowledged, clusters play a more intricate and crucial function in the modern economy. It represents a type of multi-organizational structure, which is a key factor in shaping the competitiveness of the region, and a key element of market economies. The health of an economy's clusters provides crucial information about its potential for production and the barriers to further growth. Important ramifications for businesses, the government and other institutions stem from the function of clusters in competition.

o   *The Role of Location*

Over the years, the concept of competition has been relatively static. It has been viewed as a cost-effective strategy that focuses on minimizing the impact of competition, especially in closed economies. Comparative advantage in the production factors (labour and capital) or, in more recent studies, economies of scale, were regarded as the decision-making factors.[13]

However, this picture doesn't capture the real competition that exists around the world. It is dynamic and depends on the degree to which one can find strategic differences. Factors like the increasing number of countries that are open to the global economy, expansion of the input supply, the improving efficiency of international and national factor markets and the diminishing intensity of competition can drastically reduce the value of factor inputs. Even the well-known vertical-integration method for raising productivity can be rendered ineffective, inefficient and inflexible by a more dynamic environment.[14]

According to this more expansive and dynamic interpretation of competition, location influences competitive advantage through its impact on productivity, particularly productivity growth. Productivity is the amount of value produced per hour of labour and per unit of physical resources used. Due to the increased globalization and liberalization, the factor inputs themselves are plentiful and easily accessible. It is the efficiency with which resources are utilized by firms that determines prosperity. Prosperity and productivity of a location depend on how its firms compete.[15] . In any industry, whether it's agriculture, semiconductors, or marketing, firms can be more productive if they use advanced technology, offer unique services and employ sophisticated methods. High technology and skill knowledge can be employed in all industries across all sectors. However, if any firm is unproductive, the mere presence of high technology in a sector does not ensure its prosperity. Thus, the goal should be to improve the productivity of all firms, irrespective of their kind.[16] This will create a multiplier effect as one cluster's productivity increases the productivity of others.

So, a location's success is determined by the productivity of what firms located there choose to do, which eventually determines the profits and wage levels of the region.[17] The productivity of domestic companies is frequently increased by the presence of highly developed foreign corporations and vice versa. The business environment is very important when it comes to competing in a location. It can affect the productivity and sophistication of a company's operations. For instance, if a company has a poor transportation infrastructure, it can't effectively utilize advanced logistical techniques. High-quality service is not possible unless a company has well-educated employees. This is because many businesses operate under heavy regulation and government red tape. They also face delays in resolving disputes and a lack of cooperation from the courts. These factors can affect a firm's efficiency and cost effectiveness. Various factors, such as the legal system, road system and corporate tax rates, affect the operations of different industries. These can be considered as horizontal or economy-wide areas that can hinder a country's competitiveness.[18] Consequently, more advanced economies have stronger business environments specific to the cluster-growth requirements. Close and stronger links with crucial institutions and buyers can lead to high efficiency and innovation, resulting in greater prosperity levels.[19]

o   *Importance of Economic Geography to Clusters*

The study of economic geography focuses on the global distribution of economic activity and how it has changed over time. It looks

at the elements that affect where economic activity occurs as well
as the relationships between the economy and the environment.
As previously mentioned, the homogeneity of economies and
the specialization of economies have frequently been contrasted
in the literature as two alternative theories. The former promotes
the idea that nearly everything could be transported or sourced
globally, resulting in a more unified global economy. The latter
held to the theory that competitive advantages tend to cluster
in different places, leading to intense specialization and a rise in
global economy.

The hypothesis of convergence was supported by conventional
economic theories like the neo-classical model. They contended
that increased economic integration and homogenization across
nations would come from the ease of moving products and
services due to the removal of trade barriers and the use of more
effective technology as a result of expanding liberalization and
globalization.[20] As a result, the significance of national boundaries
is diminished, and competitiveness is thought to be less dependent
on geography. Yet, the way that the contemporary global economy
is viewed has a significant impact on the issue of geography as
a source of competitive advantage. According to Alfred Weber's
well-known Industrial Location Theory, which holds that the
respective weights of three factors—transportation costs, labour
costs and agglomeration economies—determine where an industry
will be located. The spatial arrangement of economic activity was
a key component of Paul Krugman's New Economic Geography
Theory, which was strongly influenced by two variables: growing
returns to scale and transportation costs. It foresees that the core
regions, or those with the best prospects for economic growth,
will host the majority of the country's economic activity. Trade
will link these regions to periphery regions, which will be crucial
for the survival of such regions.[21]

Porter discusses the importance of location in the globalized world, going beyond the traditional idea of clustering.. He claimed that the economic geography in an era of global competition involves a paradox. The traditional view of competing in goods markets that have a comparative advantage was dominant in the pre-globalization era. The concept of generic factors of production such as capital, labour and natural resources were the key factors of competitiveness. The rivalry was mainly stagnant and relied on a strategy of cost-cutting. The increase in the exchange of goods, services, technology and information around the world diminished the traditional roles of location. In today's competitive environment, firms can easily access the resources and capital they need in global markets. They no longer need to locate near large markets. One of the first steps in globalization was to move assembly plants to low-cost regions. Anything that can be easily and efficiently sourced from a distance, however, has been essentially nullified as a competitive advantage in advanced economies.[22] Global communication and sourcing reduce drawbacks but do not produce advantages.

Furthermore, in terms of overall productivity and innovation, accessing a competitive local cluster is typically the better option when compared to distant sourcing. This is because today's competition is wider and more dynamic owing to innovation and strategic differences. The effectiveness and rate of development of the region depend on strong relationships with suppliers, customers and other institutions. Consequently, the competitive advantages of a global economy are often concentrated in local areas due to the presence of various specialized businesses and institutions in a particular region or country. Proximity in terms of institutional, cultural and geographic factors allows companies to access a wide range of benefits, such as better relationships and incentives. As a result, with time and growing globalization, the location became more important than factor endowments and size. Location influences the competitive advantage by its impact on productivity and its growth, which, in turn, influences regional prosperity. Thus, location matters, albeit in different ways at the turn of the twenty-first century than in earlier decades.[23]

Geographic proximity provides businesses with a number of benefits, including strong incentives, better knowledge and simple access to specialized inputs. It allows them to grow their operations and improve their growth. These are difficult to acquire from a distance. Despite the shift in the role of location, it is still the most important factor that businesses consider when it comes to deciding where to locate. Geographic advantages continue to be the real sources of economies' long-term competitive advantage. Due to the rise of globalization, economies have become more specialization-oriented.[24] For instance, smaller geographical regions such as cities and states are now capable of becoming major players in the global market. It is the result of the increasing agglomeration of businesses that they have reached a critical mass in a particular geographic location. It eventually leads to more positive externalities and efficiency gains, with the support of the quality of the business environment and the endowments of the dominant factors. Consequently, it provides a higher probability of attracting and retaining a large number of businesses.

o   *Competitive Advantage through Clusters*

Clusters can offer businesses and organizations a wide range of advantages that may give them a competitive edge. These advantages include access to resources, markets, and talent as well as the sharing of knowledge, resources and expertise, the development of a critical mass of businesses and institutions, the creation and development of specialized infrastructure and the provision of supportive institutions. New technologies, business models and products may be developed as a result of the interaction of all these elements. These benefits ultimately raise the region's overall levels of innovation, competitiveness and productivity. However, the majority of them depend on outside economies, spillover effects across businesses, industries, and organizations or direct interpersonal interactions between different people. Because of the strong connections between cluster members, the whole is worth more than the sum of its parts.[25] Clusters are best seen as a manifestation of the interactions among all four facets of the diamond model. However, their competitive advantages won't be uniform across all fields, even though they are widespread in all types of economies. The depth and breadth of a cluster, along with its geographical location, significantly affect its competitive advantage.

Cluster and Productivity

o *Access to Specialized Inputs and Workforce*

In addition to raising the demand for specialist inputs in a given area, the presence of clusters there also helps to expand their supply, creating a broad and specialized supplier base. In contrast to formal agreements with outside parties, vertical integration or sourcing from far-off places, firms within clusters have significantly cheaper access to higher-quality inputs. This is due to how little inventory is required, the possibility of better communication and the reduction in production-activity delays. When hiring for workers, clusters also provide comparable advantages. Since a cluster offers a pool of knowledgeable and specialized workers, the costs of recruiting and hiring are significantly lower within it. Suitable people can be paired with the right jobs and the process becomes more effective. This results in more and better employment options, which eventually lower the workforce's risk of migrating. Additionally, it has the benefit of luring specialized workers from other regions at lower costs.

o *Access to Information, Institutions and Public Goods*

Being collections of connected and related industries, clusters make it possible to gather technical and other specialized knowledge. As a result, the businesses within clusters may access this resource with more ease and affordability, increasing their productivity and bringing them closer to their productivity frontier. By creating factors like the presence of human connections, ties to the community that build trust, proximity to sources of supply and technical connections, clusters help the free flow of information. Furthermore, clusters can transform expensive inputs like specialized infrastructure and expertise into low-cost public or quasi-public commodities that are available to cluster participants.

o *Complementarities*

It describes the interdependence of several businesses, sectors and other organizations inside a cluster. Each player is reliant on the others, and the success of one can greatly influence the success of the others. At several levels, such as between products in terms of consumer needs or marketing, complementary relationships might exist. For instance, in the tourism sector, where supporting services like lodging, dining and transportation are just as important as the principal location, complementary product relationships can be seen. These can significantly raise the cluster's overall quality and effectiveness. Another form in which complementarities can arise within a cluster is marketing. Similar businesses and sectors can work together on collaborative marketing initiatives, like trade shows and marketing delegations, to increase efficiency and cut expenses. These synergies between various cluster members ultimately raise the cluster's and its location's overall productivity levels.

Clusters and Innovation

A firm's capacity to innovate and enhance its productivity growth over time is significantly influenced by clusters. Sharing resources and expertise is one of the main ways that clusters promote innovation. Due to their proximity, businesses in a cluster frequently share information and work together on R&D initiatives, which can result in the development of new goods, services and technology. Deeper insights regarding how technology is evolving, the availability of components and machinery and service and marketing ideas can be shared easily. The enterprises are able to see market prospects more clearly than independent firms because of the sophisticated buyers frequently found in clusters. They are in a better position to identify the needs of prospective customers quickly and clearly. Suppliers and other institutions are more familiar with the needs of the businesses as a result of the ongoing partnerships. Clusters also produce an environment that stimulates innovation in addition to these immediate advantages. A given industry's concentration of businesses can create a critical mass of resources and talent, which can draw in more money and talent. As a result, the cluster may experience further growth and development as new businesses and technologies are drawn to it. In contrast, the isolated firm must spend more money, overcome more obstacles to assembling insights and produce more information internally. When an organization relies on distant outsourcing, it also has more difficulties with contracting, securing delivery, receiving technical assistance and collaborating with complementary entities. Thus, clusters may have a distinct edge in identifying the demand and the possibility for innovation.

Clusters and New Business Formation

The empirical evidence across the world suggests that most new businesses are usually located within the existing clusters than in some isolated locations. Owing to a number of factors, such as the exchange of information and resources, the presence of specialized institutions and the establishment of a competitive atmosphere, networking, collaboration and a supportive community culture, clusters can result in the emergence of new businesses. The supportive environment of the clusters lowers the entry barriers to the market by facilitating easier access for business owners to resources, including manpower, assets and raw materials. New enterprises can access cutting-edge technology from well-connected institutions as well as a talent pool. Clusters frequently exhibit a strong sense of belonging and a common culture. Entrepreneurs make use of the substantial benefits offered by the quasi-public goods within the clusters and this fosters an atmosphere that encourages new firms to enter the market. They also draw in new business owners and entrepreneurs who want to take advantage of the opportunities that the competitive cluster environment is creating. A positive feedback loop is created when new businesses are formed, which increases the depth and breadth of clusters and amplifies the variety of benefits it offers. As a result, businesses within the cluster are in a better position than their counterparts in other areas.

The channels of the cluster mentioned above boost the impact of the other three diamond-shaped sections, increasing the location's competitiveness at a faster rate. The close proximity of the businesses fosters healthy competition, and the co-location guarantees that each member of the cluster benefits from any beneficial spillovers.

Clusters Initiatives: Empirical Evidence

o *Clusters and the Types of Economies*

The depth and breadth of clusters are typically stronger in advanced economies, where they are usually most pronounced. Compared to them, clusters in the developing economies have fewer and weak linkages among the participants. The potential for economic value is created by the very existence of businesses, suppliers and organizations in a place, but this potential is not always realized. Relationships, networks and a sense of common interest that undergird the social structure of clusters take on central importance. In developing economies, the lack of effective communication between existing institutions and firms is a major issue that prevents the formation of strong clusters. Cluster development is further hindered by low levels of local education and ability, flaws in technology, a lack of access to money and underdeveloped institutions. In developing nations, it is more common for industries to be based locally or be subsidiaries of foreign companies. In addition, exporting businesses is a more resource and labour-intensive task. As a result, these clusters tend to have fewer participants and have different profiles. In contrast, clusters in advanced economies are significant and prosperous as they involve a robust network of relationships.

Although developing countries can compete with their advanced counterparts, the lack of strong clusters can impede their productivity and profitability. For instance, while exporting can grow for a long time with the use of low-cost natural resources and local labour, this approach is not ideal as it limits the country's ability to improve its standard of living and productivity. One of the crucial elements in transitioning to an advanced economy is the creation of functional clusters. To become more productive, a region must develop local capabilities that can help improve the processes and products of its businesses. Eventually, a cluster should be able to innovate and grow. This is why the establishment of successful clusters, which depends on their deepening and enlarging, is very important for economic development.

Clusters Initiative: Around the World

Over time, knowledge about the cluster theory as proposed by Michael Porter has spread widely. Although there is a vast amount of theoretical literature on this subject, not much is known about its application in practice, especially in developing economies. Some developed economies, such as Sweden, the European Union and the United States have successfully used clusters to drive competitiveness and policymaking. Most of the analyses of these programmes are based on case studies.

Cluster mapping is a framework that aims to identify and analyse the various factors that contribute to the presence and growth of clusters in different geographical locations. Most countries use this approach to identify the critical clusters in smaller regions like states, counties and cities. Cluster initiatives offer a fresh approach to planning economic development activities that go beyond conventional efforts to lower business costs and improve the general business climate. Through identifying key clusters, policymakers, business leaders and other key stakeholder groups can improve their understanding of the local economy's strengths and weaknesses and develop effective policies to support their growth.

In the United States, the Economic Development Administration (EDA) and other organizations are working together with the Harvard Business School Center for Strategy and Competitiveness to lead the cluster-mapping programme throughout the country. It has been referred over time to guide federal, state and local policy decisions. At the state and local levels, the data and insights from the initiative are used to inform economic development strategies and target resources to support particular industries and regions. Whereas at the federal level, they are used to inform its programmes and funding decisions. Currently, it is being popularly used at the city level to pinpoint important clusters and evaluate the local environment. It shows the successes, knowledge gained, difficulties and chances faced by the numerous clusters in the area. The cluster has been crucial in supporting regional economic growth and competitiveness in addition to its role in guiding governmental decisions. The EDA, the Small Business Administration (SBA), the Department of Labour, the Department of Education, the Department of Energy and other agencies have provided financing to assist growth initiatives based on greater regional clusters of innovation.

In addition, the European Union has been aggressively pushing cluster mapping through a number of initiatives and funding schemes over the years. During the past thirty years, support for clusters has been a cornerstone of most national and regional competitiveness programmes, and cluster organizations currently operate in virtually all of Europe. The European Cluster Collaboration Platform (ECCP), a project supported by the European Union with the goal of increasing competitiveness and creativity of European enterprises by encouraging collaboration within clusters, is another platform working in the same direction. It promotes cross-border cooperation between companies, research centres and clusters, with an emphasis on SMEs. It offers a variety of instruments and services, such as matching occasions, online platforms and training courses, to promote cooperation amongst clusters. In recent years, it has also played a vital role in establishing resilient, green and digital industrial ecosystems in order to improve the innovation and competitiveness of enterprises and regions. Around 80 per cent of cluster organizations in the EU 27 support firms in their digital transformation and over 60 per cent in their green transition due to the transversal nature of greening and digitization across all industries and industrial ecosystems.[26] One of the other key platforms that aim to promote cluster growth and policymaking through the gathering, analysis and distribution of data is the European Cluster Observatory (ECO).

Sweden and Catalonia are among the first few economies where the cluster programme was replicated. The government of Catalonia supports some vital clusters via a variety of initiatives. With the assistance of the government, Catalonia's Industrial Technological Plan was created with the goal of enhancing the competitiveness of the region's industry, with a special emphasis on advanced industrial clusters like the aerospace industry. The Cluster of Health and Life Sciences of Catalonia, a public-private collaboration that supports the competitiveness of the health and life sciences industry in Catalonia, is another illustration of government support. Overall, 30 per cent of the region's GDP* is produced by the approximately thirty clusters in the Catalan Clusters Programme, which includes about 2600 businesses. Over 300 clusters in Sweden have also been mapped as part of the Swedish Cluster Mapping Project, a collaboration between the Swedish government and a number of universities and research institutions. The project has also identified important clusters in

---

* https://clustercollaboration.eu/news/catalan-clusters-mobilized-against-covid-19

fields like advanced engineering, biotechnology and the creative industries. Vinnova, another Swedish government organization for innovation, uses cluster analysis to identify and support important innovation areas. The Swedish Life Science Cluster, Cleantech Cluster and the ICT Cluster are a few other illustrations of the cluster endeavour in the country. The European Union and the Swedish government support all of these projects. Clusters have also been used to assess the potential for growth in less developed regions and to drive regional development strategies. This includes offering cash and assistance to clusters in these areas so they can expand and prosper.

Mexico has also been working towards promoting regional development through its cluster initiative, which is also based on the theory of competitive clusters put forth by Michael Porter. Mexico's cluster initiative is a public policy that focuses on the development of regional clusters to improve productivity, increase competitiveness and create jobs, like in other countries. The government has established the National Cluster Program in collaboration with the European Cluster Collaboration Platform, which is responsible for supporting the development of clusters throughout the country. According to ProMéxico, there are 155 clusters representing nine sectors throughout the country.[*] Renewable energy, sophisticated engineering (manufacturing technologies, automotive and aerospace components or specialized alloys) and biotechnology have been identified as the key areas of focus for cluster-to-cluster cooperation. Mexico's cluster initiative has already had significant success in several regions of the country.

---

[*] https://clustercollaboration.eu/sites/default/files/mexico_preparatory_briefing.pdf

Examples of such successful clusters can be found across the developed world. They help us understand the potential of clusters to help improve the competitiveness of regions and firms, thereby increasing the prosperity and development levels of the same.

Clusters in India

A cluster has been understood and defined as the concentration of firms producing the same or similar products or strategic services in a common geographical area* in India for decades. It is considered among the most effective strategies for boosting economic growth and competitiveness, especially in the context of the country's industrial and manufacturing sectors. Over the past couple of decades, the country has seen the emergence of various modern industrial clusters, mainly focused on software development and IT. One of these is the Bangalore software cluster, which is regarded as the Silicon Valley of India. It is home to several of the country's leading software companies such as Tata Consultancy Services, Infosys and Wipro. Another example of a modern cluster is the automobile cluster in the city of Pune, which is dedicated to manufacturing automobiles. However, even before these clusters, India has a long history of traditional artisanal clusters. These include the Banarasi silk sarees cluster in Uttar Pradesh, the Mysore brassware and jewellery cluster in Karnataka, the hand block printing cluster in Jaipur, the brassware and leather cluster in Delhi and many more. These agglomerations are majorly based on a particular industry or skill and are supported by local institutions and entrepreneurial activities. Over time, these clusters evolved naturally due to the support provided by local networks and organizations.

---

* https://www.clusterobservatory.in/clustermap.php

The government has adopted a number of steps to assist cluster development in the country over the last few years. The Ministry of Micro, Small & Medium Enterprises has established several policies and programmes, including the National Manufacturing Competitiveness Programme and the Industrial Cluster Development Programme. The majority of manufacturing companies in a variety of industries, including textiles, leather, handicrafts, electronics and vehicles, are supported by these programmes. One such example is the Cluster Observatory, which was formed in 2005 in association with the European Cluster Collaboration Platform. It lists more than 5000 clusters in India.[*] However, these clusters are broadly classified into two categories: industrial clusters and micro-enterprise clusters. The former includes all types of firms of all sizes, whereas the latter comprises micro-sized, household-based businesses. Other such initiatives are the Horticulture Cluster Development Programme, engineering clusters and science and technology clusters. These programmes aim to create strong connections between various stakeholder groups, such as government ministries, research laboratories, international organizations and academic institutions. The government also encourages the establishment of clusters through the establishment of special economic zones (SEZs). These areas are designed to provide various benefits to businesses. SEZs are commonly established to support the development of various industries. These areas often have clusters of related businesses.

To increase the clusters' productivity, competitiveness and export potential, these programmes offer them financial and technical support. In recent years, the government has been focusing on supporting the development of clusters in different regions of the country. Clusters have become a significant strategy

---

[*] https://clustercollaboration.eu/content/india

in India as they can simultaneously encourage employment, growth and innovation across numerous industries. However, the main factor is the strong and widespread linkages between the various stakeholders in the cluster. Thus, the need of the hour is to define and understand clusters as more than the simple agglomerations of the firms in a common region. As a result, we use Michael Porter's concept of clusters, which is widely used in developed and many developing nations.

Porter's Clusters Initiative: India

Cluster mapping is a unique method for identifying the concentration of economic activities linked through backward and forward connections in various geographical locations.[27] It is the quantitative assessment of cluster presence throughout smaller regions of a country in terms of size, productivity, specialization and dynamism. This exercise aims to provide comprehensive insights into the geographic footprint of a specific cluster category across different regions and sectors of the economy. In addition, it enables in building cluster portfolio of any region that can be compared systematically with its peers.

Type of Clusters

The economic geography of cities, states and countries, particularly prosperous ones, is characterized by specialization, which grows as an economy develops. The economy within a region is typically dominated by a limited number of clusters, which also make up the vast majority of the region's export-oriented economic activity (for example, exports to other locations and investment in other locations by locally based firms) and outward-oriented economic activity. These outward-oriented clusters are usually found with two other types of clusters: locally focused industries and clusters like restaurants, entertainment, logistical services, real estate and construction; local subsidiaries of competitive firms, which are based elsewhere but are focused on serving the local market like sales offices, customer support centres and assembly plants.

The former is the type of cluster known as traded cluster. It can grow beyond the area's market size and absorb workers from other industries and firms. They are considered the region's primary source of economic growth over the long run as it focuses on the global market. The latter, known as the local clusters, in contrast, are innately constrained and primarily survive directly or indirectly from the success of outward-oriented clusters. They produce goods and services serving the local market only. As a result, it is crucial to distinguish the two types of clusters present in the region, to identify the true engine of growth and prosperity.

The traded clusters are like the engine: if they are not successfully competing in national or international markets, a location cannot reach higher levels of prosperity. Whereas local clusters are like powertrains and tires; if they are not efficient and supportive, traded clusters are unable to lift the region's prosperity to higher levels.[28]

Among the developed economies, the share of traded industries in employment is relatively low as they are not very labour-intensive; however, their share in the payroll is significant, about 50 per cent or more. This pattern is observed in countries like the United States, Sweden, the United Kingdom and others. India being a developing country shows a slightly different composition. Traded clusters' share of the national employment and payroll is just about 24 per cent and 35 per cent, respectively. Almost 75 per cent of the workforce is employed by either local or agricultural clusters, which also make up 65 per cent of the national payroll.

Figure 30: Contribution of Clusters: India vs US Economy

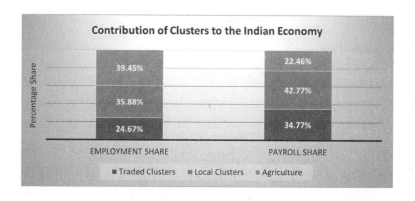

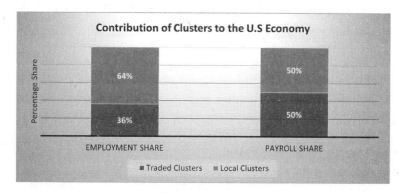

Source: The 2023 India Cluster Panorama[29]

The other economies classify agriculture as a traded cluster because of its extensive commercialization and use of technology. But unlike them, India still heavily relies on its agricultural industry, which employs more than 40 per cent of the country's workforce and makes a significant contribution to exports. Key characteristics of traded and local types of clusters are present in India's agriculture. Hence, the third broad type of cluster for India was introduced: agricultural inputs and services.

These three broad categories of clusters are further divided into narrow categories, each related to provide a more granular perspective of the national and regional economy. There are fifty traded, seventeen local clusters and one agriculture cluster. The graph below represents India's cluster portfolio of narrow categories. It shows where each of the sixty-eight cluster categories stands in terms of employment, payroll and average earnings.

Figure 31: India's Cluster Portfolio of Narrow Categories

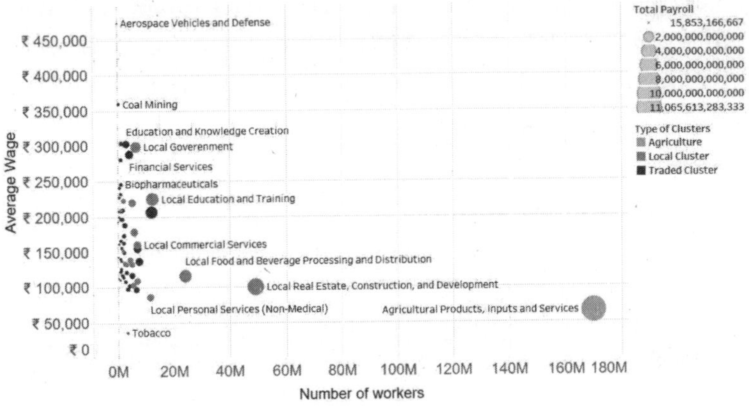

Source: The 2023 India Cluster Panorama[30]

The snapshot further supports the empirical literature that shows that local clusters, including agriculture in this case, increase the size of the economy, whereas traded clusters have a substantial impact on productivity and economic well-being. The majority of local and traded clusters produce more than the national average (Rs 1.14 lakh), which is a sign of an expanding economy. Among all the clusters, agriculture appears to be the most significant employment-intensive clusters in India.

Business services, transportation and logistics, distribution and electronic commerce, textile manufacturing and food processing and manufacturing are the top five clusters providing the highest employment among traded clusters. They contribute to about 36 per cent of employment in traded clusters. Concerning productivity, the top five traded clusters are aerospace vehicles and defense, coal mining, insurance services, education and knowledge creation and financial services. These clusters are very different from each other. Coal mining is a resource-dependent cluster; aerospace vehicles and defense is a very specialized cluster; the other three are service-oriented clusters. Other crucial clusters like information technology, analytical instruments and biopharmaceuticals are also among the top ten productive clusters in the country.

Composition of Clusters

To understand and leverage these broad and narrow categories of clusters better with respect to the labour market, one must study their composition in terms of sectors, gender, type of employment and skill level.

The urbanization rate is a crucial aspect of economic geography and development since urban areas are the primary drivers of the country's economic performance and dynamism. The National Commission on Population, Ministry of Health and Family Welfare, predicts that 35.07 per cent of the country will be urbanized by 2023.

Figure 32: Sectoral Distribution of Employment and Payroll

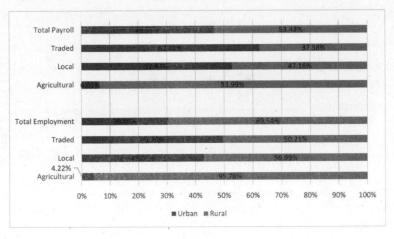

Source: *The 2023 India Cluster Panorama*[31]

India's economy is dominated by agriculture, which provides employment and income in rural areas. Only 30.5 per cent of jobs are in the urban sector, accounting for 47 per cent of the national payroll. Traded and local clusters are well-represented in rural areas, but most of their payroll is concentrated in the urban sector. Resource-dependent clusters, such as forestry, tobacco, non-metallic mining and wood products, are the few exceptions. Local clusters are equally present in both urban and rural sectors, but a large share of payroll is primarily concentrated in the urban sector.

Figure 33: Employed Population by Gender in India

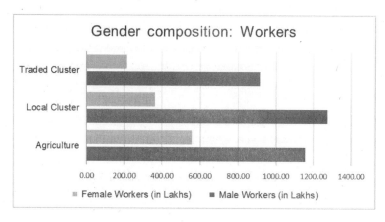

Source: *The 2023 India Cluster Panorama*[32]

Figure 34: Gender Composition: Payroll

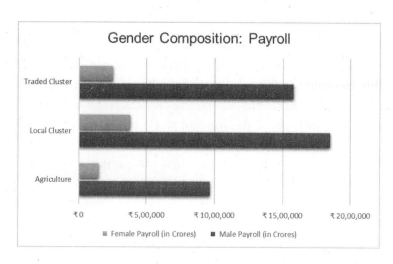

Source: *The 2023 India Cluster Panorama*[33]

The biggest proportion of women work in agriculture, where they make up roughly 33 per cent of the workforce, followed by local clusters at 22 per cent. Nonetheless, in all three types of cluster groupings, the proportion of women on total payroll is still under 20 per cent.

Figure 35: Share of Female Employment vs Relative Female Wage

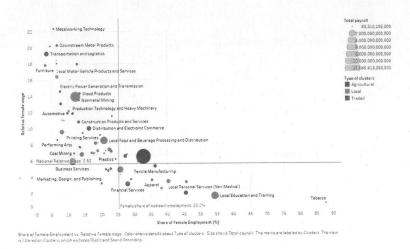

Share of Female Employment vs. Relative Female wage. Color shows details about Type of clusters. Size shows Total payroll. The marks are labeled by Clusters. The view is filtered on Clusters, which excludes Music and Sound Recording.

Source: The 2023 India Cluster Panorama[34]

This inequality in terms of payroll and employment is further magnified among the narrow clusters. There are only a few clusters where the share of female employment is larger than the national average of 25.5 per cent. They are on the right quadrant of the graph shown. Traded clusters—textile manufacturing, apparel, financial services, tobacco—and local clusters—personal services (non-medical), education and training— are among the few clusters where the gender inequality in terms of payroll and employment is relatively less. They are highlighted in the bottom right quadrant.

In terms of employment type and skill level,* the mix of cluster categories also differs. Moreover, 50 per cent of the workers in

---

* The different type of skills has been created from the National Classification of Occupation—2004 codes. Skill 4 and 3 are highly skilled workers, skill 2 and 1 reflects semi-skilled or low-skilled workers.

all three broad cluster categories fall into the Skill-2 category, which is regarded as a low skill level. Surprisingly, the skill level composition of traded clusters and local clusters in India is quite similar. About 23 per cent and 20 per cent of the workforce in the traded cluster and local clusters are made up of Skill-4 workers.

Figure 36: Skill Composition: Workers

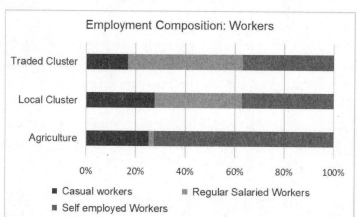

Source: The 2023 India Cluster Panorama[35]

Figure 37: Employment Composition: Workers

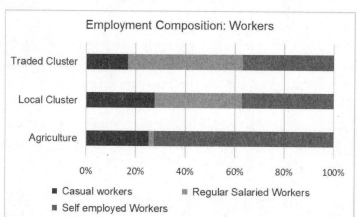

Source: The 2023 India Cluster Panorama[36]

However, there are a few differences between them in terms of type of employment. Traded clusters have the largest portion of regular salaried workers, followed by local clusters. Both clusters have a similar number of self-employed workers; however, casual workers have a significant presence in the local clusters, followed by the agriculture cluster. Seventy-five per cent of workers in the agriculture sector are self-employed. Throughout all the narrow cluster categories, higher average wages are significantly correlated with more formal employment, as measured by the fraction of regular salaried workers. The association tends to be stronger among the local clusters than the traded clusters. Moreover, there is a positive correlation between skill intensity and differences in wages.

By simultaneously examining each cluster's composition through various lenses, it is possible to fully comprehend each cluster's peculiarities. For example, when it comes to gender diversity in the workforce and payroll, tobacco has an odd mix. It is the only cluster with a higher proportion of female employees. The proportion of women in the workforce is significantly higher than that of men by a factor of four. As a result, women make up around 60 per cent of the cluster's overall payroll, but male workers make more money on average than female workers do. Most of the workers in the cluster are low-skilled and either self-employed or casual employees. It is majorly rural dominant in terms of employment, though like most other clusters, a significant portion of its payroll is concentrated in the urban sector. Thus, female employment, especially low-skilled and casual, can be linked to high rural employment. Similar patterns were observed in the agriculture cluster as well.

We can also compare the two clusters to identify the factors that contribute to their prosperity. Aerospace and defence, and coal mining are the two clusters with the highest national productivity. However, they differ in their characteristics, with the former being a highly specialized cluster, while the latter is a resource-dependent cluster. In terms of both employment and payroll, the aerospace and defence cluster is predominantly concentrated in urban areas. It comprises regular salaried employees and a substantial number of highly skilled professionals falling into Skill Categories 3 and 4. In contrast, the coal mining cluster has a significant presence in both rural and urban sectors. The majority of its workforce falls within Skill Categories 1 and 2, indicating a prevalence of unskilled or semi-skilled workers, though 75 per cent of them are regularly salaried. On comparing the two clusters, we observe that clusters of different compositions, irrespective of their high level of urbanization, skill and type of employment, can become productive and prosperous.

Figure 38: Cluster Profile

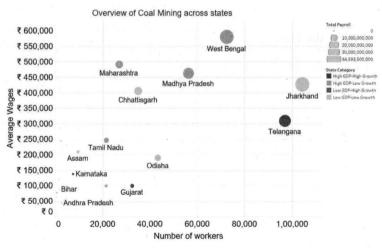

Source: *The 2023 India Cluster Panorama*[37]

Figure 39: Cluster Profile

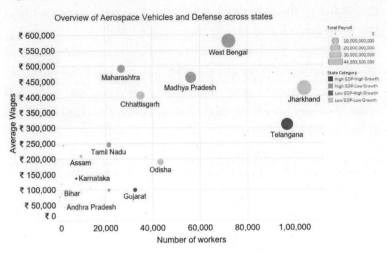

Overview of Aerospace Vehicles and Defense across states

Source: The 2023 India Cluster Panorama[38]

Growth over Time

As expected, the employment and productivity growth rates differ between the cluster types. Agriculture and local clusters are the main drivers of employment growth in the nation, although the traded cluster is more important for productivity growth. Other economies have also noticed this similar pattern in the board cluster categories.

Local clusters saw a productivity growth of about 2.2 per cent, which was a little less than the agriculture cluster. The small local market limits their prospects for growth, which contributes to the low rate of productivity growth. On the other hand, the size of traded clusters increased at the lowest rate, roughly 1.2 per cent, while their productivity increased at the highest rate, 4.7 per cent. As compared to the local cluster, the traded cluster's average wages are about 25 per cent more. This is because the traded clusters

---

compete in cross-regional marketplaces and are less constrained by the size of the local markets. In addition, during the past four years, the payroll disparity between traded and local clusters has grown. In the agriculture cluster, despite the significant change of labour in favour of it, productivity has not increased. Its moderate 2.4 per cent annual growth rate over the past four years has resulted in the lowest average wage and payroll among the three different types of clusters.

Type of Cluster	Employment Growth	Productivity Growth
Agriculture	5.85 per cent	2.41 per cent
Traded	1.24 per cent	4.67 per cent
Local	4.41 per cent	2.29 per cent

The graph below shows how employment and average income for specific cluster groups have grown through time. The productivity of the narrow cluster categories has generally increased more substantially than its size. Over the past four years, the size and payroll of about thirty clusters have increased. Examples of a few of them are downstream chemical products, 8.2 per cent in size and 9.2 per cent in productivity; recreational and small electric goods, 9.3 per cent in size and 10.8 per cent in productivity and environmental services, 11.3 per cent in size and 7.69 per cent in productivity. Other clusters with growth rates greater than 5 per cent in both dimensions include local food and beverage processing and distribution, metalworking technology, information technology and analytical instruments. They might be regarded as the economy's growing clusters.

Figure 40: Compound Annual Growth Rate (CAGR) of Average Wages and CAGR of Employment

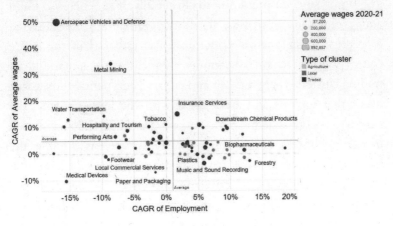

Source: The 2023 India Cluster Panorama[39]

Though not all clusters have grown, few of them have either shrunk in size or productivity or both. The size of the twenty-three clusters has decreased but their productivity has increased. The use of technology has increased significantly, and clusters have benefited from beneficial spillover effects, which eventually reduce reliance on the labour force. Examples of such clusters include the defence industry, metal mining and aerospace vehicles. On the other hand, clusters including forestry, local community and civic organizations, local health services and local personal services (non-medical) have shown an exceptional growth in size, over 9 per cent, but not in productivity. To improve certain clusters' contribution towards the economy in terms of size and productivity, special attention must be paid to them.

Regional Economy and Strong Clusters

The significance of proximity to cluster advantages helps to build and create critical masses of industries that are concentrated in particular regions or economic zones rather than the entire country. Each regional economy frequently has a handful of trading clusters where it excels and enjoys a competitive advantage over other nations and areas along with the local clusters. The region's traded goods and services are largely concentrated in traded clusters, supported by the local type. As a result, the national economy is made up of a number of regional economies, each of which has a distinctive mix of cluster specialization and composition. It engages in commerce with the rest of the world and one another. It boosts national productivity and growth, making regional economies an important unit to analyse and understand the economic performance of the nation.

The critical mass of workers in a particular region, which forms a strong cluster, significantly influences the dynamics of clusters. They are essential to boosting local development. Quantitative studies conducted in a number of different nations have shown a high and positive correlation between employment in strong clusters and regional economies. To identify strong clusters, the Delgado (2014) methodology[40] was used, which defines it as the top 20 per cent of regions by location quotient within each cluster category. Differences in the strength of cluster specialization in Europe and North America can be used to explain, on average, around one-third of the GDP per capita differential between areas. Empirical research also demonstrates that strong clusters typically account for 40 per cent to 70 per cent of all payroll and employment within a specific cluster category. In India, the strong clusters of each narrow cluster category lie in the range of 17 per cent to 67 per cent and 16 per cent to 72 per cent of employment and payroll, respectively.

Most of the local clusters have a low share of strong clusters, lying in the lower end of the above-mentioned range. On the other hand, overall, a significant number of traded clusters have a high share of strong clusters.

Figure 41: Number of Districts vs Number of Strong Clusters

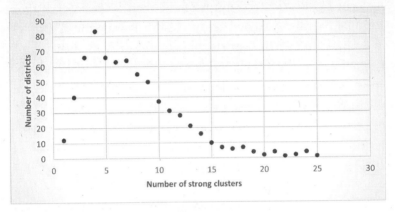

Source: *The 2023 India Cluster Panorama*[41]

The significant concentration of economic activity in particular geographic areas is clearly visible. The distribution of districts by the number of strong clusters is strongly lopsided, with many districts having a small number of strong clusters and a small number of districts having a large number of strong clusters. Just 181 districts have more than ten strong clusters, which account for 47.17 per cent of strong cluster payroll and 29.35 per cent of strong cluster employment. More differences are observed among the different narrow cluster categories. Traded clusters are typically defined by their propensity to concentrate activity in fewer geographic areas. This spatial concentration manifests itself over a wide range of categories in India. There are a handful of cluster categories with active employment in fewer districts; IT and analytical instruments, for instance, are present in only 191 of India's 680 data-covered districts, and the top 20 per cent of districts by Location Quotient (LQ)* account for 57.3 per cent of its national payroll. The same category also includes clusters for metalworking technology, coal mining, metal mining and footwear. Being present in less than 230 districts, their top 20 per cent LQ districts account for more than 50 per cent of their national payroll. A second set of clusters is widespread, present in a large number of districts, but the majority of their payroll is generated in the top 20 per cent of LQ districts, which are the areas with the highest employment specialization. For instance, the top 20 per cent of districts by specialization account for 67.1 per cent, 51.8 per cent and 67.6 per cent of the national payroll in business services, distribution and electronic commerce and apparel, respectively. Food processing, transportation and logistics, wood products, furniture and other clusters form a third group of clusters, which is even more distributed across the nation. More than 500 districts have their presence; however, the top districts by specialization are less dominating in terms of payroll, making up just around 40 per cent of the total. This can be observed in the graph given below.

---

* It measures the region's specialization in a cluster by capturing the degree of concentration of the cluster in a particular region with respect to the nation. It is computed as the ratio of a) share of region's cluster employment in its total employment b) share of cluster employment in overall nation's employment.

Figure 42: Share of Payroll in Top 20 Per Cent of Districts by LQ vs Number of Active Districts

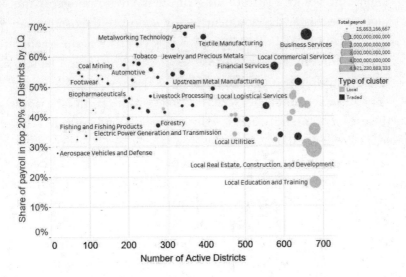

Source: The 2023 India Cluster Panorama[42]

Clusters and Regional Economic Performance

All of the world's major economies share the striking but common feature of having significant regional economic variance. The same is also present in India. States and districts vary greatly in their economic performance. In terms of GDP per capita, Goa is 9.6 times richer than Bihar, according to RBI data (2019–20). When we move to a more granular level, i.e., from the state to the district level, the prosperity disparity at the regional level is far more pronounced. The average wage in the wealthiest district is eighteen times higher than in the poorest district. Studies in other countries have found cluster presence and its strength to matter for regional prosperity, with data showing a meaningful relationship between clusters and economic outcomes.[43] Others also suggest the role and importance of the surrounding business environment in the success of cluster development in the region.[44] They state that the availability of skilled labour, access to finance, the quality of infrastructure and supportive policies are the critical factors in determining firm productivity in the region.

Clusters cannot be seen in isolation from the broader theory of competitiveness. All industries are impacted by some common business environment elements, such as the transportation system, corporation tax rates, income distribution and the legal system. Empirically, clusters are observed to thrive in situations where a particular combination of business environment characteristics generates a distinctive value for a certain collection of related industries. To comprehend the role of clusters in enhancing the competitiveness of the firms and the region as a whole, it is crucial to recognize the components of the regional environment. The enabling and supporting ecosystem in which clusters function has a significant impact on clusters' existence and success, which eventually reflects in the regional prosperity levels.

The diamond model is robust in the way that it can be fitted into any size and type of economic structure, be it an industry, a sector, a company, a county, a state or even a country. The other components of the diamond framework—factor conditions, demand conditions and the context for strategy and rivalry—facilitate the establishment of a successful cluster. Each factor in this model and the interplay of the four together affect essential ingredients for achieving competitive success. Sub-national regions witness an interplay of these four factors that creates an environment conducive to growth for certain companies.

Therefore, for Porter, 'a cluster is the manifestation of the diamond at work.'[45] We move forth to understand the essential component of the microeconomic aspect of competitiveness, i.e., the quality of business environment and related and supporting industries or the presence of clusters. We use the diamond model to understand locational competitiveness for Maharashtra and Uttar Pradesh.

Maharashtra vs Uttar Pradesh: How Do Locational Advantages Differ?

Maharashtra has the locational advantage of bordering the Arabian Sea with a 720 km long coastline. The early development of railways, trading of cotton and bullion and its closeness to the Suez Canal and the stock exchange led to the transformation of Bombay into the financial capital.[*] It had a GDP of Rs 18,89,30,666 lakh in the year 2020–21. It is one of the largest states in terms of area—with over 30,00,00 square km and a population of more than 11 crore (2011 census)—as well as in terms of exports—with over Rs 4.31 lakh crore of total export value in the year 2020–21.[†]

Uttar Pradesh, on the other hand, had a GDP of Rs 12,48,18,912 in the year 2020–21. It is a landlocked state and covers a large area of over 2.4 lakh square km[‡] and has a high population of over 19 crore (2011 census). Its export value was

---

[*] 'When Bombay overtook Calcutta: A history of India's financial geography', *Mint* (livemint.com)

[†] Maitri Maharashtra Industry, Trade and Investment Facilitation (mahaonline.gov.in)

[‡] https://knowindia.india.gov.in/states-uts/uttar-pradesh.php

over Rs 2000 crore from April 2021 to March 2022.* This section analyses differences between the two states in terms of the four components of the diamond model as elaborated upon in the previous chapter.

Factor Conditions: The inputs that drive the trajectory of productivity and economic growth are the factor conditions, i.e., land, labour, capital and natural resources. However, this stock of endowments is not utilized to the fullest unless a high-skilled workforce, infrastructural developments and technological upgrades and innovations accompany it and contribute to the competitiveness of the state. They are sustainable resources for maintaining a competitive edge. In the context of India, it is important to understand how the skilled workforce capacity varies across regions. The workforce of a region must possess the required skills of the current job market and have access to specialized courses.

This can be understood using the region's performance on parameters such as enrolment of students in engineering and technology and Gross Enrolment Ratio (GER) in higher education. Engineering-related courses offer professional training and provide in-demand job market skills, guaranteeing students jobs right after higher studies. In the engineering and technology-related courses, Maharashtra had an intake of 2.5 lakh students, and it enrolled 1.7 lakh students in 2021–22. Similarly, Uttar Pradesh had an intake of 2.1 lakh students, and it enrolled 1 lakh students[†] in the technology-related courses, slightly lower than Maharashtra, in 2021–22. In this period, over 75,000 students in Maharashtra and 51,000 in Uttar Pradesh were placed. The

---

[*] State-wise Export Data April 2021 to March 2022.xls (upepc.org)
[†] https://facilities.aicte-india.org/dashboard/pages/dashboardaicte.php

GER in higher education in Maharashtra has seen a sluggish increase over the years, with a few basis points change, with 32.2 per cent in 2018–19, 32.6 per cent in 2019–20 and 34.9 per cent in 2020–21. In UP, there is a fluctuating trend with a relatively lower GER, with 23 per cent in 2018–19, 22.5 per cent in 2019–20 and 23.2 per cent in 2020–21. This indicates a lower consideration of higher education among the population in both the states.

Another factor is infrastructure development, which is a driving force for a seamless business environment and for stimulating economic growth. Maharashtra boasts an extensive network of roads, comprising 32,005 kilometres of state highways[*] and 18,317 kilometres of national highways[†] with a railway track running 11,631 km[‡] long across the state. Uttar Pradesh has a 7427-km-long state highway, a 12,245-km-long national highway and a railway track running 16,001 km long. Similarly, air cargos are an essential part of the global supply chain as they facilitate trade, creating jobs and bringing in foreign investments. There are ten air cargo terminals in Maharashtra and eight in Uttar Pradesh as of 2020–21. Electricity is the fuel supporting the whole business ecosystem, and as of December 2022, Maharashtra has a total installed capacity of 43,188.10 MW for electricity generation, and its peak demand of 27,234 MW was met by the power supply position. Uttar Pradesh has an installed capacity of over 31,364 MW and met its peak demand of 19,970 MW as of December 2022[§] as well. Fulfilling the power demand indicates a promising foundation for businesses to function smoothly. Access

---

[*] Reserve Bank of India—Publications (rbi.org.in)
[†] Reserve Bank of India—Publications (rbi.org.in)
[‡] LEADS-2021-Report_Final.pdf (commerce.gov.in)
[§] https://cea.nic.in/dashboard/?lang=en

to ICT infrastructure is another pivotal part to support factor
conditions. Maharashtra has 127.93 million wireless and wireline
telephone subscriber bases, lower than Uttar Pradesh's 161.35
million. However, it has a 101.55 per cent total tele-density,[*]
indicating a good penetration of communication services in the
region, while Uttar Pradesh has a 68.75 per cent tele-density.
Thus, innovation created by human resources should translate
into output. Output can be understood through intangible
assets such as patents and trademarks and input through its
expenditure on R&D. Maharashtra with 4566 patents filed and
Uttar Pradesh with 3622 patents filed rank second and third in
the country respectively for most patents filed.[†] Maharashtra had
the highest number of trademarks, 83,148, and Uttar Pradesh fell
short with 36,475 trademarks in the year 2021–22. In 2017–18,
Maharashtra spent Rs 221.77 crore and Uttar Pradesh spent
Rs 471.02 crore in R&D.[‡]

Demand Conditions: The demand conditions of an industry
prepare the firms through the emerging needs of the buyers and
force them to innovate, upgrade and nurture their innovation
capabilities to compete in the international landscape. Demand
conditions investigate the demography of buyers and their income
distribution to understand how their demands and spending
are influenced.

It is noted that there is a correlation between urbanization
and wealth quintiles. Wealth quintiles give us insights to
understand demand conditions as it is a composite measure of
households' living standards in a region. A higher percentage

[*] QPIR_03022023_0.pdf (trai.gov.in)
[†] Eng Annual Report 2022.pmd (ipindia.gov.in)
[‡] S&T Indicators Tables 2019-20.pdf (dst.gov.in)

of population in the highest wealth quintile is observed usually in urban areas. For instance, as per the National Family Health Survey—NFHS 5—Maharashtra has an 8.6 per cent population in the lowest wealth quintile and a 27.9 per cent population in the highest wealth quintile, but its degree of urbanization is 45.22 per cent. Uttar Pradesh, on the other hand, has a lower rate of urbanization, i.e., 20.78 per cent, relative to Maharashtra. It is also reflected in its lower population of 17.8 per cent in the highest quintile and 23.9 per cent population in the lowest wealth quintile. GST collection is also a good reflection of the demand sophistication and income distribution of a region. A higher GST collection indicates that there is a high level of consumption of goods and services, showing strong demand conditions. The GST collection in Maharashtra in the year 2022 was approximately Rs 2,40,518 crore, while in Uttar Pradesh, it was approximately Rs 78,308 crore.

Firm Strategy, Structure and Rivalry: The determinants of firm strategy, structure and rivalry are specific to industries, firms and regions. A region's strategy depends on how the state decides to invest in its development. The attitude of people towards authority, their interactions with each other, and their behaviours in an individual and in a group influence their organizational structure.[46]

To understand their strategies for competitiveness, we look at the states' diverse industries and their contribution to the state's economic activities. In the fiscal year 2020–21, the state of Maharashtra made a significant contribution to the Gross Value Added (GVA) in the manufacturing sector, amounting to Rs 3,32,08,674 lakhs. In comparison, Uttar Pradesh (UP) contributed Rs 1,43,14,129 lakhs to the GVA in manufacturing during the same period.[*] Through the SEZ Act of 2005, Maharashtra has a total of thirty-seven functional Special Economic Zones (SEZs), the second highest in the country[†], and Uttar Pradesh has fourteen functional SEZs. The presence of SEZs benefits the economy in various ways. In terms of Foreign Direct Investment (FDI) inflows, Maharashtra stands out with FDI inflows amounting to 6.33 per cent of its GDP. From October 2019 to December 2022, Maharashtra received the highest FDI equity inflow, totaling Rs 3,74,091.74 crore. This constitutes a significant 27.88 per cent of the total FDI inflows in the country, underscoring a high level of investor confidence in the region. In contrast, Uttar Pradesh (UP) received FDI inflows of Rs 9,434.85 crore during the same period, making up only 0.6984 per cent of the total FDI inflows in the country.[‡]

Related and Supporting Industries: The related and supporting industries are the geographically concentrated companies and other institutions or clusters that enjoy high levels of productivity and innovation due to their proximity.[47] A cluster of firms creates an environment of competition in regard to securing their respective market share of buyers as well as an environment of collaboration as suppliers invest in research and create a knowledge base for the upstream enterprises.

Both states have a similar composition of employment in the three broad cluster categories. The differences are seen in terms of payroll contribution. In Maharashtra, the share

---

[*] Reserve Bank of India—Publications (rbi.org.in)

[†] http://sezindia.nic.in/upload/uploadfiles/files/State%20wise%20%20SEZ.pdf

[‡] FDI Factsheet 3rd quarter 2022-23.xlsx (dpiit.gov.in)

of traded and local clusters are 40 per cent and 39 per cent, respectively. In Uttar Pradesh, local clusters have a substantial contribution of 43 per cent, and the rest is made up of traded and agriculture clusters, equally. Overall, the traded cluster's contribution in terms of employment and payroll is greater in Maharashtra than in Uttar Pradesh. The cluster differences between the two regions are more visible when we focus on the narrow cluster categories. Maharashtra's cluster profile, in terms of productivity, is dominated by the mining of natural resources, metal and coal. The two clusters' average wages, which are roughly 2 lakh and 3.6 lakh, respectively, are higher than the national average. It can be associated with the high export value of iron, steel products and precious and semi-precious stones. Other clusters having a high productivity in the state are marketing, design and publishing and electric-power generation. In terms of employment, service-oriented clusters like business, finance and transport contribute more. On the other hand, Uttar Pradesh's cluster profile, in terms of employment, is dominated by agriculture and related clusters like textile, wood products and food processing, which tend to be more of manufacturing clusters. The region exports a lot of processed foods, cotton products and textiles, which creates many job opportunities in these industries. Specialized clusters like aerospace, medical devices and financial services have high productivity in the state. The local government cluster is also one of the top productive clusters in Uttar Pradesh.

Figure 43: Cluster Portfolio, Maharashtra

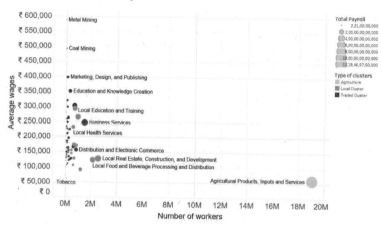

Source: The 2023 India Cluster Panorama[48]

Figure 44: Cluster Portfolio, Uttar Pradesh

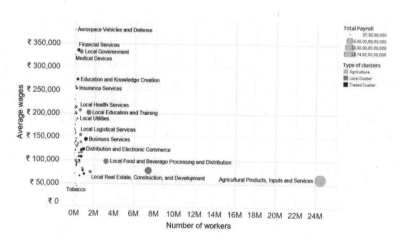

Source: The 2023 India Cluster Panorama[49]

A few important economic variables forming the business environment in both states in the context of the diamond model are given in the below table.

Table 1: Economic Variables forming the Business Environment in Maharashtra and Uttar Pradesh

Dimension	Parameters	Maharashtra	Uttar Pradesh	Year
Factor Conditions	National-highway length	18,317 km	12,245 km	2019
	State-highway Length	32,005 km	7427 km	2019
	Railway line	11,631 km	16,001 km	2019
	Air-cargo terminals	10	8	
	Electricity generation installed capacity	43,188.10 MW	31,364 MW	2022
	Tele-density	101.55 per cent	68.75 per cent	2022
	Enrolment in engineering and technology-related courses	1.7 lakh	1 lakh	2021–22
	GER	34.90 per cent	23.20 per cent	2019–20
	Patents filed	4566	3622	2021–22
	Logistics Ease Across Different States (LEADS) Index score	3.32	3.25	2021

Dimension	Parameters	Maharashtra	Uttar Pradesh	Year
Demand Conditions	Degree of urbanization	45.22 per cent	20.78 per cent	2011
	Population in the highest wealth quantiles	27.90 per cent	17.80 per cent	
	State GST collection	Rs 2,40,518 Cr*	Rs 78,308 Cr**	2022
Context for Strategy	FDI equity inflows	Rs 3,74,091.74 Cr	Rs 9,434.85 Cr	Oct 2019– Dec 2022
	GVA in manufacturing	Rs 3,32,08,674 lakh	Rs 1,43,14,129 lakh	2020–21
	Number of MSMEs	25,04,408	11,10,173	
	Number of Special Economic Zones	37	14	2022
Related and Supporting Industries	Cluster strength	80	62	

The data shows a significant difference in practically all the parameters when the figures are compared, proving that Maharashtra has a more favourable business climate than Uttar Pradesh. This enables deep and diverse cluster-portfolio

---

* GST collection excluding January (data not available for January)
** GST collection excluding January (data not available for January)

formation in the Maharashtra region, especially of traded clusters, which is evident from the above discussion. It highlights the existence of a strong positive relationship between a healthy business environment and clusters, which helps us to understand the locational advantages in driving competitiveness among the states.

These significant regional economic variances are further magnified when we move from the state to the district level. Six hundred and eighty districts in the PLFS data were divided into quartiles, based on the districts' value-generation concentration, which here is measured by the share of payroll (total wages). The upper quartile of the districts turns out to be the epicentre of significant economic activities. It contributes 49.47 per cent and 57.26 per cent to employment and payroll, respectively. In contrast, the lower quartile districts have a meagre concentration of economic activities, contributing only 6.83 per cent and 5.23 per cent to national employment and payroll. Fifty per cent of the national employment and payroll is concentrated in the top 160 and 132 districts, respectively. This shows that only a limited number of districts in India are actively and significantly contributing to its value formation and growth. To delve deeper and simplify matters, the 680 districts have been classified based on their average wages, which serve as an indicator of prosperity, into three categories: top seventy, middle and bottom. The top-seventy category consists of the most prosperous districts, while the bottom category includes the least prosperous districts.

The economic inequality between districts can be further comprehended by examining the cluster portfolio of the three district groups. Each group, representing a different level of economic development, has a distinct coexistence pattern of traded and local clusters, primarily due to micro-environmental factors and natural resources in the regions. The contribution of traded clusters to payroll and employment significantly increases as we move up from the lower prosperity group. In the top-seventy group, the average wage of the traded cluster category is approximately 30 per cent higher than the local average wage, whereas they are almost the same in the middle and bottom district groups. Agriculture is a crucial cluster in all three groups, providing the highest employment. However, the payroll share of agriculture is approximately six times higher in the bottom category than in the top seventy, despite its average wage being considerably lower than traded and local clusters across all districts in the group. Additionally, the given snapshots also illustrate the presence of different types of narrow clusters and their position in terms of employment and average wages across all three groups. The cluster-portfolio composition of each group is unique, varying in terms of sector, gender, skills and type of employment, highlighting significant differences among the three groups. The bottom group has a greater concentration of clusters that primarily rely on natural resources and abundant low-skilled labour. In contrast, the prosperous group (top seventy) is strongly associated with clusters driven by capital and high-skill labour. This is supported by data revealing that more than 75 per cent of workers in the bottom and middle districts are considered low-skilled workers, falling under Skill Levels 1 and 2. On the other hand, the top-seventy group has a substantial portion of workers categorized as medium and high-skill workers, falling under Skill Levels 3 and 4. Additionally, more than 50 per cent of workers in the prosperous group are regular salaried employees.

Figure 45: Cluster Portfolio, Top 70

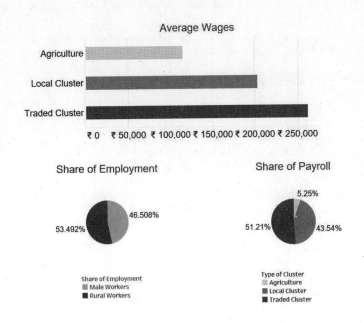

Source: The 2023 India Cluster Panorama[50]

Figure 46: Cluster Portfolio, Middle

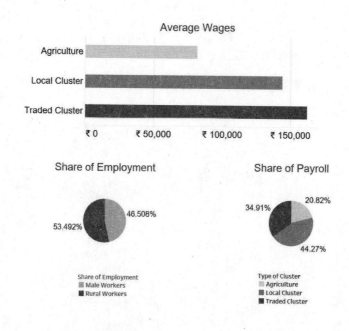

Source: The 2023 India Cluster Panorama[51]

Figure 47: Cluster Portfolio, Bottom

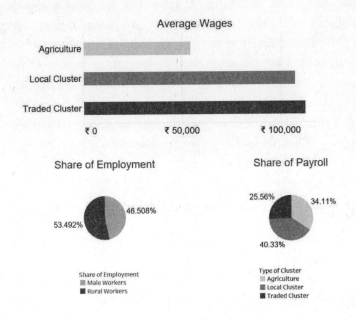

Source: The 2023 India Cluster Panorama[52]

The divide between urban and rural areas is another crucial factor in understanding the economic variations across regions. While all three district groups have urban and rural areas, the proportion varies. The middle and bottom districts are mostly rural, while the top-seventy group has only 26 per cent of its workforce in rural areas. In some rural-dominated districts in the prosperous group, such as Palwal in Haryana and Muktsar in Punjab, agriculture is a significant cluster with an average wage three times higher than the national average wage for the sector. Agriculture is considered a prime driver of local economic growth in these regions. On the other hand, in the middle- and bottom-district groups, employment in each sector (rural and urban) is driven by agriculture and local clusters. However, the average wage for agriculture and local clusters is significantly low, hindering the growth of the local economy, especially in rural areas. Clusters in less prosperous regions tend to be limited and fragile as they concentrate on specific activities, especially related to agriculture or any other natural resource. The business environment also is not very developed to support the existing clusters. However, in more prosperous regions, a positive business environment and strong connections among related and supporting industries lead to a more extensive and robust range of clusters, which further enhances their prosperity levels.

Cluster Strength and Economic Performance

It is a common notion in economic development theories that regions that support the existence of diverse types of economies will be advantageous. Here, the geographical patterns of cluster concentration are identified across regions using the 'total number of stars' measure* of cluster-portfolio strength.[53] The given maps show the hotspot regions of diverse and strong economic activity at the state and district level.

---

* Definition: The strength of a region's cluster portfolio is measured by giving weights to the type of stars and finally summing them. The highest weight of three is given to '3-star cluster', followed by two and one. If a region has six '3 stars' clusters, fifteen '2 stars' clusters and twenty-five '1 star' cluster, the total cluster strength of the region will be 73 (3*6+2*15+1*25). The greater the number of 'stars', the higher is the cluster strength of the region.

Figure 48: Cluster Strength, State-Wise

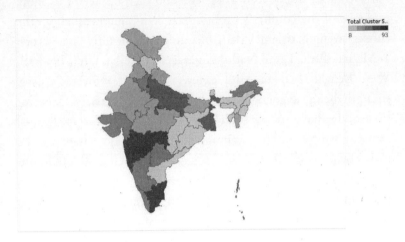

Source: The 2023 India Cluster Panorama[54]

Figure 49: Cluster Strength, District-Wise

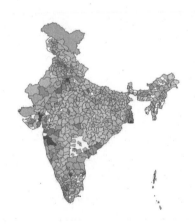

Source: The 2023 India Cluster Panorama[55]

The distribution of cluster strength among the nation's thirty-six states and union territories and 680 districts serves as more evidence of the country's pronounced economic inequality. The cluster strength is larger than fifty in the high-GDP states such as Maharashtra, Tamil Nadu, Gujarat, Karnataka, Uttar Pradesh, West Bengal, Haryana and a few others. It indicates cluster strength being a good measure of economic activity. Most of these states have strong three-star clusters and two-star clusters, showing strong cluster development in the region. However, the high cluster strength of a few states such as Uttar Pradesh and West Bengal is driven majorly by one-star clusters. It reflects that most of the clusters in the latter states have been able to compete with the rest of the region's clusters in only one of the following dimensions of cluster strength: size, average wages and location quotient. The less prosperous regions can be associated with the states with the lowest cluster strength, such as Odisha, Chhattisgarh, and most of the north-eastern states. They are usually driven by a one-star cluster only.

The same pattern is observed at the district level. The range of district cluster strength is zero to seventeen, which again emphasizes the substantial variability at the granular regional level. While the impoverished districts like Dindori, Guna of Madhya Pradesh, and Bijapur of Chhattisgarh have cluster strengths of only two, the wealthier districts like Mumbai Suburban, North-West Delhi and Bangalore have cluster strengths of over 100. In general, many of the districts in the bottom and middle groups have cluster strengths of less than thirty, whereas districts in the top-seventy group have cluster strengths greater than seventy. In terms of composition, two-star and one-star clusters are mostly responsible for the cluster strength of districts with low and moderate levels of prosperity (middle and bottom groups of districts). On the other hand, the most prosperous group has a considerable concentration of three-star clusters in addition to two-star and one-star clusters. It is a sign of the robust business climate in the area, which fosters and supports the emergence of a range of clusters. The graph illustrates how the mix of cluster strength varies across different types of districts. Overall, it is observed that the degree of spread among clusters at various locations is linked to the presence of diversified and deep clusters in the high-GDP-growth states and the districts that fall within the top-seventy and middle groups.

Figure 50: Distribution of Cluster Strength

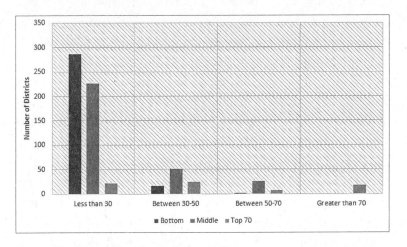

Source: The 2023 India Cluster Panorama[56]

Clusters have a clear positive impact on regional growth through their strong interconnections and spillover effects. They are essential in enhancing a region's ability to innovate and export, leading to better economic growth and living standards as they offer an environment that is conducive to research and knowledge production. This phenomenon has been observed across multiple economies, including India, where there is a positive correlation between cluster strength and innovation scores. There is a positive correlation between the 2021 innovation scores and the cluster strength of the states. Additionally, other economic indicators such as export performance (Export Preparedness Index scores 2021), GDP and GDP per capita are positively correlated with cluster strength, particularly in traded clusters that serve broader markets. The relationship between cluster strength and District Domestic Product (gross) remains consistent even at the district level. Furthermore, cluster strength is also positively correlated with social progress in the region. The results are in sync with the other studies exploring the positive and strong relationship between cluster strength and economic performance indicators.[57, 58]

The section uses the cluster-mapping methodology* to provide a comprehensive view of the presence of clusters in various states and districts of the country, using data from the Periodic Labour Force Survey (PLFS). It highlights the structure and distribution of traded, local and agriculture clusters and emphasizes their role in employment and productivity growth. Each category of a cluster contributes significantly to the dimensions of employment, payroll and productivity at the national level, and, thus, each plays an equally important role in improving competitiveness and prosperity. A detailed study shows that various clusters can have high productivity levels despite significant variation in terms of their geographical spread, sectoral presence, gender, skills or type of employment. States with a high GDP and districts belonging to the top-seventy and middle groups have diverse and deep clusters, reflected by a high number of three-star clusters and the total cluster strength of the regions. Economic outcomes such as gross domestic product, innovation and exports are positively related to cluster

---

* Here, the methodology of Clusters: The Drivers of Competitiveness (2018), with few modifications was used to calculate the cluster strength

strength, as confirmed by the theoretical literature. Therefore, the role and nature of clusters can help explain differences in economic performance among locations, as demonstrated in the existing literature. A tool to access and measure the unique cluster characteristics is necessary to design distinct cluster policies and initiatives. Thus, cluster mapping becomes a crucial step in understanding the cluster portfolio of a region. Cluster-related policies have gained the interest of many policymakers, and there is an emerging consensus on the usefulness of clusters as an analytical tool for policymakers around the globe.

Public Policy and Clusters

Policymaking is undergoing a paradigm shift, with a greater focus on microeconomics rather than macroeconomics. A macroeconomic approach to development focuses on the overall performance of the economy, such as GDP growth, inflation and employment rates. This approach tends to emphasize top-down policies and interventions by the central government. While monetary and fiscal policies are widely recognized and implemented in daily planning, they alone are inadequate for improving the economy's overall prosperity.[59] A microeconomic bottom-up approach to development focuses on improving the conditions of individual businesses, industries and clusters. This approach emphasizes the role of local actors, such as entrepreneurs, business associations and local governments, in identifying and addressing the specific needs and challenges of their respective areas. While both approaches have their merits, a microeconomic bottom-up approach is often seen as more effective in promoting sustainable economic growth and development. Targeted microeconomic efforts and planning are necessary to translate macroeconomic achievements into tangible productivity improvements for micro-players. The microeconomic circumstances of a particular region have a significant impact on a company's survival and operation, shaping its business environment.

In today's contemporary economy, clusters are a key economic unit, boosting the competitiveness of the firms and improving the prosperity levels of the region. Clusters have significant potential as a microeconomic force for driving economic and social progress, making it crucial to consider them when setting long-term growth goals. Clusters enable companies to be more innovative and productive than they would have been in isolation, recognizing the diversity of conditions and challenges across different regions and sectors. By focusing on the specific needs and opportunities of each area, the cluster approach can help to leverage the effective implementation of policies and initiatives, as well as greater buy-in and support from local communities. Usually, clusters tend to form naturally due to the interaction of many market forces along with the support of a strong business environment. Emerging new businesses, growing suppliers, and developed infrastructure all result in the speedy process of cluster formation.[60] Being made up of a group of interconnected firms, suppliers and supporting institutions that share common markets, technologies and skills, clusters are highly responsive to market signals. In a well-functioning cluster, market signals such as changes in consumer demand, technological advancements or shifts in the global competition are transmitted quickly and efficiently throughout the cluster. It enables firms to adapt quickly to changes in the market environment and to take advantage of new opportunities. Nonetheless, the same responsiveness can make the clusters vulnerable to market failures as well. It can result in under-investment in specialized infrastructure, scientific knowledge and specialized skills in the presence of positive externalities.[61] Given such spontaneous economic processes responding to market signals, clusters should not be left alone to develop naturally. The government has a crucial role in facilitating this responsiveness by providing the necessary infrastructure, institutions and policies to support the cluster's growth and development, minimizing the probability of any market failures. In addition, by examining the economy through a cluster-focused approach, it is possible to identify opportunities for development and gain valuable insights into each cluster's strengths and weaknesses with respect to the region. This information is essential for developing policies that are tailored to the specific needs and potential of each cluster.

Clusters and the Role of Government and Other Actors

The immense potential held by clusters as a microeconomic driver of the economy has added a new role and responsibility for the government. The primary function of a government in an economy is to achieve stability in macroeconomic and political conditions. This requires establishing reliable government institutions, a consistent economic framework and sound macroeconomic policies that ensure responsible government finances and low inflation. The government is also responsible for enhancing the overall microeconomic capacity of the economy by improving the efficiency and quality of general-purpose inputs to businesses, such as skilled labour, appropriate infrastructure and reliable economic information. These inputs are necessary for the success of the regional and entire economy. The onus of providing general microeconomic guidelines and competitive incentives that will promote productivity growth falls within the functions of government as well. A fair and effective legal system, laws providing consumer recourse, corporate governance rules and an efficient regulatory process promoting innovation.[62] Although the mentioned government functions are essential for economic development, they might not be enough.

However, all these factors form a crucial part of the diamond model and the broader framework of competitiveness, supporting the presence and growth of clusters in the region.

The government now also plays a crucial role in cluster upgrading and development, and its involvement is often more than necessary to achieve the desired outcomes. Although the general business environment is important for competitiveness, the specific circumstances of clusters are increasingly important in moving beyond factor-cost competition. Clusters present opportunities to enhance productivity and support wage increases, regardless of whether they compete with other locations or not. Each cluster contributes to national productivity and has the capability to create a positive impact on the productivity of other clusters. Thus, instead of creating new clusters, the government should reinforce and build on established and emerging ones, as new industries and clusters emerge best from them. Therefore, traditional clusters such as agriculture should not be abandoned but upgraded. Cluster development usually prioritizes pursuing competitive advantage and specialization, rather than copying what is present in other locations. This involves leveraging local differences and sources of uniqueness, and turning them into strengths. It is more effective to find areas of specialization than to compete head-on with established rival locations. Specialization also provides opportunities to meet new needs and expand the market. The development of clusters can be initiated and strengthened by inbound foreign direct investment (FDI). The most effective approach for attracting FDI is to focus on attracting multiple companies in the same field, with parallel investments in specialized training, infrastructure and other aspects of the business environment. Upgrading clusters involves recognizing the presence of a cluster and addressing constraints that impede productivity and innovation, including those related to human resources, infrastructure and regulation. While private initiatives can address some of these constraints, most of them require intervention through government policies and institutions.

Commonly, many governments address these constraints by focusing on the industry-level policies, which often ignore modern competition, distort markets and use government resources inefficiently. Industrial policy is based on the view that only a few industries offer higher wealth-creating prospects than others, and targeted support is given to these industries through subsidies, import protection and restrictions on foreign investments.[63] In contrast, cluster policies promote healthy competition and cooperation among firms and locations, focusing on productivity growth instead of supporting individual firms. Cluster-based policies strengthen the competitiveness fundamentals of clusters and cater to all clusters, not just emerging ones. Unlike industrial policies, the cluster theory recognizes the value of imports and foreign firms entering the market. It emphasizes that foreign firms enhance the clusters' externalities and competition, leading to increased productivity and employment generation. Policies that improve the business environment in clusters can have high benefits for the overall upgrading of the cluster and the spillover effect on regions with that particular cluster.[64] A cluster-focused approach encourages competition and facilitates the development of public or quasi-public goods that impact many linked businesses. Therefore, government investments aimed at improving the business environment in clusters can earn a higher return compared to those aimed at industries, or the broader sectoral economy, all other things being equal. However, a cluster-based policy cannot replace an industrial policy, as their foundations and implications are fundamentally different.

The government can also play a crucial role in building the capacity of the firms and institutions and facilitating collaboration and networking within the cluster. They can provide funding for research and development, innovation and technology transfer, which will result in the enhancement of the skills and knowledge of the workforce. The exporting capacity of the country can also be increased through clusters by providing support for firms to enter international markets and promoting the cluster as a source of high-quality products and services. The government can also negotiate trade agreements that benefit the firms within the cluster. Furthermore, the government can play a role in promoting social and environmental sustainability within the cluster. They can provide incentives for firms to adopt sustainable practices and ensure compliance with environmental and social regulations. By promoting sustainability, the government can enhance the reputation of the cluster and attract more socially responsible firms and consumers as well as investment.

This new economics of location and competitiveness, which is built on mutual dependency and collaborative accountability, has a role for leaders of private firms and educational and research institutions as well. Private-sector firms are critical players in the development of clusters, as firms in related industries collaborate and compete with one another to create new products and processes, improve efficiency and capture market share.[65] They are responsible for investing in research and development, building supplier networks and competing on a global scale. Additionally, they are often involved in the creation of industry associations and other networking groups that bring together firms and institutions within the cluster to share knowledge, ideas and best practices. The majority of cluster projects are effective, according to experience from around the world, when public-private partnerships are involved. It serves as a forum for improved communication between the public and private sectors with the goal of enhancing a region's cluster-specific business climate. As a result, the chance to rethink how the public and private sectors contribute to economic growth and policy can be seen in the context of cluster initiatives. Educational and research institutes, such as universities and technical schools, also play an important role in cluster development. These institutions are responsible for developing and educating a skilled workforce, conducting research and development and providing technical assistance to firms in the cluster. They serve as a catalyst for innovation, as they bring together researchers, educators and entrepreneurs to collaborate on new ideas and technologies. In addition, educational institutes can serve as a hub for networking and collaboration within the cluster, as they offer opportunities for firms and researchers to connect and share knowledge.

Cluster Policy around the World

Many nations have created cluster programmes and policies to increase the effectiveness of their research and innovation strategies. With company growth and innovation-assistance programmes, clusters give governments and other stakeholders a strategic chance to address social and economic problems. India's economy is diverse, with different sectors and regions facing varying circumstances. While national policies like Make in India and the Skills India Initiative are pivotal in enhancing the overall business environment and laying a solid foundation for progress, promising endeavours like the Smart Cities Mission and One District, One Product demonstrate the nation's commitment to holistic development. Smart cities focus on enhancing urban living with essential infrastructure, while ODOP's district-centric approach fosters value chain development and aligns support infrastructure. While these initiatives mark a positive start, there's room for further refinement to effectively address the distinctive needs of each sector and cluster. To promote growth and competitiveness, India should create new initiatives that are specific to sectors and regions, which draw on appropriate policy tools and tailor policies to the specific context. These initiatives require close collaboration between public and private sector leaders. Data on female employment in different clusters can provide valuable insights for identifying job opportunities. Effective policy implementation requires alignment with the specific needs of each location, sector and cluster. As India moves beyond basic development needs, it is increasingly important to address location- and cluster-specific issues due to the diverse landscape. [66] Analysis has shown that different locations have varying cluster compositions, and certain sectors are dominant in particular areas. Thus, policy actions must be tailored to address these unique factors. A bottom-up approach that identifies specific opportunities and challenges at the location or cluster level is needed. This approach can then use a suitable combination of national and state-level policies to address them.

Examples from other countries demonstrate how a location- and cluster-based approach can be effectively implemented. Peru, for instance, has successfully mobilized its agricultural sector around a specific initiative centred on asparagus. Latin America and Europe have hundreds of cluster initiatives that act as a strategy interface between general policy instruments and the specific needs of locations, sectors and clusters. [66] Colombia has also established a system of national and regional competitiveness councils focused on policy design and coordination, with the regional councils playing a critical role in translating national policies into location-specific actions. A parallel private-sector competitiveness council serves as a national contact point for these public-sector structures. China and Vietnam are examples of emerging economies that have successfully utilized location-specific policies and regional experimentation to drive economic development. In

China, a strong central government provides direction, resources and incentives while delegating implementation responsibilities to local leaders. In Vietnam, regions have had more policy influence, and there has been direct competition across regions without a controlling central-government voice. [68] While there is a range of institutional models, effective cluster organizations should align with existing political institutions and structural circumstances. For large countries like India, it is crucial to combine efforts to encourage local action with efforts that connect with the national policy debate. Studying economic clusters necessitates a heightened focus on regional economic dynamics. It encourages us to adopt a bottom-up approach to policymaking and delve extensively into the variations and diversity present within a nation.

6

India through a Bottom-Up Perspective

'Figuring out how a country can prosper as a country, particularly a large, complex country like India, is one of the hardest problems ever to be solved on the face of the earth. Most countries around the world don't do that well; they struggle, the performance is very uneven, it's very hard to come up with an overall plan that works, and if we look at the data, a lot of countries are relatively poor and they're not moving forward, so what we have to do is figure out what key steps to take. What's the key analysis? How do we think about this very complex problem?'

—Michael Porter on Launch of Competitiveness
Roadmap for India@100

A nation's primary goal is to provide a high and improving standard of living for its citizens. The primary purpose of economic policy is to boost competitiveness. We have provided a comprehensive explanation of the concept of competitiveness, its foundational elements or fundamentals and its emphasis on the regional drivers of economic growth. To reiterate, competitiveness's central tenet as defined by Michael Porter is productivity. This is also the primary determinant of standard of living in the long run and cause of national per-capita income. Porter's research[1] pointed out that competitiveness and economic development studies have tended to focus on the nation as a whole as the unit of study and on national characteristics and policies as the drivers. However, there are significant disparities in economic and social development performance across regions in almost every country, as recognized by regional scientists and economic geographers for a long time. Our discussion on clusters made it amply clear that there exist wide variations among regions in terms of potential, opportunities and needs. This implies that many of the important drivers of economic success may be identified at the regional level. The previous chapters expounded on how the source of competitiveness is the home country 'diamond,' which is made up of four major attributes. Cluster theory centralizes clusters as a key economic unit and proposes the benefits of a granular approach to understanding competitiveness. In this context of the existence of 'Many Indias,' this chapter goes beyond to shed light on the reasons behind India's performance by examining the heterogeneity in performance at sub-national levels, since the major engines of development in India are found at the sub-national levels.

Regional prosperity is most effectively stimulated by individual firms and clusters rather than top-down policy initiatives. While national policies do foster regional competitiveness, it is ultimately up to the states' and union territories' enterprises and sectors to boost productivity and innovation. This is because they are seen as the foundation of competitiveness. The competitiveness approach emphasizes the necessity of capitalizing on a region's strengths and creating a competitive advantage as a result. Hence, it is important to examine what drives or hampers competitiveness in different regions across India.

Each of India's states and union territories contribute to the country's overall economy. Despite the fact that Indian states have traditionally shared identical political structures and national economic policies, there is wide geographical, demographic and economic variation. Therefore, one of the goals of planning in India as a developing country is to reduce regional disparities in economic performance. An obvious inquiry emerges here, namely, how the different regions of the country have done in terms of per capita income over time. Beyond per capita income, there are other indicators that need to be used as metrics of analysis to assess reginal performance. These indicators can be related to the broader aspects of human development and thus, they can complement purely economic metrics. Taking from the theory of economic convergence that underscores the potential for catch-up growth and reduced economic disparities, it becomes important to understand whether the performance of various regions on economic and human development 'converges' or not.

This section examines the heterogeneity that exists in India; we delve deeper by understanding differences across states based on prosperity levels, economic activities and labour markets. Further, by examining literature specific to Indian states, it seeks to answer why certain states are becoming richer and why poorer regions are not meeting convergence. Variation at different parameters directly impacting a region's competitiveness fundamentals is studied at state and district levels. Lastly, an insight is reached that, since the liberalization policy, states have been in the spotlight for their development strategies, which have included everything from exports and innovation to human development paradigms. These initiatives have effectively improved results at the state level on both the social and economic fronts, closing the gap between richer states over a period of time. However, significant disparities are prevalent even now; hence, it requires promoting regional economic and social development at the sub-national level, which necessitates a bottom-up approach.

Heterogeneity in India: A Challenge and an Opportunity

Regions have resurfaced as a critical place for the control of economic development and wealth creation. According to Michael Kitson et al. (2004),[2] regions should be compared in terms of economic performance, since such a comparison may provide an explanation for why regions vary in economic success. Moreover, per-capita GDP is seen as the primary outcome of competitiveness factors as discussed by the findings of Gina Dimian and Aniela Danciu (2011).[3] Insights from the study reveal that the productivity or efficiency with which inputs get translated into commodities and services, determines competitiveness. It may be examined in terms of revenue, employment and its drivers, ranging from traditional production variables to soft factors like human capital, research and development and information dissemination. Finally, it concludes that countries such as China, India, Brazil, the Czech Republic and Poland have profited from macroeconomic stability, investment in education and research and sound economic policies in the present economic climate.

Indian states are larger than most of the countries not just in terms of population but also in terms of GDP. India is home to some of the most populated states, such as Uttar Pradesh and

Maharashtra, (often termed as provinces/ counties) in the world.
Previously, we have discussed differences between Maharashtra
and Uttar Pradesh in terms of the four aspects of the diamond
model. To examine differences across regions in India, we take
up the case of the two states once again. Home to more than
23.3 crore people, the size of the population of Uttar Pradesh
is equivalent to the European Union's three major countries,
Germany, France and the United Kingdom combined. In
2019–20, Uttar Pradesh's GSDP was equivalent to Algeria
(about $167 billion). Maharashtra's population is equivalent
to that of Russia's, and its GSDP was equivalent to that of
Vietnam's (about $313 billion). If we examine differences in
district domestic products for both states, we find that four out
of thirty-four districts—Mumbai, Thane, Pune and Nashik—
together contribute to more than 50 per cent of Maharashtra's
GSDP. Out of this, about 20 per cent of the contribution is
directly from Mumbai (including Suburban). Whereas in
Uttar Pradesh, Gautam Buddha Nagar has the highest share,
i.e., 8.91 in Uttar Pradesh's GSDP, and the share of the rest
of the 65 districts is less than 4 per cent. Maharashtra's per
capita income in 2019–20 was Rs 1,45,165, with 45.22 per
cent of its population living in urban areas. Uttar Pradesh's
per capita income, on the other hand, is Rs 43,503, and the
state's population is predominantly rural, with 22.6 per cent of
the population living in urban areas. On external factors such
as exports, Uttar Pradesh's contribution was 5.61 per cent,
whereas for Maharashtra it was 19.9 per cent in 2020–21. These
differences magnify further at the district level when we look
at exports data for both the states. We observe that Gautam
Buddha Nagar of Uttar Pradesh contributed more than 2.1 per
cent to India's exports, while the rest contribute less than 1 per
cent. On the other hand, the combined contribution of the five

districts of Maharashtra—Mumbai Suburban, Mumbai city, Pune, Thane and Raigad—to India's export share was about 13.5 per cent.* A compact comparison of these two states itself outlines the issue of heterogeneity, which reflects in about 100 districts (when combined for Uttar Pradesh and Maharashtra).

Just 100 districts out of over 760 have substantially contributed to India's progress. There is a noticeable difference across Indian districts. As discussed above, even Maharashtra, the state with the greatest degree of wealth in the country, with a GDP equivalent to Vietnam's, has a significant economic difference across its districts. Its top three districts account for more than 30 per cent of the state's GDP. Similar trends may be seen in districts across the nation. These variances in trajectory will vary from district to district across states, and the discrepancies will become apparent when we look at the districts' rural-urban gap. These differences further magnify when we move to the northeastern part of the country. Given the challenge and opportunity at hand, it is imperative to examine the differences at a sub-national level. There is a need to concentrate on the state's growth-paradigm landscape in order to resolve differences in district growth, wealth and other key features. Fostering regional economic and social development requires a bottom-up strategy considering the many differences at the sub-national level across several measures. The district population of India is comparable to that of several economically successful countries, reflecting the country's tremendous untapped potential. In this regard, it is clear that the goal of a $5 trillion economy can only be reached by realizing the full potential of the states.

---

* 2020–21 https://dashboard.commerce.gov.in/commercedashboard.aspx

Variations in Prosperity Levels at Sub-National Levels

The per-capita income in India varies greatly among regions. The figure below plots GDP per capita* to CAGR of GSDP per capita (2011– 12 to 2019–20) at a constant rate based on base years (2011– 12). Even when urban cities are excluded, the varying economic performance of Indian states and territories demonstrates the significant regional disparities that exist within the country. In fact, prosperity levels vary by a factor of four, which is a significant deviation from the variances observed between EU member states or US states. As shown by the data, it is concerning that these disparities have been growing over time. It is essential to acknowledge that states with higher incomes, such as Haryana and Karnataka, have significantly outperformed states with lower incomes, such as Uttar Pradesh, West Bengal and Bihar. The former have grown by an average of more than 6 per cent annually, while the latter have grown by 3 to 4 per cent annually. If nothing is done, such significant development disparities could contribute to a further widening of the prosperity disparity. These trends of growing regional disparities in economic performance are not unique to India but are evident in nations with advanced economies. In most of the world, convergence has been the norm, with developing economies growing at a quicker rate and catching up to wealthier regions.

---

* Data sourced from RBI

Figure 51: GDP per capita to CAGR of GSDP per capita (2011-12 to 2020-21)

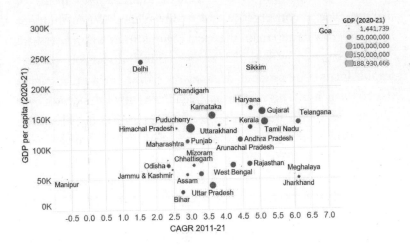

Source: *Competitiveness Roadmap for India @100*

Extant Research on Convergence between States around the World

Economic theory provides one gauge for making these comparisons based on 'convergence' (or unconditional convergence). Convergence implies that a state that begins with low performance levels on an important outcome, such as income or consumption, should experience quicker growth on that outcome over time, increasing its performance so that it catches up with states that began with higher starting points. This essentially suggests that faster growth occurs when there is greater room for expansion. It is therefore an easy metric of absolute and relative performance, enabling comparisons across states. It assesses the pace of catch-up, namely whether less developed states have caught up with wealthier ones and whether regional dispersion is expanding. There is little indication of convergence between states or union territories in the extant research on Indian development.

The 'growth' empirical evidences examine two forms of convergence: b-convergence and s-convergence. When the poor regions grow faster than the rich regions, it is known as beta (b)-convergence. When the cross-sectional dispersion of per-capita income or product declines over time, it is called sigma (s)-convergence. This indicates a negative trend of dispersion over the period, which implies that inequalities are fading. However, if the dispersion shows an increasing trend, there is s-divergence, meaning inequalities among the economies are rising. Robert J. Barro and Xavier Sala-i-Martin (1992)[4] investigated whether impoverished nations or areas develop quicker than prosperous ones. They examined convergence throughout the forty-eight contiguous states in the US using the neoclassical growth model as a framework. The evidence of data on personal income since 1840 and on GDP since 1963 provides convincing evidence of convergence but only if falling returns to capital occur gradually. Further, it is noted by Xavier Sala-i-Martin (1996)[5] that b-convergence is required but not a sufficient condition for s-convergence.

Moreover, researchers from all across the globe have contributed to the convergence theory. In their paper, OlaOluwa S. Yaya et al. (2020)[6] examined income convergence in nine Asian nations using a novel unit root test—the Fourier unit-root test with break. It divided the nations into three regions: Northeast Asia, Southeast Asia and South Asia and selected three main economies from each region for empirical examination. The empirical data show that South Asia has considerably stronger income convergence, whereas Northeast and Southeast Asia have a mixed tendency of income convergence and income divergence.

Hartmut Lehmann et al. (2020)[7] discovered a convergence across Russian regions between 1996 and 2017. Similarly, María Florencia Aráoz et al. (2020)[8] discovered b-convergence in per-capita GDP among Argentine regions. This paper presents the first consistent quantitative analysis of the regional dimension of that story, using estimations of provincial GDPs for ten benchmark years between 1895 and 2004. In his study, Ram (2020)[9] fills several gaps in the existing literature by focusing on the most recent period, 1997–2018, using official data on real GDP per capita compiled by the US Bureau of Economic Analysis (BEA), comparing the convergence scenario for 1997–2018 with that for 1977–1997 and orienting the observed patterns within the context of Piketty-like propositions about high returns to capital and rising income inequality. One notable finding is evidence of sigma-divergence among US states, as measured by increasing standard deviation of logs and coefficient of variance with time.

Growth Convergence: A Case for India

In the Indian context, the variation in economic performance among states has captivated the curiosity of scholars, policymakers and economists alike. As a consequence, various empirical studies on state or regional convergence in India have been done. These studies on the convergence of Indian states or regions provide diverse conclusions based on various samples of states or regions collected across different time periods. Paul Cashin and Ratna Sahay (1996)[10] discovered 100 per cent b-convergence across Indian states between 1961 and 1991. This paper also finds out that dispersion of actual per capita net domestic product (NDP) across Indian states has widened over the same period. This pattern stands in stark contrast to that seen in industrialized nations, such as Australia, Japan and the United States. Transfers from the Central government of India to the states guaranteed that the dispersion of states' real per-capita disposable incomes was smaller than that of the states' real per-capita incomes since more funds were sent to impoverished states than to affluent states. Taking the sectoral structure of the twenty states into consideration, about 1.5 per cent of the difference between wealthy and poor states was narrowed each year between 1961 and 1991. This suggests that it would take around forty-five years in India to bridge half the difference between each state's beginning per capita income and the states' common long-run per capita income. It would only take thirty-five years in an industrialized nation. Similarly, Nirupam Bajpai and Jeffrey D. Sachs (1996)[11] found convergence in per-capita income levels during the first sub-period, 1961–71. For the last two sub-periods, 1972–82 and 1983–93, however, they found evidence of divergent per-capita income levels. According to the study, convergence occurred between 1961 and 1971 principally as a consequence of the green revolution's tremendous expansion in the agriculture sector. The 1970s saw a slowdown of industrial growth and the formation of a city-based pattern of industrial development that was focused exclusively on a few places, and this seems to be the cause of the divergence seen during this period. Buddhadeb Ghosh and Prabhir De (1998)[12] further noted that states in India have diverged during the previous thirty-five years. Around the same period, M. Govinda Rao et al. (1999)[13] explored the developments in interstate income disparities in India since mid-1961. The investigation demonstrated growing interstate gaps, which contradicts the neoclassical growth theory. It investigated the causes of interstate disparities in growth rates and the significance of interstate transfers in influencing the geographical distribution of investment and income. It concludes that income disparities are mostly the result of inequitable distribution of private investments and infrastructure.

Montek S. Ahluwalia (2000)[14] emphasized on enabling state-level efforts to attract investment since the degree of control held by the Centre in many sectors was lowered as a result of liberalization. He argued that state-level performance and policies need more scrutiny, and it is critical to investigate variances in performance across states in order to understand what works and what does not. A greater understanding of the causes behind certain states' higher performance would aid in spreading success from one region of the nation to the next.

Dipankar Dasgupta et al. (2000)[15] discovered a definite tendency for Indian states to differ in per-capita state domestic product. An examination of the period 1960–61 to 1995–96 reveals a definite trend for states to vary in terms of per-capita domestic output but converge in terms of the proportions of various sectors in state domestic product (SDP). The empirical findings offered by R. Nagaraj et al. (2000)[16] emphasized on the relevance of disparities in physical, social and economic infrastructure endowments as well as variances in production structure, in accounting for the observed variety in Indian state-development performances. As a result, economic policies aimed at improving physical, economic and social infrastructure may have a significant influence on long-run development potential and convergence among Indian states. Their findings imply that directing public infrastructure investment towards certain states might boost the overall payout in terms of improved economic performance. The six states that should be prioritized are those where the per capita SDP growth disparity about the India average is mostly accounted for by a lack of infrastructure. Increasing infrastructure availability in certain states might have a greater influence on the aggregate economy than a public investment programme that does not account for such variances in infrastructure restrictions encountered in different jurisdictions.

The research done by Jeffrey D. Sachs et al. (2002)[17] assessed whether per capita incomes in the states were converging or diverging using two measures of convergence. India displayed overall divergence between 1980 and 1998 as well as during the pre- and post-reform periods. Surprisingly, the richer states had some degree of convergence throughout the post-reform era, whilst the poorer ones did not. The poorest group of states saw the most divergence.

Adabar Kshamanidhi (2004)[18] aimed to re-examine the problem of convergence and economic development by concentrating on disparities in the fourteen major Indian states from 1976–77 to 2000–01. According to this paper, conditional convergence has been shown in India after controlling the investment per capita, population growth rate, human capital and state-specific impacts at a rate of roughly 12 per cent in each five-year period. These factors alone might explain almost 93 per cent of the difference in the per-capita real-income growth rate among fourteen large states from 1976 to 2000. This demonstrates the significance of policy activity in achieving balanced development and regional convergence. According to B. Bhattacharya and Sakthivel (2004),[19] the regional disparity in SDP among major Indian states has expanded, and there is no evidence of convergence of growth rates across these states.

Using the Malmquist Productivity Index, Gaurav Nayyar (2008)[20] presented empirical evidence of patterns of Total Factor Productivity (TFP) development among Indian states in the post-liberalization period. It discovers that the average degree of inefficiency in India has decreased during the period of liberalization, but there is substantial regional variance. From 1993 to 2005, ten states had increased production, mostly due to advances in technological efficiency. Even if only efficient states remain inventive, there is a tendency for states' productivity growth to converge throughout liberalization. States with a higher standard of living utilize resources more effectively.

Ghosh[21] found that per-capita income in Indian states has differed in the post-reform era. This paper analysed long-run growth performance and geographical disparities in per-capita income across fifteen major Indian states before and after reform. Research suggests that the difference has grown due to inter-state differences in production systems, human resources and infrastructure. More public investment in human capital and infrastructure for states with lower steady-state growth rates could boost overall growth performance and minimize regional inequities.

Sanjay Kalra and Piyaporn Sodsriwiboon (2010)[22] examined convergence and spill-overs across Indian states using non-stationary panel data techniques. The findings are consistent with prior research, with evidence of divergence throughout the entire sample period (1960– 2003), convergence during structural breaks and club convergence. Club convergence is clearly evident in high- and low-income states, while data for middle-income states is inconsistent. There is evidence of three growth cycles in India, with high-income states seeing strong and sustained growth on average, medium-income states expanding quickly and some low-income states catching up. From a policy standpoint, states that advanced were those that profited from advancements in the services sector, greater infrastructure and credit availability as well as those who spent development funds effectively. The absence of dynamic spill-overs may indicate a need for improved infrastructure and connection across the country to enable the advantages of development to be distributed throughout the country.

Utsav Kumar and Arvind Subaramanian (2012)[23] evaluated the growth performance of Indian states from 2001 to 2009, throughout the global financial crisis. It includes four main findings. Growth in virtually all major states increased, yet there was still a disparity or growing inequality between states. During the crisis years, nations with the highest growth rates from 2001 to 2007 saw the greatest slowdown, indicating that openness breeds dynamism and vulnerability. The demographic dividend was visible before 2000, but there is no indication of a dividend in the 2000s. Demography alone cannot guarantee future economic development.

Surender Kumar and Shunsuke Managi (2012)[24] focused on neoclassical and endogenous growth theories in addressing the heterogeneity in Indian state productivity. They examined the yearly rates of change in productivity and technological efficiency in each Indian state from 1993 to 2004. They presented empirical evidence of patterns of total factor productivity (TFP) development among Indian states in the post-liberalization period using the Malmquist productivity index. According to the findings of this research, the yearly rate of productivity growth has increased on average throughout time despite the fact that certain states have witnessed a slowdown or even a drop in output. The findings show that the disparities in productivity across states are a consequence of the policies and institutions that contribute to raise the human development index (HDI). Increases in TFP at the state level are also shown to be favourably related to the degree to which a state has embraced economic reforms. They also discovered that states with a higher quality of life utilize resources more effectively. In light of the convergence and divergence theories, the research also explores the sources of productivity divergence among states.

Samarjit Das, Chetan Ghate and Peter E. Robertson (2015)[25] investigated the hypotheses of conditional convergence using a new data set of district-level income and socioeconomic data as well as using distance as an indicator of internal geographical trade and migration costs. This paper aims to explain the pattern of Indian development at the district level using two new data sets on per-capita incomes and social and economic features for 575 districts. It draws on the research on economic geography to develop a model of conditional convergence across districts, and it incorporates distance as an explanatory variable. Notwithstanding absolute difference, the rate of convergence is less than half the value of Barro's Iron Law of convergence, indicating that India faces additional major regional economic hurdles to convergence. Infrastructure disparities, urbanization and electricity and state-level policy variances are all essential factors in understanding regional income and growth rates. The findings imply that variations in trade and transportation costs, infrastructure, literacy rates and state-level factors have contributed to India's lack of absolute convergence.

Arfat Ahmad Sofi and Raja Sethu Durai S. (2016)[26] examined the convergence theory across twenty-two Indian states from 1980–81 and 2010–11. The findings show that income distribution is multimodal, with considerable evidence of club creation across various income levels. According to quantile estimation, Indian states are separating in absolute terms while converging in conditional terms. Going from lower to higher quantile, the absolute divergence reduces but conditional convergence strengthens.

An examination of regional convergence in fifteen major Indian states by Prerna Sanga and Abdul Shaban (2017)[27] revealed that the aggregate GDP diverged from 1970–71 and 2013–14. This contradicts the neoclassical convergence theory, which predicts that impoverished countries would eventually catch up with advanced regions. The convergence puzzle was discussed in Economic Survey 2017 as it examined states on two broad economic indicators and three indicators of health and demographic outcomes. It noted that while rising significantly on average, there are signs of increased regional disparity across Indian states. This is perplexing since the underlying dynamics in favour of equalization inside India are clearly evident. One explanation is that there are governance stumbling blocks impeding the process of catching up, and if such traps exist, labour and capital mobility may exacerbate underlying inequality. However, there is considerable evidence of state convergence in health and demography in the 2000s, and the worldwide disparity is stark. In terms of life expectancy, the Indian states are near to where they should be given their level of wealth, but this is not the case for IMR, indicating that the 'mother and child' face the burden of poor health-care delivery.[28]

Lekha Chakraborty and Pinaki Chakraborty (2018)[29] find no unconditional or conditional convergence in economic growth across Indian states. Pranab Mukhopadhyay and Aparna Lolayekar (2020)[30] identified a positive b-convergence coefficient and conclude that income disparities exist in India. Suryakanta Nayak and Dukhabandhu Sahoo (2021)[31] investigated the convergence in per-capita income of Indian regions from 1990–91 to 2017–18. Two assessments were conducted to determine the impact of India's second phase of economic liberalization, and a panel data analysis was conducted to estimate absolute and conditional b-convergence and s-convergence across seventeen Indian regions. The research found that areas with low starting per-capita income have risen quicker than regions with high beginning per-capita income. It also found that FDI inflows and the availability of electricity boost growth across geographies. However, the prevalence of s-divergence suggests that economic inequality has spread over time, requiring governmental interventions to encourage development in backward areas.

We may conclude from the examination of literature on India's economic development that there is a need to concentrate on strengthening state convergence and addressing the dilemma of shared prosperity. Despite recent improvements, gaps in economic growth and development exist across states and union territories, impeding the accomplishment of inclusive and sustainable growth as a country. Delving now into the analysis of several key indicators, including economic activity, the labour market, Gross Fixed Capital Formation (GFCF), infrastructure, innovative capacity, education attainment, exports and FDI inflows, we attempt to gain a better understanding of the variations in economic performance and development across Indian states. These indicators are crucial for analysing the state of economic and social development. We examine economic indicators as well as the degree of human development among states and union territories, using the Human Development Index (HDI) as a standard. The HDI gives an in-depth analysis of a state's growth in categories such as health, education and income. It can help identify regions where focused measures are needed by state governments to foster convergence by analysing variances in the HDI between states and union territories.

Furthermore, using the SPI, the differences in social advancement among states and union territories is further investigated. The SPI assesses a state's ability to provide citizens basic and fundamental human needs, such as access to healthcare, education and safety, as well as access to opportunity and rights. This index assists in identifying areas for development to create greater social inclusion and shared prosperity. Finally, using income distribution statistics from NFHS, the changes in wealth quintiles and Gini coefficients between states and union territories to shed light on wealth inequality are investigated.

Variations at the State Level

o   *Economic Activity and Labour Market*

Labour mobilization, labour productivity and labour share in production are all significant aspects in Porter's competitiveness theory that contribute to a location's overall competitiveness. A location that can mobilize a skilled and educated population, boost productivity and creativity and pay people equitably is more likely to attract investment and generate economic growth.

To reiterate, the competitiveness of a location is driven by the diamond model—encompassing four main factors: factor conditions, demand conditions, related and supporting industries and firm strategy, structure and rivalry. Labour mobilization, labour productivity and labour share in production are all key aspects that might affect a location's overall competitiveness under the area of factor conditions. For example, a location with a highly educated and competent workforce may have a competitive edge in high-tech sectors, while a region with a less educated population may have a competitive advantage in low-tech manufacturing. Similarly, highly automated sectors may demand less labour and, therefore, have a lower labour share in production, while labour-intensive businesses may have a larger labour share in production. Because various locations and industries may have distinct competitive advantages and difficulties, variances in labour mobilization, productivity and labour share in production may contribute to a country's heterogeneity. We use the graph[*] below to illustrate differences on these key factors.

---

[*] For graphical representation only 22 states are used. This excludes Union territories, north eastern states other than Assam as their projected population from Population Projection Report 2011–2036—upload_compressed_0.pdf (mohfw.gov.in) is not available for these states.

Figure 52: Labour Productivity vs Labour Mobilization, States of India

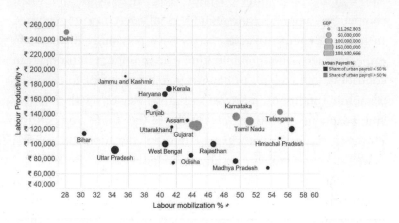

Source: Competitiveness Roadmap for India @100

In most states, labour mobilization rates, or the share of employees in the working-age population, range from 28 per cent to 50 per cent. The age profile is also important; here, the disparities are relatively minor, with other states between 50 per cent and 56 per cent within working age. It must be noted that this differs from state to state. The states with the highest employed workforce, such as Bihar and Uttar Pradesh, have lower mobilization rates, i.e., 30.42 per cent and 34.35 per cent as the employed population is relatively lower to available total workforce in these regions. However, there are states such as Andhra Pradesh and Tamil Nadu that have higher mobilization rates, i.e., 56.49 per cent and 51.19 per cent, where more than the 50 per cent workforce is employed. Such states become important locations as a highly trained and mobile workforce is better equipped to attract investment and generate economic growth in terms of labour mobilization. A location may have a competitive advantage that attracts enterprises and supports economic growth because of an educated and mobile workforce. It can be influenced by factors such as education and training programmes, labour laws, diversity of industries, competition among businesses and social safety net programmes. In terms of competitiveness, as we have previously discussed in earlier chapters, labour mobilization is an important factor that can contribute to a region's or country's ability to adapt to changing economic conditions, innovate and grow. Regions with a flexible and adaptable workforce are likely to be more competitive. However, this necessitates expenditures in education and training as well as labour mobility and flexibility policies.

Labour productivity is also an important factor in competitiveness since it allows businesses to create more products and services in a given period of time. A location must invest in technology, infrastructure and innovation to enhance productivity and establish a corporate climate that stimulates competition and innovation. A location may attract investment and offer a competitive advantage that fosters economic development by improving productivity. It must be noted that wages range between Rs 68,000 and Rs 2,50,000. Delhi has the highest average wage, and it is observed that it is the only urban region where the employed workforce's payroll share is more than 50 per cent for the age bracket of 15–59 years. Further, it is observed that larger and relatively less developed states, such as Chhattisgarh, Jharkhand and Bihar, which have the lowest average wages, i.e., Rs 68,000, Rs 75,000 and Rs 84,615 and have lower employed workforce's urban payroll share, which is less than 20 per cent. A detailed analysis reveals that about 60 per cent of the difference between a regional and the national average is explained by economy-wide locational factors and 40 per cent by the mix of sectors in the respective economy.

Finally, in Porter's view, the labour share in GDP is significant because it influences the distribution of economic rewards and stimulates demand for products and services. The labour share of GDP refers to the percentage of state revenue that is paid to labour in the form of wages, salaries and other forms of compensation. A higher labour share indicates that a greater proportion of national revenue is sent to employees in the form of wages, salaries and benefits. Capital income accounts for a larger share of GDP in higher-income households and urban regions, which is commensurate with the factor input needs of these regional economies. A location may create a more equitable business climate that fosters economic development by advocating regulations that favour better employee pay and benefits. This may lead to greater demand for products and services, which can boost economic development even more.

In 2020–21, the labour share* of GDP in Bihar, one of India's least developed states, was about 64.81 per cent. This might suggest that wages, salaries and other types of labour remuneration accounted for half of the state's GDP. On the other hand, in Maharashtra, an industrialized state with a more diverse economy, the labour share of GDP in 2020–21 was about 24.35 per cent. This signifies that wages, salaries and other kinds of labour remuneration accounted for less than half of the state's GDP. The disparity in labour share between Bihar and Maharashtra is due to the difference of industries based on their economic activity that dominate each state's income. Based on economic activity, GVA estimates of 2020–21[†] reveal that Bihar contributes around 3 per cent, with agriculture's GVA being the highest. It must be noted that the agriculture sector employs a

---

* This is in reference to income extracted from PLFS 2020–21 data, not with respect to compensation of employees from Macro aggregates
[†] Reserve Bank of India, Publications (rbi.org.in), GVA relative to particular economic activity

large share of Bihar's workers, and it is a labour-intensive sector with poor earnings.

In contrast, Maharashtra has a larger concentration of knowledge-based businesses such as information technology, pharmaceuticals and engineering, which are capital-intensive and provide higher returns for capital owners. Its relative contribution to GVA of agriculture, manufacturing and services is 12.2, 16.52 and 16.91 per cent respectively, with the services sector's contribution being the highest in the country, whereas the manufacturing contribution is second highest only to Gujarat (19.81 per cent). Another factor contributing to the disparity in labour share between Bihar and Maharashtra are the productivity levels of their respective workforces.

Dibyendu Maiti (2019)[32] in his paper, argues that the share declines more in the states that hold pro-workers labour legislation than those with pro-employer legislations. In contrast, the paper finds that the number of strikes and lockouts as well as man days lost per factory from such lockouts, have declined substantially during this period in all the major states. Moreover, the share of contract labour has increased in all the major states in India irrespective of their degree of labour legislations. It also finds a drop in labour bargaining power with the interaction of trade, more in the so-called pro-employer states than in others, suggesting that the labour legislation does not matter unless it is effective enough. The specialization effect, arising out of heterogeneity in productivity distribution between trading partners, out-weights the joint effects of market size and competition, depressing the demand for labour and, hence, their bargaining power. This suggests that legislative reform is unnecessary for workers' welfare, but competitive policies encouraging entry can benefit workers and increase economic growth.

o   *Gross Fixed Capital Formation (GFCF)*

Gross fixed capital formation (GFCF) is a crucial economic indicator for measuring investment in fixed capital assets, such as infrastructure, buildings and machinery in a given period. Higher levels of GFCF are generally associated with greater economic growth and development, as investment in capital assets can increase the efficiency of production processes, improve infrastructure and lead to the development of new technologies. Simon Kuznets is credited with popularizing the concept of GCFC, making it a more widely used measure of investment in fixed assets. His work on GFCF has had a lasting impact on economics, and his insights have informed policy discussions on investment and economic development. He believed that investment in physical capital was a key driver of economic growth and saw GFCF as an important measure of investment in fixed assets. This allowed for the creation of new products and services, leading to higher output and employment.[33, 34]

Due to their emphasis on industry and infrastructural development, Indian states such as Maharashtra, Gujarat and Karnataka have historically been among the top contributors to GFCF. Policymakers and investors may use GFCF data to identify locations that are investing heavily and prioritize them for future growth. They can also use it to choose where to concentrate their efforts to boost a region's competitiveness. Gujarat has the highest share in GFCF, i.e., 17.3 per cent, Maharashtra closely follows it with 16.7 per cent and Tamil Nadu with 11.02 per cent. Other states' and union territories' GFCF shares lie below 6 per cent. These figures indicate that these states are making substantial investments in fixed capital assets and infrastructure, which are essential for economic growth and development. Given their status as one of India's most industrialized states, it is not surprising that they are distinct leaders in terms of GFCF. Most of the northeastern states except Assam have less than a 0.07 per cent share in GFCF.*

It is important to note that Kuznets also recognized that investment in human capital or investments in education and training was critical for sustained economic growth. He argued that investment in human capital allowed workers to acquire the skills and knowledge necessary to adapt to changing economic conditions and technological advancements, and a well-educated and trained workforce was necessary for continued economic growth and development. Therefore, it is essential for states to recognize that GFCF alone cannot provide a comprehensive picture of a region's competitiveness. Other determinants of a region's competitiveness include human capital, technological advancements, the business environment and the availability of natural resources.

o   *Infrastructure*

Infrastructure development is critical for economic growth and expansion. In recent years, particularly since 2014, India has made substantial investments in infrastructure, notably in the areas of road infrastructure and electricity supply. India's infrastructure development has prioritized transportation, communication and energy infrastructure. Expansion of the road network, port development and construction of airports has increased connectivity, resulting in decreased business transaction costs and improved market access.

---

* Share in GFCF has been calculated by GFC of state divided by all India GCFC, expressed in percentage Reserve Bank of India—Publications (rbi.org.in)

While progress has been made across the nation, the rate and scope of development vary between states and territories. Rajarshi Majumder (2005)[35] in his paper, talked about the imbalances in regional infrastructural availability as a major reason behind lopsided development in India. The main findings of this paper are that regional disparities have increased in the post-Structural Adjustment Programme era, indicating that the state should play the role of a facilitator, while private actors should primarily undertake the expansionary endeavour. It is also evident that the availability of physical, financial and social infrastructure is a significant determinant of a region's current and prospective development levels. Nevertheless, as the degree of development increases, the infrastructure-development causality appears to be diminishing. At lower development levels, the causality between infrastructure and development may be simple and linear, whereas at higher development levels, the relationship may be complex, non-proportional and non-linear. It is possible that infrastructure availability is a crucial factor required to surpass a critical minimal level of development, beyond which other factors assume the role of development's propelling force.

We will investigate road infrastructure and electricity supply differences across Indian states and territories. These two examples illustrate how a national trend manifests itself differently across Indian states and territories. Over the years, the density of the road network has increased. This is evident in all locations, but improvements have occurred at varying rates. Regarding electricity, India has made significant strides in matching capacity and demand. However, there are still vast disparities in transmission and distribution losses, which have significant economic implications for each location's electricity system.

Road Infrastructure: The Ministry of Road Transport and Highways publishes an annual publication titled *Basic Road Statistics of India* on the road sector. It provides data on various aspects of road statistics. India has over 63,31,757 kilometres of roads as of 31 March 2019, making it the second-largest road network in the world. The total length of roads constructed increased by 1.9 per cent from 62,15,797 km in 2018 to 63,31,757 kilometres in 2019. In India's transport sector, road transport is the dominant subsector, contributing 3.06 per cent of GVA in 2019–20. State highways account for 2.8 per cent of the total road network, with a length of 1,79,535 km.[*] However, the pace of development has varied across different states and territories. For instance, the state of Maharashtra has the highest density of national highways, with 12.67 kilometre of state highways per 100 square kilometre of area, followed by Kerala and Karnataka, with 11.17 kilometre and 10.18 kilometre per 100 square kilometre. On the other hand, states like Himachal Pradesh and Jharkhand have a much lower density of national highways, with just 1.49 km and 1.45 km per 100 square kilometre, respectively.[†] Whereas, rural roads comprise 71.4 per cent of the total road network, with Maharashtra having the largest network, 4,26,327 km (11.7 per cent), followed by Assam at 3,72,510 km (10.2 per cent), Bihar at 2,59,507 km (7.1 per cent), Uttar Pradesh at 2,55,576 km (7 per cent) and Madhya Pradesh at 2,32,344 km (6.9 per cent). These five states account for about 42 per cent of the nation's total rural roadways. It is important to note that, in addition to the density of the road network, the quality of roads is another important factor to be considered.

---

[*] Basic Road Statistics in India 2018–19
[†] BISAG 2022 Welcome to BISAG-N

Electricity Supply: Uninterrupted power supply is critical for industrial and commercial operations. It allows companies to run more effectively, lowering manufacturing costs and boosting competition. The availability of contemporary conveniences like air conditioning, refrigeration and communication devices, thanks to an uninterrupted power supply, also enhances the quality of life for inhabitants. In the last eight years, the Indian power industry has made significant progress, from being a country with a power deficit to one with a power surplus. Several coordinated actions caused the generating capacity to rise by 45 per cent, from 275 GW in March 2015 to almost 400 GW on March 22. India was able to lower its energy and peak deficits from 4.2 per cent and 4.5 per cent in 2014 to 0.4 per cent and 1 per cent in 2022, respectively, thanks to a parallel growth in electricity generation at a compound annual growth rate (CAGR) of around 4 per cent. This indicates that there has been a significant expansion in the electricity-generation capacity in the country.[*]

However, the availability of electricity [†] varies across different states and territories. For instance, there is variation in per capita consumption. The combined union territory of Dadra and Nagar Haveli and Daman and Diu has the highest per capita electricity consumption, with 18,163 kWh per capita, followed by Goa with 3,735.51 kWh per capita and Punjab with 2350 kWh per capita. On the other hand, states such as Bihar, Manipur and Assam have a much lower per capita electricity consumption, with just 328 kWh, 361 kWh and 384 kWh per capita, respectively.[‡] At least ten

---

[*] Meeting of the Consultative Committee of the Members of Parliament for Ministry of Power held

[†] *RBI 2021–22, 2019–20*

[‡] Data for 2021–22 from—Dashboard—Central Electricity Authority (cea.nic.in)

states and union territories, Chandigarh, Dadra and Nagar Haveli
and Daman and Diu, Goa, Lakshadweep, Manipur, Nagaland,
Puducherry, Sikkim and Tripura, met the power demand in
their respective regions in 2021–22. Electricity produced but
not used by the intended consumers is known as transmission
and distribution (T&D) losses. India has one of the highest levels
of T&D losses in the world. It is more than twice as great as the
global average and almost three times as large as T&D losses in
the United States, India's T&D losses account for about 20 per
cent of generation.[*]

Figure 53: Availability of Electricity Across States of India

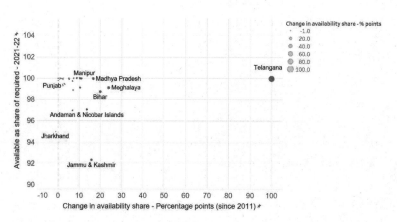

Source: Competitiveness Roadmap for India @100

---

[*] US Energy Information Administration—EIA—Independent Statistics
and Analysis

Figure 54: Losses in Distribution and Transmission as a Share of Production

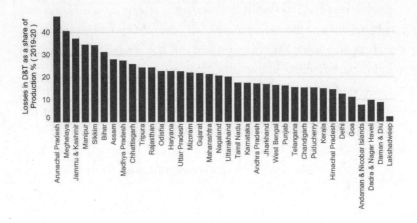

Source: Competitiveness Roadmap for India @100

According to the 2019-20 data from RBI, Arunachal Pradesh, Meghalaya, Jammu and Kashmir, Manipur, Sikkim and Bihar account for more than 30 per cent T&D losses, i.e., 47.05, 40.55, 37.24, 34.54, 34.27 and 31.09, respectively. Theft and technological inefficiencies cause electricity losses. The resistance of cables and other equipment as electricity goes through causes technical losses. While some loss is unavoidable, T&D losses typically fall between 6 per cent and 8 per cent at locations with strong technological efficiency and negligible theft. Most T&D losses in India are due to theft, which happens when used power is not accounted for. The usual methods of stealing electricity include circumventing or tampering with metres and paying off utility metre readers or billing representatives.

Differences exist also in other dimensions of the regulatory framework. For the cost of doing business, these differences have been shown to exist in the comparison of high- and low-growth states. Across all indicators, from setting up a business and getting environmental approvals to connecting to infrastructure and paying taxes, the time it takes and the obstacles reported are significantly higher in low-growth states.

Overall, the role of the state government is critical in ensuring uninterrupted power supply, mitigating loss in power during transmission and other infrastructure-development related initiatives within their respective states. They are responsible for implementing policies and programmes to improve the availability and quality of power supply and for investing in the development of infrastructure. Additionally, they are responsible for the development of transportation infrastructure, energy infrastructure and private investment in infrastructure development.

o *Innovative Capacity*

There are differences in the innovative capacity of states as well. Indicators of innovative capacity in an area include patenting, degree of R&D expenditure and rise of start-ups.

When people or businesses apply for patents, they are actively involved in research and development and have created innovative ideas or technology. Therefore, a region's ability to innovate may be shown by the number of patents it has received. Maharashtra alone accounts for 17 per cent of all Indian patenting. In 2021, the top five states, i.e., Maharashtra, Tamil Nadu, Karnataka, Uttar Pradesh and Telangana, by absolute patenting accounted for about 60 per cent of Indian patenting,[*] compared to a 40 per cent share of GDP. Their per-capita patenting rate is five times higher than the average for the rest of the country.

It is crucial to remember that patenting anything does not automatically signify innovation. A region may award a large number of patents, but it does not guarantee that they will be profitable or lead to important technological developments. Similar to the last example, a location with few awarded patents might yet be quite creative, with its inventive activity going to trade secrets, copyrights or trademarks rather than patents.

Over the years, sustained Central government efforts to improve India's rank in the global innovation index and the pledge to improve innovative capacity have resulted in increasing the number of DPIIT-recognized start-ups from 452 in 2016 to 84,012 in 2022.[†] For DPIIT-recognized start-ups in particular, innovation is a major factor in the start-up success. To be considered for recognition, these firms must concentrate on creating cutting-edge goods or services, and innovation is essential to their long-term expansion and success. It should be noted that about 63 per cent of DPIIT-recognized start-ups are present mostly in the following states : Maharashtra (18.43 per cent), Karnataka (11.61 per cent), Delhi (11.24 per cent), Uttar Pradesh (9.21 per cent), Gujarat (7.19 per cent) and Tamil Nadu (5.86 per cent).

Lastly, it is important to note that at the national level and state level, we have consistently seen lower overall spending on R&D. This is reflected in the overall expenditure of R&D as a percentage of GDP, which is between 0.01 to 0.54 per cent[‡] for

---

[*] https://ipindia.gov.in/writereaddata/Portal/IPOAnnualReport/ 1_112_1_Final_English_AR_2020-21_for_Net.pdf

[†] Ministry of Commerce & Industry (pib.gov.in)

[‡] Research and Development Statistics 2019-20_0.pdf (dst.gov.in)

states and union territories. It is important to note that states that spend less on R&D will fail to retain their human capital in the long run. The ability to innovate in a region is dependent on the quality of human capital. However, if people move from one region to another, it will lead to brain drain and ultimately reduce the competitive edge of the state.

o   *Educational Attainment*

There are differences not just in education expenditure, but also in the broader functioning of the educational system. In India, teacher absenteeism is a persistent problem that affects the quality of education and learning outcomes of students. It is also highlighted in successive rounds of the National Assessment Surveys, which demonstrated that student learning results are below grade level, and that the percentage of children attaining grade-appropriate learning decreases as they go through the grades.[36]

The figure below is based on learning outcomes of all states and union territories based on the Class X NAS survey assessment on five subjects: English, mathematics, modern Indian language, science and social studies. This figure reveals that the national average for most of the subjects for Class X except for English is less than 40 per cent, reflecting overall low learning outcomes. The national average for English is 48 per cent; however, it is still far from satisfactory. Overall, there is a trend of falling scores. A recent report[37] on foundational literacy supports this finding as well. It presents a complete evidence-based picture of the causes behind India's low early learning outcomes for Classes 3 and 5 and reform options. However, it goes well beyond teacher absenteeism and other factors, which, although significant, may often restrict policy consideration and debate about the needs of this age group. Its insights on the learning outcomes pillar at the primary and preprimary levels suggest that, of all states, Punjab got the highest score of 96.36 in the small-state category. The state's high score may be attributed to its greatest performance in all disciplines of the NAS 2021 results for Classes 3 and 5. Overall, fifteen of the thirty-six states or UTs outperformed the national average in terms of learning outcomes, i.e., 44.78. In the large-state category, Rajasthan and Madhya Pradesh scored 77.93 and 64.14, respectively. In the union territory category, Chandigarh had a high score of 68.74. These findings are in line with the NAS 2021 data.

The following figure shows how the country performed in the NAS 2021 survey. However, it must be noted that the survey was administered in November 2021, when most schools started to recover from the learning loss due to pandemic.

Figure 55: NAS Class X Assessment Scores: Learning Outcomes

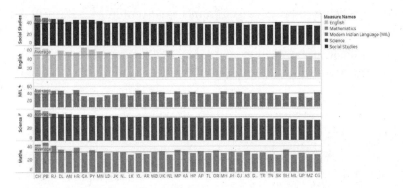

Source: Competitiveness Roadmap for India @100*

Overall, it may be asserted again that Indian states need to adapt a strategy to enhance teaching in the long run, allowing the children to catch up with learning gradually and improve their

---

* NAS 2021

outcomes. This necessitates understanding the well-established relationship between teacher absenteeism and student learning outcomes. When teachers are not in the classroom, students lose out on essential learning experiences and are more likely to lag in their studies. This may negatively impact their learning outcomes and prospects in the long run. From a legal perspective, the RTE Act has outlined the obligations placed on teachers but reduced the quality of education till Class 8. Government schoolteachers are seen to lack responsibility, and states in India struggle to hold them responsible. Teacher absenteeism has been frequently cited in literature as a serious problem when addressing a fall in learning outcomes.

Michael Kremer et al. (2005)[38] research revealed that during unannounced visits to a nationally representative sample of government elementary schools in India, 25 per cent of teachers were not present and just approximately half were teaching. Absence rates in states ranged from 15 per cent in Maharashtra to 42 per cent in Jharkhand. The research further found that there was no correlation between greater salary and decreased absenteeism. It was noted that contractual teachers are compensated poorly than regular teachers but have similar absence rates, and while relative teacher salaries are higher in poorer states, absence rates are also higher.

Karthik Muralidharan et al. (2017)[39] research further using nationally representative panel data set on education quality in rural India revealed that there has been a substantial improvement in several measures of school quality, but teacher absenteeism rates continue to be high. They discovered two robust correlations in the panel data that lend external validity to results established in smaller-scale experiments: Decreases in student-teacher ratios are strongly correlated with increased teacher absence, whereas increases in inspection frequency are strongly correlated with decreased teacher absence. In addition, they determined that the annual cost of teacher absence exceeds $1.5 billion and estimate that investing in improved governance by increasing the frequency of monitoring would be over ten times more cost-effective than hiring additional teachers to increase student-teacher contact time. The results suggest that the Indian education system has made significant progress on the former but less progress on the latter, and that shifting public expenditure away from merely augmenting inputs and towards policies that increase the efficiency of inputs could significantly increase the productivity of education expenditures.

State and UT performance on educational infrastructure has been comparatively strong. States must understand that although making investments in or improving educational infrastructure is important, concentrating only on it will not lead to better learning results, especially against the background of the pandemic-related learning loss that children have experienced.

o   *Exports*

In the past, researchers focused on analysing and investigating the export performance of particular domestic economies at the national level, frequently with a sector emphasis or firm-level examination. Traditionally, the starting point for tracing the origins of national export flows has been considered to be a country, both in academic studies of international commerce and in the practice of international trade. Nevertheless, using large and geographically extensive territories such as India as one spatial unit for the research ignores substantial regional variations that characterize the development of national exports.

India's engagement in international trade has increased substantially as it opened up to globalization in the early 1990s. In 2022, trade accounted for up to 45 per cent of India' s GDP, a threefold increase from the 15 per cent in 1990. India's export growth can be attributed to a broad range of factors, including increased efforts by the central and state governments to improve the production of existing products, promote investment in the industries and identify new products for export, among others.

Although many studies have concentrated their attention on exports at the national level, not much research has been done to address the performance of exports at the subnational level. Economies, such as India and China, are recognized to have a wide range of subnational geographies with large interregional disparities in development and economic growth levels. Yet, research on the subnational geographical origins of exports from developing countries remains scarce. Despite this, persisting regional disparities in India make it necessary to have a solid understanding of the state's export landscape and the factors that influence export performance.

States in the northeast and hilly terrains have a harder time influencing the world's export footprint than coastal and landlocked regions. It has been noticed that the coastal states, particularly Gujarat, Maharashtra and Tamil Nadu, are the most important exporters in the country throughout the course of many years. In 2021–22, their respective shares in India's total exports were 30.05, 17.32 and 8.33 per cent. In all, the combined contribution of these three states to overall exports accounted for more than 50 per cent. In addition, it is important to note that their contribution to exports has only increased over the years. According to the statistics provided by DGCIS throughout the course of the previous decade, their share has increased from 52.80 per cent in 2011–12 to 55.71 per cent in 2021–22.

On examining the three states' CAGR from 2011–12 and 2021–22, we observe that only Gujarat's performance on exports has improved with a rate of 3.52 per cent, while Maharashtra and

Tamil Nadu's share in exports has only reduced by 2.5 and 0.8 per cent, respectively, indicating reduction in the overall share of exports over the last decade. However, this also signifies that at the same time, the share of other states has increased over a period of time. For instance, Karnataka and Uttar Pradesh closely follow these states with 6.13 and 4.98 per cent share in exports and have exhibited a positive CAGR of 1.8 and 3.6 per cent.

Other states have exhibited a higher growth rate in exports over the last decade with a CAGR of more than 10 per cent. These states are Bihar, Sikkim, Manipur, Chhattisgarh, Jharkhand, Odisha, Mizoram, Arunachal Pradesh, Dadra and Nagar Haveli and Daman and Diu . Odisha is the only state that has significantly improved. In 2011–12, Odisha's share in exports was only 1.13 per cent; however, it has increased to 4.04 per cent in 2021–22. We can further deep dive into these variations by understanding the district-level export landscape. The DGCIS 2021 data suggests that 683 districts out of 749 districts export from India. However, only nineteen of these 683 districts contribute to around 50 per cent of exports in India. At the same time, the top 100 districts contribute to about 87 per cent of exports from India, whereas the other 583 districts contribute to about a 12.78 per cent share in exports. It must be noted that the export share of Jamnagar, a district from Gujarat, is equivalent to 12.18 per cent, exhibiting a huge regional variation across districts within Gujarat and the rest of India. The limited data examined above implies that broad patterns in national exports may disguise considerable regional variation, especially in emerging economies' export activity.

It must be noted under the Districts as Export Hubs Initiative, items and services with export potential have been selected for all districts across the country. The list of such specified items and services is continuously updated based on feedback from the states or territories. Under this initiative, district export action plans have been developed for such identified products and services destined for international markets. These plans detail the steps that need to be taken to help local exporters and manufacturers produce the products in sufficient quantity and with the necessary quality to attract buyers from outside India. These strategies also include identifying and addressing problems for such identified products or services' exports and enhancing supply chains, market accessibility and handholding to increase exports.

o   *FDI Inflow*

Foreign direct investment (FDI) has long flowed to India, dating back to the twentieth century. It was a favourite destination for FDI in the early twentieth century. It dropped out of favour in the 1970s and 1980s but has regained popularity since the 1990s. It's fascinating to observe how FDI has evolved in India through time as well as what has spurred investment in specific states and how it has changed overall.

India was one of the first countries in Asia to realize that the Export Processing Zone (EPZ) model was a good way to boost exports. In 1965, Asia's first EPZ was set up in Kandla. Since then, seven more EPZs have been set up in different regions of the country, but none of them has been successful in terms of export performance, job creation and foreign direct investment (FDI). Due to a plethora of regulations and clearances, rigid labour laws, a lack of infrastructure and an unstable fiscal climate, the 1991 economic reforms did not result in long-term development in manufacturing.

To address these inadequacies and attract further foreign investment, the SEZ was integrated into India's Export-Import (EXIM) strategy in April 2000, and the SEZ Act was passed in

2005. The SEZ programme provided advantages such as tax breaks, single-window clearance, export and import restrictions flexibility and preferential land policy. Growth in terms of foreign investment, exports and employment was rather moderate in the early stages of the SEZ programme. The transition from EPZs to SEZs occurred in two stages: conversion of existing EPZs to SEZs from 2000 to 2003 and new approvals of new SEZs after 2003. To achieve the goals, the entities were granted unique powers to specifically attract investment into the SEZs, including FDI.

This experience is also in line with, China's phenomenal success in SEZs for attracting FDI. Jin Wang's findings of panel data from 321 municipalities demonstrated that from 1978 to 2007, SEZs in China boosted foreign-owned capital. Together with SEZs, there were a slew of other elements to consider, such as private property rights protection, tax advantages and land-use policies. These have all contributed to a growth in FDI.[40] FDI's percentage of total investment gradually climbed from 12 per cent in 1989 to slightly more than 18 per cent in 2000.[41] In 2004–05, India's SEZ exports accounted for 5 per cent of overall exports. In the same year, they accounted for barely 1 per cent of industrial sector employment and 0.32 per cent of factory investment.[42] However, after 2005, the growth of SEZs in India has been phenomenal with faster increases in FDI inflows. Using panel data from 321 prefecture-level municipalities, Wang demonstrated that SEZs boosted foreign-owned capital in China from 1978 to 2007. There are presently 376 notified SEZs, out of which 272 are operational in different states of India. Total investment and employment in these zones amount to Rs 6,55,995.45 crore and 28,69,083 persons, respectively, as on 31 December 2022. Exports in 2021–22 stood at Rs 9,90,741 crore, which grew by 30 per cent over the 2020–21 figure. This further increased to Rs 3,64,477.73 crore in 2011–12, registering a growth rate of 15.39 per cent over the 2010–2011 figure.[*] It must be noted that most of the operational SEZs are in the more industrialized states. With the highest percentage, 18.52 per cent, being in Tamil Nadu, followed closely by Maharashtra (13.70 per cent), Telangana (13.33 per cent), Karnataka (12.59 per cent), Andhra Pradesh (9.26 per cent) and Gujarat (7.78 per cent).

To begin with, Shraddha Sathe and Morrison Handley Schachler (2006)[43] found that FDI is economically advantageous in the Indian context, with states with greater levels of FDI seeing better growth rates as a consequence. M.R. Murty et al. (2006)[44] investigated the distribution of FDIs by states in the post-liberalization period. It showed that states in the western and southern areas garnered the majority of authorized FDIs despite several backward states drawing foreign investment offers based on their natural resources. Therefore, manufacturing investment will not flow to relatively underdeveloped states except for extractive and natural resource-based businesses. Generally, FDI has favoured developed countries, and the two variables together may increase the disparities between developed and developing countries. To attract investment, states must enhance the entire investment environment, with public investment playing an obvious role.

Vani Archana et al. (2014)[45] examine the effect of FDI on eight major Indian states from 1991 to 2004 using the Fixed Effects (FE), Random Effects (RE) and Seemingly Unrelated Regression (SUR) models. The FE and RE models provide a comprehensive perspective, whilst the SUR model provides a more specific image of India's eight states. The findings suggest that the overall FDI had a favourable influence on labour productivity and employment over the time period studied. Yet, FDI across states is

---

[*] SEZ India Fact Sheet

more productive only when the states have more absorptive ability; and labour productivity is increasing at the price of employment.

Bhanumurthy and Manoj Kumar (2014)[46] in their research outlined that the two most important criteria for evaluating the performance of the Indian economy in regional terms are efficiency and equity. Efficiency in FDI means it tends to go to places with efficient production, while equity focuses on equitable resource allocation. This paper contends that states with low-cost economic production systems, among other variables, have made efficient use of FDI investment. FDI complements domestic investment; therefore, states that are more efficient in general would have a higher efficiency parameter. This specifies the notion of efficiency, and a Centre or state that demonstrates additional production in terms of GSDP deserves to obtain a bigger share of FDI in the following round of FDI distribution. Hence, states that are efficient must be rewarded.

Tamali Chakraborty et al. (2017)[47] sought to determine if the construction of SEZs was successful in drawing greater FDI to the state. Towards that purpose, a panel data study of sixteen states, from 2001 to 2014, was conducted to determine the relationship between FDI inflows and SEZ policies after accounting for other state-specific factors (such as market size, infrastructure and so on). FDI inflows are influenced by factors including location and labour availability.

The findings were consistent with the literature and demonstrated that FDI inflows are considerable. Urbanization and coastal infrastructure are more prevalent in states with greater per-capita wealth (market size and nearness to the ports). Coastal states, such as Maharashtra, Karnataka, Gujarat, Tamil Nadu and Andhra Pradesh, garnered the most FDI. Nonetheless, Bihar and Jharkhand have a low number of SEZs and FDIs. It can also be seen that operational SEZs are mostly concentrated in states with a larger investment, thereby exacerbating regional inequality. The findings show a positive and substantial association between FDI inflows and SEZ policy formation. Further, the findings imply that the SEZ policy and operational SEZ favourably influence attracting FDI to a state.

From a policy viewpoint, to conclude this section, the purpose of creating SEZs is to bring in more equitable development across the states. This does not appear to coincide with the outcomes. FDI remains focused in those states, which have certain geographical advantages. FDI inflows have the ability to improve impoverished states, but these states cannot attract FDI because investors prefer states that provide them infrastructure, market advantages and a risk-free environment. Although SEZs had a significant role in giving a boost to the Indian economy, their contribution in the national figures is below the expected level. Its comparison with other countries shows its potential in attracting FDI and in promoting exports and economic activities has not been fully exploited.

Convergence on Human Development: A Case for Indian States

Before moving into understanding disparities in India when it comes to social progress, we look to a discussion on human development with this excerpt from Hirschman (1973)[48]:[*]

---

[*] His influential works on economic development and social change include *The Strategy of Economic Development* (1958) and *Exit, Voice, and Loyalty* (1970). In these works, he examined the role of individual behaviour and collective action in influencing economic and political outcomes and argued that the decisions people make in response to social and economic changes could have a significant impact on the trajectory of development.

In the early stages of rapid economic development, when inequalities in the distribution of income among different classes, sectors, and regions are apt to increase sharply, it can happen that society's tolerance for such disparities will be substantial. To the extent that such tolerance comes into being, it accommodates, as it were, the increasing inequalities in an almost providential fashion. But this tolerance is like a credit that falls due at a certain date. It is extended in the expectation that eventually the disparities will narrow again. If this does not occur, there is bound to be trouble and, perhaps, disaster.

Albert Hirschman, an economic thinker, drew attention to the tunnel effect over fifty years ago. When individuals become preoccupied with their immediate concerns and neglect to address larger systemic issues, the tunnel effect occurs. This can result in a dearth of innovation, an inability to resolve systemic issues and a deterioration of social cohesion. Initial gratification can lead to a lack of investment in long-term objectives or collective action to address larger systemic issues if it is overemphasized. Because ultimately the initial gratification caused by the hope-inducing tunnel effect, when studied in the context of human development, is something we as a collective society need to be worried about.

Since Hirschman theorized about the tunnel effect, a lot has changed and is continuing to change in India. In a developing country like India, which has huge disparities existing at subnational levels, be it across indicators that measure economic development or social development, individuals may get so consumed with addressing their immediate wants in a society, i.e., basic needs and foundations of wellbeing, such as food, housing and healthcare, that they fail to address the wider systemic flaws that are generating the situation. This might result in people being unable to overcome poverty or enhance their ease of living. It is noted that there is improvement in India over the last decade. It has lifted a staggering 271 million out of multidimensional poverty. The country continues to improve on access to clean water, sanitation and affordable clean energy. India has also improved access to social protection for vulnerable segments of the society, particularly during and after the pandemic, with a 9.8 per cent increase in funding for the social services sector in 2021–22 over 2020–21.[*]

However, the larger question remains the same: Will there be any convergence on human development across Indian states? Have things improved substantially? To examine this, we glance through the literature on HDI. It is observed that HDI-specific studies on India as a whole have been carried but not much literature focuses on Indian states and union territories. It is crucial to investigate the convergence of HDI across Indian states and UTs as this could be the possible answer to addressing the differences across regions in a nuanced manner.

Using a state-by-state HDI decadal data from 1981–91 and 1991–2001, Hiranmoy D. Roy's and Kaushik Bhattacharjee's (2009)[49] paper examines the convergence of human development among the main Indian states. It intends to answer an important question on whether low HDI states will be able to catch up with the high HDI states, using convergence analysis. The analysis results cast doubt on the hypothesis that low HDI states are truly growing quicker than high HDI states, resulting in HDI convergence. However, the dispersion of their cross-sectional HDI is not decreasing over time, indicating that convergence in HDI among Indian states may not be attained over time.

---

[*] India ranks 132 on the Human Development Index as global development stalls | United Nations Development Programme (undp.org)

Ajit Nag and Jalandhar Pradhan (2023)[50] in their study look at the convergence theory for HDI in thirty-six Indian states and union territories from 1990 to 2019. The authors used club convergence method and kernel density estimates to figure out if states tend towards a single steady-state equilibrium or towards various groups. From 1990 to 2019, the figures from thirty-six Indian states show that, on average, human development has moved forward steadily. From 1990 to 2019, HDI has gone up on average at the state level. All signs show that India's different states are getting closer together in terms of their social and economic growth, but this seems to be happening more slowly than before. The results show that states with the lowest HDI get closer together more quickly than states with a higher HDI. The values of kernel density show that HDI stratifies, becomes more polarized and becomes unimodal over time, even though it stays in the same steady state. From 1990 to 2019, the Gini and Theil indices show that the difference in HDI between Indian states and UTs has been getting smaller and smaller. Inequality has gone down a lot in the last twenty-nine years. From 1990 to 2019, the HDI of India's states and UTs shows a small drop in inequality and a weak tendency towards unity. Taking into account all the results, the study recommends promoting regional growth and eliminating inequality.

Social Progress: Variation at the State Level

In this section, we use the findings of the SPI to identify whether states or UTs are translating economic growth into social progress with improved outcomes on non-economic parameters. SPI is a tool that aims to provide a rigorous and complete measure of social development based on social and environmental variables, which may be used to supplement GDP as a measure of well-being. It is based on the assumption that economic expansion without social progress would result in marginalization, environmental deterioration and social unrest. The index is the first comprehensive instrument developed to quantify social growth independently of GDP. Separating the assessment of social advancement from economic growth aids in creating an empirical link between the two ideas, giving individuals a clearer image of how their nation is doing. It contributes to our knowledge of how economic growth promotes social advancement and vice versa, a topic that has long been contested.

The index assesses the social progress of regions based on three dimensions: basic human needs, foundations of well-being and opportunity. The first dimension, basic human needs, evaluates a population's ability to live with appropriate nutrition and basic medical care as well as clean water, sanitation, affordable housing and personal protection. Many impoverished nations still do not meet these demands, and several richer ones frequently fall short. Although necessities have been the primary focus of development economics research, the second pillar of social growth, foundations of well-being, merits equal consideration. It emphasizes the degree to which citizens of a region may receive a basic education, access information, communicate freely, benefit from a contemporary healthcare system and live in a healthy environment conducive to a long life. Almost every country struggles with at least one of these issues. Finally, any assessment of social progress must include the freedom and opportunity for a country's citizens to make their own choices and seek higher education. Personal rights, personal freedom and choice, inclusivity and access to advanced education contribute to a society's degree of opportunity.

The index uses a bottom-up assessment approach to capture diversity in India, providing a granular and holistic perspective at the state and district levels. By identifying and comparing states with identical GSDP and SPI scores, a comparative analysis is presented between states that have been able to outperform and achieve a better degree of social advancement with the same amount of per-capita income. The overall results of the SPI at the state level reveal that even at equivalent levels of GDP per capita, states and UTs experience radically different degrees of social progress.

Figure 56: Correlation GSDP Per Capita vs SPI Scores

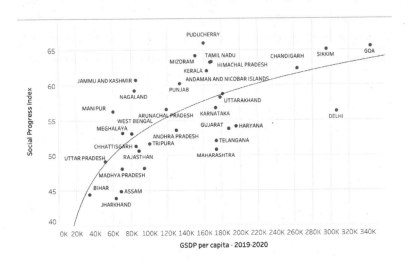

Source: Social Progress Index 2022

For example, a state with a higher GSDP per capita may outperform other states with equivalent incomes in terms of absolute social development, reflecting the benefits of higher income. On the other hand, a state with a lower per-capita income may only achieve minor social advances while surpassing regions with similar levels of prosperity.

According to the Global SPI report (2014)[51] (there is significant evidence that the link between economic development and social progress is caused, at least in part, by the availability of additional resources for public and private support for social challenges as a result of economic growth. Yet, it also observes a definite inverse causal link. Improved health, education, personal safety, opportunity and other health outcomes are critical for high productivity and prosperity levels. As a result, the relationship between economic growth and social advancement is complex, and causation may exist in both ways. There are clearly two findings in the Indian context presented in the report[52] by Amit Kapoor and Michael Green; The first is that SPI scores and GSDP per capita have a positive and strong relationship, and the second is the link between economic growth and social improvement is not linear. At lower income levels, minor variations in GSDP per capita are connected with considerable increases in social progress.

Puducherry, for example, achieves a substantially better degree of social progress (65.99) than Delhi (56.28) in terms of GSDP per capita (Rs 1,59,804 vs Rs 3,06,385). Himachal Pradesh achieves much higher SPI score (63.28) than Uttarakhand (58.26), while having a somewhat lower GSDP per capita (Rs 1,66,895 vs Rs 1,78,050). Telangana has a slightly greater SPI score (52.11) than Maharashtra (50.86), with almost the same GSDP per capita (Rs 1,73,757 for Maharashtra and Rs 1,73,672 for Telangana).

The SPI reveals significant differences between states and territories when non-GDP-related dimensions of well-being are considered. We have observed significant disparities in well-being across India's states and territories. While economic prosperity tends to be positively correlated with higher SPI scores, some states perform significantly better than their GDP-per-capita levels would indicate. Kerala, Tamil Nadu and Puducherry are states that perform well in terms of social progress despite having lower economic prosperity than other states. The urbanization rate is a key factor associated with higher social progress. Access to education, healthcare and other social services is typically greater in urban areas than in rural areas. In addition, urban areas typically have superior infrastructure and a more diverse economy, which can contribute to greater economic prosperity. As shown in the figure below, the majority of states with urban payroll shares exceeding 50 per cent perform well on the SPI.

Figure 57: Urbanization as One of the Drivers of Social Progress in States

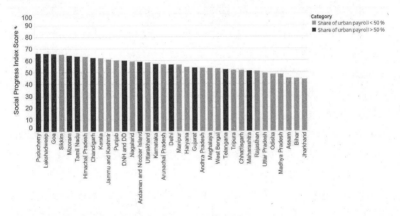

Source: Competitiveness Roadmap for India @100

It is essential to observe, however, that urbanization alone is insufficient to advance social progress. Also essential are policies and investments that promote access to education, healthcare and social services. Moreover, if not properly managed, urbanization can also result in environmental degradation, social inequality and other negative externalities. To enhance overall well-being,

---

* Data sourced Social Progress Index and PLFS—2021

a comprehensive approach that balances economic growth with social and environmental considerations is required.

An examination of social progress was also done at the district level, which further revealed the mixed performance of districts across states on social progress on key indicators that has been explored in the report thoroughly and can be viewed as a tool for state governments to address the issues of social development.

Wealth Quintiles and Gini Coefficient

To analyse the heterogeneity in income between different socioeconomic groups in different regions of India, we use the NFHS-4 and NFHS-5 surveys conducted in 2015–16 and 2019–21. NFHS provides data on the wealth quintiles of households in each state. Wealth quintile data is created based on household asset ownership, access to basic amenities and housing quality on the basis of which score is calculated in NFHS. The assets of ownership may range from a television to a bicycle or automobile, as well as dwelling attributes such as source of drinking water, bathroom facilities and flooring materials, using principal component analysis to calculate weightages. National wealth quintiles are calculated by giving a score to each typical household member and rating each individual based on their score. Each group contains 20 per cent of the population. The wealth quintiles are split into five equal categories, each representing 20 per cent of the population. The data may be used to uncover patterns of inequality and income discrepancies across socioeconomic categories.

The NFHS 2019–21 insights give wealth quintiles based on urban-rural residence and state. Urban regions in India are home to the majority of the country's wealthiest households. Seventy-four per cent of the urban population is in one of the two richest quintiles. More than half of the rural population, 54 per cent, is in the two lowest wealth quintiles. While comparing with NFHS-4, we find that there is not much deviation as the proportion of households in respective wealth quintiles have only slightly decreased by 0.3 per cent in urban areas (in case of richest quintiles), whereas in the case of rural areas, the proportion of population (in case of lowest quintiles) has decreased by 1.1 per cent.

When we look at insights from the state or union territories level, it is found that the largest proportion of the population who reside in the highest wealth quintile is found in Chandigarh, i.e., 79 per cent, followed by Delhi at 68 per cent and Punjab at 61 per cent. Jharkhand, Bihar and Assam have the largest proportion of the population in the lowest wealth quintile, i.e., 46, 43 and 38 per cent respectively.

In this case, we can compare the wealth quintile data for selected states based on similar GDP per capita in 2019–20, reflecting the same prosperity level. This helps us examine the patterns of inequality and disparities in income between two states. To compare the wealth quintile data for the selected five states and one union territory, we can start by looking at the overall distribution of households across the five quintiles and each state. The table below shows the percentage of households in each quintile in selected states.

Group	State/Union Territory	Lowest (1)	Second (2)	Middle (3)	Fourth (4)	Highest (5)	Gini Coefficient
1	Delhi	0.2	2.6	9.2	20.3	67.7	0.08
	Goa	0.5	2.7	9.8	25.7	61.3	0.11
2	Maharashtra	8.6	15.3	22.1	26.1	27.9	0.17
	Tamil Nadu	4.8	15.2	26.4	29	24.6	0.10
3	Bihar	23.9	23.6	18.3	16.4	17.8	0.21
	Uttar Pradesh	42.8	26.1	15.4	10.3	5.4	0.22

Source: NFHS -5

Goa has a per capita income of Rs 3,13,973, whereas Delhi has a per capita income of Rs 2,60,541. The insights reveal that the distribution of households across five quintiles is similar in both regions. In both states, most of the households (over 88 per cent) are in the wealthiest quintiles (4,5), while the poorest quintiles represent around 3 per cent of households each. Maharashtra and Tamil Nadu have almost similar per capita income, i.e., Rs 1,45,165 and Rs 1,44,845. The insights reveal that the distribution of households across five quintiles is similar in both regions. In both states, over 53 per cent of households are in the wealthiest quintiles (4,5), while the poorest quintiles represent around 20 per cent of households each. Uttar Pradesh has a per-capita income of Rs 43,053 and Bihar has a per-capita income of Rs 29,794. The insights reveal that the distribution of households across five quintiles is not similar in both regions. In Uttar Pradesh, over 42.8 per cent households are in the lowest quintile (1), while the wealthiest quintiles (4,5) represent around 16 per cent of households each. Whereas, in Bihar, over 23.9 per cent households are in the lowest quintile (1), while the wealthiest quintiles (4,5) represent around 34.2 per cent of households each.

We now examine the Gini coefficient, a measure of income inequality, for this wealth quintile data. The Gini coefficient varies from 0 to 1, with 0 indicating perfect equality (every family earns the same amount) and 1 suggesting perfect inequality (every household earns the same amount). The table shows a distinct aspect in their Gini coefficient. Before we go any further, it's worth noting that the Gini coefficient is based on household income, which may not represent the entire spectrum of assets and resources accessible to families. As a result, the Gini coefficient may underestimate the real amount of income inequality in any state.

The NFHS Gini coefficient may be computed for each Indian state to assess income disparity within each state. According to the NFHS 2019–21, the states with the highest Gini coefficients are Jharkhand (0.27), Assam (0.25), Meghalaya (0.25) and West Bengal (0.25). Delhi, Kerala, Punjab and Tamil Nadu have the lowest Gini coefficients. Only Delhi has a lower value of 0.08; the others have the same Gini coefficient of 0.10.

An examination of Gini coefficients for Indian states shows some intriguing patterns. To begin, the states with the highest Gini coefficients are those with a big population, such as West Bengal, Bihar and Uttar Pradesh, which have values of 0.25, 0.22 and 0.21, respectively. As a result of the additional complexity of managing a big population and a varied variety of economic activity, larger states may have more difficulties establishing income equality. Second, the states with the lowest Gini coefficients, 0.10 and 0.11, tend to be those at a high degree of development, such as Kerala and Chandigarh. This implies that expenditures in social development, such as education, healthcare and social welfare programmes, may aid in the reduction of economic disparity. Finally, an examination of Gini coefficients for Indian states indicates large regional differences in income inequality. States in India's northeastern area, for example, have lower Gini coefficients. States having Gini coefficients greater than or equal to 0.20 include Assam, Meghalaya, Arunachal Pradesh, Nagaland and Tripura. These states also have a relatively high proportion of households in lower quintiles compared to other northeastern states like Sikkim and Mizoram. This reflects the need for policies that address wealth inequality.

While states in the northern and western areas have higher Gini coefficients, Delhi and Punjab have lower Gini coefficients. This shows that regional disparities in economic and social development may have a role in income disparity. To further understand the heterogeneity of wealth across the various socioeconomic classes in each state, we must look beyond the overall distribution and examine the characteristics of households in each quintile, which is beyond the scope of this section.

Policy Actions: Do States Have Adequate Tools?

Let us talk about the Tinbergen Rule[*] that states that there must be a one-to-one correspondence between the number of policy targets and the number of policy instruments used to achieve those targets. This is because using a single policy instrument to achieve multiple objectives can lead to unintended consequences or ineffective outcomes. However, governments typically have numerous objectives but limited instruments. Consequently, trade-offs are an integral component of government operations. Choices are contingent on preferences and a knowledge of trade-offs. Then, how do we resolve this since trade-offs never change? There is no clear definitive answer, but we know that in its seventy-five years as an independent nation, India has developed using suitable national and state-level policies. So, to solve the economy's imbalances is critical to address the heterogeneity-related issues in the country through policy actions by both the Central and state governments. But before we get into this, it is important to understand the current dynamic relationship between the union and state governments in India, especially in terms of resource allocation and policy tools.

It should be noted that decentralization of powers is of significant importance in addressing issues of heterogeneity in India. This is because state governments have great leverage over the industrial sector at the ground level through their control of land, water, electricity and labour and environmental regulations. The speed with which each state implements these rules reflects

---

[*] Named after Jan Tinbergen, the Dutch economist who was awarded the first Nobel Prize in Economics in 1969 for his work on economic policy.

internal political tensions, as do the divergent views on how best to encourage private investment. There is also growing consensus that the state should refocus its role away from public ownership and control of business enterprises and towards a greater emphasis on health, education and other basic social services for the poor. This is true even when the state is to be the primary funding agency for some of these services; however, this does not mean that the state must be directly involved in the provision of these services. But even though there has been some progress, the policy implementation of this view in many parts of India has been slow and inconsistent. So, more needs to be done by state governments to address these issues. However, over the last few decades, through liberalization, the Fourteenth Finance Commission (FFC) and the Goods & Services Tax (GST), there has been a significant reduction of the discretionary powers of the Central bureaucracy, that resulted in more autonomy to state governments.

The FFC was instrumental in improving the availability of resources to states, enhancing the role of state governments in the general development of the nation. The commission's proposals resulted in a large rise in the percentage of tax money handed to states, giving them more budgetary autonomy and decision-making ability. As outlined in the budget of 2015–16,* the FFC has increased the states' portion of the central divisible pool from 32 per cent to 42 per cent, the largest rise in vertical tax devolution ever. The FFC has also recommended a new horizontal method for allocating the states' portion of a divisible pool. Several different sorts of transfers have been suggested, including grants to rural and urban local governments, a performance grant, disaster relief grants and revenue deficit grants. The introduction of the GST in 2017 represents a significant departure from the constitutional

---

* Vol1-Chap10.pmd (indiabudget.gov.in)

scheme for the distribution of fiscal powers. The proposed dual GST calls for the simultaneous taxation of the same taxable event, i.e., the supply of commodities and services, by the Centre and the states. Therefore, the Centre and the states will be authorized to impose GST across the entire value chain, from manufacturing to consumption.[*] The Aspirational District Programme in 2018[†] exemplified the national government's strategy for mobilizing state and local funds for development. This programme seeks to improve the performance of some of the most disadvantaged districts in India by providing local action and initiative-driven analytical and technical support. The programme is intended to provide these districts with assistance and direction in identifying and addressing their unique development challenges. Recently in 2021, the Fifteenth Finance Commission recommended reducing the share of states in the net tax proceeds from 42 per cent to 41 per cent. This was offset by the creation of a new finance allocation known as vertical devolution. In addition, the Commission suggested the use of demographic factors, performance-based incentives and grants to local governments to encourage fiscal responsibility. This was intended to enable local administrations to provide improved services to their citizens and empower local governments.[‡]

Variances and Convergences

Overall, we examined the variation of Indian states and union territories based on selected indicators for economic development and social progress indices. This becomes important when

---

[*] Concept Note on GST | Department of Revenue | Ministry of Finance | Government of India (dor.gov.in)
[†] Aspirational Districts Programme | NITI Aayog
[‡] Committee Reports (prsindia.org)

policymakers and state governments want to identify areas for improvement and design focused actions to promote shared prosperity and inclusive development by evaluating these variances. As a country, we are stuck between two distinct but linked issues: is development geographically concentrated to the point that just a few states profit from it, and has it resulted in improved social progress in critical areas such as education and health? The former issue necessitates another level of examination of growth and poverty reduction. Moreover, since education and health are primarily state issues under the Indian Constitution, the latter requires a thorough examination at the state level.

This section conducts a comprehensive analysis of disparities and commonalities at the sub-national level in India. It advocates for a more robust and efficient form of cooperative federalism, where the central and state governments collaborate to tackle challenges unique to each state. India's socio-economic landscape is distinguished by its significant diversity. In addition to the policy measures states should adopt, the significance of institutions in bolstering regional competitiveness cannot be understated. Institutions serve as the essential backdrop against which all actions unfold. What lies ahead is to examine the role of institutions in tackling challenges related to heterogeneity, and harnessing opportunities presented by economic heterogeneity for enabling growth.

7

Rewiring the Institutions in India

Throughout this book, our central focus has consistently revolved around the quest to comprehend the underlying factors contributing to economic growth trajectories across nations. Following this, we have conducted a detailed analysis of India's fundamental competitiveness, shedding light on the significant variations in prosperity between nations. Moreover, we have explored how these disparities persist even at the regional level within a country. In the case of India, a nation with a diverse geographic landscape and distinctive cultural traditions, this heterogeneity offers a chance to close the gaps in competitiveness fundamentals at the national level. However, bridging these disparities hinges on addressing the critical policy implementation gap, which is intrinsically linked to the quality of institutions within a nation. The efficacy and outcomes of policy initiatives are, in essence, contingent on the state of institutions. This line of inquiry naturally leads to the pivotal question: How do institutions act as drivers of economic growth? Our ongoing analysis delves into this question, providing a critical backdrop for understanding India's unique policy landscape.

Recognizing the significance of the relationship between institutions and economic growth in India, we must consider how this dynamic resonates within the framework of India's policy history. India's policy trajectory, since achieving independence, has traversed three distinctive phases, each characterized by its own distinct challenges. The initial phase immediately post-1947 witnessed a government-controlled economy, which, despite its best intentions, led to the dominance of capital-intensive industries and limited private sector participation. Subsequently, in the era of economic liberalization and international openness, new challenges emerged as the prevailing conditions posed barriers for new entrants to the market, particularly those lacking the competitive edge of price competitiveness. It is against this backdrop that the policy landscape in India has taken a transformative turn, notably since 2014. The government has strategically focused on mitigating market distortions, employing policies aimed at attracting FDI, fostering the start-up ecosystem and nurturing small and medium-sized enterprises (SMEs). Furthermore, structural reforms, such as demonetization and the implementation of the GST, have been introduced to address issues surrounding informality and trade barriers. The pivotal bridge connecting these policy endeavours and their ultimate success lies in the domain of institutions. Strong institutions serve as the linchpin for the effective implementation of these reforms, thereby ensuring the sustainability of economic growth in India. This connection underscores the significance of institutional quality in shaping the future trajectory of India's economic growth, making it an important aspect of this book.

What Are Institutions?

Institutions in a country establish structures that influence human interaction and activity. In the context of a country, examples of institutions are the policies, government with its executive, legislative and judicial branches, and regulations or laws that shape a country. These are political (political parties, a municipal corporation, political bodies etc.), social (religious organizations, vocational clubs or sports associations), economic (firms, trade unions, cooperatives, corporations), or educational (schools, universities and training centres). These organizations serve a certain purpose in the country, and their success over time is dependent on how well they model themselves according to the overarching institutional framework of the country. Thus, an efficient institutional framework nurtures efficient organizations, whereas an inefficient institutional framework produces similar organizations. The relationship, however, is not unidirectional as organizations are often the driving forces behind institutional changes.[1] In other words, inefficient organizations may drive institutional change in an opposite direction, thereby influencing the trajectory a country takes. Therefore, it is imperative to trace the evolution of institutions in a country to understand its development or the lack of it.

Institutions perform various economic functions that have an impact on efficiency and equity objectives in the market system. Institutions establish markets initially. By safeguarding property rights, ensuring contractual sanctity and maintaining law and order, they establish a conducive atmosphere for the growth and success of private investment and commerce. Therefore, the police, bureaucracy and judiciary are crucial institutions in promoting the growth of markets. Institutions then substitute for and/or regulate markets. The necessity for these functions stems from the need to address market failures and/or the pursuit of other societal objectives, such as the distribution of income. Particularly, markets fail to provide what is deemed socially desirable. For instance, regulatory oversight is necessary to prevent banks and other financial institutions from assuming excessive risk, which may result in bank runs or collapses that impose significant social costs. Water and education may not be provided by the private sector to the most impoverished due to their inability to pay for these services. In addition, fiscal and inflation stability, as well as the prevention of financial crises, are functions of institutions, including central banks and fiscal institutions, which serve to stabilize markets. In conclusion, institutions legitimize markets by means of social protection and insurance mechanisms, and most significantly, by means of redistribution and conflict management mechanisms.[2]

Understanding Institutions' Role in Economic Growth

'Countries with better "institutions," more secure property rights, and less distortionary policies will invest more in physical and human capital, and will use these factors more efficiently to achieve a greater level of income'—Douglass Cecil North[3]

The dominant approach in the social sciences around institutionalism has often been associated with the work of Douglass C. North (1990).[4] His work on institutionalism primarily focuses on the external rules that shape behaviour and outcomes in institutions, guiding individuals' actions and shaping incentives in external settings. In his book he outlines that: 'Institutions are the constraints devised by humans which in turn shape how humans interact with other in a society. In other words, institutions represent the rules that govern a society.'

They can be formal—codified laws, regulations and frameworks, or informal—conventions, traditions or codes of conduct. Since they encompass all the conditions that shape human interaction, their impact can be seen in all aspects of life.

In a country, with a certain set of institutions, an individual undertakes activities, ranging from complex decisions such as contesting an election or applying for a driving licence to mundane, everyday activities such as visiting a bank or driving, all within the rules devised by these institutions. To understand this better, we can utilize an analogy of a sport. A sport has written or codified laws that oversee how the sport will be played. For example, in football, touching the ball with one's hand or harming another player is prohibited. These are the examples of formal constraints. Informally, disrespecting another player verbally is not acceptable; however, there is no written law that prohibits it. In essence, good sportsmanship is an informal constraint that impacts the way a sport is played. In cases of violation, a certain cost is paid by the culprit. Constrained by these rules, the objective of each team in football is to win by using strategy, coordination and skill. The strategies and skills are therefore devised and modelled as a consequence of the rules of the sport. Similarly, in a country, the evolution of its political, economic or social systems is dependent on the kind of institutions that govern it.[5] Just as football teams adapt their strategies and skills within the confines of the rules to secure victory, countries must evolve their political, economic and social systems in alignment with the nature of their governing institutions to achieve success and progress.

Robert. E. Hall and Charles Jonas[6] touched on institutional economics in their work, although it wasn't their main focus. They noted that in the long term, countries achieve higher levels of output per worker due to their capacity to attain substantial rates of investment in physical and human capital, coupled with their ability to employ these resources with a high degree of productivity. Their empirical analysis indicates that success in each of these aspects is intricately tied to the state of a country's social infrastructure. They further note that country's long-term economic performance is largely influenced by its institutions and government policies, which shape the economic environment where individuals and firms invest, create ideas and produce goods and services. Majorly, the paper's findings suggest that differences in social infrastructure across countries significantly influence capital accumulation, educational attainment, productivity and, consequently, income levels across countries. The extent to which countries have adopted different social infrastructures is related to their historical and cultural influences. The paper uses factors like distance from the equator and language data to demonstrate the robustness of the finding that differences in social infrastructure have a substantial impact on income levels.

Daron Acemoglu and other authors in their paper 'Institutions as the fundamental cause of long-run growth'[7] articulated the challenge in the realm of economic theory, noting that despite the foundational contributions of eminent scholars such as John Locke, Adam Smith, John Stuart Mill, Douglass North and Robert Thomas, the intellectual landscape still lacks a comprehensive framework for comprehending the determination and divergence of economic institutions across nations. This body of scholarly work, although instrumental in elucidating the mechanics of economic growth, falls short in delivering a satisfactory account of the divergent growth trajectories observed among different countries. While there exists a well-founded belief in the profound impact of economic institutions on economic growth, there remains an absence of essential comparative static results that would enable the elucidation of the underlying reasons for variations in the equilibrium of economic institutions. It is contended that this deficiency has led to a conspicuous focus within the economics literature on the proximate causes of economic growth, with a corresponding neglect of the fundamental institutional determinants. The paper argues that the available empirical evidence supports the contention that a society's growth trajectory is contingent upon the organizational structure of its economy, which is inextricably linked to its economic institutions. The authors then proceed to propose the foundational elements of a theory of institutions, illustrating their thesis through a series of historical exemplars. Importantly, they stress that any comprehensive theory explaining the diversity of economic institutions among nations must be grounded in the domain of politics, specifically examining the configuration of political power and the characteristics of political institutions.

Overall, the discourse on institutions has also evolved and is not limited to the authors discussed. As discussed above, while institutions are indeed rule-based, they are not merely abstract sets of rules. Institutions also function as complex organizations with their own internal dynamics. They have their own internal norms, cultures, financial resources, systems for hiring and firing and methods for selecting leadership. These internal workings of institutions are often overlooked or treated as a 'black box' in institutional analysis. They are considered both the outcomes of institutional arrangements and factors that contribute to the causal processes.[8]

India's Growth Story through the Lens of Institutions

Understanding the role of institutions in India's growth story requires examining historical legacies. India has a colonial past and it has made significant strides, as we enter the seventy-sixth year of independence, it needs to be acknowledged that our past still haunts our present institutions. Acemoglu, one of the prominent economists in the field of institutionalism, in his paper mentioned colonial experience as one of the many factors affecting institutions. It is useful to point out that his findings do not imply that institutions today are predetermined by colonial policies and cannot be changed. Since mortality rates faced by settlers are arguably exogenous, they are useful as an instrument to isolate the effect of institutions on performance. In fact, the paper suggests that these results suggest substantial economic gains from improving institutions, for example as in the case of Japan during the Meiji Restoration or South Korea during the 1960s.[9]

Roberto Rigobon's[10] paper, which does not primarily focus on institutions, still touches upon aspects related to institutions, particularly addressing the role of institutions in the broader context of economic development and growth. In his paper, he examines the relationship between economic institutions, political institutions, openness (measured by trade/GDP) and income levels using a cross-national dataset. The research uses identification through heteroskedasticity (IH) and divides the dataset into two sub-samples: colonies versus non-colonies and continents aligned along East-West versus North-South axes. The findings show that both democracy and the rule of law have positive impacts on economic performance, with the rule of law having a stronger influence on income levels. Greater openness, measured by trade/GDP, negatively affects income levels and democracy but positively affects the rule of law. Elevated income levels contribute to increased openness and improved institutional quality, with modest effect sizes. The study also highlights the complementary relationship between the rule of law and democracy, suggesting that these factors tend to reinforce each other.

In the context of India, Arvind Subramanian's research provides further insights into the historical evolution of public institutions and their significance for economic growth, Arvind Subramanian[11] investigated the historical evolution of public institutions in India, with a particular focus on the efficacy of customs administration, governance measures based on public perceptions and institutional outcomes. Drawing attention to two paradoxes, the paper examines the two-way relationship between institutions and growth. The first paradox concerns the reason why India experienced a 'dramatic turnaround' in its economic growth despite reforms that have been comparatively modest in scope, particularly in comparison to those of other countries. The second paradox is why institutions have not improved adequately, despite nearly three decades of accelerated growth. The paper argues that pre-independence leaders of India established fundamental market-creating public institutions that are crucial to the country's long-term development, but which may not have kept pace with the economic realities of India today. Certain institutions, particularly those associated with regulation, may not have to be fatally decisive in terms of their influence on growth because alternatives exist in the private sector. Nonetheless, India might be depleting the reserves left by its historical core institutions. This is concerning because the weaknesses in the intangible aspects of these institutions, such as administrative systems, could impede progress just as much as the deterioration of physical infrastructure like roads, power plants and ports.

In his paper, Lant Pritchett (2009)[12] underscores the intricate relationship between India's democratic tradition, its governance and economic growth. He posits that while India has a longstanding democratic heritage, it grapples with challenges in effectively adopting administrative modernism, particularly in the context of its society and politics.* Pritchett's commentary delves into the concept of a 'flailing state', which characterizes a state with weakened governance and implementation capabilities. He points out that India's economic growth, while substantial, has occurred at relatively low absolute income levels. This is indicative of the country's ability to advance from a low-income base, even in the presence of governance weaknesses. Furthermore, he makes a comparative observation by looking at India's neighbours with weaker governance, such as Bangladesh, which has shown that for sustaining economic growth, one only needs 'good enough' governance. He further highlights that many reforms undertaken over the last decades were 'administrative capability-saving' reforms, which create an inhibiting force on private sector efforts through policy implementation uncertainty. He attributed India's economic growth to capital accumulation, capital efficacy and overall productivity growth. It has managed to maintain high levels of savings and investment, partly due to the elite economic policy institutions that are less susceptible to 'flailing' than activities requiring large-scale implementation. He further argues that many post-1991 reform actions have sustained rapid growth by reducing the need for a government agency to improve investments. The relative weakness of the Indian state in implementation capability has also affected the pattern of economic growth, with the growth of the outsourcing industry being an example. Further, Pritchett's concern is that India's 'administrative modernism' is misaligned with the country's politics and society, as political competition often centres around loyalty to identity groups rather than the effective provision of public services. He suggests that India will

---

* Pritchett's original quote in his paper says that 'India was born and has always lived in a democratic tradition, but has increasing weakness in the adoption of administrative modernism in its society and politics.'

navigate its challenges through incremental reforms and learning by doing.

Devesh Kapur et al. (2017)[13] in their book *Rethinking Public Institutions in India* present an alternate perspective on this subject. They discuss the challenges of India's public institutions and address the ideas put forth by Lant Pritchett. In their book the authors note that the major issue recognized by Pritchett and others is the weak accountability of government employees is right. Accountability can be internal (within the organization) or external (to citizens as voters). Some of the bureaucrats themselves suggest in their paper that various ways accountability can be improved i.e., via structural changes, such as allowing more decision-making below the top bureaucratic level, providing better career incentives for elite bureaucrats' performance and incorporating more expertise into policymaking.[14] All these changes can be seen as embodying two fundamental principles: decentralization enhances skill matching and task alignment by implementing modest structural changes at the top, such as pushing decisions down the hierarchy. Competition includes performance expectations, appraisals and potential competition from outsiders to the bureaucracy.[15] These micro reforms can be applied at the state government level as well. More macro reforms are needed to apply decentralization and competition principles across different tiers of government. The 'flailing state' issue, in their view, results from over-centralization, and more expenditure authority needs to be devolved to state and local governments, particularly city and town governments. Decentralization is crucial for fostering effective external accountability, which in turn can enhance internal accountability. Even though they acknowledge that decentralization raises concerns about inequity, corruption and capacity issues. But they further argue that these problems can be directly addressed and are not inherent to decentralization.

How Did India's Institutions Evolve?

After gaining independence from British rule, India opted to construct a parliamentary democratic form of government. To lay its foundation, the Indian Constitution was adopted on 26 January 1950, thereafter commemorated as Republic Day. The foundation of our governance mechanism lies within the Constitution, which is the collection of all rules and laws that govern our country. To enforce the Constitution, various organizations were created such as ministries, armed forces and trade organizations, all functioning under the constitutional framework. To understand the evolution of institutions, we elaborate using the example of one of our foremost institutions: the Parliament.

o   *The Parliament*

Constructed in the heart of New Delhi, the national capital, our Parliament was tasked with enacting legislations and amending the existing legislations as per the needs of the country. The structure of our Parliament makes it a representational organization, where the lower house (Lok Sabha) constitutes of 543 elected members from all parts of the country. The upper house of the Parliament (Rajya Sabha) is composed of representatives from all states and union territories of the land. The purpose of such a representative forum is to aggregate public opinions and discourse into efficient policy and laws. Representatives of each constituency put forth the opinions of their constituents and comment on proposed policies and laws from the perspective of the people who elected them. This is facilitated in two ways in the Parliament. Firstly, by the provision of a Question Hour, the members of Parliament (MPs) can put forth questions to the government at the beginning of every meeting for one hour.[16] These questions are then either brought to the floor for discussion or answered in a written manner. This allows the members to scrutinize various laws and policies passed by the government, facilitating their responsibility of representing their constituents' opinions and preferences. Secondly, any member of the Parliament can present a bill in the Parliament, as long as it does not have any implication on expenditure and taxation, and this bill is termed as a private member's bill. The majority of these bills may not pass; however, it provides an opportunity for the member to put forth an issue in the forum that can later be picked up by the government and thus become a legislation. At the least, public discussion on an issue brings attention to it and contributes to raising awareness towards it. However, despite these provisions, the ability of an elected member to represent their constituents is severely handicapped.[17]

As discussed previously, the efficiency of a framework is also determined by the prevalent norms and customs. In other words, the role of informal constraints is equally important. Firstly, the government exercises immense control over the agenda, which determines the issues that get discussed, when and for how much time. The Business Advisory Committee determines the agenda for the Lok Sabha under the chairmanship of the speaker. The current committee has eight out of fifteen members from the ruling party,* thus holding substantial control over the agenda setting in the lower house. Secondly, despite all members of Parliament enjoying the freedom to present a bill, the government is responsible for the majority of the bills being presented in the Parliament. Thirdly, amendments or recommendations to a presented bill require cabinet approval to be incorporated before the final vote and, thus,

---

* https://loksabha.nic.in/Committee/CommitteeInformation.aspx?comm_code=39&tab=3

are again influenced by the incumbent government. Fourthly, the government holds the power to suspend a debate, by majority vote, or to pass bills without discussion since it mostly holds the necessary voter strength to pass a bill, weakening the opposition's role. Lastly, the members who are representing their constituents and their grievances get no research staff to construct an educated and well-informed argument for the Parliament.[18] This severely inhibits the members in raising the grievances of their electors in a well-informed manner.

This dysfunction in the Parliament is represented by data from various agencies. For example, in 2006, 40 per cent of the total bills in the Lok Sabha, with less than an hour of debate and nearly 65 per cent of members, had nothing to add to the discussion on various legislations. Another expert estimated that only 20 per cent of the total time in the Lok Sabha was spent on debates across seven previous sessions till 2006. As far as representation is concerned, the first-past-the-post electoral system creates its own issues. In 2004, 60 per cent of the elected members secured less than 50 per cent of the votes from their constituency.[19] Thus, their representation is often that of a minority from their constituency, and with the aforementioned issues, even their representation is severely compromised. Similar issues crop up at the state level as well, and thus reduce the scope of addressing local issues and achieving the desired goals of aggregating public opinion through representation to shape India's policies. The failure of the Parliament as a representational organization has given rise to other ways in which the public seeks redressal or shapes the discourse on policymaking.[20] One such way is through Public Interest Litigation (PILs), which uses courts as a venue to shape policymaking in the country. Thus, owing to the lack of representation of local issues in the national forum, the institutional framework of the country was altered to make way for a more decentralized form of governance, i.e., the emergence of local governments.

Role of Decentralization

The Indian Constitution, despite being federal in structure, predominantly concentrated fiscal power with the central government from the 1950s to the 1980s. It wasn't until 1991 that states gained increased authority over their economic and social policies. In 1992, the third tier of government received constitutional recognition in India and truly the story of decentralization in India began.

Decentralization, in theory, refers to the devolution of decision making, resources and political power to democratically elected lower-level authorities.[21] The emergence of the decentralized form of governance can be traced back to the need of location-specific policymaking and the lack of fulfilment of such requirements by the existing levels of government. Thus, by empowering local administration with resources, there is an expectation of better identification and redressal of local issues by efficient implementation of policies. Identifying this, the government of India passed a series of constitutional reforms in 1993 that recognized local governments in urban and rural areas as the third tier of government in the country.[22] The seventy-third and seventy-fourth Constitutional amendments, therefore, named rural bodies—panchayats and urban bodies—and municipal corporations or councils as a form of government. This was to be followed by fiscal decentralization from states, empowering the local governments to better administer their regions. However, this alteration led to different outcomes across the country due to varied response by states. The level of decentralization has varied across regions in India, leading to disparities in the delivery of public services and resource mobilization.[23] Some states have been more successful in this regard. Decentralization has allowed local elites to exert more control over public resources, raising concerns about inequality.[24] On the other hand, some argue that decentralization has promoted equitable development across states, especially through health and education expenditures.[25] Thus, decentralization not only affects growth but also has distributional consequences.

Fernanda Xavier et al. (2021)[26] in their study specifically focused on sub-national (state-level) decentralization due to a lack of data regarding the local (third-tier) level during our study period. Although India has undertaken expenditure decentralization to sub-national governments, there hasn't been substantial progress in tax devolution. Their study spans a thirty-five-year period from 1981–82 to 2015–16, a time during which India underwent significant institutional changes. The early 1990s saw the implementation of open-market policies, and the seventy-third and seventy-fourth constitutional amendments devolved more powers to lower tiers of government. The study finds that an increase in capital expenditure alongside a reduction in revenue expenditure, without affecting the fiscal deficit, positively influenced economic growth. Social sector expenditures, including education and health, played a crucial role in promoting growth and development by enhancing competitiveness, productivity, labour efficiency and poverty reduction. They contribute to existing literature by employing a two-pronged approach. First, they use regression models, employing both expenditure decentralization (ED) and revenue decentralization (RD) as covariates, along with social and capital expenditures. They also employ the Dumitrescu and Hurlin Granger non-causality test to establish causality between growth and decentralization. Second, they augment the regression-based approach with a distribution dynamics model that overcomes issues related to the normality assumption. This approach aids in identifying convergence clubs and polarization among states. The study concludes that both RD and ED have a positive impact on growth, and the influence of social and capital expenditure on economic growth increased after the liberalization period. These findings hold substantial implications for public policy concerning the distribution of powers among different tiers of government in India.

Despite this development, the existing fiscal arrangement between the Centre and states has various shortcomings that prevent efficient fiscal decentralization. Firstly, the expenditure of states is far in excess of their revenue sources, leading them to seek financial help from the Centre.[27] However, states cannot borrow independently from financial institutions as they have to get it approved by the Union Ministry of Finance, thus leaving the fiscal power in the hands of the Central government itself. The general and specific transfer of funds from the Centre to the states is overseen by central bodies. However, often, the transfer has little to do with the revenue-generating capacity of the state and, thus, does not offset the existing fiscal shortages. Secondly, centralized planning in essence negates the effect of federalism and reduces the impact of decentralization.[28] Thirdly, the lack of clear definition of power of the local governments often reduces their ability to act in a meaningful manner. Although the Constitution lists out twenty-nine subjects as the responsibility of local governments, in practice, their corresponding actions are not carried out by them. A few states, such as Karnataka and Kerala, have transferred the responsibility to the local government for all twenty-nine subjects, and the transfer has either been partial or missing in other parts of the country.[29] The institutional framework laid out to efficiently decentralize these powers is not adhered to sufficiently since the pre-existing state organizations have a stronger presence and override such alterations that dilute their powers. Thus, despite having an institutional framework, the desired impacts have not been observed, leaving more to be desired.

How Has the Fiscal Framework Fared?

The fiscal framework in India has demonstrated remarkable stability over time, even with a somewhat fragmented transfer system. This consistency can be attributed to the continued alignment of the fifteen Finance Commissions* approaches since the inception of the Constitution. These commissions play a pivotal role in transferring funds from the central government to the states. Their consistent approach has resulted in relatively steady post-transfer revenue and expenditure shares for both the Union and the States within the general government. While the Constitution outlines the fundamental responsibilities of the Finance Commissions in intergovernmental transfers, each Commission has adapted to contemporary challenges and macro-fiscal conditions to address the evolving development goals of the nation. Each Finance Commission is expected to maintain a degree of continuity in the basic framework while making necessary changes to accommodate changing circumstances. G. Ram Reddy and Y. Venugopal Reddy, in their book[30] on fiscal federalism, have identified five enduring principles in the approach and recommendations of the fourteen previous Finance Commissions. These include a focus on the revenue account, attempts to reduce inequalities among states, a preference for tax devolution over grants, the provision of revenue gap-filling grants without conditions and the use of the 1971 population as a basis for calculations from the Sixth

---

* The Finance Commissions will be referred to as FC-I, FC-II and so on up to FC-XV.

Commission onwards. These overarching principles align with the constitutional spirit and intent and have served the interests of both the Union and the States, promoting fairness among the States. Most of these recommendations have been universally accepted, with the President endorsing them.

Until the 1980s, public institutions in India primarily compensated for market failures by providing essential services such as industry, education, power and water. After liberalization, the blossoming of the private sector was enabled as public sector ceded ground in the economy and created regulatory institutions to oversee markets. Examples of these regulatory institutions include the Securities and Exchange Board of India (SEBI), Telecommunications Authority of India (TRAI), Insurance Regulatory and Development Authority (IRDA), Central Electricity Regulatory Commission (CERC) etc. The National Institution for Transforming India (NITI) Aayog was established on 1 January 2015, with the purpose of replacing the Planning Commission. However, unlike the Planning Commission, NITI Aayog does not possess a role in resource allocation. In the Union Budget of 2017–18, the distinction between plan and non-plan expenditures was eliminated, coinciding with the conclusion of the Twelfth Five-Year Plan in March 2017. Instead, these categories were substituted with the more widely accepted classifications of revenue and capital expenditures.[31]

However, a significant departure from this paradigm occurred with the Fourteenth Finance Commission (FC-XIV) and the Fifteenth Finance Commission (FC-XV). This shift resulted from the abolition of the Planning Commission in August 2014, which marked the end of sixty-five years of central planning and paved the way for structural changes in the transfer mechanism to the States. Until then, from the Third Finance Commission

(FC-III) to the Thirteenth Finance Commission (FC-XIII), with the exception of the Ninth Finance Commission (FC-IX), recommendations had largely pertained to the non-plan revenue accounts of both the Union and the States. The introduction of the nationwide GST in India in July 2017 brought about a substantial transformation in the country's indirect taxation system. To oversee the formulation of the tax's structure, design and operation, the GST Council was established, consisting of representatives from both the Union and the States. Simultaneously, recognizing the need to address the structural and procedural modifications resulting from the dissolution of the Planning Commission, the Fifteenth Finance Commission (FC-XV) was instituted in December 2017.[32]

Overall, India's fiscal framework has shown stability, but it is now acknowledged that further changes to its institutional framework are needed to become a developed economy. The shift from central planning to a market-oriented approach has contributed to India's economic growth. Despite perceptions of institutional decline, India has experienced remarkable economic growth in the past three decades. Some public institutions have shown positive growth, such as the judiciary, which has become an avenue for citizen participation in policymaking. Constitutional amendments, such as the seventy-third and seventy-fourth amendments, have promoted decentralization and transparency, and legislation like the Right to Information (RTI) has further enhanced public access to information. However, some institutions, like Parliament, have faced challenges, while others have remained stagnant.[33, 34] To achieve developed economy status, India needs comprehensive reforms, promoting transparency, efficiency and accountability. But most importantly it needs competitive architecture.

Institutions as the Beacons of Progress: Representatives across the Globe

As discussed, institutions play a critical role in the effective implementation of policies that promote national competitiveness. The success of policies depends not only on the content of the policies themselves but also on the ability of institutions to implement them efficiently and effectively. Effective institutions provide a stable and predictable environment that enables individuals and businesses to plan for the future with confidence. They also ensure that policies are implemented in a manner that enhances the competitiveness of the country. Countries that invest in developing effective institutions are more likely to attract foreign investment, create jobs and improve the quality of life for their citizens.

By understanding the good practices of institutions around the world, countries can adopt policies and strategies that promote effective policy implementation and enhance their competitiveness on the global stage. Continuing with this line of thought, this section explores good practices from around the world that highlight the role of institutions in promoting national competitiveness through effective policy implementation. Specifically, this section will examine the Economic Development Board (EDB) in Singapore, the competitiveness councils in Colombia, the institutionalization of public-private dialogue in Peru and the adoption of Sustainable Development Goals (SDGs) at a local level in India. By examining these examples, we will identify the factors that contribute to the success of effective institutions and explore how they contribute to national competitiveness. Before delving into examples, we will briefly discuss the role of institutions in policy implementation.

Examples of good practices from around the world:

a.   Economic Development Board (EDB) in Singapore

The first example explores how capacity building by institutions helps a country improve its competitiveness. For this, we go to Singapore and its EDB. The EDB is a government agency in Singapore that promotes economic growth and attracts foreign investment. The EDB is responsible for implementing policies that encourage businesses to invest in Singapore and create jobs for its citizens. The EDB provides a range of services to companies, including market intelligence, business advisory services and investment facilitation.[35] The EDB is widely recognized as one of the most effective institutions in promoting economic growth and attracting foreign investment.

The success of the EDB is attributed to several factors. First, the EDB has a clear mandate and operates with a high degree of autonomy, which allows it to respond quickly to changing economic conditions. The EDB's sole purpose is to promote economic growth and attract foreign investment, which allows it to concentrate its efforts and resources effectively. Second, the EDB has a strong institutional framework that ensures coordination and collaboration among stakeholders. The EDB has a strong focus on building partnerships with businesses and other government agencies, which enables it to implement policies that are responsive to the needs of stakeholders. Third, the EDB has a customer-oriented approach that prioritizes the needs of businesses. The EDB provides customized services to companies, which has helped it to establish a reputation for responsiveness and flexibility. Finally, the EDB is committed to developing a highly skilled workforce, which makes Singapore an attractive destination for businesses that require a skilled workforce. Along with these features, one of the key factors that contributes to the success of the EDB is its ability to provide a stable and predictable environment for businesses to operate in. Singapore has a well-developed legal and regulatory framework, which provides businesses with the confidence that their investments will be protected.[36] Therefore, the ability of institutions to foster a conducive environment and enable innovation is directly reflected in a country's competitiveness.

b.   **Competitiveness Councils in Colombia**

Moving to the continent of South America, the second example highlights the role of institutions in improving coordination and collaboration among diverse stakeholders. In Colombia, the Competitiveness Councils were established in the late 1990s as a public-private partnership to promote economic growth and competitiveness. The councils are composed of representatives from the public and private sectors and are responsible for developing policies and strategies to improve competitiveness. The councils have been successful in promoting public-private dialogue and collaboration, which has led to the development of several successful initiatives.[37] The Competitiveness Councils' success can be attributed to several factors. First, they provide a platform for public-private dialogue, which promotes collaboration and consensus building. The councils bring together stakeholders from different sectors and allow them to work together towards a common goal. The councils provide a platform for businesses, academia and government officials to collaborate and identify opportunities for growth, and their ability to bring and channel different stakeholders towards a common goal has been a key factor towards its success. Second, the councils have a clear focus on competitiveness, which ensures that policies and initiatives are aligned with the goal of improving competitiveness. Third, the councils have a flexible institutional framework that allows for adaptation to changing circumstances. The councils have been able to adjust their strategies and initiatives in response to changes in the global economic environment.

c. Institutionalization of Public-Private Dialogue in Peru

Continuing in South America, the next example highlights the impact of effective stakeholder engagement. In Peru, the government established the National Council for Competitiveness and Formalization (CNCF) to create a space for dialogue between the private sector and the government. The CNCF is an inter-institutional body composed of representatives from the executive, legislative and private sector. The council's main objective is to improve the country's competitiveness by promoting the formalization of economic activities and reducing informality. The CNCF is composed of various working groups that focus on specific areas such as labour, education, justice and finance.[38] These working groups are responsible for analysing the issues related to their respective areas and proposing solutions. Once a solution is proposed, it is then evaluated by the council and, if approved, forwarded to the government for implementation. The institutionalization of public-private dialogue through the CNCF has been successful in improving policy implementation in Peru. For example, the council proposed a reform to the labour market that aimed to increase the flexibility of labour contracts while also protecting workers' rights. This reform was passed by the government and resulted in an increase in formal employment and a reduction in informality. The institutionalization of public-private dialogue has also been successful in promoting transparency and accountability by requiring the publication of reports on the activities of the public-private dialogue mechanisms.

d. The Role of Effective Policy Research in Ireland

For our fourth example, we move to Ireland to look at the impact of informed policy recommendations based on sound research in promoting competitiveness. The National Competitiveness Council (NCC) in Ireland plays a critical role in enhancing the country's competitiveness. As an independent advisory body, the NCC provides evidence-based policy recommendations to the Irish government on how to improve economic competitiveness and the quality of life for its citizens. Established in 1997, the NCC's work is based on rigorous analysis of the Irish economy and benchmarking against other countries.[39]

One of the key contributions of the NCC to national competitiveness is its economic analysis. The NCC conducts research and analysis of the Irish economy, identifying the key factors that impact its competitiveness. The analysis is based on a wide range of economic indicators, such as productivity, innovation, infrastructure, education and healthcare. Through this analysis, the NCC provides valuable insights into the strengths and weaknesses of the Irish economy and identifies areas where improvements can be made to enhance competitiveness. The NCC also provides policy recommendations to the Irish government on how to improve competitiveness. These recommendations are based on the analysis of the economic environment and focus on areas where improvements can be made. The NCC works closely with the government to ensure that its recommendations are implemented effectively. This collaborative approach helps to ensure that the policies recommended by the NCC are aligned with the government's priorities and that they are implemented in a way that maximizes their impact. Another important contribution of the NCC to national competitiveness is its benchmarking reports. The NCC benchmarks Ireland's performance against that of other countries to identify areas where the country is falling behind and where improvements can be made. These reports provide valuable insights to the Irish government and other stakeholders on how to improve national competitiveness. The reports arc widely used by policymakers and other stakeholders to inform decision-making and to guide the development of policies and initiatives that promote competitiveness.[40]

The NCC is also involved in promoting education and training in Ireland. It identifies skills gaps in the economy and makes recommendations to improve education and training policies to address these gaps. The NCC also promotes lifelong learning and encourages workers to upskill to meet the changing needs of the economy. Through these efforts, the NCC helps to ensure that the Irish workforce is equipped with the skills and knowledge needed to compete in the global marketplace.[*] In addition to education and training, the NCC also identifies infrastructure gaps in Ireland's economy and makes recommendations to improve the country's infrastructure. This includes recommendations on transportation, broadband and energy infrastructure, which are essential for attracting foreign investment and supporting the growth of indigenous businesses. By identifying these gaps and recommending improvements, the NCC helps to ensure that Ireland's infrastructure is equipped to support economic growth and competitiveness. Finally, the NCC promotes innovation in the Irish economy and encourages businesses to adopt innovative practices. Innovation is a key driver of competitiveness and is essential for maintaining a competitive edge in the global market.[41] The NCC's promotion of innovation helps to foster a culture of

[*] http://www.competitiveness.ie/media/ncc090309_statement_on_education_presentation.pdf

creativity and entrepreneurship in Ireland, which is vital for the country's economic future.

Therefore, the National Competitiveness Council (NCC) in Ireland is a critical player in enhancing the country's competitiveness. Through its economic analysis, policy recommendations, benchmarking reports, promotion of education and training, infrastructure recommendations and promotion of innovation, the NCC helps to ensure that Ireland remains competitive in the global marketplace.

e. Adoption of Sustainable Development Goals (SDGs) at a Local Level in India

Coming to India for our final example, we explore the role of strong decentralized institutions. The SDGs are a set of seventeen goals adopted by the United Nations in 2015 to be achieved by 2030. The SDGs are designed to address various global challenges such as poverty, hunger, health, education, gender equality, clean water and sanitation, affordable and clean energy, decent work and economic growth, industry, innovation and infrastructure, reduced inequalities, sustainable cities and communities, responsible consumption and production, climate action, life below water, life on land, peace, justice and strong institutions.

While the SDGs are a global agenda, their implementation and achievement depend on actions taken at the national and sub-national levels. To this end, India has adopted the Sustainable Development Goals (SDGs) at a local level to promote sustainable development and improve the quality of life for its citizens. The SDGs provide a framework for governments, businesses and other stakeholders to work together to achieve common goals. Bringing in an institution-level change, in India, the adoption of the SDGs at a local level has been institutionalized through the creation of District Sustainable Development Goals (DSDGs).)[42] The DSDGs are a set of goals and targets developed at the district level in India to ensure that the SDGs are implemented in a manner that is tailored to the specific needs and context of each district.

Incorporating effective stakeholder engagement, the DSDGs are developed through a consultative process that involves various stakeholders such as government officials, civil society organizations, community leaders and citizens. Once developed, the DSDGs are integrated into the district's planning process, and the progress towards achieving the goals is monitored regularly. The institutionalization of the DSDGs has been successful in improving policy implementation and competitiveness at the local level in India. For example, in the district of West Godavari in the state of Andhra Pradesh, the DSDGs have helped to improve access to clean water and sanitation by constructing new toilets and improving existing ones. Additionally, the DSDGs have helped to promote sustainable agriculture practices by encouraging farmers to adopt organic farming techniques.[43]

The success of the adoption of SDGs at a local level in India is attributed to several factors. First, the adoption of the SDGs has been led by local governments, which enables them to develop policies that are responsive to the needs of their communities. Second, the adoption of the SDGs has been supported by businesses and other stakeholders, which has enabled the development of partnerships that promote sustainable development. Finally, the adoption of the SDGs has contributed to the country's competitiveness by promoting sustainable development and improving the quality of life for its citizens.

After discussing these examples, the importance of effective institutions in promoting national competitiveness through effective policy implementation can be understood. The success of these institutions is attributed to several factors, including a clear mandate, a high degree of autonomy, a focus on building partnerships with stakeholders and a commitment to developing a highly skilled workforce. By adopting these practices, countries can create an environment that attracts foreign investment, creates jobs and improves the quality of life for their citizens. Furthermore, the examples discussed illustrate the importance of public-private partnerships in promoting national competitiveness. By bringing together government officials, business leaders and other stakeholders, these partnerships create an environment that is conducive to economic growth and development. They enable the development of policies that are supported by stakeholders and promote innovation and entrepreneurship.

Need for Institutional Evolution for National Progress

Institutions play a significant role in promoting effective policy implementation, which, in turn, determines a country's success. Institutions are the points in a country where ideas converge and change happens, making their role tremendously crucial to a country's economic and social landscape. Indian institutions have embarked on this journey across these seventy years, with most of them evolving and becoming the harbingers of change. The vitality of the Parliament as an institution is not a matter of debate, as is not its dysfunction. There is a need for the Parliament to serve as a more effective representative institution. A landmark institutional change has been decentralization. Constitutionalized in the 90s, the third tier of government was given formal powers and responsibilities, effectively paving the way for local governance. Although marred by somewhat ineffective implementation—states acting reluctant when asked to relinquish and unclear demarcation of roles leading to dispute at times—decentralization has been a welcome institutional change and can be leveraged to drive change in the country. Building on this, we explored how institutions effectively contribute to a nation's progress and how they can mitigate the challenges that exist in the country. India has witnessed significant growth over the past years; however, widespread inequality has made the disparity between the rich and the poor starker, which reproduces itself with rising poverty, low rates of education, unproductivity, etc. Furthermore, the lack of jobs, especially productive jobs, has hampered the growth of the country. To address these challenges, India has consistently formulated targeted policies, but there is an opportunity for improvement in implementing these initiatives more effectively. This is where institutions come in. They ensure that policies are implemented efficiently and effectively, which also contributes to the competitiveness of a country. This is achieved by establishing clear procedures for policy implementation, monitoring the implementation process and holding individuals and organizations accountable for their performance. When policies are implemented efficiently and effectively, they are more likely to achieve their intended outcomes, which can contribute to national competitiveness. For businesses, effective institutions provide a stable and predictable environment that enables individuals and businesses to plan for the future with confidence. This stable and predictable environment is created by establishing and enforcing rules that govern the behaviour of individuals and businesses. For example, a strong legal system ensures that contracts are enforced, property rights are protected and individuals are held accountable for their actions. When individuals and businesses have confidence in the legal system, they are more likely to invest in the country and take risks that promote economic growth. Effective institutions also play a role in promoting innovation and entrepreneurship. By providing support for research and development, institutions can create an environment that fosters innovation and entrepreneurship. For example, institutions may provide funding for research and development, create tax incentives for businesses that invest in research and development or provide training and mentorship for entrepreneurs. Building institutions along these lines enables a country to drive towards progress. India has to make concerted efforts towards overhauling its institutional framework by understanding its shortcomings and addressing them in a swift and effective manner. For this exercise, India can look towards its Asian neighbours such as Singapore, which has effectively established an institution aimed at fostering and maintaining a business-conducive environment. Similarly, the examples of Peru and Colombia highlight the role of effective stakeholder management, facilitating their coordination and collaboration to drive policy change. The example from Ireland illustrates the role of informed policy decisions in improving national competitiveness. Thus, India has immense potential and a robust foundation of institutions. However, to stay abreast with changes, the institutions need to evolve. This section was an attempt to pave a guideline on how we can achieve that and build our country to ensure a progressive future.

Tryst for New Institutional Framework

The significance of robust and effective institutions for fostering economic development and growth cannot be overstated. In recent years, institutions and property rights have garnered substantial attention as key factors in explaining economic growth. The literature we have examined on institutions in India suggests that India's economic growth has undergone a remarkable turnaround despite modest reforms when compared to most countries. However, the quality of institutions has not improved significantly, even after nearly three decades of accelerated growth.

Regardless of the underlying causes, a notable observation emerges: India's economic growth has outpaced the enhancement of its institutions. This observation raises concerns, as weak institutions have the potential to hinder long-term economic growth and overall development. The relationship between institutions and economic growth is complex, lacking a straightforward and unequivocal explanation. Nevertheless, the chapter attempts to convey a compelling message: India needs to undertake substantial efforts to strengthen its institutional framework to ensure the enduring sustainability of its economic growth. This underscores the critical imperative for India to address the persistent institutional challenges that may hinder its continued economic progress.

While this chapter introduces a myriad of complex inquiries, it is essential to acknowledge its limited scope, which is focused on examining the current state of Indian institutions. This chapter attempts to shift focus on the need for India's economic growth to be accelerated through institutional reforms. Thus, its aim is not to provide an exhaustive survey of the literature but to outline some primary conceptual needs, particularly the necessity for India to establish a set of principles on which a new institutional framework can be built. For this no doubt, strong institutions will serve as guiding principles for the future growth story of the Indian economy.

8

The Guiding Forces

As we journey through the various facets of India's development trajectory, we recognize that our exploration of competitiveness fundamentals, the bottom-up approach to growth and institutional efficiency has laid the foundation for understanding the guiding forces that will shape India's forward path. What lies ahead for India? The answer to this question depends on our understanding of India's key challenges to and potential for growth. With the onus of lifting over a billion of its people into prosperity, India faces a daunting challenge. According to projections from the IMF, India is on track to become the world's third-largest economy by 2027, surpassing both Japan and Germany, with a GDP exceeding $5 trillion. If the goal is to become a developed economy by 2047, Deloitte estimates that India will need to maintain a growth rate of at least 6.5 per cent by 2027 and between 8 per cent to 9 per cent in the lead-up to 2047[1]. The country today falls under the lower middle-income category and to match the prosperity levels of a developed or upper middle-income country, there has to be an increase of at least 80 per cent in the prosperity levels measured at PPP terms. There are two sides to the path ahead—one, maintaining consistent growth on economic indicators (like GDP, growth rate, etc.) and two, improving performance on development indicators (encompassing quality of life, standard of living, etc.). To contextualize, India stood 40th (in 2022 as well as in 2023[2]) among the 132 countries assessed under the Global Innovation Index released by WIPO signalling a massive improvement from its 81st rank in 2015. On the contrary, India ranked 110th (in 2022), among the 169 countries assessed under the SPI. India's SPI score was 60.19, below the global average of 65.24*. This juxtaposition of India's performance on two conceptually different assessments highlights the fact that to attain holistic development, improvements in both the economic and social dimensions of competitiveness are essential. The current economic vitality is instilling confidence that these targets are achievable, at least in the short term. However, the pace of growth in the initial years will be pivotal for establishing a sustained and rapid growth trajectory in the long term.

While India showed a high GDP growth rate (6.8 per cent) in 2022, the wealth inequality was also high with a Gini coefficient of 82.5. Additionally, the top 1 per cent share of wealth was 40.4 per cent[3]. This necessitates the need for interventions towards enabling equitable growth and equitable distribution of wealth among the population. The percentage of poor people remains very high in the country, with over 16 per cent of the population classified as poor according to the Global Multidimensional Poverty Index (GMPI) 2023. Although the income levels have improved, about 21.9 per cent of the population are living below the monetary poverty line (national). This indicates an opportunity for India to

---

* https://www.socialprogress.org/

enhance the well-being of its citizens, ensuring that it mirrors the substantial economic and social progress achieved. In addition to addressing income disparity, India is actively working to bridge regional gaps, ensuring that all states benefit from favourable trade policies and contribute to overall development. Although progress has been made towards taking basic services such as water, power and fuel to people, large parts of the country remain unconnected to the global economy. To use an example, despite a centralized focus on exports across the country, the top ten states of the country, in terms of export value, contributed to nearly 85 per cent of all the exports.[4] Thus, in order to achieve further growth and boost competitiveness, India needs to focus on a holistic model of development as various regions across the country are unable to fulfil their potential.[5] Before we delve into what these guiding forces are, it is important to recall the competitiveness framework and its fundamentals, which will form the basis for a discussion on the guiding forces.

Alluding to Michael Porter's competitiveness framework as detailed in Chapter 4 of this book, competitiveness lies at the core of wealth creation and economic performance. It hinges on the efficient use of resources and productivity, with the metric of output per potential worker serving as a key indicator. The competitiveness framework encompasses a wide range of factors, categorizing them into macroeconomic and microeconomic dimensions. Macroeconomic competitiveness considers factors like social infrastructure and political institutions, addressing vital aspects, such as education, healthcare, the strength of rule of law and security and monetary and fiscal policies, collectively shaping the overall economic landscape. On the other hand, microeconomic competitiveness includes determinants such as factor conditions, which assess the quality and quantity of available labour, access to capital, administrative practices and the state of physical infrastructure, and demand conditions that gauge the sophistication of consumer demand and expenditure patterns. The difference between macroeconomic and microeconomic factors of competitiveness lies in their scope and focus. Macroeconomic factors are broad and affect overall productivity at the country level, such as the rule of law and healthcare. In contrast, microeconomic competitiveness focuses on specific advantages that local businesses and industries can leverage to succeed both domestically and globally, focusing on factors like business management, operational efficiency and regional clusters. Essentially, macroeconomic factors shape the broader economic environment, while microeconomic factors pertain to the competitive advantages of individual firms within a region. Understanding competitiveness in this holistic manner provides a nuanced view of a country's strengths and weaknesses, highlighting the interplay of macroeconomic and microeconomic factors in driving productivity and fostering economic growth.

To explicate the competitiveness fundamentals crucial for India's journey towards shared prosperity, this chapter presents a brief analysis of key dimensions like skills and education, access to capital, infrastructure, market regulations, costs of doing business and trade and FDI policy. Skills and education, infrastructure, trade and FDI policy and market regulations address the macroeconomic fundamentals and costs of doing business and access to capital address the microeconomic fundamentals necessary for improving competitiveness. The attempt is to understand the core issues prevalent in these areas and highlight the policy actions that can be directed towards addressing them. The later sections of the chapter put forth the 4Ses – the new guiding forces, as outlined in the Competitiveness Roadmap for India@100 report, as an approach towards addressing the challenges that the state of India's competitiveness fundamentals highlight. This is further substantiated by a list of new policy priorities and a new institutional architecture that have the potential to increase India's prosperity levels.

India's Competitiveness Fundamentals: An Overview

As highlighted earlier in Chapter 4, labour productivity and labour mobilization determine a country's competitiveness. The fact that the very definition of competitiveness as outlined by Porter is output per potential worker, indicates the centrality of labour in the competitiveness approach. The rationale for choosing the following six dimensions (skills and education, access to capital, infrastructure, market regulations, costs of doing business and trade and FDI) for this analysis is that each of them have one common input factor—labour. These dimensions have many direct and indirect linkages that can potentially improve or deter labour productivity and labour mobilization. Therefore, to improve competitiveness, addressing the challenges in these key dimensions is necessary. The World Economic Forum measures global competitiveness assessing the set of institutions, policies and factors impacting productivity levels in the country.[6] This assessment is released in the form of the Global Competitiveness Report (GCR) that entails four sub-indices, enabling environment, human capital, markets and innovation ecosystem, covering 12 pillars and 103 indicators. The report examines the nation's policies enabling conditions conducive for entrepreneurship and research and development. In the 2019 edition of the report, India ranked 68th among 141 countries. However, on innovation India's rank was 35th, on the financial sector, it was 40th, and on macro-economic stability, 43rd.[7] Overall, by international measures of competitiveness, as in the Global Competitiveness Report, India's competitiveness is considerably higher than most of its lower middle-income peers in the South-Asian region.

Figure 58: India's Competitiveness to Prosperity Gap

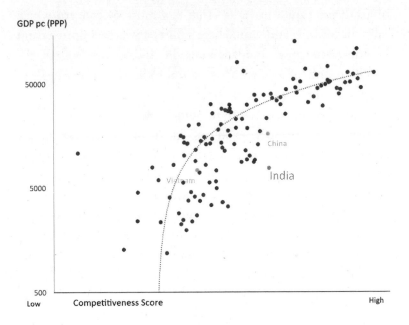

Source: Competitiveness Roadmap for India @100

Despite a good score on these assessments, there exists a mismatch between the prosperity levels measured in terms of GDP per capita (PPP) and the competitiveness levels that India exhibits. China's competitiveness levels are similar to that of India but in terms of prosperity, India lags behind. Similarly, Vietnam

---

* Data sourced from Global Competitiveness Report data for 2018, ISC analysis based on Delgado et al. 2008

with competitiveness levels lower than India's, is way ahead of India in prosperity levels. This gap between competitiveness and prosperity levels in India's case, seems to have increased. While higher growth rates reflect high levels of competitiveness, and offer potential for firms to achieve higher productivity and value creation, this improvement in not adequately reflected in GDP per capita in India. That is a cause of concern which calls for sincere and immediate efforts towards improvement of competitiveness fundamentals in India that reflect the overall health of competitiveness in India and translate into improvements in prosperity levels. In order to truly understand why competitiveness levels in some cases do not adequately translate into prosperity advancement, we must investigate underlying reasons. The focus should not just be on the mere presence of certain rules and regulations for business environment in a country but also on the way they are implemented on the ground. There is a need to address inefficiencies and gaps in Indian market structures to ensure that high levels of investment lead to higher outcomes. In this context, the 2019 GCR edition revealed that key productivity aspects were being overlooked in their assessment of competitiveness. Thus, in 2020, the GCR rankings were paused to shift focus to recovery, revival and creating new economic systems that prioritize 'productivity', 'people' and 'planet' targets. The report planned to return to its benchmarking exercise in 2021, emphasizing long-term prosperity over short-term gains.[8] India, also, thus requires to not only focus on what policies to pursue but also on how to design and implement them comprehensively across the various segments of the economy.

A Closer look at Key Dimensions of India's Competitive Fundamentals:

o *Skills and Education*

Education has always been a key focus area in the Indian economy through the years. In the recent years, there has been a remarkable emphasis on education by the government as education is allocated around 10.02 per cent of the total budget in the period between 2017–22.[*] India's expenditure on education as a percentage of GDP in the year 2020, stood at 4.5 per cent, remarkably higher than the South Asian region combined. Although the statistics have experienced an upward trend in the years since 2015, it significantly lies below the target of 6 per cent set under the New Education Policy, 2020.[9] The increased public expenditure on education has proven fruitful for the masses as it has led to improved access to education. The primary school enrollment rate stood at a staggering 108.1 per cent for the year 2022.[†] The high levels of primary school enrollment can be attributed to the implementation of the Right to Education Act in 2009. The Act mandates the Government to provide free and compulsory primary education to all children between 6 and 14 years of age. As per 2021–22, 97.9 per cent of the population of the country had access to primary schools in the country.[10] The secondary and tertiary school enrollment rates in the country also reached its highest in the year 2021 at 78.5 per cent and 31.3 per cent respectively.[‡] Thus, it can be concluded that students have considerable access to education in the country.

---

[*] Union Budget documents, 2017–22.

[†] https://databank.worldbank.org/reports.aspx?source=2&series=SE. PRM.ENRR&country=

[‡] https://databank.worldbank.org/reports.aspx?source=2&series=SE. SEC.ENRR&country=

The primary challenge encountered in the Indian education sector revolves around the need for enhanced quality and better alignment of skills with the job market. Even though the country has made significant strides in ensuring access to education for all, there is a need to improve the learning outcomes of children for quality education. As discussed in Chapter 6, the level of learning of the Indian students in various subjects has been subpar, with the students scoring less than 40 per cent for all subjects in Class X except English. This can be attributed to many factors in the Indian context. As pointed out in Chapter 6, teacher absenteeism in the educational institutions, especially in public/government schools, is a major factor for the poor performance of students, indicating the lack of sufficient number of teachers. As a result, these schools have become enormously ineffective. Therefore, because public schools are so inefficient, private schools have emerged as an alternative for the students in the country, but a higher cost of education in the private sector makes it unfeasible for the financially deprived to access high quality education. Although the RTE mandates 25 per cent of the seats in private schools to be reserved for the disadvantaged sections, the cost of education in private schools remains high owing to high secondary costs involved in education in the private sector, making it impossible for poor sections of the society to access high quality education.[11]

With about 353 new universities established in the country,[12] access to higher education for students has expanded, as seen from the increasing enrolment rates in higher education in the country. However, students in higher education face a distinct problem of skill mismatch with the job market, as the skills taught at this level of education do not align with the skills required by the job sector. The trend among the unemployed youth of the country is a true depiction of the same as 42.3 per cent of the graduates below the age of 25 were unemployed in the year 2021–22.*As per the World Economic Forum, one in ten graduates in the country lack the skills to be employed in the formal sector in the country[13]. The lack of vocational training and low education attainment were identified as the key reasons for the underlying situation.[14] India has taken significant steps in the direction of improving the quality of education and reducing the mismatch in the Indian education and job market. The New Education Policy (NEP), 2020 is a significant step taken in this direction. In order to achieve better learning outcomes in the nation, NEP aims to reduce the teacher pupil: ratio in primary schools to 30:1 to enable teachers to give more attention to each child in the classroom, and to achieve the aim of attaining Foundational Literacy and Numeracy in primary schools by 2025[15]. For higher education, NEP focuses on developing a multidisciplined structure in universities and colleges, bridging the gap between academic and vocational training to diversify the skillsets available to the younger population, making them more employable for the current job market. To facilitate the skill development of the population even further, the Government of India launched the Skill India Mission in 2015. The mission comprises of four schemes focusing on reskilling and upskilling of the workforce with Pradhan Mantri Kaushal Vikas Yojana, being the key scheme under the programme. Between 2017 and 2023, 1.1 crore people were trained, and 21.4 lakh people were placed under the second phase of the PMKVY scheme.[16]

Despite the continued efforts of the Government of India, the education sector still faces significant challenges. The onset of the COVID-19 pandemic caused a huge amount of learning

---

* State of Working India 2023, Azim Premji University, 2023.

loss for the students in the country. In-person learning, which is a critical requirement during the foundational years of education, faced challenges during the pandemic and it negatively impacted the student's ability to acquire basic competencies. As a result, many students who have been promoted to higher grades after the schools resumed do not have the adequate basic knowledge and skills necessary to proceed further. Therefore, if these gaps are addressed in the initial years, the learning disparities can be significantly reduced. In addition, the implementation of the NEP faces significant challenges, which includes inadequate financial expenditure and digital infrastructure. Many schools require basic infrastructure needed to implement the policy's guidelines. One of the key goals of the NEP is to develop the technological skills of children in the economy. However, only 33.9 per cent of schools have access to the Internet, which poses a major challenge in achieving this goal.[*] The emphasis of the policy in focusing upon a state's mother tongue as a medium of education has raised several issues among the states and may further aggravate the gap between the English speaking and non-English speaking population in the nation as there is lack of reading/learning materials in different languages.[17] To overcome this challenge, there is a need for better training of teachers and development of a thorough curriculum to equip the teachers with the necessary pedagogical skillsets. Along with it, the country's focus should also be on developing digital infrastructure amongst schools as it will not only facilitate the successful implementation of the NEP 2020, but also lead to an increased exposure of the students to high technology skills that are the need of the hour. Also, considering the dire need to improve learning outcomes in the country, advances in

---

[*] Flash Statistics, Report on Unified District Information System For Education + 2021-22.

foundational learning should be emphasized. The launch of the National Initiative for Proficiency in Reading with Understanding and Numeracy (NIPUN) scheme is a significant step in this direction and India has the potential to achieve the objectives with appropriate measures and strategies and ensure foundational literacy and numeracy among the students.

o **Infrastructure**

Infrastructure is a prerequisite for every country in achieving economic growth. An extensive infrastructure in an economy leads to an increase in its productive capability and facilitates its economic integration with the world. This leads to enhanced opportunities for its population. For a country like India aiming to become a 5 trillion-dollar economy by 2025, infrastructure investment holds great significance, as its level of infrastructure enhancement will play a pivotal role in determining whether or not India can attain this target. However, India has long been suffering from an infrastructure deficit over the years. Infrastructure enhancement is the need of the hour for the country with its growing population, especially in the urban centres. According to a recent World Bank report, $840 billion needs to be pumped into urban infrastructure in the next fifteen years to keep up with the growing needs of the increasing population in the urban areas in the country.[18] While India still suffers from a deficit in infrastructure, it has made significant strides in key areas such as energy, transport, telecommunications and digital infrastructure.

Figure 59: Electricity Capacity—over the last decade

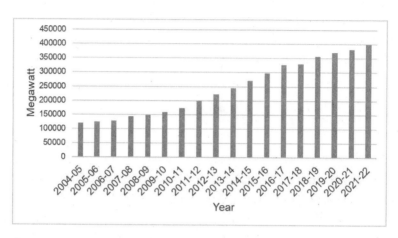

Source: Competitiveness Roadmap for India @100

In the energy sector, India has significantly increased its energy capacity in the recent years. Since 2014, 1,90,285 MW of electricity generation capacity has been added in the country. It has also seen an impressive CAGR of 9.2 per cent over the last decade, transforming India into a power surplus nation. There has been a considerable increase in the participation of the private sector within the industry. The private sector contributed to 85 per cent of the investment in renewable energy during the year 2012–17.[19] India also achieved its target of generating 40 per cent of its power through renewable sources in the year 2021, signalling a move of the Indian energy sector towards sustainable energy.[20] However, there is still a long road ahead as 56 per cent of India's energy capacity is still derived from fossil

---

* Data sourced from World Bank

fuels, with coal contributing 49 per cent.[21] The heavy reliance of the various public entities of the power sector on fossil fuels has led to widespread coal shortages in the country in the recent years. In the third quarter of 2022, coal supply fell 42.5 million tonnes below its demand owing to increasing power demands in the economy.[22] Seeing the uncertainty regarding the availability of coal and the geopolitical situations in the world impacting fossil fuel prices globally, it is the need of the hour for India to focus more towards renewable energy sources leading to a sustainable growth of the Indian power sector. Even though India may have evaded its deficit of electricity generation in the past years and is no longer facing capacity constraints in the generation of electricity, the availability of energy to the population is a key issue. The availability of electricity to the population is not continuous due to frequent power outages, which can impede the manufacturing sector as electricity cuts causes a loss of 5–10 per cent of the industrial units in the country.[23] The irregular supply of electricity is also coupled with high electricity costs for the Indian manufacturers. According to the International Energy Agency (IEA), India has one of the highest costs of electricity for industrial as well as residential users, leading to a major hurdle for the industry to grow and increase their scale and productivity. A major reason for this is the cross subsidization of electricity in the industry, leading to free electricity for some sectors and high costs for other sectors of the industry.[24] There is a dire need for policymakers to look at reducing the cross-subsidization burden on the industry and reducing the cost of electricity for the masses.

Figure 60: Source of Funding by Infrastructure Category, 2012–17

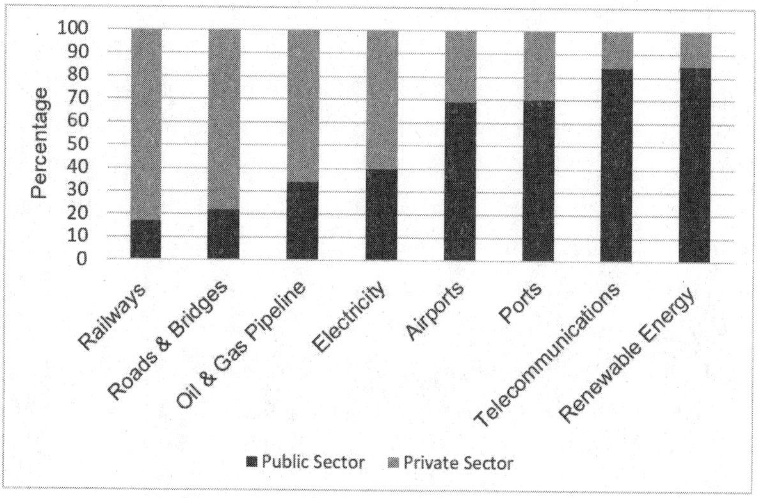

Source: Competitiveness Roadmap for India @100

In telecommunications, India has witnessed a huge improvement in the availability of cheap and high-performing Internet to the majority of the population. The intense rivalry among the major players in the market has driven down the prices of mobile Internet data to the seventh cheapest in the world.* The reduction in mobile data costs has significantly improved the accessibility of citizens to the expanding digital infrastructure initiatives spearheaded by the government, fostering greater inclusivity in the process. To take this a step forward, India needs to undertake the process of large-scale fiberization, i.e., connecting radio towers with each other using optical fibre to enhance data networking and telecommunications. As of March 2023, only 35 per cent of the towers in India are fiberized leading to delays in the proper

---

* Worldwide mobile data pricing: The cost of 1GB of mobile data in 237 countries.

implementation of 5G network in the entire country.* Another key issue in the telecommunications market is the demand of retrospective payments from the telecom operators, often based upon judicial decisions leading to uncertainty regarding the amount of payments made by some operators. The intense competition and hefty telecom duties have led to the exit of many operators from the market and India's telecom sector seems to be moving towards becoming a duopoly in the immediate future, which would lead to a fewer number of options available to the common people and may lead to a rise in the cost of the Internet in the future as the remaining players try to bank upon their market share and charge hefty prices to recover for the low data prices now and increasing telecom duties in the future.

The transport infrastructure in the economy has seen an improvement in recent years. The road network of the country stands as the second largest road network in the world and it continues to significantly improve as the construction of national highways and rural roads in the country is moving at an impressive rate of 28.3km and 90km per day respectively. The railways saw its highest ever capital expenditure in the year 2023, resulting in the introduction of new railway lines and the continued electrification of existing railway lines in the country.[25] Despite witnessing major improvements in the transport infrastructure, the congestion of roads, poor service quality in railways and low amount of air traffic capacity emerge as key issues faced by the realm, leading India to be ranked 38 among 139 countries of the world in the Logistics Performance Index, 2023.[26] Financing of infrastructure projects, delays in land acquisition and non-

---

* 65 per cent telecom towers need fiberization; 12L towers to be deployed to make India 5G-ready

performance of contractors are key challenges facing the transport industry in the country.

Through the years, the Government of India has launched various schemes and policies for addressing the issues in the infrastructure sector. Through the National Investment Pipeline, the Government of India has planned an infrastructural investment of Rs 111 lakh crore through FY 20-25. The investments are to be made in key sectors, such as energy, transportation, urban development, etc. As the financing of public projects has been identified as a key challenge for infrastructure development in the country, the government aims to raise funds for investment through the monetization of its core assets and aims to raise Rs 6 lakh crore during FY 20–25 through a National Monetization Pipeline initiative.[27] The government has also recognized the need for improving the logistics scenario of the country and launched a National Logistics Policy (NLP) in September 2022. The NLP envisions a future where India's logistics sector is integrated, seamless, efficient, reliable, green, sustainable and cost-effective. This will be achieved by leveraging the best-in-class technology, processes and skilled manpower. The NLP will reduce logistics costs and improve performance, which will drive economic growth and business competitiveness. The introduction of the NLP and the National Investment Pipeline are good first steps in addressing some of the challenges facing India's infrastructure development. However, several important issues remain overlooked. Land acquisition delays and slow judicial processes have stalled the commencement of key infrastructure projects. Additionally, the government's cross subsidization of energy has contributed to low profitability among manufacturers in various industries. The reliance on traditional energy sources also remains a key issue. The government must address these challenges to create a complete and efficient infrastructure network that will drive productivity and economic growth in the coming years and lead to higher level of prosperity for the people in the economy.

o **Access to Capital**

Reforms since the 1990s have aimed at making the Indian financial system viable and have attempted to continually adapt to the growing needs of this dynamic country. Between the period of 2005 to 2008, there was a substantial surge in the credit extended by the banking system. During the global financial crisis, the RBI reacted with cutting policy interest rates and providing liquidity. Challenges began to accumulate when debt-funded infrastructure projects encountered obstacles related to land titles and regulations. Additionally, the telecom sector faced its own set of issues, with substantial capital expenditure requirements and uncertainties surrounding regulations and taxation, giving rise to growing apprehensions regarding non-performing assets (NPA).

Extending from these earlier financial developments, the examination of the existing state of India's financial environment is necessary. In recent years, the debt-to-GDP ratio, which provides a comprehensive gauge of a country's financial market depth, has been on the rise and stood at 58.3 per cent of India's nominal GDP as of June 2023*. The equity market in India boasts a high market capitalization for listed domestic firms, whereas the bond market is virtually non-existent. Venture capital investment has experienced substantial growth, ranking behind only the United States, China and the United Kingdom in absolute terms. Large companies and segments of business conglomerates have ready access to credit, whether through the well-established equity markets, the banking system or their

---

* India Government Debt: percentage of GDP.

internal capital markets within the group. Entrepreneurs with ambitious growth goals and high-risk capital now have easier access to a growing pool of investment capital. As of 2023, India has more than 1,00,000 start-ups, making India the world's third largest start-up ecosystem,[*] among these, 111 are unicorns.[†]

In contrast, a significant portion of the economy is unable to gain access to these financial sources. Easy access to formal means of credit is one of the fundamental principles of financial inclusion. Vulnerable sections of society can leverage formal credit to secure sustainable means of income such as businesses and small-scale enterprises and improve their lives. One of the sections of society that relies heavily on channels of credit is the farmers, as they are often at risk of crop failure and incurring losses. The Kisan Credit Card (KCC) scheme, initially launched in 1998, facilitated the issue of electronic Kisan Credit Cards. As of March 2020, the total amount outstanding under operative KCCs stood at Rs 6970.176 billion, as compared to Rs 6682.563 billion in 2019, while the total number of operative KCCs stood at 65,280 in March 2020. The Pradhan Mantri Jan Dhan Yojana (PMJDY) has made significant strides in promoting financial inclusion since its launch in 2014. It aims to provide universal access to banking services, including basic banking accounts, financial education and access to credit, insurance and pension facilities for every household. Over 46 crore bank accounts have been opened, with more than 80 per cent of them being actively used. Notably, PMJDY has led to a substantial increase in women's bank account ownership, with nearly 46 per cent of these accounts belonging to women. In 2021, 79 per cent of women reported having a bank account, a significant jump from the 53 per cent reported in 2015.

---

[*] Ministry of Commerce and Industry
[†] Private start-ups that have reached a valuation of $1 billion

Digital infrastructure has played a crucial part in facilitating the transformative journey of India's financial industry, enabling the cost-effective provision of financial services. This innovative technology proposes a prospective scenario in which individuals engaged in both the official and informal sectors of the Indian economy are able to conveniently make contactless payments through a few simple interactions with a screen. This achievement was facilitated via the implementation of two significant systems, namely the JAM trinity initiatives and the India stack, along with supporting government policies. The JAM trinity is among the major initiatives implemented by the Government of India. The goal of adopting the JAM trinity was to encourage large-scale, technology-enabled, direct benefit transfers to enhance people's economic life, particularly in low-income families. In addition to the India stack, the open digital infrastructure platform of India has established the groundwork for enhancing the availability of digital financial services. The India stack has successfully established an infrastructure that effectively minimizes the involvement of intermediaries, allowing stakeholders to directly engage with one another. The distinguishing characteristic of the India stack lies in its exceptional level of interoperability. The open-ended architecture of the system enables banks and financial technology companies (Fintechs) to establish payment banks. The UPI, which is a component of this framework, has had significant achievements. According to the National Payments Corporation of India (NPCI), the UPI witnessed a significant growth in transaction volume. From a starting point of 1,00,000 transactions in 2017, the number of transactions completed using UPI escalated to 782 crores by December. Notably, in May 2023, UPI achieved its highest-ever number of transactions, reaching 9.41 billion. This data highlights the substantial expansion and adoption of

UPI as a popular payment method in India.* Digitization has had a significant impact on MSMEs as well. It has led to increased scalability and enhanced access to knowledge and capital, thanks to various initiatives such as the Udyam Portal, MSME Champions Portal, SIDBI's digital lending platform (PRAYAAS), Udyam Mitra Portal and the recently launched ONDC Portal, among others. However, it's worth noting that, despite these advancements, only 1.3 crore MSMEs have officially registered on the Udyam Portal, which is a fraction of the approximately 6.3 crore MSMEs estimated to be in operation across India, as per the data from the NSS 73rd Round. This difficulty in accessing credit restricts the expansion of micro-enterprises to small or medium-sized enterprises, which gives rise to what's known as the 'missing middle.' This phenomenon primarily occurs because micro-enterprises face difficulties in accessing credit for their growth, largely due to traditional loan procedures. These procedures typically require MSMEs to demonstrate their creditworthiness through collateral, such as evidence of digital financial transactions and property ownership. Their limited access to affordable formal credit results in insufficient working capital, hindering their productivity and impeding their progression into mid-sized enterprises. This concerning situation, in turn, negatively impacts the overall economic growth of the country[28].

Despite significant advancements, the problem of fraudulent operations persists. Transparency and adherence to proper procedures in the management of public sector banks have often been lacking. Instances of fraudulent activities and insider trading have been observed in both public and private banking institutions, leading to instances of law enforcement taking assertive measures against bank officials. The Reserve Bank of

---

* npci.org.in

India's (RBI) Asset Quality Review conducted in 2015,[29] unveiled a notable proportion of Non-Performing Assets (NPAs), resulting in a decline in the availability of credit. The majority of these NPAs were owned by banks in the public sector. The settlement process faced challenges despite the initiation of measures to resolve this issue from late 2015 to early 2018. Non-Bank Financial Corporations (NBFCs) assumed a more assertive role by procuring short-term funds from the banking industry and redirecting them towards longer-term lending activities. The crisis that occurred in late 2018 with IL&FS brought to light significant worries over NPAs within this particular sector of the banking system. Consequently, NPAs currently account for around 10 per cent of the total outstanding loans within the Indian banking sector, representing a much larger proportion in comparison to other nations of similar economic position. The primary objective was to provide a well-defined procedure for addressing NPAs under the Insolvency and Bankruptcy Act of 2016. The Insolvency and Bankruptcy Code (IBC), along with the establishment of the Insolvency and Bankruptcy Board of India (IBBI) in 2016, signifies a significant milestone in India's legal framework. The IBC was introduced to streamline insolvency laws, replacing older legislation to ensure a consistent and transparent process for various stakeholders affected by insolvency[30]. The IBBI, as a unique regulatory body, oversees both the insolvency profession and the insolvency resolution procedures, with a focus on fostering the growth and regulation of insolvency professionals, agencies and information utilities. The IBC's core objectives revolve around achieving insolvency resolution, optimizing the value of assets for corporate debtors, promoting entrepreneurship and facilitating access to credit while maintaining a fair balance among all involved parties. This transformation shifts the balance of power towards creditors, promoting financial discipline and contributing to

India's economic stability and progress[31]. Efforts have been made to facilitate the privatization of public banks, primarily through the consolidation of these institutions to establish more capable companies capable of effectively managing NPAs. In recent times, the government has made an announcement on the establishment of a 'Bad Bank' with the purpose of acquiring NPAs.

Numerous endeavours have been undertaken to enhance the governance of public sector banks; however, the execution of these initiatives has been inconsistent. There has been an observed increase in the occurrence of fraudulent incidents in the realm of digital payments as well. It is critical to prioritize the implementation of comprehensive safety mechanisms that go beyond mere awareness campaigns. Although some progress has been made in clearing congested credit channels, there remains a pressing requirement for resolutions to fundamental challenges that significantly impede the development of the financial sector.

o   *Cost of Doing Business*

The cost of doing business directly impacts market competitiveness through its heavy influence on factor inputs and demand conditions. Though India is emerging as a hub for business and trade, the cost of doing business has remained high. The World Bank's Doing Business Project offers a comprehensive framework for objectively evaluating business regulations and their implementation in 190 economies and in selected cities at subnational and regional levels. This evaluation is achieved through the use of quantitative indicators. The Ease of Doing Business score is calculated on the basis of performance parameters under Doing Business[32]. India has focused immensely on Improving the Ease of Doing Business (EoDB), especially since the last decade.

The effort to improve the business environment in India can be traced back to the 1990s. Liberalization in the 1990s was a monumental step in the fairness of price determination, foreign investment and industrial investments, all driven by the private sector.[33] Since Doing Business 2008, India has implemented several reforms to improve the costs and ease of doing business by addressing the main concerns regarding starting of a business, procedural complexities in obtaining permits, cross-border trade, insolvency issues, electricity and credit facilitation, employment of workers and so on.[34] In 2019, India significantly improved its EoDB ranking, jumping 23 positions to 77th place among 190 countries, according to the World Bank. This achievement follows a thirty-place improvement in the previous year. Over the past four years, India has climbed sixty-five positions, with notable advancements in six out of the ten assessed indicators. The most remarkable progress was seen in 'Construction Permits' and 'Trading across Borders'. India is also moving closer to international best practices in seven of the ten indicators.[35]

Indian business environment faces several challenges, including the need for more flexibility in labour laws and streamlining judicial processes, among other aspects.[36] However, the prevalence of heterogeneity across all levels of the government is the most significant challenge. The heterogeneity is first observed in the nation's federal structure. Ineffective demarcation between responsibilities of the state government leads to botched implementation of policies and decision-making. Along with this, dependency on funding rather than creating capacity for revenue generation through long-term planning of state governments makes them burdened by debt. On the regional level, heterogeneity is seen in fragmented, unconcerted policies. Effective collaboration and coordination across the tiers of government will lead to smooth inter and intra-regional and sectoral linkages. These linkages will effectively reduce the costs and complexity while increasing accessibility, building an enabling environment for businesses. These issues have a much more detrimental impact on smaller companies, keeping them informal and reducing their growth. In India, where the majority of enterprises come under MSMEs, high cost of business, high compliance costs, barriers to credit access, complex regulatory framework and mismatch of policy efforts to on-ground challenges, disrupt the entire business fabric of the nation.

India's current position on the costs of doing business is quite comparable to peer countries. In Doing Business 2020, India and China are amongst the top improvers who adopted the Doing Business indicators as a core component of their reform strategies. The 'Make in India' campaign has significantly contributed to increasing the competitiveness of the nation by drawing in foreign investment—mainly focusing on the manufacturing sector. Corporate tax rates in India have undergone a significant transformation, going from 45 per cent in the landmark 1991 budget to roughly half of that at present. This reduction effectively lightened the tax burden on companies, making them pay a smaller share of profits in taxes than the statutory rate. Notably, Indian companies now face lower statutory tax rates than their counterparts in countries like Brazil, Argentina and Mexico, enhancing India's competitiveness. However, larger companies pay just about 22 per cent, which is lower than what smaller firms pay, implying an unequal burden.

India is characterized by one of the highest logistics costs that range from 14–18 per cent of GDP as compared to the global benchmark of 8 per cent.[37] To address this, reprioritizing the implementation of robust infrastructure solutions by addressing complaints by foreign investors about suboptimal physical and virtual infrastructure in India, to remove deterrence from manufacturing operations, is necessary.[38] Prime Minister Narendra Modi introduced the National Logistics Policy in 2022, which aims to create a favourable environment for conducting business in India. Its goals include lowering the costs related to both domestic and international trade, streamlining licensing through technology and promoting the long-term development of the nation's infrastructure. Creating an enabling business environment with a low cost of doing business is essential to tapping India's potential to become a dynamic business hub.

o   *Market Regulations*

India, before the mid-1980s and 1990 reforms, had a dirigiste economic model. The governments of the developing world, including India, followed the import substitution policy. It encouraged reliance on the domestic production of goods and discouraged imports to protect the infant domestic industries[39]. Also, tariffs were imposed on imports to make them uncompetitive compared to domestic production. However, the industries lacked the machinery and technological know-how to manufacture goods, so they depended on imports to make ends meet. At the same time, currencies were devalued (in relation to the dollar) to make exports more profitable, but it also made imports costlier. The result was that the costs of domestic manufacturing went up because any import carried with it the costs of tariffs, import duties and higher procurement expenditure resulting from higher currency outflow, in turn, caused by currency devaluation.

However, numerous market rules, particularly pertaining to licensing requirements, have been eliminated since then. In the late 1990s, emerging economies like India started to restructure their economic systems towards three main goals: sustainability, efficiency and accessibility. This primarily consisted of switching from using state command and control structures to market-based mechanisms to provide these services.[40] The only rules that remain in effect today pertain to governing factor markets, such as labour and land, as well as restrictions governing utilities like water and electricity. These select market regulations have been employed in India for a long time to address perceived imbalances in market transactions and seem to hold societal and political relevance. While India has made notable advancements in opening up product markets to competition, there remains a significant concern about the degree to which regulations support fair competition.[41]

Labour laws have a significant influence on the business environment. In India, the labour laws that are designed to offer protection and room for growth to smaller firms, have inadvertently placed a heavier financial burden on larger enterprises, discouraging the expansion of small and medium-sized businesses. While very large companies have managed to circumvent this through the use of contract labour, growth-oriented small and medium-sized enterprises still bear significant costs. In South Asia and especially in India, labour laws lack uniformity, have different legislative applicability for different sizes of enterprises and have a lack of protection for enterprises employing less than ten workers.[42] A significant portion of labour laws in India are determined at the state level, and differences in their policies are clearly associated with differences in labour market outcomes. Often overlooked but equally significant are the regulations related to the educational qualifications required for specific professions. India has taken a similar approach to many advanced economies by demanding relatively high levels of formal education for jobs in specific fields like healthcare.

This, in turn, leads to higher wages for professionals in short supply and encourages the development of technology that can replace low-skilled workers. Consequently, certain segments of the labour market become inaccessible to individuals with lower skills, and technology-driven advancements in skill-intensive industries limit their employment opportunities, which contradicts the current characteristics and requirements of the Indian workforce. There is a need for simplification of business and labour laws, and a restructuring wherein schemes including policies for skill development, access to credit and information and facilitation of factor inputs, are incorporated.[43]

Land regulations often present obstacles when it comes to the acquisition of land for development. While a more active rental market has alleviated some of these distortions in certain areas, the associated costs remain significant and act as a deterrent to investments in infrastructure and production facilities that rely on land. The removal of such barriers, for instance, through the opening up of agricultural land for industrial use, has demonstrated a substantial positive impact on economic development outcomes.

In the realms of water and energy resources, the issues revolve around pricing regulations that disrupt efficient market dynamics. Agricultural users benefit from unrestricted access, resulting in resource wastage, while industrial users, in contrast, bear elevated costs to offset the subsidies provided for production. In certain areas, the government has implemented a strategy of providing direct transfers to households in need, as opposed to offering subsidized access. This approach has yielded favourable outcomes, as demonstrated by the successful distribution of LPG containers to rural households through the Pradhan Mantri Ujjwala Yojana (PMUY) programme.[*]

---

[*] https://www.pmuy.gov.in/

The regulation of agriculture in India was established during a period characterized by a substantial disparity between output and demand, leading to considerable deficits. Consequently, the primary objective of these regulations was to provide affordable pricing for agricultural commodities. The market was subject to government regulation through various measures, such as the establishment of guaranteed prices for certain commodities that exceeded or fell below global market values. Additionally, the government imposed restrictions on the entry of industrial agro-businesses and provided subsidies for certain resources like water, electricity and fertilizer. These policies are evaluated to impose adverse financial consequences on farmers, which sets them apart from the policies in many other nations. Consequently, there has been a dearth of reforms in the agricultural sector, leading to widespread rural hardship, with numerous farmers vulnerable to poverty, and an increasing set of environmental restrictions, notably on water utilization. In sum, it can be determined that these policies have been evaluated to have an adverse financial effect on farmers, which stands in striking contrast to the situation in several other nations. The outcome has shown a deficiency in the reorganization of the agricultural sector, leading to a significant prevalence of rural distress whereby several farmers are prone to poverty. Additionally, there is a growing environmental limitation, particularly pertaining to water utilization. On the contrary, India's food production is enough to fulfil internal consumption requirements and has substantial potential to cater to international markets.

In 2004, the Indian government initiated discussions about a policy to ensure that all levels of government and regulatory agencies consider the competitive dimension when formulating policy. Subsequently, the Planning Commission released a report considering the merits of an Act of Parliament that outlines overarching regulatory principles aimed at enhancing competition, improving efficiency and reducing costs (Planning Commission, 2006). It transformed product and service markets by harmonizing tax rates across Indian states and reducing trade barriers. The consolidation of 38 previous labour codes into four now provides greater flexibility for Indian states to liberalize their labour markets. Additionally, there has been a shift towards direct transfers to impoverished farmers through the expansion of the PM-KISAN programme since 2018 and efforts to reform agricultural laws aimed at removing barriers faced by firms in agricultural markets However, these reforms faced strong opposition due to concerns that they might empower large private firms at the expense of farmers, and eventually, the reforms were repealed. The success of a reform often hinges on local implementation rather than just national legislation or decisions taken by the local body. In addition to this, administrative bottlenecks and corruption undermine the effectiveness of well-designed policies. In a study of 194 countries by Bellver and Kaufmann (2005),[44] institutional and political transparency are closely associated with competitiveness and inversely correlated with corruption. India ranked 86th out of 180 countries in Transparency International's 2022 Corruption Perceptions Index. Eliminating administrative barriers and enhancing regulatory transparency can have a substantial positive impact on overall economic competitiveness through various channels, including increased FDI. Overly complex administrative procedures also increase discretion within government bureaucracy, thereby facilitating corruption.

In conclusion, India's economic landscape has undergone significant transformations since the late 1990s, with a shift towards market-based mechanisms. However, the persistence of specific market regulations, particularly in labour, land and utilities, continues to raise concerns about their compatibility with fostering fair competition. Labour laws, land acquisition hurdles and pricing rules for water and energy remain significant challenges. The complexities of reform are amplified by political tensions, administrative bottlenecks and corruption, emphasizing the need for transparent and well-implemented policies that can drive economic competitiveness and growth at both the national and local levels.

o   *Trade and FDI*

Trade and FDI are important sources for investment and have a direct impact on the propensity and pattern of consumption and savings in an economy. FDI is not only important to balance deficits but has a significant impact on the adoption of technology, levels of efficiency and competitiveness of the host country.[45] The Indian economy now displays a much higher level of openness to foreign trade and investment than in the past. After a decade of India's aversion from free trade agreements (FTAs), India is now actively reevaluating its foreign policy, revitalizing trade relationships with multiple nations. Following a series of unsuccessful trade deals and years of isolationism, India's recent surge in FTA signings reflects a commitment to transform itself into a global economic powerhouse, while ensuring the benefits of its newly opened economy reach all segments of society. In a world post-Brexit where countries seek to diversify their supply chains towards the Indo-Pacific and global businesses seek alternatives to investing in China, India finds itself in an excellent position to integrate into the global landscape. Leveraging its abundant, English-speaking, skilled workforce and cutting-edge technology solutions, India is poised to become an attractive outsourcing hub and manufacturing destination.

Since 2015, the government has moved away from the gradual pace of liberalization that characterized the 1990s.

This shift is a response to the increased dynamism in the global market and China's growing assertiveness on the global stage. Free trade agreements have now again gained prominence in the Indian economy. As of 2022, India has thirteen FTAs with its trading partners including Sri Lanka, SAFTA countries, Nepal, Bhutan, Thailand, Singapore, ASEAN countries, South Korea, Japan, Malaysia, Mauritius, UAE and Australia.[46] The India–UAE CEPA, which came into force on 1 May 2022, is aimed at increasing bilateral trade in goods to over $100 billion and trade in services to $15 billion in the following five years[47]. The India–Canada CEPA negotiation was re-launched in the fifth India–Canada Ministerial Dialogue on Trade & Investment (MDTI) with the possibility of Early Progress Trade Agreement (EPTA).[48]

The Make in India Initiative, introduced in 2014, primarily focuses on attracting FDI, eliminating obstacles to FDI in specific sectors and reducing the overall cost of doing business. Between 2014 and 2022, the FDI inflow in India amounted to $525.10 billion. This constitutes about 62 per cent of the FDI inflow India received since ($848.68 billion)[49].

Studying the FDI statistics from DPIIT, on a sectoral level, non-manufacturing sectors received over 90 per cent of this investment[50]. During the fiscal year 2021–22, the top sectors that saw the highest FDI equity inflow in India were computer software and hardware, accounting for 24.60 per cent of FDI, followed by the services sector, which includes a wide range of financial and business services, at 12.13 per cent. The automobile industry attracted 11.89 per cent of FDI, while trading and construction (infrastructure) activities received 7.72 per cent and 5.52 per cent of FDI, respectively. Notably, FDI in India during this fiscal year came from 101 different countries, an increase from the 97 countries reported in the previous fiscal year of 2020-21. In the fiscal year 2021–22, the top states attracting the highest FDI inflows were Karnataka (37.55 per cent), Maharashtra (26.26 per cent), Delhi (13.93 per cent), Tamil Nadu (5.10 per cent) and Haryana (4.76 per cent). Though Karnataka and Haryana are in the top five, the difference in FDI performance between Karnataka and Haryana stands at a significant 32.79 per cent.[51]

Figure 61: Year-wise FDI inflow since 2014–15

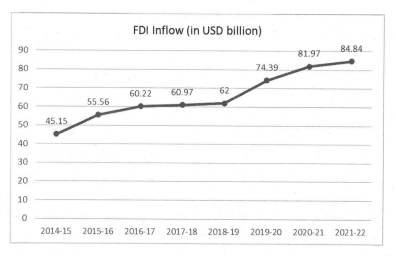

Source: DPIIT Annual Report 2023

Starting in 2017, new procurement laws have been implemented, favouring the use of domestic inputs; data localization requirements have mandated the processing of Indian operation-related data within the country, some tariffs have been raised and stricter FDI regulations have been enacted, particularly concerning FDI from China. Presently the Government has allowed 100 per cent automatic-route FDI under the FDI Policy 2022 in many sectors including agriculture, industrial parks, construction development, petroleum and natural gases and so on.[52] The Self-Reliant India (Aatmanirbhar Bharat Abhiyaan) doctrine, was launched in 2020, with the objective of promoting Indian goods in the global supply chain markets. Negotiations on trade and investment agreements have been largely put on hold, although discussions with the United States and the European Union are ongoing. Along with this, the government is taking a number of steps to improve exports including a merger of the Council of Trade and Development and the Board of Trade providing a common platform for addressing stakeholder concerns. Infusion of funds for export support, resolutions to boost gem and jewellery exporters, promoting ease of doing business and so on.[53]

However, there is still a long way to go. In 1990–91, India's exports amounted to a modest $18 billion, and it took nearly a decade for this figure to double, reaching $36.8 billion by 1999–2000. During this period, India's contribution to global trade was a meagre 1 per cent.[54] As per WTO data, released in 2019, in the year 2018, India's global exports stood at 3.5 per cent and imports at 3.2 per cent.

On exports, India has seen an impressive increase in goods exports, with $420 billion in trade in goods in 2021–22[55]. The services sector, particularly software and professional services, has exhibited remarkable growth, with Indian service exports reaching their highest value at $254.4 billion in 2021–22, representing a substantial 23 per cent increase over the previous year. This can be attributed to the IT and service industries, which have become significant contributors to the country's export revenue. This is exemplified by the fact that computer services, software and professional services, including consulting and research services, account for a major portion of India's service exports. Another positive in India's exports is the 'One District One Product' (ODOP) initiative, the objective of which is to diversify exports by focusing on districts across the country and the formation of District Export Promotion Councils (DEPCs) to boost local exports. These measures aim to create unique market positions for local products, opening new export opportunities and enhancing the overall competitiveness of Indian exports[56].

On the other hand, the challenges in India's export performance are multifaceted and include several key issues. First, there is a significant concentration of goods exports in non-manufacturing sectors and brownfield projects. For example, while India has made substantial progress in boosting goods exports, much of this growth has been in non-manufacturing sectors, leading to concerns about the country's dependence on these specific sectors and its limited diversification. Second, there is a risk of over-dependence on foreign investments, which can make India susceptible to global economic fluctuations. The Export Preparedness Index 2022 highlights the adverse effect of the COVID-19 pandemic, where the value of Indian exports declined by 6.7 per cent in 2020-21 due to disruptions caused by the pandemic. This situation signifies the vulnerability that can arise from reliance on foreign investments, which can be influenced by global economic conditions. Third, the transfer of ownership of Indian companies to foreign entities is another challenge. For example, despite India's efforts to increase exports, foreign entities may acquire controlling stakes in Indian companies during the process. Lastly, there exist regional disparities, as most FDI concentrate in major cities, leaving less-developed areas behind. This geographical imbalance in FDI inflows perpetuates economic inequalities within the country, with the benefits of export-led growth disproportionately favouring urban areas over rural or underdeveloped regions[57].

Despite decades of reforms, progress remains minimal. The latest data released by the Ministry of Commerce and Industry shows a further widening of India's trade deficit in August

2022;* the increase was attributable to crude oil, coal, coke, silver and vegetable oil imports. The journey to shrinking the deficit and promoting self-reliance would involve the adoption and widespread availability of renewable energy and hybrid and electric vehicles. Additionally, enhancing the capabilities of MSMEs to produce good-quality competitively priced products will not only nudge Indian consumers to go local but also ensure that local goes global via the FTA route. With the global value chains under transition and India being in an economically and strategically favourable position to capitalize on this opportunity, FTAs undoubtedly serve as an expedient to India's growth target. The challenge for India is to establish a set of policies that enables the attractiveness of India as a base to serve global markets without stifling local rivalry and access to more competitive foreign goods and services.

Navigating Challenges

The Indian government has duly recognized challenges in specific sectors and has initiated various schemes and initiatives to address them. The primary challenge, however, is to ensure the effective implementation of these measures across all three tiers of government: the central government, state governments and local governments, including grassroots levels such as panchayats and local bodies. Ineffectiveness in implementation is largely attributed to vertical and horizontal imbalances within the economy. These imbalances manifest through the unequal distribution of monetary and decision-making powers, a lack of collaboration between different tiers of government, the localization of solutions and an insufficient public-private dialogue. Sustained economic growth cannot be achieved by individual stakeholders alone. In the context of public-private partnerships, the public sector tends to prioritize

---

* https://commerce.gov.in/trade-statistics/latest-trade-figures/

social welfare, while the private sector leans towards economic benefits. The pressing need is to establish efficient partnerships that encourage both sectors to engage, collaborate and leverage each other's strengths while mitigating their respective weaknesses. When it comes to coordination between different government levels, local bodies are responsible for addressing location-specific issues at the grassroots level, while higher-level tiers of government manage macroeconomic factors and possess fiscal and political authority. The lack of coordination between these government levels is a significant impediment to the translation of policies and initiatives into improvements in socio-economic parameters. Discerning the domains where bottom-up measures yield greater impact, while identifying where top-down policies are essential, holds the key to optimizing resource allocation and driving more effective resource mobilization. Addressing the disparities and coordination issues among these stakeholders will reduce the constant mismatch in resource allocation. Efforts will then be directed to the right areas, effectively allocating resources to address deficits in the economy.

At this stage, India cannot afford to falter due to ineffective policies that do not contribute to its aspirations of becoming a global superpower. It must ensure sound implementation and coordination to achieve equitable growth. In this section, we present the three challenges that pose as obstacles in the path towards better competitiveness in the Indian economy—the shared prosperity challenge, the jobs challenge and the policy implementation challenge.

o   *The Shared Prosperity Challenge*

Despite India being one of the fastest-growing economies in the world, social inequality remains a major challenge, roadblocking the attainment of shared prosperity. Shared prosperity refers to the equitable distribution of economic gains across society, ensuring that no one is left behind. One of the most prominent forms of inequality is income inequality. As per the World Inequality Report 2022 released by the United Nations Development Programme, the top 10 per cent and the top 1 per cent hold 57 per cent and 22 per cent of the total national income, respectively. In contrast, the income share of the bottom 50 per cent has dwindled to just 13 per cent. This highlights a significant concentration of wealth in the hands of a few, while the majority of the population struggles to make ends meet. Income inequality, however, is far from the only form in which inequality exists. As highlighted by the SPI, India also has lower scores on environmental quality, inclusiveness and health and wellness dimensions. There is a positive and strong relationship between the SPI and GSDP per capita.[58] Our analysis in Chapter 6 revealed that on average, states with a higher income tend to have higher social progress. For example, Goa and Sikkim rank high on social progress, while Bihar ranks the lowest. Additionally, the relationship between economic development and social progress is non-linear. At lower income levels, minor differences in GSDP per capita are associated with significant improvements in social progress. Therefore, to foster inclusive and equitable growth and achieve shared prosperity levels, addressing the various forms of inequalities within the different regions of the country becomes essential.

A structural hindrance to mitigating these inequalities is the organization of the Indian polity. India is a quasi-federal country, with policy areas falling either under the central or state government's domain or under the concurrent domain, which makes both the levels of government responsible for them. The diversity embedded in the country requires a structure where state-level governments are empowered to deal with the local issues in a more efficient manner. However, as discussed previously, the fiscal arrangement between the central and state governments leaves much to be desired. Firstly, states need to be given opportunities to improve their capability of revenue generation. Rather than funding their immediate needs, long-term planning needs to take place to help them establish streams of revenue via trade, tourism, industries or other means depending on the state's proficiency. This can also be done by the identification of key sectors in a state and leveraging the centre's resources to develop that sector. For example, a state rich with natural resources shall be provided education and skill-development programmes to benefit from its resources. The Pradhan Mantri Van Dhan Yojana (PMVDY), aimed at retail-based development of tribal people, was one such initiative where the centre and state governments assisted each other to uplift the tribals. Furthermore, the channels for fiscal borrowing should be streamlined as states' often function in a debt and fund-deficit, leaving them handicapped in efficiently fulfilling their constitutional duties. The establishment of centre and state councils for goods and service tax is a right step in the direction of better fiscal sharing between the two tiers of government.

Another crucial issue is the ineffective demarcation of responsibility between the centre and the state. Increased planning at the central level negates the fundamentals of federalism where states are to be treated as autonomous regions that are capable of planning themselves. In addition to that, the policies launched by the centre should be clear on the role of the state government in their implementation. Often, ineffective coordination between the two levels of government leads to botched implementation of the policy, and this hampers its desired impact. A key step in improving centre–state cooperation can be to establish councils at a regional level, which are composed of ministers from the centre and respective state governments. These councils can be the forum in which policies, key plans of action and other relevant issues can be discussed between the central and state government. Similarly, these forums can become the place of knowledge transfer between the centre and states. Effectively, India's diverse resources and skills can be leveraged with effective planning and coordination. In order to achieve that, the institutional changes discussed above need to be addressed.

In an attempt to alleviate inequality, the Indian government has implemented various measures to address income inequality over the years, such as the Mahatma Gandhi National Rural Employment Guarantee Act (MGNREGA) and the National Rural Livelihood Mission (NRLM). These programmes aim to provide employment opportunities and financial assistance to rural households, with a focus on women and marginalized communities. However, their impact has been limited, as many households still lack access to basic services and social protection. After India gained independence, it faced numerous challenges, including famine, de-industrialization and widespread poverty. At that time, a significant portion of the population lived in chronic poverty, and the country had food shortages, limited financial infrastructure, weak economic growth and basic technology for programme administration. Consequently, Indian policymakers concentrated primarily on developing anti-poverty and protective measures. However, India has undergone substantial changes since then, with a transformed demographic landscape and a different set of risks. As a result, the country's social protection system must adapt and align with the evolving needs of its population and the current risk profile[59]. The regional disparities in economic growth and development are largely attributed to historical and structural factors, such as access to education, healthcare and infrastructure. The Government of India has implemented various policies to address regional disparities, such as the special category status granted to certain states for development and the Backward Regions Grant Fund (BRGF) for infrastructure development. However, these policies have not been sufficient to bridge the gap between the different regions. Achieving shared prosperity in India remains a major challenge, despite the country's high economic-growth rates. Income inequality, regional disparities and social exclusion are the main obstacles to achieving equitable economic growth and development.

o   *The Jobs Challenge*

India is confronted with a significant challenge in generating productive jobs, despite having one of the largest potential workforces globally, with over 660 million people aged between eighteen and thirty-five.[*] Alarming statistics reveal that the country's unemployment rate stands at around 7 per cent, a concerning figure given the sheer size of the workforce.[†] Furthermore, the quality of jobs in India raises concerns, as most of the population is engaged in low-value-added and low-paying employment. The State of Inequality in India Report 2022 points out that an individual earning over Rs 25,000 per month belongs to the top 10 per cent of earners in the country, emphasizing the dearth of well-compensated positions.

Female labour force participation remains strikingly low at just 23 per cent, significantly below the global average of 47.4 per cent, presenting a substantial hurdle to India's economic development

---

[*] https://worldpopulationreview.com
[†] https://unemploymentinindia.cmie.com

due to cultural and societal constraints.[*] The country's youth unemployment rate is notably high at 23.2 per cent,[†] reflecting deficiencies in the education and training systems that fail to equip the youth with the necessary skills for the job market.

India's industrial sector has not grown at par with its services sector. While the manufacturing sector shrank to 15.3 per cent of overall GDP in 2021–22, the service sector contributed to over 50 per cent in the same financial year.[60] This trend indicates that the country has not realized the Kuznetsian structural transformation, which is denoted by the mobility of economic resources from agriculture to manufacturing and finally to services as an economy develops.[61] The economic phenomenon of deindustrialization can arise due to a lack of investment in manufacturing capabilities and the resultant lack of competitive advantage of the sector.[62] The aftermath is India becoming a net-importer of manufacturing while the service sector growth in productivity outpaces its manufacturing counterpart. Moreover, the agricultural sector, employing 43 per cent[‡] of the working population, exhibits disguised unemployment, leading to low productivity and wages due to limited non-agricultural opportunities in rural areas. The service sector's significant growth has outpaced the industrial sector, indicating a lack of investment in manufacturing capabilities and a reduced potential for high-productivity, high-wage jobs in the formalized economy.

Furthermore, significant disparities in the quality of jobs persist in India, characterized by the glaring contrast between

---

[*] Labor force participation rate, female (per cent of female population ages 15+) (modeled ILO estimate) - India

[†] https://data.worldbank.org/indicator/SL.UEM.1524.ZS

[‡] https://tradingeconomics.com/india/employment-in-agriculture-percent-of-total-employment-wb-data.html

highly skilled, well-compensated jobs and low-skilled, low-paying positions. Informal employment, accounting for over 80 per cent[63] of India's workforce, results in poor working conditions, low wages and job insecurity. Gender-based discrimination further compounds the issue, relegating women to low-paying, low-skilled jobs with limited access to formal employment opportunities. Women in India face significant cultural and social barriers to entering the labour force, including discrimination and lack of access to education and job training. Addressing these challenges requires a coordinated effort from the government, civil society and the private sector. We have seen previously in this chapter how educational and skill imbalances create a mismatch between the supply and demand of labour in the job market, with a growing demand for skilled workers in high-paying positions. Despite having a vast reservoir of young workers, both low skilled and highly skilled, many remain out of formal employment and engage in low-paying and low-value-added activities. Unprecedented policy changes are required to improve the learning outcomes of those currently in the education ecosystem and create better linkages between jobseekers and employers.

While India's economic growth is commendable, addressing these multifaceted challenges is essential to harness the full potential of its workforce and ensure more equitable and productive employment opportunities for all citizens.

o   *The Policy Implementation Challenge*

To overcome the aforementioned challenges, policymaking is an efficient tool. India's economic growth has been the result of policy changes, such as liberalization in the 90s, to more business-friendly policies that fostered environment for market forces to grow and meet the economic realities of the country.

The opportunities thus created by these policies have been the drivers of change in the Indian economy. Furthermore, since 2014, policies have been aimed at unlocking the underlying competitiveness of the economy.[64] To meet the jobs challenge, various incentivized schemes, such as Make in India and Skill India, have been launched in the country. For these schemes to translate into greater outcomes, there is scope to address institutional inefficiencies. Policy implementation is a complex process that involves a range of actors, institutions and factors. Its impact often depends not simply on executing given policies uniformly across the country but on adapting them to the specific circumstances in each state, district or city. One of the major challenges of policy implementation in India are the resource constraints and lack of capacity at the state and local levels. While policies are formulated at the national level, the actual implementation is carried out at the state and local levels. However, many states and local governments lack the necessary resources to implement policies effectively. This results in poor implementation, which undermines the intended impact of policies.

The implementation process requires coordinated action among various levels of government as well as identification of the target group of these policies at every level—state, district and village—of the country. The challenge, thus, is not limited to the identification of issues and addressing them with policy changes but extends to the next step, where the benefits of the drafted policies reach the targeted beneficiaries. Expecting only the public institutions, with the current framework, to meet these responsibilities by themselves is not a healthy approach. In addition, corruption and red-tapism often undermine policy implementation in India. Bureaucratic inefficiency, complex regulations and lack of accountability create opportunities for corruption, which can deter the effectiveness of policies. Another factor is the complexity of the Indian society and economy. India is a diverse country with a complex social structure and a large informal sector. This makes policy implementation challenging, as policies may not always be suitable for different social and economic contexts. Moreover, the lack of data and evidence-based policymaking is another contributing factor to the challenge of policy implementation in India. Many policies are formulated without a clear understanding of the local context and the potential impact of the policy. This can lead to poor implementation and limited impact.

Poor implementation, therefore, has hampered the intended growth of the economy. Therefore, a need to rectify the implementation mechanism is crucial to reap the benefits of India's policymaking. Furthermore, India needs to adapt to the changes occurring globally and prepare itself beforehand so as not to lag in the global economy. One such example is the increased digitalization across various spheres of life in the world. Opportunities that arise out of such changes need to be leveraged in order to create a robust growth profile for the country. India, therefore, needs to make efficient policy choices that can help it advance in tandem with the world. Furthermore, the policy choices need to be backed by sound implementation to ensure equitable growth and high levels of productivity across the country.

India stands at a crucial juncture in the current times where one misstep could cost its aspiration of establishing itself as a leading superpower. Overcoming these challenges is therefore necessary and vital at this time. Based on the discussion so far, the diagnostics about India's competitiveness make the need for a newer approach to attaining shared prosperity extremely evident. The next section outlines the new guiding forces that have the potential to drive India's growth at an accelerated pace.

The New Guiding Forces

As we move towards the final sections of this book, it is important, at this point, to reiterate the objective of this in-depth analysis of India's current competitiveness. The goal was always to delve deeper into finding ideas that could translate into structures and processes that can work for twenty-five years and not just two years in India's journey towards becoming an upper middle-income country. The goal is not just attaining a certain GDP number but a sense of quality of life that is more encompassing, one that prioritizes social progress, is about shared prosperity, focuses on sustainability and shows resilience to external shocks. How do we integrate these ideas into one approach rather than having multiple entities working individually towards separate goals? How do we achieve equitable growth? How do we benefit from the demographic dividend? It is crucial now to recognize that we will only be able to address these challenges if we address them simultaneously. That is the goal. What we need to do is create a new growth agenda that brings together the new type of structural prosperity and structural transformation with an agenda that equally prioritizes economic and social progress. Rather than just focusing on the jobs at the top, for example, digitization and IT, we now need to create a roadmap for others, a ladder that allows those at the lower sections of the society to move up the system. That is going to be an effective social policy that enables economic growth. At this juncture, we introduce to you the India@100 strategy, a set of new guiding principles, new priority policies and a new implementation model aimed at fostering economic as well as social progress as India moves towards becoming an upper middle-income country by 2047. Based on the challenges detailed in the previous sections, the India@100 strategy offers guidelines towards equitable growth. We draw heavily from the Competitiveness Roadmap for India@100 report published by the Economic Advisory Council to the Prime Minister (EAC-PM) in 2022. However, it should be noted that this is an exploratory exercise and more work examining the components of this strategy is needed for it to be treated as a strategic plan. The India@100 strategy rests on the new guiding principles, the 4S.

The 4S Framework

Four dimensions that succinctly integrate economic- and social-progress goals and lay the foundation for the journey towards fulfilling the ambition of being an upper middle-income country form the crux of the 4S framework. Prosperity, being the core of these four principles, reflects the country's drive to achieving the economic-development goals. However, the diagnostics in the previous chapters have revealed that measuring prosperity as an average of the GDP per capita is insufficient. Prosperity measures are equally interwoven with other aspects like ease of living, regional development and renewable-energy production etc. The 4S framework articulates these concerns coherently and is reflective of the overall goals India is striving to achieve.

- Prosperity growth needs to be matched by **social** progress.
- Prosperity needs to be **shared** across all parts and regions of India.
- Prosperity growth needs to be environmentally **sustainable.**
- Prosperity needs to be **solid** and resilient in the face of external shocks.

o   ***Prosperity Growth Needs to be Matched by Social Progress***

The Stiglitz-Sen-Fitoussi Commission report in 2009 brought forth fundamental concerns about GDP being a measure of economic development and social progress and reiterated the need to move beyond GDP when trying to assess the growth trajectory of a country.[65] The aim of the report by the Commission was multi-fold.

> [It was] to identify the limits of GDP as an indicator of economic performance and social progress, including the problems with its measurement; to consider what additional information might be required for the production of more relevant indicators of social progress; to assess the feasibility of alternative measurement tools, and to discuss how to present the statistical information in an appropriate way.[66]

They postulated that statistical indicators enable the assessment of the implementation of social policies as well as the performance of economic markets of a country. It is thus essential to work towards developing statistical indicators that are robust enough to reflect the reality of economic and social progress to examine the quality of life in a country. To this end, the SPI, introduced by Michael Porter and his colleagues, quantitatively encompasses the social and environmental variables that may be seen as supplementing GDP as the measure of prosperity.

The first S in the 4S framework stands for 'social.' Growth in prosperity needs to be matched by social progress. Currently, India is 110* among 169 countries on the overall measure of social progress as per the SPI report of 2022. The index examined sixty social and environmental indicators to reveal that the performance of India on dimensions like environmental quality, gender equality and quality of basic education showcases much room for improvement. Air quality in India is categorically poor in many cities. The inefficiency of the energy system, the heavy reliance

---

* https://www.socialprogress.org/global-index-2022-results/

on carbon-based energy and stubble burning are the key reasons behind the state of air pollution in the country. Water scarcity is another major cause of concern. Additionally, agricultural practices that encourage soil erosion also need addressing. While India's CO_2 emissions are relatively modest in comparison to China and most OECD countries, the increasing need for energy production could be an imminent challenge. India still fares low on gender-quality assessments internationally despite some progress in recent years. What is striking is that over 186 million women in the country lack the ability to read or write in any language. The testimony to this is the female literacy rate, which is 65 per cent while the male literacy rate is 80 per cent[*].

On the contrary, Morgan Stanley predicts that by 2031, India's GDP could more than double from $3.5 trillion to $7.5 trillion or more and per capita income can go from $2000 now to about $5000. This contrast in the economic and social progress of India is precisely what the country should address to develop holistically. The need for equitable focus on economic and social progress could not be more evident.

In its attempt to reach out to the poor sections of society, lately, the government has worked on modifying the policies to address the underprivileged better while rectifying the flaws of the previous policies. Conventionally, the policies for the poor offered subsidies on consumption goods (food and energy) and provision for reservation in employment in the public sector. Recently, there has been a shift towards offering direct financial transfers for those in need. With Aadhaar as the personal identification number, the Indian government now has a direct channel of ensuring that financial transfers are efficiently done for those they are meant for. The Pradhan Mantri Jan Dhan Yojana (PMJDY) is another

---

[*] https://www.careindia.org/blog/literacy-rate-in-india/

policy intervention enabling greater financial inclusion. More examples of these direct policy interventions are the Aspirational Districts Programme launched in 2018, aimed at improving the social performance of the most challenged districts in India; the Swachh Bharat Abhiyan, aimed at ensuring better standards of cleanliness and sanitation; the Ayushman Bharat scheme, aimed at improving access to healthcare; the POSHAN Abhiyan, aimed at eliminating malnutrition, and the Mahatma Gandhi National Rural Employment Guarantee Scheme (MGNREGS), aimed at ensuring jobs for the rural population.

o   *Prosperity Needs to Be Shared across All Parts and Regions of India*

The second S in the 4S framework stands for 'shared'. Prosperity needs to be shared across all parts and regions of India. The heterogeneity in India lays the basis for the second S being a guiding principle. The economic performance of states and territories across India differs greatly, as has been substantiated in the earlier chapters of the book. Discussing the variations in prosperity levels at a sub-national level in Chapter 6, we saw that prosperity levels vary by a factor of four. This number is striking because this is double that of the countries in the European Union. The difference in prosperity levels across the country has grown over time. It is noted that states with average higher-income levels grew by 1 per cent more than the states with average lower-income levels annually. While such differences have occurred in other countries, it is important to realize that the way to overcome this difference is achieving convergence and that is precisely the focus under the second S. Prosperity is measured in terms of labour mobilization, labour productivity and labour share in production. These dimensions also vary greatly across the states and territories in India. On labour mobilization, only about 25 to 40 per cent of the working-age population are employees in most states.[67] Overall, labour mobilization, labour productivity and labour share in production significantly influence the economic performance of a region. About 60 per cent of the differences between national and regional averages in this aspect can be understood by analysing the economic factors specific to those regions or locations while the other 40 per cent can be understood by studying the various sectors in that economy. Economic activity across the Indian states also differs. Gujarat and Maharashtra account for 50 per cent of all exports. Gujarat also accounts for 25 per cent of India's gross fixed-capital formation. There are significant differences on the levels of innovation too. Maharashtra alone accounts for 25 per cent of patenting. Additionally, 65 per cent of Indian patenting is accounted for by the top five states while their share of GDP is 40 per cent. This is so because the per-capita patenting rate in these states is five times that of the national average. Differences between the regional and national economies can also be studied if one considers the traded and local industries and in India's case, agriculture too. For example, in Bihar, 20 per cent of all jobs and wages paid are accounted for by traded activities, while in Gujarat, traded activities account for 50 per cent for payroll and 40 per cent for employment. More strikingly, about 30 per cent of all jobs in four states are accounted for by agriculture, whereas the same figure is less than 10 per cent for more than twenty other Indian states.

Heterogeneity in India is vast and there exist numerous explanations for the same. So far, the attempt has been to highlight the contrast in terms of regional economic outputs. Recapitulating the analysis on wealth quintiles and Gini coefficients across Indian states, we studied the data from NFHS 4 and 5. According to NFHS 5 (2019–21), 74 per cent of the urban population lies in the two richest quintiles, while 54 per cent of the rural population lies in the two lowest quintiles. Chandigarh accounts for the largest proportion of the population in the highest wealth quintile, 79 per cent. For Delhi, the same figure was 68 per cent followed by Punjab at 61 per cent. On the other end of the spectrum, Jharkhand accounts for the largest share of the population in the lowest quintile, 46 per cent. This is followed by Bihar at 43 per cent and Assam at 38 per cent. Moving on the examination of the Gini coefficient, which is a widely recognized measure of income inequality, where 0 indicates perfect equality and 1 perfect inequality, the NFHS 5 revealed that Jharkhand has the highest Gini coefficient, 0.27, closely followed by Assam, Meghalaya and West Bengal at 0.25. On the contrary, Delhi has the lowest value at 0.08, followed by Kerala, Punjab and Tamil Nadu at 0.10. The Gini coefficient reveals that there exists immense inequality among the Indian states and territories, highlighting the fact that prosperity is not shared equitably.

The competitiveness approach for attaining equitable growth and prosperity rests on the need for capitalizing on regional strengths to create competitive advantage. As seen in Chapter 5, individual firms and clusters are more effective in fostering regional prosperity than top-down policies. It is the enterprises in the regions that have the ability to increase productivity and innovation. Therefore, it becomes essential to study the heterogeneity in prosperity among the regions in India to work towards a shared prosperity.

o   *Prosperity Growth Needs to Be Environmentally Sustainable*

The third S in the 4S framework stands for 'sustainable.' Prosperity growth needs to be environmentally sustainable. The IPCC Sixth Assessment Report found that the global temperature has increased by 1 degree in comparison to the pre-industrial levels. The cause is also evident: greenhouse gas emissions from human activity resulting in climate change. The report emphasizes the urgency for immediate policy actions aimed at limiting the global warming temperatures to 1.5°C above pre-industrial levels in order to contain the ill effects of climate change. The erratic changes in weather patterns due to climate change hugely contribute towards the worsening of the natural environment and biodiversity. These planetary pressures hamper the progress towards development, especially in terms of reduction of multi-dimensional inequalities such as poverty. The United Nations Environment Programme (UNEP) recommends that global emissions be decreased by 45 per cent by 2030 and eventually be net zero by 2050 if we are to achieve our climate goals. Currently, the progress and commitments made by national governments fall short of the mark, and gradual or incremental changes will not suffice. There is a need to reimagine our society and lives radically. Our long-standing assurance with respect to having enough for everyone is waning and fast. Accelerating economic growth while fulfilling our environment and climate targets is the transformative shift that will be instrumental in delivering a breakthrough for the people and the planet.

So far, the policy actions in response to the imminent climate crisis have been regulations, investments towards carbon neutrality, newer fiscal treatments of energy sources leading to carbon emissions and, most recently, the carbon-border taxes that are aimed at relocating the emissions to countries with lower standards. While the effort towards the implementation of these policies is urgent and needed, there are certain implications that follow, directly affecting development objectives across countries, industries and markets. The worst affected are the energy-intensive sectors: automotive industry and steel production. Firms and enterprises are constantly working towards discovering new products and production processes that meet the climate goals as well as the development objectives. To this end, humongous investments in the renewable-energy sector show some hope while the conventional coal-based energy production has started to become less and less economically viable. Overall investments in the oil and gas industry have also shifted focus towards natural gas production.

Prosperity growth is hindered significantly owing to the vulnerabilities brought to the surface by climate change. India's experience with global policy changes on climate change are quite paradoxical. While the low per-capita carbon emissions mark the country as high performing on climate change, India is one of the largest contributors to future carbon emissions given its low efficiency on current energy production and the increasing energy needs[68]. For India, the challenges in combating these planetary pressures are manifold. The most evident is the challenge posed in agriculture. Changing environmental conditions negatively impact agricultural productivity. A cushion to these negative impacts can be created by way of certain market regulations that penalize and discourage the wasteful use of natural resources. Another cause of concern in this regard are the increasing energy needs of the country. The need of the hour is to shift reliance towards solar energy and other renewable energy sources in an attempt to minimize the effects of climate change while fulfilling the country's energy requirements. Thirdly, eliminating all carbon-based energy productions should be the focus of policy actions.

For the latter, India needs different technology than Europe, given its lower wind speeds. Ambitious policy action is required in order to enable a transition towards carbon-free energy that meets demand and avoids disruptions. There is evidence of the increasing efficiency of renewable energy sources and India should look to adopting strategies to eliminate all coal-based utilities over the next two decades. If India strongly pursues avenues of global investments in the renewable energy sector and attracts collaborators on technology with the objective of minimizing carbon emissions, there will be immense economic and environmental gains. National competitiveness is constituted of both ecological and economic prosperity, and climate change has a direct impact on the worsening of both. As noted earlier, climate change can adversely affect agriculture and natural resources such as water, the direct consequence of which can be scarcity of food and water in many regions across the country. The result will be increase in malnutrition, hunger and conflicts over natural resources. Similarly, worsening air quality in Indian cities is the major cause of rising respiratory illnesses and directly affects the quality of citizens' life. Moreover, the growing incidence of environmental catastrophes like floods and droughts has contributed to displacement and destruction of life and property. What this really changes is people's identities, which further disrupts prosperity growth. The focus, thus, needs to be on prosperity growth that furthers environmentally sustainable economic goals.

o   ***Prosperity Needs to Be Solid and Resilient in the Face of External Shocks***

The fourth and the final S in the 4S framework is 'solid.' Prosperity needs to be solid and resilient in the face of external shocks. The last four years since the COVID-19 pandemic in 2019 have been the most tumultuous for the world. The pandemic brought with it a global financial crisis, what the experts now qualify as a deep macroeconomic shock. The crises were twofold: a challenge to healthcare across the world and an equally serious economic slump whose repercussions are still felt in the economy. The world had only begun to recover from the 2020 crises when the Russian invasion of Ukraine sent geopolitical shock waves across the world. The ongoing conflict led to significant increases in energy costs worldwide while also negatively impacting the global supply chains for essential goods[69]. This series of external shocks bring to notice the urgency of being extremely solid and resilient politically, socially and economically. India's prosperity is bearing and will bear the direct impact of these externalities if the competitiveness fundamentals are not strengthened. Macroeconomic conditions and the new and upcoming changes in technology, geopolitics and climate change are all factors that have the potential to affect the value of India's competitiveness fundamentals. However, India's growth prospects are far more positive in comparison to the rest of the world, which is predicted to face another economic slump soon. According to the IMF and the World Bank, India is better set to face the global changes than other emerging markets because of its robust macroeconomic fundamentals, healthy domestic demand and relative insulation from international trade flows. As per the World Bank, a decrease of 1 per cent in the U.S growth rate results in a 0.4 per cent decrease in India's growth rate, whereas for the other emerging economies, the impact is 1.5 times that of India.[70]

The global economy is experiencing a significant change currently. With market growth moving from North America and Europe to Asia on the demand side and the flattening out of the global labour force on the supply side, the global economy will be majorly restructured. Consequentially, the global markets, trade and economic geography are also undergoing major alterations. One important cause behind this is China and its shift from being a production site for the rest of the world to now focusing on domestic consumption and services. The country is now growing as a market as opposed to being a production site[71]. These changes present a great number of opportunities for India. Experts claim that a global post-pandemic growth bump is a very favourable period for India to work on policy reforms focused on prosperity growth. Now, with Asia gradually becoming the major market-growth driver on the demand side, India is at the forefront in the global growth story. The reason for this is India's demographic advantage or its growing labour force, to be more precise. When the global markets face a crunch, India will be able to emerge stronger due its labour force. India is set to attract global resources, energy markets and huge investments given the changes in China's growth model[72].

One major phenomenon reshaping the global economy is digitalization. Digitalization has had massive effects in restructuring multiple industries, stimulating the growth of new products, services, business models and value chains. Artificial intelligence (AI) and similar digital technologies have created the need for highly skilled human capital. These technologies have also raised the value of access to big data given that big data forms the basis of their processes. It is crucial that we realize the importance of integrating such technologies in our existing systems to develop innovative solutions to serious problems. Doing so will enable the effective and efficient use of digital technologies like AI. India, despite being very active in the global IT market, needs to adopt newer strategies for digitalization. The most evident challenge is the growing demand for skills required for digitalization in the workforce. India, for sure, needs digital solutions that enable the leveraging of capital and skills. The focus should be on integrating digital technologies into its existing strengths and capabilities. Another assertion at this point is that while doing so, India needs to be cautious about protecting its data.

Ultimately, at the core of all policy actions should be the guiding principles as described above. Articulating the goals and objectives under this framework encourages transparency in the discussion on how to weigh the trade-offs against the goals. The 4S framework is multidimensional and hence cannot be just limited to one measure like the average GDP per capita. The objective now of the leadership should be to define metrics that envelope the 4S more directionally and aid the process of tracking performance and decision making for future goals. The diagnostics of India's current competitiveness reveal that there is a long way to go before India achieves equitable growth and shared prosperity. What makes the process more complicated and complex is India's heterogeneity in terms of social progress and income levels. We also examined India's progress on environmental sustainability, and we know now that the ambition to have net-zero carbon emissions is equally challenging given the country's increasing energy needs. Finally, harnessing resilience to better face the externalities like global economic changes or unforeseen health emergencies is also of utmost importance for moving towards shared prosperity. Policies enveloping these dimensions need to be prioritized now for materializing the India@100 dream.

An Integrated Approach to Economic and Social Progress: The Foundation of Structural Transformation 2.0

The task now for India is to articulate an underlying development approach outlining the hypothesis on how India plans on tackling the specific challenges in its economy to translate the same into attaining the India@100 ambitions. As per the Competitiveness Roadmap for India@100 report, this new development approach rests firmly on two pillars. The first is the integration of social and economic agendas. These agendas are intrinsically linked and share fundamental linkages. The single-eyed focus on economic growth fails to invoke similar growth on the social development front and that ultimately disrupts the foundations of prosperity. One of the ways of integrating the economic and social progress agenda is by creating competitive jobs for those who are currently not part of the active labour market. Shared prosperity through competitive jobs is the way to open up pathways for low-skilled and female workers and foster social development. The second pillar under this approach is Structural Transformation 2.0. The idea here is ensuring that individual sectors in the economy contribute to job creation and growth. The India@100 strategy acknowledges the need to move beyond the old model of industrialization, given the ways in which it limits economic power and fails to incorporate the recent advancements in technology and globalization. The paramount need for India at this moment is the creation of job opportunities across a mix of service and industrial sectors. The first task priority to do so is the identification of sectors that can offer entry-level job opportunities to those outside the active labour force—low-skilled workers and women in particular. What follows is the creation of policy actions within these sectors that foster growth for job creation while also enabling upgradation to better job opportunities. Understanding India's current and future competitive advantages while systematically developing such sectors is extremely essential to this process. The sectors identified for creating entry-level jobs for the unskilled are agriculture, textile and clothing, education, healthcare, construction and logistics and distribution. Similarly, sectors that can nurture India's competitive advantages to enable high employment productivity are IT services, biopharmaceuticals, telecommunication, renewable energy equipment and electronics.[73]

New Policy Priorities under Structural Transformation 2.0

Policies must focus on three essential aspects: enabling competitive jobs, growing competitive firms and creating a competitive government. Chapter 7 discussed the need for a competitive government while acknowledging the specificities of the government model in India. Avoiding a repetition of arguments, this section will refrain from discussing the role of competitive governments. However, it was important to point out that competition in the government is a new policy priority under the new approach for growth.

o   *Competitiveness-driven Job Creation*

In order to generate jobs through specific initiatives targeting particular industries and regions, as well as to improve the overall conditions for doing business, India must focus on promoting the expansion of companies that are highly productive. The country needs to support and enable the growth of businesses that can operate more efficiently, deliver higher-quality goods or services and, in turn, create more job opportunities. Enabling the growth of competitive firms hinges on a comprehensive approach that encompasses both supply and demand-side factors. On the supply side, the cost of doing business is a critical consideration. Governments must work on reducing the regulatory burden and improving the efficiency of their judicial systems. Furthermore, investment in infrastructure and the development of a highly skilled workforce are imperative to ensure businesses can operate efficiently and remain competitive. Access to capital is another essential element, necessitating collaboration between financial institutions and businesses. Robust competition policies should be in place to foster an environment where companies can thrive, based on merit and innovation. On the demand side, the focus should be on opening up the domestic market, removing barriers to trade and investment and implementing public procurement policies that encourage competitive firms to participate. These principles should be underpinned by effective implementation and an environment that allows experimentation, learning and scaling of policies. Additionally, alignment between national policies and sectoral growth initiatives is crucial to achieving policy synergies that benefit the growth of competitive firms. In essence, a multifaceted strategy, involving both supply and demand-side elements, is essential for the sustained growth of firms that ultimately lead to better job creation.

The creation of competitive jobs is crucial for any economy to prosper. Different policies are required to create competitive jobs depending on the target group, determined by the labour's status. Low-skilled female workers and those without active employment should be given priority in India's new development strategy. A second category can consist of jobs with better productivity that use recent and upcoming competitive advantages in India. They will be essential in achieving greater prosperity in the future, even though they only offer partial solutions to India's current employment challenges. Children and young people in education who will join the labour market in the future make up a third category; the capabilities profile of this group can still be in line with the changing demands of the Indian economy.[74]

o   *Sector and Location-Specific Growth Initiatives*

India must introduce new economic initiatives tailored to specific sectors and locations. Through these initiatives, an effective strategy for improving growth and competitiveness can be pursued by first identifying the specific needs in a given context and then using the appropriate set of generic policy tools. The public and private sectors will need to work closely together on these efforts because they bring complementary skills and insights essential for creating and pursuing an efficient action agenda. The selection of viable areas for these efforts must be an open, competitive and evidence-based process. Low entrance barriers for women and low-skilled workers, market opportunities and the availability of existing competitive advantages are crucial requirements for attracting these workers in specific sectors. Data on female employment shed light on potential job opportunities within cluster categories or industry sectors. Some jobs are in sectors focused on exports, such as clothing and textiles. Although India has a strong presence in international markets, it has yet to catch up to competitors such as China, Vietnam and Bangladesh. Other work is in the domestic sectors, such as education and healthcare. For instance, the coverage of healthcare services can be expanded, and the low-skilled and female workforce can be leveraged to support the delivery of the services. This can be achieved by changing regulations to allow the participation of low-skill workers in numerous activities, using digital tools, increasing public spending and investment in healthcare services, enabling public and private providers to engage in service delivery and using pilot approaches to scale up effective initiatives. According to diagnostics, India has significant requirements in these sectors, but the present healthcare spending is relatively low. The specific steps required to unlock the potential for producing competitive jobs in this area can be determined by conducting a sector-specific analysis. Additionally, entry barriers for low-skilled employees are lowest in industries like agriculture, construction and logistics and transportation. For female and low-skilled workers, the primary opportunity would be to increase employment prospects and support these industries while improving current occupations' standards.[75]

o   *Priority Actions for Enabling Social Policies*

Enabling social and economic policies is required to assist efforts in stimulating job creation. The Competitiveness Roadmap for India@100 laid out five priority actions enabling social policies: (1) To take action to end childhood poverty for growth and productivity; (2) To reduce obstacles for women entering the workforce, create career opportunities and provide childcare services; (3) To invest in a value-based healthcare system to deliver better medical services and open up employment opportunities in a more technologically enabled, low-skilled delivery framework; (4) To improve public safety that would further help in eliminating obstacles for women entering the workforce; and (5) To enhance the efficiency of the educational system by giving K–12 pupils the necessary skills for entering the workforce successfully.

Focusing on education policies that enhance the long-term employment prospects and development opportunities for children and young people is crucial in India. Childhood poverty remains a significant obstacle, affecting children's potential productivity throughout their lives. Although stunting rates have declined, India lags behind many of its peers in addressing this issue. The need to combat childhood poverty is both a social and economic imperative. Drawing inspiration from Indonesia's successful conditional cash-transfer programme, called 'Programme Keluarga Harapan', India can expand its efforts and incorporate innovative technological approaches like the India Stack in social policy domains. The quality of education and the alignment of available skills with the demands of the Indian economy are major concerns. These challenges have been highlighted in the New Education Policy and Skill India initiatives. Maximizing their impact requires effective implementation. Enhancing workforce skills requires a location- and sector-specific approach, similar to the sectoral growth initiatives previously mentioned. Peru's 'Innova Schools' model, providing high-quality education to low-income families affordably, offers a promising example for India to adopt. Collaborating with NGOs and social entrepreneurs working to elevate educational standards across the country will be instrumental in this regard.

Creating new employment opportunities, particularly in healthcare, is a significant avenue for growth. With a substantial percentage of women already engaged in the healthcare industry, their labour force challenges are relatively lower. However, existing regulatory requirements often demand skill-intensive healthcare delivery from low-skilled personnel. Legislative adjustments should prioritize a few highly skilled doctors for critical tasks and incorporate technology to enhance healthcare services while generating new job prospects. In parallel, social policies enabling women's access to the workforce play a vital role. Providing childcare facilities and improving public safety are essential for women to actively seek employment. Initiatives like Shared Value India support major corporations' CSR efforts to address societal issues like child poverty and skill development for disadvantaged communities, exemplifying the ethos behind facilitating social policies. Mobile learning experiments, using digital technologies and regional languages, showcase the potential for expanding educational access[76].

o   *Creating Value through Effective Market Competition*

India has made substantial progress in enhancing its business environment by addressing factor input conditions and reducing the cost of doing business over the last few years. To further boost economic competitiveness and job creation, the focus must expand beyond addressing input conditions and cost reduction. The key to this lies in unlocking market competition as a driver of value generation. This involves the creation of a regulatory framework that incentivizes value creation for customers, promotes allocative efficiency and encourages innovation. It is crucial to effectively enforce competition policies, taking into consideration the dynamics of digital markets and existing market structures. Encouraging the entry and scaling of competitive new firms becomes imperative to balance the dominance of large incumbents. Market regulations should provide incentives for firms to compete based on productivity and value. In markets heavily influenced by government intervention, it is necessary to establish governance and incentive structures that mimic market dynamics.

The success of these policies depends on recognizing India's political economy, conducting regional experiments to assess the implications of reforms and ensuring that markets reward value creation aligned with societal needs. Encouraging the scaling up of more productive firms is essential for job creation, along with an increasing number of companies transitioning from informality to complying with public rules and regulations. India's current policies emphasize entrepreneurship, cost reduction and support for MSMEs. While these efforts are positive, they need to address India's primary challenges in its firm demographics. Entrepreneurship thrives in India, but many small companies struggle to achieve scale, leading to a divide between highly skilled tech-based startups and a large segment with limited opportunities for low-skilled workers. Similarly, reducing the cost of doing business is important but must go beyond formal changes to address systemic regulatory issues. Digitalization of government services has been a positive step. Existing MSME policies often lack a clear focus on scaling the most competitive SMEs, highlighting the need for a comprehensive national policy for MSMEs. To foster the growth of competitive firms, both supply-side and demand-side policy levers must be deployed coherently[77].

In summary, India grapples with multiple challenges in translating its policies into effective impact. While the country has been active in policy formulation, there is often a gap between the intended goals and the outcomes achieved. To overcome this challenge, there's a need to reframe core policy directions. This requires harmonizing social and economic policies to better achieve key objectives and broadening sectoral focus through approaches like Structural Transformation 2.0 to align with changing realities. Improving the quality of policy design processes is essential. This entails fostering a more constructive public-private dialogue during policy formulation and implementing location- and sector-specific policies. Moreover, enhancing government coordination is equally critical. This requires clearly defining the roles and responsibilities of different government levels and addressing fragmentation across functional areas, ensuring that policies deliver the intended results. The next section builds more on this while elaborating on the need for competitive government as part of reforming the institutional architecture.

New Institutional Architecture

As discussed in the previous sections, India has shown sustained economic growth over the years; however, it is still far from meeting its actual potential. The institutional overhaul thus proposed aims to achieve just that. India requires a new institutional framework to drive more effective implementation, as many recent policies, while having commendable aims, have often fallen short of achieving their intended impact. If we approach the policies outlined in this strategy with the same methods as those in the past, they are likely to face similar outcomes. The following section elaborates on the pillars vital to the new institutional framework that can be implemented to improve the growth trajectory of the country. The pillars are formulated on crucial aspects of policymaking in the Indian context.

o   *Public-Private Dialogue*

Sustained economic growth cannot be undertaken by the public or the private sector alone. The public sector often compromises on economic advancement for social welfare, which can lead to a country not realizing its full potential. An example of such a situation was the dominance of public institutions in the Indian market until the 1980s. The country showed growth, but the pace was far behind the global standard. After the opening up of markets in the 1990s, the country witnessed meteoric growth. The private sector, therefore, holds the key to unlocking a country's economic potential and thus, bringing it face to face with its economic realities. However, if left unchecked, market forces often disrupt the social progress of the country and exacerbate the existing inequalities. Therefore, for efficient and holistic progress in a country, public-private partnerships are important. A healthy relationship between public and private institutions, where public institutions nurture an environment that helps the private sector to thrive while exercising a regulatory authority, is a key driver of a country's growth. In India, with its diverse population and varied set of opportunities, the role of the private sector in utilizing India's potential is crucial. However, given our existing socio-economic disparity, robust public institutions are required to ensure that the growth is equitable and its benefits are enjoyed by all.

In India, there are deep-seated reservations among both sectors towards collaborating with each other. These reservations often come in the way of widespread partnerships between the two sectors and, therefore, hamper the potential growth India could witness.[78] Often business practices are seen as anti-public and are thought to be driven only by profits and neglect social welfare. Furthermore, the private sector often finds public institutions difficult to work with, owing to their perception about bureaucracy and corruption. These reservations, although having supporting arguments, need to be worked past for a meaningful dialogue between the public and private institutions. Currently, infrastructure projects, such as highways, ports or railways are some successful large-scale examples of public-private partnerships.* However, if the channel between the two sectors is strengthened and collaborations are improved, the expertise brought in by the private sector along with the caution exercised by the public sector could be beneficial for the economic growth of the country. Various projects suffer at the hands of bureaucracy, whereas, similarly, many private projects often neglect social norms and, thus, drive the public against them. Forging an efficient partnership where both sectors engage and collaborate and leverage each other's benefits while mitigating each other's drawbacks is the need of the hour. Therefore, institutionally, we should strive towards actively striking and increasing public-private partnerships for the benefit of the country.

o   *Location-Based Policy Approach*

India's heterogeneity is rather spread across sectors and locations. These locations can be regions spread across states, within a state or localized to a city or district. However, leveraging their potential with effective policymaking is equally important. Under

---

* https://www.niti.gov.in/verticals/ppp

the current government, this need has been identified in terms of policies such as Smart Cities or One-District-One Product, which focus on promoting the local goods to generate economic growth and improve productivity. The identification of these locations is a responsibility that falls to local-level bodies, the state government and the private sector of the region. To maximize their potential, effective collaboration and coordination across the three tiers of government and the private sector is necessary. Furthermore, the governments can identify key sectors where the entry barrier is low to create productive jobs. This shall also be useful to improve the labour force participation rates. Furthermore, the development of human capital is essential to sustain the productivity of the jobs thus created and improve their long-term value creation. Similarly, the identification of sectors with high export value or established industries whose products can be exported shall be undertaken. This will improve the trade output from these locations and contribute to the diversification of India's export basket, making India's trade more resilient to economic shocks.

Institutionally, the empowerment of local governments is necessary to effectively implement these localized policies. In order to do that, the local governments require a certain political clout. The political clout here refers to fiscal decentralization, which enables the local governments to hold certain financial power. The objective of decentralization was to increase the productivity at the local level by using local goods, thereby bringing prosperity. However, the local governments often suffer from the lack of mobilization of resources at a local level and lead splintered actions in the absence of hard power. Thus, the need of devolution of power and fiscal responsibility to local governments is crucial to location-centric policymaking. Similarly, this location-centric approach brings the necessary bottom-up perspective to policymaking in the country. Various locations have their own challenges and opportunities, which often cannot be addressed by top-down measures. Policy actions such as the Aspirational Districts Programme and Smart Cities Mission serve this very purpose in the current discourse. Coupling the current constitutional framework around decentralization with favourable policy actions would emerge as a crucial step towards achieving the desired economic goals.[79] In addition to that, economic prosperity at the local level would bring with it social development. Policies often suffer from last-mile delivery of their benefits, but with this approach, social development at the grass-roots level can occur in tandem with economic development. With this approach, the role of other government levels is also crucial. Local governments should plan efficiently and target specific levers from the state and Central government to improve the coordination among the three levels. Moreover, the necessary devolution of power can only take place through higher levels of government. At last, the identification of clusters and opting for a cluster-centric-development approach can be the logical next step after the successful implementation of location-centric policies. Thus, opting for a bottom-up approach and leveraging India's heterogeneity in terms of opportunities are essential to accelerate the growth of our economy.

o   *Policymaking Architecture*

India's current policy implementation infrastructure is splintered across various ministries and levels of government. This leads to coordination challenges both vertically among different government levels and horizontally among various departments and ministries at the same government level. Often, policies involve a multi-dimensional approach as the issues are multiple, which requires a coordinated effort. For instance, a programme that offers free healthcare services in rural areas follows a path starting at the central level, going through the Ministry of Health and Family Welfare, Ministry of Finance and Ministry of Women and Child Development. It then extends to state governments and ultimately engages local bodies for implementation. Along with this, various departments are mobilized, which entails bureaucracy and thus creates a puzzle that is often not easy to solve. This method is riddled with inefficiencies and, thus, inhibits the desired effect of the policy. Therefore, there is a need for better implementation mechanisms.

A long-term solution to this can be the creation of new agencies that are tasked with aligning various bodies for a coordinated action. This would reduce the bureaucracy involved in the current structure and enable more efficiency of implementation. Furthermore, the policymaking process should encompass the desired implementation process and have a goal-based approach to implementation rather than the current splintered efforts that are an entanglement of various issues. These actions would enhance the impact of policies, which will become more targeted and efficiently implemented.[80] [81] The creation of a body to coordinate action can be done as a pilot for a certain policy and can be rolled out in a phased-out manner to other policy areas. Furthermore, these bodies can be the forum in which public-private dialogues can take place. Along with that, since these bodies should be empowered to work across ministries and levels of government, they can be used to implement sector-specific policies at a later stage. In this manner, the policy-implementation mechanism of the country can be slowly overhauled, leading to a better, more efficient mechanism.

o   *Whole of Government Approach*

The transformative potential of ICT in the delivery of government services has unlocked novel trajectories of institutional development, which can solve a host of problems faced by government institutions. These problems, namely, the lack of collaborative approaches, inability to deliver personalized services to end users and accessibility issues, can be solved by adopting an integrative approach to governance like 'one-stop government' or 'whole-of-government.' The concept was originally introduced by the Tony Blair Government in 1997 as 'Joined-up Government'; it aspired to achieve better horizontal and vertical coordination and positioned itself as the opposite of departmentalism or operating in silos. On similar lines, one definition of the 'whole-of-government' approach is, '. . .[it] denotes public services agencies working across portfolio boundaries to achieve a shared goal and an integrated government response to particular issues. Approaches can be formal or informal. They can focus on policy development, program management, and service delivery.'[82] An integrated and integrative approach allows separate government institutions to break patterns of siloed thinking and practice and enables more active engagement and dialogue with the government on the part of the end users who may be citizens or businesses. The lack of an integrated approach can negatively affect the delivery of services, especially social services in large countries like India. This approach differs from e-government, which is solely concerned with the integration of ICT with already existing institutional practices.[83] An integrated whole-of-government approach, on the other hand, calls for the reorganization of government institutions in such a manner that government institutions are integrated with respect to objectives, design and delivery of services. It shields the end user from the complexities of the internal workings of government agencies by providing a single point of contact.

The implementation of such an integrated and integrative approach to governance requires a national framework and strong, national-level backing. The appointment of an official with necessary powers across departments who can facilitate the development and integration of the required ICT infrastructure is critical to the success of these efforts. This role should be given enough flexibility to respond to the evolving nature of such an institutional framework. Another key requirement for this approach to be effective and cost efficient is interoperability across already existing systems, especially legacy systems. Different departments and agencies across the government might have developed their own ICT infrastructure, and it may not be cost effective to replace these already existing infrastructure given sunk costs, which may include technical as well as training costs.[84] Thus, interoperability, based on common standards, can effectively resolve the problem of legacy architecture in a cost-efficient manner. Another level of integration would involve the integration of online services. The already existing services can be organized around common themes or service types under a one-stop-shop model.

The significant initial investment involved in setting up such an integrated architecture requires a complementary strategic framework to ensure the sustainability of this architecture. Instead of siloed and fragmented planning, this framework should be based on horizontal and vertical integration of government departments and agencies and should be aimed at improving transparency and accountability, apart from designing a sustainable architecture. Parallel architectures need to be eliminated to avoid duplication of efforts and transform the traditional hierarchical model of governmental organizations. This integrated architecture should also include networks as well as partnerships within as well as outside the government.

Significant long-term and sustainable integration requires extensive cooperation, which, in turn, requires effective training and a flexible approach. A Government Information Infrastructure, which integrated existing networks across the government requires cross agency planning and active cooperation amongst individual units. Cloud computing can enable sharing of ICT resources across departments and agencies and can save costs while implementing such a large information infrastructure. Private service providers can be roped in to provide the ICT backbone for this architecture as this will save infrastructural as well as training costs.[85] This, coupled with a specialized framework for security and privacy protection would ensure efficiency as well as infrastructural safety. However, the major organizational as well as political challenge would be to ensure collaboration and cooperation amongst different agencies and departments with divergent and often conflicting priorities. Without effective cooperation, such an integrated and integrative approach would be impossible to achieve.

The India@100 strategy should transition from a rigid plan of fixed government policy initiatives to a more inclusive approach that engages all government bodies and departments over time. This approach prioritizes, adapts or introduces specific policies, tools and programmes in alignment with the strategy's objectives. It underscores the importance of dedicated strategic agencies and project teams to execute these policies and programs in line with the strategy's goals. Moreover, it stresses the need for announcing policies and programmes that align with the strategy's objectives and priorities. The strategy is designed to guide India's responses to external shocks and new circumstances, ensuring unified government responses.

To maintain its relevance and adaptability to changing circumstances, the strategy should remain dynamic, subject to periodic updates reflecting new insights and shifts in the strategic landscape. Given the strategy's ambitious goal of guiding India towards its 100th independence anniversary, it must utilize multiple impact channels that influence actions and outcomes over an extended period. These channels encompass specific policies and action initiatives, which have the most immediate impact, as they address near-term objectives. The proposed institutional structures and process changes have a more extended influence, shaping both current policy actions and the design and implementation of future policies. Finally, the conceptual approach and framework underpinning the strategy can have the most enduring impact, influencing India's long-term thinking about its circumstances and strategies for improvement, even as circumstances evolve and priorities change over time.

9

The Road Ahead: India's Odyssey to Prosperity

There was a time when a multipolar world could have seemed unfathomable. Such is the unpredictability of time and its ebbs and flows that a multipolar world is now not only fathomable but also rather closer in sight, if not already here. India is positioned as a key influencer in the global landscape. It is spearheading strategies to show the way to not just the developing nations but also the developed world. The world is faced with multidimensional crises in the form of rising debt, rising inflationary pressures, price volatility of essentials, climate change risks, fragmented geopolitical terrain and a slowed-down progress towards the SDGs. A multipolar world must be led by responsible and capable leaders who understand the complexities of the challenges facing us and are able to overcome them with nuanced solutions, enabling a more equitable and just world.

The India@100 strategy transcends mere policy analyses to understand India's competitiveness. Albeit crucial, such analyses serve only as the foundation to derive policy recommendations to enhance India's competitiveness. The aim of this book is to challenge conventional norms, explore untrod trajectories and provoke forward-looking thought. The policy prescriptions laid out in this roadmap are meant to act as a compass. Whether the guiding principles mentioned earlier can influence and, wherever necessary, alter the national discourse about competitiveness. These more general concepts are especially important for a roadmap that intends to determine India's growth strategy for the following twenty-five years, which is far longer than the time frame of any given policy or programme.

At this juncture, it is imperative that the new India be governed by a unified value system driven by the principles of social progress, shared prosperity, sustainability and resilience to external shocks. We need not chart small, straitjacket fragmented packets of policy underscoring prosperity but a broad set of ideas that utilizes an all-encompassing approach above and beyond fixed policy initiatives to be implemented by designated parts of government. A novel all-of-government approach underpins the India@100 strategy. The onus should lie on ministries and government agencies across levels to evaluate how their policies and operations align with the strategy's stated objectives. Based on the outline of the action plan, their goals should include producing more competitive jobs, firms and, thus, government. New policies and legislative proposals should be rigorously evaluated for their capacity to advance these objectives, capitalize on the specific actions outlined in the action plan and work with the systems and procedures put in place to make them a reality. The strategy's success is dependent not just on an action plan that seeks to anticipate and prepare for the future but is also motivated by the strategy's capacity to give effective advice and structures to advise policies that adapt to new situations in ways that are compatible with and rely on the actions and structures already established.[1]

The objectives and guiding principles laid out in the India@100 plan are designed to aid the country in managing its reactions to its changing circumstances. The strategy should be updated on a regular basis to reflect changes in conditions and new insights, as well as how these changes influence the plan. Programmes and legislative responses should be routinely evaluated for their capacity to advance the objectives of the strategy, make use of the particular actions outlined in the action plan and rely on the systems and procedures put in place to carry them out during times of crisis like the current rise in food and energy prices. Numerous components of the India@100 action agenda are time bound; thus, activities will only be carried out temporarily until they have either achieved their objectives or have otherwise lost their significance. The capacity to use additional impact channels that have the potential to have a long-term impact on actions and results is essential to the achievement of a plan with the highly ambitious objective of assisting India in celebrating its hundredth anniversary of achieving freedom.[2]

The suggested policies and action plans will have an effect in the near future. The suggested institutional structures and process improvements will have a longer time to take effect, impacting not just the creation and execution of current policies but also those that will be developed in the future. The strategy's conceptual approach and underlying structure offer the greatest potential for long-term effects. They have the power to shape how India views its problems and potential solutions, even when those problems and corresponding policy objectives are vastly different from what they are now. The year 2047 may seem far away but it is less time than there was between the early 1990s economic reforms and now. India cannot afford to wait. There are a few first initiatives that may be taken to gain momentum towards putting the strategy provided in this study into action. The beginning of a public conversation on this plan has to be one of the initiatives. It will be crucial to raise awareness and buy-in for the strategic roadmap and the competitiveness diagnostics that it is based on since the strategy is about choices. If there is agreement on the necessity and fundamental nature of a strategic roadmap and if fruitful, evidence-based talks regarding its individual components take place, much will be accomplished. A conversation with those ministries and agencies specifically referenced in particular priority policies as well as with others is necessary to investigate their reaction to the broad principles provided. This will take place, in part, inside the government. A second component will engage the business sector, with a focus on sector- and cluster-specific activities to create tangible action plans in the prioritized sectors. Overall direction for both sets of activities will be required. At the core of the India@100 strategy is an all-of-government approach based on adaptability to changing circumstances, with a focus on public engagement and multi-sectoral collaboration between government and non-government entities to foster competitiveness and sustainability. While this first edition of the book has attempted to provide the diagnostics for India's competitiveness fundamentals, we can expect a further examination into how the strategic roadmap can be concretely implemented in the second edition of the series.

India's Competitiveness Journey: A Reflective Synopsis

Starting out with a lay of the land of India, offering a brief walk through Indian economic watershed moments of the past, an awareness of our history was built to understand how we got here. Right from the time India gained independence and emerged as a democratic nation state to donning the role of the G20 presidency in 2023, it has indeed traversed a long way. Morgan Stanley predicts that India's GDP could more than double from $3.5 trillion to $7.5 trillion or more by 2031, and its per-capita income can go from $2000 now to about $5000 by then. In the initial years, as a nascent democratic state, India saw the state assuming the 'commanding heights of the economy,'[3] controlling major aspects of economic growth. The country witnessed a watershed green revolution in the 1960s, after suffering from crippling food crises. Going from these phases to an initial slow opening up of the economy in the 1980s, India had seen major ups and downs. Moving forward, 1991 stood for more comprehensive liberalization reforms that changed the face of the country forever. Slowly, the new liberalized country moved into the run up to India's IT boom. The stark shift from agriculture to services without having first substantially industrialized caught the attention of many minds. It continues to be a topic of huge interest as it went against popular economic thinking. During the boom preceding the 2008 financial crisis, the presiding mindset was that India is largely divorced from the developed world to be affected by any negative spillovers. The India of 2008 was substantially different from the one that saw the 1998 Asian economic crisis. It was more integrated with the world in the latter time period. On the back of recalibrated macroeconomic policies, including the usage of stimulus packages, India got onto a recovery path. Early on in the 2010s, the two major trends in the economy were high levels of inflation and low lingering growth rates. A major change in terms of approach to policymaking came in the latter half of the decade. Comprehensive, far-reaching and people-centred socio-economic reforms came into play.

Demonetization, the GST roll-out, the Jan Dhan Yojana and many reforms focusing on last-mile implementation have been brought in.

There is a noteworthy trend one can point to; nowadays, exchanges on India's potential as a superpower or a global leader almost always mention its potential to lead in the context of the current changing external context. This was not the case even until a few years ago. Some major changing contours are shaping uncharted but promising waters for India. The Asian Development Bank has posited a massive doubling of Asia's share of the global GDP by 2050, while the IMF and World Bank have identified India as a 'bright spot' in the global economic scenario, attributing it the potential to tackle any external shocks better than other emerging economies. Two trends that stand out are digitalization and climate change. The Internet evolutionary tale has gone from being a rarity to being indispensable. India is now home to 692 million Internet users with Internet penetration at 48.7 per cent, social media users close to 33 per cent of the population and 1.1 billion active cellular mobile connections. Additionally, in a short time span, the country has pioneered a digital revolution of the kind that is rare to have been seen in developing economies. Be it the JAM trinity or UPI, India stands testimony to real last-mile digital connectivity. We are also given a glimpse into how developing economies are leveraging technology for growth and digital adoption in Asian economies. We discussed how the online space has proven to be a boon, particularly in our quest to recover from the pandemic. Where conventional trade suffered, e-commerce and digital sales surged, helping sellers and consumers across the world. In terms of digital sales in retail e-commerce in 2021, the Asia-Pacific region emerged as the biggest market. Countries such as China are boosted by a massive digital buyer base. Similarly, India is also emerging as a huge market for e-commerce, with growing purchasing power among buyers. This digital progress continues to have a positive impact on social progress. India has been able to protect itself from data colonialism, which is when advanced countries are able to benefit from cross-border data flows at the expense of the interests and welfare of developing or less-developed nations. Owing to our enhanced digital capacities, India has been able to bring public services to its people through digital means. It is hard to grasp that just over a few decades ago, citizens had to grapple with phone calls, standing in long queues or make trunk calls. From this perspective, it gets clear as to what a massive revolution the mobile phone has brought about. Through a smartphone, a farmer in a remote village is able to find information on the weather, best agricultural practices and ways to access financial inputs.

The climate-change phenomenon is yet another behemoth of a trend that requires the world to take urgent action. India is in a unique position to pioneer ways to balance the climate and development agenda. Its traditional way of living has always been in line with recycling, reusing and judicious use. Mission LiFE, or Lifestyle for Environment, nudges individual and community behaviour for an environmentally conscious lifestyle while facilitating this shift through responsible production and consumption. Finance, education and technology, along with international collaboration with multiple stakeholders, are key enablers for well-balanced climate and development action. A vital element of climate action and sustainable development is climate justice. Developing economies find it challenging to attain greater levels of economic growth and industrialization without adversely affecting the environment. Adapting production processes requires greater investment and capital at this point. All in all, climate justice addresses the fact that not everyone has contributed equally to environmental damage in the same manner, but all are experiencing the negative impact of climate change, more so the poor and vulnerable regions who are affected disproportionately. It is important to recall the commitment of developed nations at COP15 in 2009 to mobilize $100 billion per year by 2020 to support developing countries combat climate change. They are yet to deliver on this promise. Climate-resilient development is the way forward to address the climate-development dilemma elaborated upon in the section. Low-cost technologies transfer and knowledge sharing are key factors in a climate-resilient future, especially for developing nations, least developed countries and small island developing nations.

There are myriad examples through history of countries that have performed to the best of their abilities and gone above and beyond, delivering exceptional economic growth and development. There is scholarly work on analyses of such cases. The East Asian Tigers, Taiwan, Singapore, Hong Kong and South Korea have been subjects of extensive analysis to identify drivers of growth among these nations. The rise of the Asian bloc was associated with the rise of the tigers, although other nations in the region are also considered to be spearheading this rise today. The East Asian miracle started with Japan and was driven mainly by exports, rapid industrialization, technological advancement and government interventions. Chapter 3 explored different viewpoints towards the East Asian miracle. While some identify one factor to be the growth catalyst, some consider other aspects of greater significance. The Danish Model is yet another example of a growth strategy that has stood the country in good stead. Expounding on the Danish innovation system and its welfare state, we look to the innovative spirits among Danish businesses that are mostly SMEs. Innovations in the system are generally incremental in nature. There are multiple low and medium-tech industries that produce on the back of extensive knowledge inputs. There is also an immense flexibility in resource usage. Denmark adds to the argument by showcasing that an economy can grow by relying on its strengths and a unique strategy even if it goes contrary to the conventional mode of thought. Conventional economics adopts a pro-market line of thought that identifies huge public expenditure, progressive taxation and extensive public social welfare programmes as obstacles to growth. Denmark's comprehensive welfare state that has been able to deliver phenomenal social and economic growth stands tall as a unique model. We went on to trace historical events that have shaped Denmark's current socioeconomic system and social cohesion in the Danish society. It identifies certain key elements of the Danish model such as self-regulation of the labour market, education system and a learning economy based on continuous innovation and knowledge creation. An important takeaway is that Denmark, as a learning economy, considers rapid creation of knowledge more important than the intensive use of existing knowledge in the system. This pushes organizations and workers to constantly strive for betterment. Factoring the external context and the contemporary scenario for the economy under discussion is extremely important while doing a case study. Each nation faces its own set of growth factors, opportunities and obstacles. What may have worked for one nation may not be relevant for another. It is evident that a certain bent of policy worked in the favour of these economies. The takeaway should be that emulating policies that delivered success in one region is not the solution. Learning the process of policy formulation, of how opportunities specific to the economy's conditions were leveraged, how obstacles were overcome and re-thinking for our set of conditions, is the way ahead.

The competitiveness framework enables an economy to leverage its specific set of conditions. The term competitiveness came to be defined in different ways. Michael Porter, a pioneer in the field of competitiveness and strategy, defined competitiveness more specifically. It came to be perceived as the foundation of wealth creation and economic performance. Foundational competitiveness is the expected level of output per working-age individual or output per potential worker, given the overall quality of a country as a place to do business. By defining it in terms of productivity, Porter underscored its focus on productivity and the direct linkage to prosperity. A notable point in the framework is its emphasis on prosperity being influenced by both the productivity of employed workers and that of the potential workers as well. It reflected the importance of the economy's ability to mobilize the available labour force. The framework is built on factors that drive foundational competitiveness in an economy and is classified into two arenas: macroeconomic and microeconomic. While the macroeconomic arena includes a crucial aspect called social infrastructure and political institutions encompassing healthcare, education, law and security and monetary and fiscal policy, the microeconomic arena discusses factor conditions, demand conditions, the presence of related and supporting industries and the sophistication of company strategies. The framework factors into account endowments that a country holds inherently. This can range from natural-resource deposits and country size to locational attributes. The competitiveness framework also underscores that the mere existence of endowments does not assure competitiveness. Owing to the sheer variety of determinants that the framework holds, it offers immensely useful insights when analysing a country's growth potential and future prospects. We dove deep into a concept that forms a crucial part of the framework: the quality of the business environment in the nation and the presence of related and supporting industries. Porter's diamond model offers an insight into the dynamic interplay between factors constituting a local business environment.

When delving into country-specific circumstances, Porter's diamond model proves to be of great significance. The model, seemingly simplistic, offers insights into the complex dynamics and interlinkages within economies, regions and firms. The sheer applicability of the model renders it in a strong position to be utilized in understanding the workings and interdependencies in a system. The model answers questions such as why certain firms based in certain nations innovate more efficiently and successfully, and why they are capable of pursuing improvements, going from one level of sophistication to another. Classical theory considers labour, land, capital and natural resources to be the cornerstones of an economy. While this is still a useful lens to use, Porter offers a more relevant model that takes into consideration a vital fact: Competition is dynamic and evolving. He considers this an essential premise to begin working on a model. There has been a huge emphasis on how dynamic our external context is. A static model, in that case, would not hold much relevance. The diamond model, on the other hand, is able to provide insights into the functioning of economies or firms in a changing world. It gives scope to consider the globalization of competition, power of technology, competition in global trade and foreign investments, etc. Michael Porter's diamond model discusses four forces: demand conditions, factor conditions, firm strategy, rivalry and structure and related and supporting industries.

Having set the theoretical context of competitiveness and its significant components, the next step is to ask what India's competitiveness fundamentals look like. India does score on the higher side in many competitiveness rankings. However, when the competitiveness scores are higher compared to the current prosperity levels, it can imply that there is potential for firms to utilize favourable business conditions to drive productivity and growth. High levels of competitiveness relative to current prosperity can indicate significant potential for firms to translate favourable business environment conditions into higher productivity and value creation. While efforts are being taken to ease the process in and around business, there lies a long way ahead. At the implementation level, rules and regulations tend to pose multiple challenges to entrepreneurs. Even when we simplify or remove cumbersome regulations, a large part of the economy still cannot avail the benefits of the same. Despite being a clarion call for a long time now, Indian policies need to have a bottom-up approach to understand each and every policy from the ground up. Yet another competitiveness fundamental that is delved into is investing in human resource. The Indian education system has expanded significantly as enrolment rates across all levels of education have gone up. However, learning outcomes need to be focused on. There needs to be a lot of improvement in this area still. Quality of education and ensuring that skill levels match market requirements should be priority areas. Along with investing in education, investing in physical infrastructure is of the essence. It forms the bedrock of a strong functioning system. India has successfully ramped up infrastructure in terms of electricity capacity, telecommunications and transport. There have been massive investments focusing on the financing side, be it the National Infrastructure Pipeline or the Asset Monetization Pipeline plans for setting ambitions for investment and mobilizing private capital. Despite these investments, India needs to work on the regulation and governance side. As a case in point, land rights regulations are known to have caused delays and created a rigmarole of processes for many projects. The speedy redressal of cases is also required, and more efficient judicial processes would certainly add to the former. In terms of the financial scenario,

India is doing differently on different parameters. It has a low debt-to-GDP ratio as compared to its peers. Venture capital investment has grown by leaps and bounds over the years. While large companies have ample access to capital, a huge portion of the economy still faces challenges in the same. In the product and service markets, some reforms have hugely benefited the economy. The GST, by bringing uniformity in tax rates across states, has reduced barriers to foster trade ties across the nation. Lastly, a notable fundamental that has shown exponential growth is India's export capacity. In recent years, one can see a conspicuous change in Indian foreign trade and investment. While there still exist many barriers, we have come a long way in terms of opening up our markets and building capabilities in domestic industries to create export-oriented sectors.

Moving further down to a bottom-up perspective, the theme of clusters is explored thoroughly. To reiterate, there were a few dominant economic models back in the day, which held sway over development thought. With new economic models making a foray into mainstream policy, new approaches have found their own space. Earlier, the emphasis was more top-down, with entire nations and states being taken as a whole in policy thought. However, taking a view from the bottom-up, understanding how dynamics play out at the playing field level has become a new influential approach. This approach has helped us understand the competitiveness and productivity of a region, thus giving us far better insights into what truly drives a region's growth. It shows us how businesses function, whether successfully or not, and the reasons underlying both. As defined, a cluster is as a group of interconnected firms, suppliers, service providers and associated institutions in a particular field, often linked by commonalities and complementarities, which compete as well as coordinate. There is a distinct role of location and economic geography in giving businesses a competitive advantage and allowing for a conducive environment for clusters. There are certain differentiating traits between traded and local clusters. Traded clusters are those that can grow beyond the area's market size and absorb workers from other industries and firms, functioning as the region's main source of economic growth. Local clusters are the ones that produce goods and services serving the local markets. This demarcation helps to identify the true engines of growth and prosperity, which are the former ones.

Heterogeneity can be an opportunity and a challenge. Variations in economic performance on multiple indicators across regions can explain why some fare better than others. Home to some of the most populated states in the world, India has seen huge variations among regions in terms of per-capita income, social progress, FDI inflows, exports and inequality levels. In terms of the labour-market conditions across states, there are significant variations in labour mobilization, labour productivity and labour share in production. Even in the field of GFCF, some states, such as Maharashtra and Gujarat, fare far better than some others. It is important to level variations as GFCF measures investment in fixed capital assets, such as infrastructure, buildings and machinery in a given period. While furthering state-level variations, it is crucial to reflect on innovation at the state-level. It is noted that there is a huge scope at the national level and the state level, to increase expenditure on R&D. The ability to retain human capital in the long term depends on a state's innovation capabilities. Low expenditure on innovation has a lasting impact on a state's competitiveness. No single parameter can provide a holistic picture of a region's competitiveness. All determinants, including human capital, technology, business environment and natural resources, in tandem, constitute the basis of an economy's growth.

Convergence is an economic theory that indicates a catch-up effect wherein regions lagging in terms of growth tend to have grown at a faster pace and, eventually, came at par with developed regions. In the existing scholarly work on Indian development, there is little evidence of convergence between states or union territories. This presents a robust case for delving deeper into specific factors constraining growth in low performing regions. There needs to be a targeted focus on state-level efforts. Investigating variances in performance across states and sectors is key to unleashing their potential. This is especially important for policymakers to narrow down on areas for improvement and design strategies with focused pathways for equitable and inclusive growth. These variances among states hold the key to unlocking a multiplicity of such pathways.

The economic dynamics discussed pan out in a landscape shaped by the contours of institutional architecture in the country. They provide a structure to interactions within the country. Policies, governance structure, regulations and laws constitute the institutional apparatus. The call for institutional reforms in India has been resounded multiple times in policy circles. On the basis of an understanding of the current state of our institutions, we propose a set of new principles for a new institutional framework. The pivotal role of institutions in shaping India's economic growth and development has been highlighted and the importance of strong institutions in implementing and sustaining policies effectively has been brought to attention. Despite India's notable economic progress, the quality of its institutions has not improved significantly over the years, raising concerns about the potential obstacles weak institutions may pose to long-term growth. While recognizing the complexity of the relationship between institutions and economic growth, there is an urgent need for India to strengthen its institutional framework. India must address persistent institutional challenges to ensure sustained economic progress. Robust institutions are essential for implementing reforms, ensuring India's economic growth sustainability. The book underscores the pivotal role of institutional quality in shaping India's future economic trajectory.

An example of good practices from around the world is the Economic Development Board (EDB) in Singapore. There are factors underlying EDB's growth including its clear mandate, high degree of autonomy and focus on building partnerships, among others. Competitiveness councils in Colombia also stand testimony to the power of a productive public-private dialogue, focusing on collaboration and consensus building. India has attempted to decentralize the implementation of the SDGs through District Sustainable Development Goals (DSDGs) and involved a range of stakeholders in consultative processes to tailor the implementation as per a given context.

All in all, it is the institutional framework within a nation that decides whether a reform will deliver the intended results efficiently or not. A robust policy architecture, ultimately, contributes to strengthen the competitiveness of the country. Streamlined procedures and accountability among organizations and individuals lead to the creation of a stable and predictable environment conducive to the growth of individuals and enterprises. While there are multiple elements important to improve India's institutional framework, an integrated whole-of-government approach is foundational. In a country as diverse and massive as ours, delivering public services efficiently has been a humongous task. There is immense ground to cover on this front. For decades, lack of collaboration has created silos within the public set up. The attempt to break these down, create a holistic approach to service delivery and policymaking and identify cumbersome processes and streamline them have been an encouraging trend. It has also helped foster productive dialogue between the end users of services and the government.

The 4S framework offers a new vantage point that can aid this process. The framework redefines certain qualifications for prosperity growth by stating that prosperity needs to be shared across all parts and regions of India, matched by social progress, be environmentally sustainable and solid and resilient in the face of external shocks. It adds to a 'GDP +' thinking – a line of thought that emphasizes alternative measures of development to complement the GDP. Binding each of the four forces elaborated in a holistic manner is key to make the whole greater than the sum of the parts, or in other words, make the impact greater than the contributing factors. We delve into a multifaceted discussion centred on the imperative of balanced and sustainable prosperity within the context of India. Four critical elements are meticulously examined to outline a comprehensive strategy for the nation's advancement. We posit that economic growth should be paralleled by improvements in social progress. The need for an equitable distribution of prosperity across India's diverse regions is underscored. It is crucial for all parts of the country to benefit from economic development, thus mitigating regional disparities. In addition, environmental sustainability is championed as an essential component of prosperity. The text stresses the significance of balancing growth with ecological preservation, advocating for green and sustainable practices to mitigate the environmental impact of economic activities. Furthermore, building resilience into India's prosperity framework, recognizing the need to withstand external shocks and global economic vagaries is of paramount importance.

From digital infrastructure to clean technologies and technology-enabled social protection systems to targeted support for the marginalized, India's development story is driven by its citizens. Recent years have witnessed the resounding success of initiatives that have been implemented well, reaching every household in the country. Policy initiatives are rightly recognizing the criticality of Jan Bhagidari or people's participation. Participative governance is indeed a sine qua non of each policy reform that has been rolled out and those that will come into the picture in the future. India is truly a people's nation, and it is this quality that will render it a force to reckon with in the coming years. There are multiple arguments on India's prospects, some claiming the next decade to be India's decade and some a bit more sceptical of projections deeming it as an emergent global titan. While it is true that only time can tell, going by the current indications and India's competitiveness fundamentals, it is apparent that we have the right basis to build forward, stronger and better. In the run up to India's centennial year, recognizing the gravity of the time and tasks at hand and leveraging opportunities to their maximum potential will stand the country in good stead. In the context of the economic parlance of comparing economies to various animals and their distinct characteristics, perhaps the true wisdom lies not in compelling an elephant to partake in a tiger's pursuit but to allow it to define its own path and pace.

The dawn of India's Amrit Kaal is now upon us. This is an era defined by hope, action, tangible results and unprecedented growth. Over the past decade, India has demonstrated remarkable resilience and progress, evolving from strength to strength. As we stand at the threshold of this golden period, it is essential to acknowledge the solid foundation laid in the preceding decade, providing us with a formidable platform to capitalise on our achievements and propel the nation towards greater heights. The robust foundation established in the last decade serves as a testament to the collective efforts and strategic foresight that have positioned India as a formidable force on the global stage. As we enter this golden age, successes attained in the past decade help us gather momentum further. The Amrit Kaal is an invitation to harness the spirit of innovation, collaboration and perseverance. It is a call to build on the successes of the past, address the challenges of the present, and chart a course towards a future where India's influence continues to resonate globally. With a solid foundation beneath us, we stride confidently into this era of possibilities to make India's centennial year truly a remarkable one.

Notes

Chapter 1: Of Elephants and Tigers

1. Swallow-Carriere, Yan, and Krishna Srinivasan, 'Asia Continues to Fuel Global Growth, but Economic Momentum is Slowing', *International Monetary Fund* (2023) https://www.imf.org/en/Blogs/Articles/2023/10/13/asia-continues-to-fuel-global-growth-but-economic-momentum-is-slowing
2. Ramachandra Guha, *India after Gandhi: The History of the World's Largest Democracy*. Picador (2007).
3. Sunil Khilnani, '1950's: Era of Wrong Turnings.' *India Today* (2007).
4. R. Jagannathan, '1950s to 1970s: How India's Economic DNA Got Hard-Coded.' *Forbes India* (2019).
5. Gurcharan Das, *India Unbound*, Penguin India (2000).
6. Ibid.
7. Ibid.
8. B. Baskar, 'Bombay Plan: India's Missed Opportunity.' *Hindu Businessline* (2019).
9. Jagdish Bhagwati and T.N. Srinivasan. *An Overview: 1950–70*. National Bureau of Economic Research (1975)
10. Asim Karmakar, 'Development Planning & Policies under Mahalanobis Strategy: A Tale of India's Dilemma.' *International Journal of Business and Social Research*, vol. 3, no. 3 (2012.): 121–132.

11. Ibid.

12. Ajit Ranade, 'Building Temples of Modern India.' *Mumbai Mirror,* (2020)

13. Mohanlal Lallubhai Dantwala, 'Agricultural Policy in India Since Independence.' 1976 Conference, 26 July–4 August, Nairobi, Kenya, from International Association of Agricultural Economists (1976).

14. Ibid.

15. Anantha. V. Nageswaran, and Gulzar Natarajan, 'Can India Grow? Challenges, Opportunities and the Way Forward.' *Carnegie Endowment for International Peace* (2016).

16. John. P. Lewis, 'Quiet Crisis in India: Economic Development and American Policy', *Brookings Institution* (1962).

17. Ankit Mital, 'India and Liberalization: There Was a 1966 Before a 1991.' *Livemint* (2016)

18. Rakesh Mohan, 'Growth Record of the Indian Economy, 1950–2008: A Story of Sustained Savings and Investment', *Economic and Political Weekly*, vol. 43, no. 19. May 10–16 (2008): 61–71.

19. Arvind Panagariya, 'India in the 1980s and 1990s: A Triumph of Reforms', *International Monetary Fund* (2004), p. 7.

20. Arvind Panagariya, 'India in the 1980s and 1990s: A Triumph of Reforms', *International Monetary Fund* (2004).

21. Arvind Subramaniam and Dani Rodrik, 'From "Hindu Growth" to Productivity Surge: The Mystery of the Indian Growth Transition', *International Monetary Fund* (2004).

22. Ibid.

23. Arvind Panagariya, 'India in the 1980s and 1990s: A Triumph of Reforms', *International Monetary Fund* (2004).

24. Charan, D. Wadhva, 'India Trying to Liberalise: Economic Reforms Since 1991.' *Asia Pacific Centre for Security Studies* (2010).

25. Gurcharan Das, *India Unbound,* Penguin India (2000). p. 237.

26. B.A. Prakash, *The Indian Economy Since 1991: Economic Reforms and Performance.* Pearson (2012).

27. Ibid.

28. Namrata Anand, 'An Overview of Indian Economy (1991–2013)', *IOSR Journal of Economics and Finance,* vol. 3, no. 3, (2014):19 –24.

29. Montek Singh Ahluwalia, 'Economic Reforms in India Since 1991: Has Gradualism Worked?', *Journal of Economic Perspectives*, 16 (3), (2002): 67-88.

30. Y. V. Reddy, 'Indian Economy: 1950; 2000; 2020.' *RBI* (2000). https://rbi.org.in/scripts/BS_SpeechesView.aspx?Id=62.

31. Desh Gupta, 'Has India Escaped the Asian Economic Contagion?' *South Asia: Journal of South Asian Studies*, vol. 23, no. sup1 (2000): 179–92. https://doi.org/10.1080/00856400008723407.

32. R. Nagaraj, 'India's Dream Run, 2003–08: Understanding the Boom and Its Aftermath.' *Indira Gandhi Institute of Development Research* (2013).

33. Press Information Bureau, 'Capital Expenditure Outlay for 2022–23 Increased Sharply by 35.4 Per Cent With Approximately 67 Per Cent Spent between April–December 2022.' (2023). https://www.pib.gov.in/PressReleseDetailm.aspx?PRID=1894919.

34. Ibid.

35. Press Information Bureau, 'Digital Transactions in India.' (2023). https://pib.gov.in/PressReleaseIframePage.aspx?PRID=1897272

36. Press Information Bureau, 'Government Committed To Ensure Quality Education For All' (31 January 2023). https://pib.gov.in/PressReleasePage.aspx?PRID=1894915#:~:text=The%20availability%20of%20teachers%2C%20measured,to%2027.1%20at%20the%20Higher.

37. 'Governor's Statement: December 08, 2021', *Reserve Bank India* (2021) https://www.rbi.org.in/commonman/English/Scripts/PressReleases.aspx?Id=3344.

Chapter 2: Sailing Ahead: Keeping Abreast with the Global Winds

1. 'World Economic Outlook: Navigating Global Divergences', *International Monetary Fund*, October 2023.

2. 'India Better Positioned to Navigate Global Headwinds Than Other Major Emerging Economies: New World Bank Report.' *World Bank*, 5 December 2022.

3. Ibid.

4. Tristam Sainsbury, and Mike Callaghan (Eds.), *The G20 and the Future of International Economic Governance*, (NewSouth Publishing, 2015).

5. Paul Brenton, Michael J. Ferrantino, and Maryla Maliszewska, 'Reshaping Global Value Chains in Light of COVID-19: Implications for Trade and Poverty Reduction in Developing Countries.' *World Bank Publications* (2022).

6. 'World Development Report 2020: Trading for Development in the Age of Global Value Chains.' World Bank, (2020).

7. Thomas Helbling, Shanaka J. Peiris and Krishna Srinivasan. 'Asia Poised to Drive Global Economic Growth, Boosted by China's Reopening', *IMF* (1 May 2023). https://www.imf.org/en/Blogs/Articles/2023/05/01/asia-poised-to-drive-global-economic-growth-boosted-by-chinas-reopening.

8. Ibid.

9. 'World Economic Situation and Prospects: March 2023 Briefing, No. 170.' Department of Economic and Social Affairs. *United Nations* (March 2023). p. 4. Accessed 2 April 2023. https://www.un.org/development/desa/dpad/publication/world-economic-situation-and-prospects-march-2023-briefing-no-170/.

10. Shekhar Aiyar and Anna Ilyina, 'Charting Globalization's Turn to Slowbalization After Global Financial Crisis,' *IMF Blog* (8 February 2023). https://www.imf.org/en/Blogs/Articles/2023/02/08/charting-globalizations-turn-to-slowbalization-after-global-financial-crisis.

11. Christian Keller and Renate Marold, 'Deglobalisation: Here's What You Need to Know', *World Economic Forum* (17 January 2023) https://www.weforum.org/agenda/2023/01/deglobalisation-what-you-need-to-know-wef23/.

12. Paul Brenton, Michael J. Ferrantino, and Maryla Maliszewska, 'Reshaping Global Value Chains in Light of COVID-19: Implications for Trade and Poverty Reduction in Developing Countries.' *World Bank Publications* (2022).

13. Ibid.

14. Michael E. Porter, Christian H.M. Ketels, Amit Kapoor, 'Competitiveness Roadmap for India@100.' *Institute for Competitiveness*, 24 August 2022. https://competitiveness.in/wp-content/uploads/2022/08/Report_Competitiveness_Roadmap-25_August_2022_Web_Version.pdf.

15. Amit Kapoor and Navya Kumar, 'Budget 2023-24: Harnessing
     India's Competitiveness and Creating National Prosperity,'
     the *Economic Times* (5 February 2023). https://economictimes.
     indiatimes.com/news/economy/policy/budget-2023-24-
     harnessing-indias-competitiveness-and-creating-national-
     prosperity/articleshow/97623393.cms.

16. World Intellectual Property Organization (WIPO), *Global
     Innovation Index 2022: What is the future of innovation-driven
     growth?* (Geneva: WIPO, 2022), DOI 10.34667/tind.46596.

17. Olena Kravchenko, Maryna Leshchenko, Dariia Marushchak, Yuriy
     Vdovychenko and Svitlana Boguslavska, 'The Digitalization as a
     Global Trend and Growth Factor of the Modern Economy', *SHS
     Web of Conferences* Volume 65 (2019). https://doi.org/10.1051/
     shsconf/20196507004.

18. Hannah Ritchie, Edouard Mathieu, Max Roser and Esteban
     Ortiz-Ospina, 'Internet'. Published online at OurWorldInData.
     org. (2023) Retrieved from: 'https://ourworldindata.org/internet'
     [Online Resource].

19. Florence Jaumotte, Myrto Oikonomou, Carlo Pizzinelli, and Marina
     M. Tavares, 'How Pandemic Accelerated Digital Transformation
     in Advanced Economies', *International Monetary Fund* (21 March,
     2023) https://www.imf.org/en/Blogs/Articles/2023/03/21/how-
     pandemic-accelerated-digital-transformation-in-advanced-economies.

20. 'Digital Development Overview: Development News, Research,
     Data', *World Bank* (6 October 2022) https://www.worldbank.org/
     en/topic/digitaldevelopment/overview.

21. James Manyika, Susan Lund, Michael Chui, Jacques Bughin,
     Jonathan Woetzel, Parul Batra, Saurabh Sanghvi, and Ryan Ko, 'What
     the Future of Work Will Mean for Jobs, Skills, and Wages: Jobs Lost,
     Jobs Gained', *McKinsey and Company*, (28 November 2017). https://
     www.mckinsey.com/featured-insights/future-of-work/jobs-lost-jobs-
     gained-what-the-future-of-work-will-mean-for-jobs-skills-and-wages.

22. Karin Von Abrams, 'These Are the Top Global Ecommerce
     Markets', *Insider Intelligence* (14 July 2021). https://www.
     insiderintelligence.com/content/top-global-ecommerce-markets.

23. Bhaskar Chakravorti, Ravi Shankar Chaturvedi, Christina
     Filipovic, and Griffin Brewer, 'Digital in the Time of COVID'.
     The Fletcher School at Tufts University (December 2020).

https://digitalplanet.tufts.edu/wp-content/uploads/2022/09/digital-intelligence-index.pdf.

24. Anne Cortez and Hsiao Chink Tang, 'Paving an Even Path in Asia's Digital Economy: Role of Regional Cooperation in Inclusive Digital Transformation', *Regional Knowledge Sharing Initiative* (2023). https://rksi.adb.org/publications/paving-an-even-path-in-asias-digital-economy-role-of-regional-cooperation-in-inclusive-digital-transformation/.

25. 'How Developing Countries Can Seize "Green Windows of Opportunity" with Innovative Technologies', *United Nations Conference on Trade and Development* (October 26. 2022). https://unctad.org/news/how-developing-countries-can-seize-green-windows-opportunity-innovative-technologies.

26. Kemp, Simon. 'Digital 2023: India.' DataReportal, 13 February 2023. https://datareportal.com/reports/digital-2023-india.

27. Ejaz Ghani, 'India's Digital Revolution and Governance', *BW Businessworld* (6 March 2023). https://www.businessworld.in/article/India-s-Digital-Revolution-And-Governance-/06-03-2023-467858/.

28. 'Digital Economy Report 2021', *United Nations Conference on Trade And Development* (29 September 2021). https://unctad.org/system/files/official-document/der2021_en.pdf.

29. 'India @100 – Realizing the potential of a $26 trillion economy', *EY* (19 January 2023). https://www.ey.com/en_in/india-at-100.

30. Keyzom Massally and Manish Pant, 'Building Digital Public Goods: Takeaways from India's COVID-19 Vaccine Implementation Programme', *United Nations Development Programme* (1 February 2022). https://www.undp.org/digital/blog/building-digital-public-goods-takeaways-india%E2%80%99s-covid-19-vaccine-implementation-programme.

31. Akenji, Lewis, Magnus Bengtsson, Viivi Toivio, Michael Lettenmeier, Tina Fawcett, Yael Parag, Yamina Saheb, Anna Coote, Joachim H. Spangenberg, Stuart Capstick, Tim Gore, Luca Coscieme, Mathis Wackernagel and Dario Kenner. '1.5-Degree Lifestyles: Towards A Fair Consumption Space for All.' Hot or Cool Institute, 2021. https://hotorcool.org/wp-content/uploads/2021/10/Hot_or_Cool_1_5_lifestyles_FULL_REPORT_AND_ANNEX_B.pdf.

32. Amit Kapoor and Navya Kumar, 'Habits For A Greener Economy', *BW Businessworld* (4 March 2023). http://businessworld. inhttps://www.businessworld.in/article/Habits-For-A-Greener-Economy/04-03-2023-467785.

33. 'Green Budget Tagging: Introductory Guidance and Principles', *Organisation for Economic Co-operation and Development* (13 February 2021). https://www.oecd.org/gov/budgeting/green-budget-tagging-fe7bfcc4-en.htm

34. International Monetary Fund (IMF), 'Strengthening Infrastructure Governance for Climate-Responsive Public Investment', Policy Paper (22 December 2021). https://www.imf.org/en/Publications/Policy-Papers/Issues/2021/12/22/Strengthening-Infrastructure-Governance-for-Climate-Responsive-Public-Investment-511258.

35. Rodrigo Pizarro, Raúl Delgado, Huáscar Eguino and Aloisio Lopes Pereira, 'Climate Change Public Budget Tagging: Connections across Financial and Environmental Classification Systems', *Inter-American Development Bank,* Discussion Paper (January 2021). http://dx.doi.org/10.18235/0003021.

36. Simona Pojar, 'Environmental Assessments within Green Budgeting', *European Commission*, Discussion Paper 175 (December, 2022). doi:10.2765/745591.

37. 'Climate Change Budget Tagging: A Review of International Experience.' *World Bank.* 2021 https://openknowledge.worldbank.org/handle/10986/35174.

Chapter 3: What Makes Nations Tick?

1. Kim, Jong-Il, and Lawrence J. Lau, 'The Sources of Economic Growth of the East Asian Newly Industrialized Countries', *Journal of the Japanese and International Economies*, vol. 8, no. 3, (1994): 235-71.

2. Wong, Kar-Yiu and Chong K.Yip. 'Industrialization, Economic Growth, and International Trade.' *Review of International Economics*, vol. 7, no. 3, (1999): 522-523.

3. Porter, Michael. E. (1998). The competitive advantage of nations: With a new introduction. (The Free Press, 1998), pp. 35–722.

4. Lukasz, Pietak. 'Review of theories and models of economic growth.' *Comparative Economic Research*, vol. 7, no. 1, (2014): 46.

5.   Lukasz, Pietak. 'Review of theories and models of economic growth.' *Comparative Economic Research*, vol. 7, no. 1, (2014): 57.

6.   Gallardo Pérez, H J, M Vergel Ortega, and M C Cordero Díaz. 'Economic Growth Model in Developing Economies.' *Journal of Physics: Conference Series 1388*, no. 1 (1 November 2019): 012033. https://doi.org/10.1088/1742-6596/1388/1/012033.

7.   Robert. Jr. E Lucas, 'On the Mechanics of Economic Development.' *Journal of Monetary Economics*, vol. 22, no. 1, (1988): 3–42.

8.   Bassanini, Andrea. and Stefano. Scarpetta. 'The Driving Forces of Economic Growth: Panel Data Evidence for the OECD Countries.' *OECD Economic Studies*, vol. 33, no. 2, (2001): 10-49.

9.   Aoki, Masahiko. 'The Role of Government in East Asian Economic Development: Comparative Institutional Analysis.' Oxford University Press, 2007.

10. John Page, 'The East Asian Miracle: Four Lessons for Development Policy.' *Macroeconomics Annual*, vol. 9, (1994): 219–269.

11. Reuvan Glick and Ramon Moreno, 'The East Asian Miracle: Growth Because of Government Intervention and Protectionism or in Spite of It?', *Business Economics*, vol. 32, no. 2, (1997): 20–25

12. Coe, David T. and Elhanan Helpman. 'International R&D spillovers.' *European Economic Review*, vol 39, no. 5, (1995): 859-887.

13. Reuvan Glick and Ramon Moreno, 'The East Asian Miracle: Growth Because of Government Intervention and Protectionism or in Spite of It?', *Business Economics*, vol. 32, no. 2, (1997): 20–25

14. Ibid.

15. Ibid.

16. Ibid.

17. Joseph E. Stiglitz and Marilou Uy, 'Financial Markets, Public Policy, and the East Asian Miracle', *The World Bank Research Observer*, vol. 11, no. 2, (1996): 249–276.

18. Ibid.

19. Ibid.

20. Joseph E. Stiglitz and Marilou Uy, 'Financial Markets, Public Policy, and the East Asian Miracle', *The World Bank Research Observer*, vol. 11, no. 2, (1996): 256.

21. Ibid.
22. Joseph E. Stiglitz and Marilou Uy, 'Financial Markets, Public Policy, and the East Asian Miracle', *The World Bank Research Observer*, vol. 11, no. 2, (1996): 257.
23. Ibid.
24. William McCord, 'Explaining the East Asian "Miracle"', *The National Interest*, Summer 1989, no. 16 (1989): 74–82.
25. Page, John. 'The East Asian Miracle: Building a Basic for Growth.' International Monetary Fund, vol. 31, no. 001, (1994): 5.
26. Takada, Masahiro. (1999) 'Japan's Economic Miracle: Underlying Factors and Strategies for the Growth.' LeHigh University. March.
27. William McCord, 'Explaining the East Asian "Miracle"', *The National Interest*, Summer 1989, no. 16, (1989): 74–82.
28. Benkt-Ake Lundvall, 'The Danish Model and the Globalizing Learning Economy: Lessons for Developing Countries.' WIDER Research Paper, No. 2009/18. The United Nations University World Institute for Development Economics Research (UNU-WIDER). March (2009).
29. Ibid.
30. Ibid.
31. Ibid.
32. Ibid.
33. Ibid.
34. Madsen, Per. Kongshoj. 2006.'How Can It Possibly Fly? The Paradox of a Dynamic Labour Market in a Scandinavian Welfare State'. (2006) .CARMA Research paper 2005:2. Centre for Labour Market Research (CARMA) University of Aalborg. January.
35. Benkt-Ake Lundvall, 'The Danish Model and the Globalizing Learning Economy: Lessons for Developing Countries.' WIDER Research Paper, No. 2009/18. The United Nations University World Institute for Development Economics Research (UNU-WIDER). March (2009).
36. Madsen, Per. Kongshoj. 'Fexicurity in Danish: A Model for Labour Market Reform in Europe?' Intereconomics, Springer, vol. 43, no. 2. (2008): 74–78.
37. Benkt-Ake Lundvall, 'The Danish Model and the Globalizing Learning Economy: Lessons for Developing Countries.' WIDER Research Paper, No. 2009/18. The United Nations University

World Institute for Development Economics Research (UNU-WIDER). March (2009).

38. Ibid.

39. Madsen, Per. Kongshoj. 2006.'How Can It Possibly Fly? The Paradox of a Dynamic Labour Market in a Scandinavian Welfare State'. (2006) . CARMA Research paper 2005:2. Centre for Labour Market Research (CARMA) University of Aalborg. January.

40. Benkt-Ake Lundvall, 'The Danish Model and the Globalizing Learning Economy: Lessons for Developing Countries.' WIDER Research Paper, No. 2009/18. The United Nations University World Institute for Development Economics Research (UNU-WIDER). March (2009).

41. Ibid.

42. Ibid.

43. Ibid.

Chapter 4: Competitiveness Fundamentals

1. Porter, Michael. E., *The Competitive Advantage of Nations*. First Free Press Edition, 1990.

2. Delgado, Mercedes., Christian H.M Ketels, Michael Porter, and Scott Stern. 'The Determinants of National Competitiveness'. July 2012. https://doi.org/10.3386/w18249.

3. Ibid.

4. Ketels, Christian H.M. 'Michael Porter's Competitiveness Framework: Recent Learnings and New Research Priorities.' *Journal of Industry Competition and Trade, 6(2)*, (2006): 115–136. doi:http://dx.doi.org/10.1007/s10842-006-9474-7.

5. Delgado, Mercedes., Christian H.M Ketels, Michael Porter, and Scott Stern. 'The Determinants of National Competitiveness'. July 2012. https://doi.org/10.3386/w18249.

6. Sachs, Jeffrey D., *The End of Poverty*. New York City, Penguin, 2005.

7. Acemoglu, Daron., Simon Johnson, James Robinson, and Yunyong Thaicharoen. 'Institutional Causes, Macroeconomic Symptoms: Volatility, Crises and Growth.' *Journal of Monetary Economics*, vol. 50, no. 1, (2003): 49–123. https://doi.org/10.1016/s0304-3932(02)00208-8.

8.   Delgado, M., Ketels, C., Porter, M. E., and S. Stern, (2012). 'The Determinants of National Competitiveness.' NBER. doi:https://doi.org/10.3386/w18249.

9.   Ibid.

10. Munangagwa, Chidochasshe. L., 'The Economic Decline of Zimbabwe.' *Gettysburg Economic Review, 3*(1), (2009).

11. Ketels, Christian H.M., 'Michael Porter's Competitiveness Framework: Recent Learnings and New Research Priorities.' *Journal of Industry, Competition and Trade, 14*(2), (2014): 137–156.

12. 'Innovative Asia: Advancing the Knowledge Based Economy.' *ADB*, 2014. https://www.adb.org/sites/default/files/publication/59587/innovative-asia-knowledge-based-economy-pa.pdf.

13. Baptista, Rui, and Peter Swann. 'Do Firms in Clusters Innovate More?' Research Policy, vol. 27, no. 5 (1998): 525–539.

14. Baily, Martin N. and Nicholas Montalbano. *Clusters and Innovation Districts: Lessons from the United States Experience.* The Brookings Institute, 201.

15. Porter, Michael E., *The Competitive Advantage of Nations.* First Free Press Edition, 1990.

16. Ibid.

17. Šarić, Sasa. Competitive Advantages through Clusters: An Empirical Study with Evidence from China. Springer Science and Business Media, 2012.

18. Michael E. Porter, Christian H.M. Ketels, Amit Kapoor, 'Competitiveness Roadmap for India@100.' *Institute for Competitiveness*, 24 August 2022. https://competitiveness.in/wp-content/uploads/2022/08/Report_Competitiveness_Roadmap-25_August_2022_Web_Version.pdf.

19. Desai, Sonali., Manjistha Banerji, Debasis Barik, Dinesh Tiwari and Om Prakash Sharma. 'A Glass Half Full: Changes in Standard of Living Since 2012.' India Human Development Survey (2020):9-10 A Glass Half Full.pdf (umd.edu).

20. Chancel, Lucas., and Thomas Piketty. 'Indian Income Inequality, 1922-2015: From British Raj to Billionaire Raj?' *Review of Income and Wealth*, vol. 65, no. S1 (2019): S33-S62 https://doi.org/10.1111/roiw.12439.

21. Sutirtha, Sinha. Roy., and Van Der Weide Roy. Weide. *Poverty in India Has Declined over the Last Decade but not as Much as Previously Thought – Policy Research Working Paper.* Washington, DC: World Bank, 2022. http://hdl.handle.net/10986/37273.

22. Green, Michael. 'Social Progress Index 2022 - Executive Summary.' Social Progress Imperative, 2022. https://www.socialprogress.org/static/8a62f3f612c8d40b09b3103a70bdacab/2022 per cent20Social per cent20Progress per cent20Index per cent20Executive per cent20Summary_4.pdf.

23. Kapoor, Amit, and Michael Green. 'Social Progress Index: States and Districts of India.' Economic Advisory Council to the Prime Minister, 2022. https://eacpm.gov.in/wp-content/uploads/2022/12/Social_Progress_Index_States_and_Districts_of_India.pdf

24. Krugman, P. (1994). 'Defining and measuring productivity.' In P. Krugman, *Defining and Measuring Productivity—The Age of Diminishing Expectations*. Retrieved from OECD.org: https://www.oecd.org/sdd/productivity-stats/40526851.pdf.

25. Krugman, Paul. *The Age of Diminished Expectations*. The MIT Press, 1997. https://mitpress.mit.edu/9780262611343/the-age-of-diminished-expectations/.

26. Feenstra, Robert C., Robert Inklaar, and Marcel P. Timmer. 'The Next Generation of the Penn World Table.' *American Economic Review* 105, no. 10 (1 October 2015): 3150–82. https://doi.org/10.1257/aer.20130954.

27. 'Women's Labour Force Participation in India: Why Is it So low?' *International Labour Organization*, 2014. Retrieved from https://www.ilo.org/wcmsp5/groups/public/---asia/---ro-bangkok/---sro-new_delhi/documents/genericdocument/wcms_342357.pdf.

28. 'Game Changers: Women and the Future of Work in Asia and Pacific.' *International Labour Organization*, 2018. https://www.ilo.org/wcmsp5/groups/public/---asia/---ro-bangkok/---sro-bangkok/documents/publication/wcms_645601.pdf.

29. Hsieh, Chang-Tai T., and Peter. J. Klenow. 'Misallocation and Manufacturing TFP in China and India.' *Quarterly Journal of Economics, 124*(4), (2009): 1403–1448. http://www.jstor.org/stable/40506263.

30. Ghani, Ejaz., Kerr, William. R. Kerr and Stephen D. O'Connell. 'Spatial Determinants of Entrepreneurship in India.' Regional Studies, 48(6), (2014): 1071–1089. doi:http://www.tandfonline.com/action/showCitFormats?doi=10.1080/00343404.2013.839869.

31. 'Science, Technology, and Innovation Policy.' Government of India, 2020. https://dst.gov.in/sites/default/files/STIP_Doc_1.4_Dec2020.pdf.

32. Michael E. Porter, Christian H.M. Ketels, Amit Kapoor, 'Competitiveness Roadmap for India@100.' *Institute for Competitiveness*, 24 August 2022. https://competitiveness.in/wp-content/uploads/2022/08/Report_Competitiveness_Roadmap-25_August_2022_Web_Version.pdf.

33. Schneegans, Susan.,Tiffany Straza, and Jake Lewis, UNESCO Science Report: The Race Against Time for Smarter Development, 604–621. Paris: UNESCO Publishing, 2021.

34. 'India Innovation Index 2021.' *NITI AAYOG*. New Delhi: Government of India, 2022. https://www.niti.gov.in/sites/default/files/2022-07/India-Innovation-Index-2021-Web-Version_21_7_22.pdf.

Chapter 5: The Many Indias

1. Michael E. Porter, *On Competition,* Harvard Business Press (2008).
2. Ibid.
3. Michael E. Porter and Michael P. Porter, 'Location, Clusters, and the 'New' Microeconomics of Competition.' *Business Economics* 33, no. 1 (1998): 7–13. http://www.jstor.org/stable/23487685.
4. Ibid.
5. Saša Šarić, *Competitive Advantages Through Clusters: An Empirical Study with Evidence from China.* Strategisches Kompetenz-Management Ser (2012). https://doi.org/10.1007/978-3-8349-3554-0.
6. Ibid.
7. Ibid.
8. Ibid.

9.   Michael E. Porter and Michael P. Porter, 'Location, Clusters, and the 'New' Microeconomics of Competition.' *Business Economics* 33, no. 1 (1998): 7–13. http://www.jstor.org/stable/23487685.

10. Michael E. Porter, *On Competition,* Harvard Business Press (2008).

11. Christian H.M. Ketels and Olga Memedovic, 'From Clusters to Cluster-Based Economic Development.' Special Issue on Global Value Chains and Innovation Networks: Prospects for Industrial Upgrading in Developing Countries. Part 1. *International Journal of Technological Learning, Innovation, and Development* 1, no. 3 (August 2008).

12. Michael E. Porter, *On Competition,* Harvard Business Press (2008).

13. Michael E. Porter and Michael P. Porter, 'Location, Clusters, and the 'New' Microeconomics of Competition.' *Business Economics* 33, no. 1 (1998): 7–13. http://www.jstor.org/stable/23487685.

14. Michael E. Porter, 'Location, Competition, and Economic Development: Local Clusters in a Global Economy.' *Economic Development Quarterly* 14, no. 1 (February 2000): 15–34. https://doi.org/10.1177/089124240001400105.

15. Christian H.M. Ketels and Olga Memedovic, 'From Clusters to Cluster-Based Economic Development.' Special Issue on Global Value Chains and Innovation Networks: Prospects for Industrial Upgrading in Developing Countries. Part 1. *International Journal of Technological Learning, Innovation, and Development* 1, no. 3 (August 2008).

16. Michael E. Porter and Michael P. Porter, 'Location, Clusters, and the 'New' Microeconomics of Competition.' *Business Economics* 33, no. 1 (1998): 7–13. http://www.jstor.org/stable/23487685.

17. Michael E. Porter, 'Clusters and the New Economics of Competition', *Harvard Business Review* (November–December 1998).

18. Michael E. Porter, *On Competition,* Harvard Business Press (2008).

19. Michael E. Porter, 'Location, Competition, and Economic Development: Local Clusters in a Global Economy.' *Economic Development Quarterly* 14, no. 1 (February 2000): 15–34. https://doi.org/10.1177/089124240001400105.

20. Robert J. Barro, Xavier Sala-I-Martin, Olivier Jean Blanchard, and Robert E. Hall, 'Convergence Across States and Regions', *Brookings Papers on Economic Activity*, no. 1 (1991): 107. https://doi.org/10.2307/2534639.

21. Paul Krugman, 'Increasing Returns and Economic Geography', *Journal of Political Economy* 99, no. 3 (June 1991): 483–99. https://doi.org/10.1086/261763.

22. Michael E. Porter, 'Clusters and the New Economics of Competition', *Harvard Business Review* (November–December 1998).

23. Michael E. Porter and Michael P. Porter, 'Location, Clusters, and the 'New' Microeconomics of Competition.' *Business Economics* 33, no. 1 (1998): 7–13. http://www.jstor.org/stable/23487685.

24. Brian Snowdon and George Stonehouse, 'Competitiveness in a Globalised World: Michael Porter on the Microeconomic Foundations of the Competitiveness of Nations, Regions, and Firms', *Journal of International Business Studies* 37, no. 2 (March 2006): 163–75. https://doi.org/10.1057/palgrave.jibs.8400190.

25. Michael E. Porter, 'The Five Competitive Forces that Shape Strategy.' *Harvard Business Review*, 86(1), (2008) 25–40.

26. Susana Franco, Asier Murciego, Juan Pablo Salado, Eduardo Sisti, and James Wilson, 'European Cluster Panorama 2021 - Leveraging clusters for resilient, green and digital regional economies (2021) https://clustercollaboration.eu/sites/default/files/2021-12/European_Cluster_Panorama_Report_0.pdf.

27. Christian Ketels, Cluster Mapping as a Tool for Development.' *Institute for Strategy and Competitiveness-Harvard Business School* (2017).

28. Ibid.

29. Christian H.M. Ketels, Amit Kapoor, Bibek Debroy, Subhanshi Negi, 'The 2023 India Cluster Panorama', Institute for Competitiveness (IFC), Economic Advisory Council to the Prime Minister (EACPM), Institute for Strategy and Competitiveness, Harvard Business School and US Asia Technology Management Center, Stanford University (August 2023) https://eacpm.gov.in/wp-content/uploads/2023/08/Report_India_Cluster_Panorama_2023.pdf.

30. Ibid.

31.   Ibid.
32.   Ibid.
33.   Ibid.
34.   Ibid.
35.   Ibid.
36.   Ibid.
37.   Ibid.
38.   Ibid.
39.   Ibid.
40.   Mercedes Delgado, Michael E. Porter, and Scott Stern, 'Clusters, Convergence, and Economic Performance', *Research Policy 43*, no. 10 (December 2014): 1785–99. https://doi.org/10.1016/j.respol.2014.05.007.
41.   Christian H.M. Ketels, Amit Kapoor, Bibek Debroy, Subhanshi Negi, 'The 2023 India Cluster Panorama', Institute for Competitiveness (IFC), Economic Advisory Council to the Prime Minister (EACPM), Institute for Strategy and Competitiveness, Harvard Business School and US Asia Technology Management Center, Stanford University (August 2023) https://eacpm.gov.in/wp-content/uploads/2023/08/Report_India_Cluster_Panorama_2023.pdf.
42.   Ibid.
43.   Christian Ketels and Sergiy Protsiv, 'Cluster Presence and Economic Performance: A New Look Based on European Data.' Regional Studies 55, no. 2 (August 10, 2020): 208–20. https://doi.org/10.1080/00343404.2020.1792435.
44.   Michael Porter, *The Competitive Advantage of Nations*, New York: Free Press (1990).
45.   Michael E. Porter, 'Clusters and the New Economics of Competition', *Harvard Business Review* (November-December, 1998).
46.   Saban Esen and Hande Uyar, 'Examining the Competitive Structure of Turkish Tourism Industry in Comparison with Diamond Model', *Procedia – Social and Behavioral Sciences,* Volume 62 (24 October, 2012): 620-627 https://doi.org/10.1016/j.sbspro.2012.09.104.
47.   Michael E. Porter, 'The Economic Performance of Regions.' *Regional Studies* 37, no. 6–7 (August 2003): 549–78. https://doi.org/10.1080/0034340032000108688.

48. Christian H.M. Ketels, Amit Kapoor, Bibek Debroy, Subhanshi Negi, 'The 2023 India Cluster Panorama', Institute for Competitiveness (IFC), Economic Advisory Council to the Prime Minister (EACPM), Institute for Strategy and Competitiveness, Harvard Business School and US Asia Technology Management Center, Stanford University (August 2023) https://eacpm. gov.in/wp-content/uploads/2023/08/Report_India_Cluster_ Panorama_2023.pdf.

49. Ibid.

50. Ibid.

51. Ibid.

52. Ibid.

53. Ibid.

54. Ibid.

55. Ibid.

56. Ibid.

57. Christian Ketels and Sergiy Protsiv, 'Cluster Presence and Economic Performance: A New Look Based on European Data.' Regional Studies 55, no. 2 (August 10, 2020): 208–20. https:// doi.org/10.1080/00343404.2020.1792435.

58. Mercedes Delgado, Michael E. Porter, and Scott Stern, 'Clusters, Convergence, and Economic Performance', *Research Policy 43*, no. 10 (December 2014): 1785–99. https://doi.org/10.1016/j. respol.2014.05.007.

59. Michael E. Porter, *On Competition,* Harvard Business Press (2008)

60. Michael E. Porter, 'Clusters and Economic Policy:
Aligning Public Policy with the New Economics of Competition', *Harvard Business School* (2007) https://www.hbs.edu/ris/ Publication%20Files/Clusters_and_Economic_Policy_White_ Paper_8e844243-aa23-449d-a7c1-5ef76c74236f.pdf.

61. Ibid.

62. Michael E. Porter, *On Competition,* Harvard Business Press (2008).

63. Michael E. Porter, 'Location, Competition, and Economic Development: Local Clusters in a Global Economy.' *Economic Development Quarterly* 14, no. 1 (February 2000): 15–34. https:// doi.org/10.1177/089124240001400105.

64. Ibid.

65. Michael E. Porter, *On Competition,* Harvard Business Press (2008)

66. Michael E. Porter, Christian H.M. Ketels, Amit Kapoor, 'Competitiveness Roadmap for India@100.' *Institute for Competitiveness*, 24 August 2022. https://competitiveness.in/wp-content/uploads/2022/08/Report_Competitiveness_Roadmap-25_August_2022_Web_Version.pdf.

67. Ibid.

68. Ibid.

Chapter 6: India through a Bottom-Up Perspective

1. Michael E. Porter, 'The Economic Performance of Regions.' *Regional Studies* 37, no. 6–7 (August 2003): 549–78. https://doi.org/10.1080/0034340032000108688.

2. Michael Kitson, Ron Martin, and Peter Tyler, 'Regional Competitiveness: An Elusive yet Key Concept?' *Regional Studies* 38, no. 9 (December 2004): 991–99. https://doi.org/10.1080/0034340042000320816.

3. Gina Cristina Dimian, and Aniela Danciu. 'National and Regional Competitiveness in the crisis Context. Successful Examples.' *Theoretical and Applied Economics* 18,(11), (2011): 67–78. https://doaj.org/article/87bdc27a4b95426b972d1965d4e74a2b.

4. Robert J. Barro and Xavier Sala-i-Martin, 'Convergence.' *Journal of Political Economy* 100, no. 2 (1992): 223–51. http://www.jstor.org/stable/2138606.

5. Xavier Sala-i-Martin, 'The Classical Approach to Convergence Analysis.' *The Economic Journal* 106, no. 437 (July 1996): 1019. https://doi.org/10.2307/2235375.

6. OlaOluwa. S. Yaya, Fumitaka Furuoka, Kiew Ling Pui, Ray Ikechukwu Jacob, Chinyere M. Ezeoke, 'Investigating Asian Regional Income Convergence Using Fourier Unit Root Test with Break', *International Economics*, (2020): 120–129. doi:https://doi.org/10.1016/j.inteco.2019.11.008.

7. Hartmut Lehmann, Aleksey Y. Oshchepkov and Maria Silvagni, 'Regional Convergence in Russia: Estimating A Neoclassical Growth Model', *Higher School of Economics* (2020) http://dx.doi.org/10.2139/ssrn.3627173.

8. María Florencia Aráoz, Esteban A. Nicolini and Mauricio Talassino, 'Growth and Convergence Among Argentine Provinces

Since 1895.' *Palgrave Studies in Economic History* (2020):65–95. https://doi.org/10.1007/978-3-030-47553-6_4.

9.   Rati Ram, 'Income Convergence across the U.S. States: Further Evidence from New Recent Data.' *Journal of Economics and Finance* 45, no. 2 (August 20, 2020): 372–80. https://doi.org/10.1007/s12197-020-09520-w.

10. Paul Cashin and Ratna Sahay, 'Regional economic growth and convergence in India', *Finance and Development, International Monetary Fund* 33, (1996): 49–52. https://www.imf.org/external/pubs/ft/fandd/1996/03/pdf/cashin.pdf.

11. Nirupam Bajpai and Jeffrey D. Sachs, 'Trends in Inter-State Inequalities of Income in India.', *Trends in Inter-State Inequalities of Income in India* | Academic Commons, (1 January 1996). https://doi.org/10.7916/D8988DVS.

12. Buddhadeb Ghosh, and Prabhir De, 'Economic Growth and Regional Divergence in India, 1960 to 1995', *Economic and Political Weekly* 33, (1998): 1623–1630. https://www.jstor.org/stable/4407415.

13. M. Govinda Rao, R. T. Shand and K. P. Kalirajan, 'Convergence of Incomes across Indian States', *Economic and Political Weekly* 34, no. 13 (1999): 769–78. http://www.jstor.org/stable/4407797.

14. Montek S. Ahluwalia, 'Economic Performance of States in Post-Reforms Period', *Economic and Political Weekly* 35, no. 19 (2000): 1637–48. http://www.jstor.org/stable/4409264.

15. Dipankar Dasgupta, Pradip Maiti, Robin Mukherjee, Subrata Sarkar, and Subhendu Chakrabarti, 'Growth and Interstate Disparities in India', *Economic and Political Weekly* 35, no. 27 (2000): 2413–22. http://www.jstor.org/stable/4409475.

16. R. Nagaraj, A. Varoudakis, and M.-A. Véganzonès, 'Long-Run Growth Trends and Convergence across Indian States', *Journal of International Development* ,12, no. 1 (January 2000): 45–70. http://dx.doi.org/10.1002/(sici)1099-1328(200001)12:1<45::aid-jid586>3.0.co;2-z.

17. Jeffrey D. Sachs, Nirupam Bajpai, and Ananthi Ramiah, 'Understanding Regional Economic Growth in India', *Asia Economic Papers* (January 1, 2002):32-62 https://doi.org/10.1162/153535102320893983.

18. Adabar Kshamanidhi, 'Economic growth and convergence in India,' Working paper. *Institute for Social and Economic Change* (2004). https://www.isid.ac.in/~planning/ka.pdf.

19. B. Bhattacharya and S. Sakthivel, 'Regional Growth and Disparity in India: Comparison of Pre- and Post-Reform Decades', *Economic and Political Weekly* 39, no. 10 (2004): 1071–1077.

20. Gaurav Nayyar, 'Economic Growth and Regional Inequality in India', *Economic and Political Weekly* 43, no. 6 (2008): 58–67. http://www.jstor.org/stable/40277103.

21. Ghosh, Madhusudan. 'Economic Reforms, Growth and Regional Divergence in India.' Margin: The Journal of Applied Economic Research 2, no. 3 (August 2008): 265–85. https://doi.org/10.1177/097380100800200303.

22. Sanjay Kalra and Piyaporn Sodsriwiboon, 'Growth Convergence and Spillovers Among Indian States: What Matters? What Does Not?' *SSRN Electronic Journal* (2010). https://doi.org/10.2139/ssrn.1590709.

23. Utsav Kumar and Arvind Subramanian, 'Growth in India's States in the First Decade of the 21st Century: Four Facts', *Economic and Political Weekly* 47, no. 3 (2012): 48–57. http://www.jstor.org/stable/41419741.

24. Surender Kumar and Shunsuke Managi, 'Productivity and Convergence in India: A State-Level Analysis.' *Journal of Asian Economics* 23, no. 5 (October 2012): 548–59. https://doi.org/10.1016/j.asieco.2012.05.002.

25. Samarjit Das, Chetan Ghate, and Peter E. Robertson, 'Remoteness, Urbanization, and India's Unbalanced Growth', *World Development* 66 (February 2015): 572–87. https://doi.org/10.1016/j.worlddev.2014.09.013.

26. Arfat Ahmad Sofi and Raja Sethu Durai S., 'Income Convergence in India: Evidence from Nonparametric Panel Data', *Journal of Economic Studies* 44, no. 3 (14 August 2017): 400–411. https://doi.org/10.1108/jes-04-2015-0065.

27. Prerna Sanga and Abdul Shaban, 'Regional Divergence and Inequalities in India', *Economic and Political Weekly* 52, no. 1 (2017): 102–10. http://www.jstor.org/stable/44166096.

28. Government of India, 'Chapter 10 - Income, Health, and Fertility:

Convergence Puzzles.' In *Economic Survey 2016-17*. New Delhi: Government of India (2017). Retrieved from India Budget: https://www.indiabudget.gov.in/budget2017-2018/es2016-17/echap10.pdf.

29. Lekha Chakraborty and Pinaki Chakraborty, 'Federalism, Fiscal Asymmetries and Economic Convergence: Evidence from Indian States', *Asia-Pacific Journal of Regional Science* 2, no. 1 (April 2018): 83–113. https://doi.org/10.1007/s41685-018-0087-z.

30. Aparna P. Lolayekar and Pranab Mukhopadhyay, 'Understanding Growth Convergence in India (1981–2010): Looking beyond the Usual Suspects.' Edited by William Joe. *PLOS ONE* 15, no. 6 (2 June 2020): e0233549. https://doi.org/10.1371/journal.pone.0233549.

31. Suryakanta Nayak and Dukhabandhu Sahoo, 'Regional Economic Growth in India: Convergence or Divergence?' *Competitiveness Review: An International Business Journal 32*, no. 1 (19 July 2021): 155–78. https://doi.org/10.1108/cr-10-2020-0131.

32. Dibyendu Maiti, 'Trade, Labor Share, and Productivity in India's Industries', *Tokyo: Asian Development Bank Institute* (Working paper 926) (2019). https://www.adb.org/sites/default/files/publication/487696/adbi-wp926.pdf.

33. Simon Kuznets and Elizabeth Jenks, 'Capital in the American Economy: Its Formation and Financing' *Princeton University Press* (1961). http://www.jstor.org/stable/j.ctt183pr7r.

34. Simon Kuznets, 'Quantitative Aspects of the Economic Growth of Nations: VIII. Distribution of Income by Size', *Economic Development and Cultural Change* 11, no. 2, Part 2 (January 1963): 1–80. https://doi.org/10.1086/450006.

35. Rajarshi Majumder, 'Infrastructure and Regional Development: Interlinkages in India' *Indian Economic Review* 40, no. 2 (2005): 167–84. http://www.jstor.org/stable/29793842.

36. Padma M. Sarangapani, Bindu Thirumalai, Anusha Ramanathan, Ruchi Kumar and Mythili Ramchand, *'No Class State of the Education Report for India.'* UNESCO (2021) https://unesdoc.unesco.org/ark:/48223/pf0000379115?posInSet=1&queryId=3ec427ea-e67c-400e-aa55-e36adafc1ff6.

37. Amit Kapoor, Natalia Chakma and Sheen Zutshi, 'Foundational Literacy and Numeracy', *Economic Advisory Council to the Prime Minister* (2023). https://eacpm.gov.in/wp-content/uploads/2023/02/FLN-report-For-Web.pdf.
38. Michael Kremer, Nazmul Chaudhury, F. Halsey Rogers, Karthik Muralidharan, and Jeffrey Hammer, 'Teacher Absence in India: A Snapshot.' *Journal of the European Economic Association* 3, no. 2 (1 April 2005): 658–67. https://doi.org/10.1162/1542476054473143.
39. Karthik Muralidharan, Jishnu Das, Alaka Holla and Aakash Mohpal, 'The Fiscal Cost of Weak Governance: Evidence from Teacher Absence in India', *Journal of Public Economics*, vol. 145, (2017): 116–135. doi:https://doi.org/10.1016/j.jpubeco.2016.11.005.
40. Jin Wang, 'The Economic Impact of Special Economic Zones: Evidence from Chinese Municipalities', *Journal of Development Economics* 101, (March 2013): 133–47. https://doi.org/10.1016/j.jdeveco.2012.10.009.
41. Aradhna Aggarwal, 'Export Processing Zones in India: Analysis of the Export Performance.' *Indian Council for Research on International Economic Relations*, 2004. https://icrier.org/pdf/wp148.pdf.
42. Sarbajit Chaudhuri, and Ujjaini Mukhopadhyay, 'FDI, SEZ and Agriculture.' *In Foreign Direct Investment in Developing Countries,* 79–100. New Delhi: Springer India (2014). https://doi.org/10.1007/978-81-322-1898-2_4.
43. Shraddha Sathe and Morrison Handley-Schachler, 'Social and Cultural Factors in FDI Flows: Evidence from the Indian States', *World Review of Entrepreneurship, Management and Sustainable Development* 2, no. 4 (2006): 323. https://doi.org/10.1504/wremsd.2006.010217.
44. R Murty and K S Chalapati Rao, 'Towards Understanding the State-wise Distribution of FDI in Post Liberalization Periods.' *ISID Working paper* (2006).
45. Vani Archana, Narayan Chandra Nayak, and P Basu, 'Impact of Fdi in India: State-Wise Analysis in an Econometric Framework', *Global Journal of Human-Social Science: E Economic* 14, no. 2, (2014): 15–24.

46. K. V. Bhanumurthy and Manoj Kumar Sinha, 'Equity and
     Efficiency of Foreign Direct Investment in Indian States', *Publishing
     India* (2014). http://www.publishingindia.com/GetBrochure.
     aspx?query=UERGQnJvY2h1cmVzfC8yMjA1LnBkZnwv
     MjlwNS5wZGY=.

47. Tamali Chakraborty, Haripriya Gundimeda and Vinish Kathuria,
     'Have the Special Economic Zones Succeeded in Attracting
     FDI?—Analysis for India', *Theoretical Economics Letters* 07, no. 03
     (2017): 623–42. https://doi.org/10.4236/tel.2017.73047.

48. Albert O. Hirschman, 'The changing tolerance for income
     inequality in the course of economic development', In *World
     Development,* Vol. 1, no. 12,(1973): 29–36.

49. Hiranmoy Roy and Kaushik Bhattacharjee, 'Convergence of Human
     Development across Indian States: Quantitative Approaches to
     Public Policy' Fourth Annual International Conference on 'Public
     Policy and Management', IIM, Bangalore, (9-12 August, 2009)
     http://www.igidr.ac.in/pdf/publication/PP-062-22.pdf.

50. Ajit Nag and Jalandhar Pradhan, 'Does Club Convergence
     Matter? Empirical Evidence on Inequality in the Human
     Development Index among Indian States,' *Humanities and Social
     Sciences Communications* 10, no. 1 (19 January 2023). https://doi.
     org/10.1057/s41599-023-01518-z.

51. Michael E. Porter, Scott Stern, and Michael Green, 'Social
     Progress Index 2014.' *Social Progress Imperative* (2014).
     https://www.socialprogress.org/static/d4f7102775ee71
     fa6ebab1926009072a/2014-social-progress-index.pdf.

52. Amit Kapoor and Michael Green, 'Social Progress Index: States and
     Districts of India.' *Economic Advisory Council to the Prime Minister*
     (2022). https://eacpm.gov.in/wp-content/uploads/2022/12/Social_
     Progress_Index_States_and_Districts_of_India.pdf

Chapter 7: Rewiring the Institutions in India

1.   North, Douglass Cecil. *Institutions, Institutional Change and
     Economic Performance: Political Economy of Institutions and
     Decisions* (Cambridge: Cambridge University Press, 1990).

2.   Subramanian, Arvin. 'The Evolution of Institutions in India and Its Relationship with Economic Growth.' *Oxford Review of Economic Policy 23*, no. 2 (1 June 2007): 196–220. https://doi.org/10.1093/oxrep/grm014.

3.   North, Douglass C., and Robert Paul Thomas. *The Rise of the Western World: A New Economic History*, 1976. https://doi.org/10.1604/9780521290999.

4.   Ibid.

5.   Ibid.

6.   Hall, R. E., and C. I. Jones. 'Why Do Some Countries Produce So Much More Output Per Worker than Others?' *The Quarterly Journal of Economics 114*, no. 1 (1 February 1999): 83–116. https://doi.org/10.1162/003355399555954.

7.   Acemoglu, Daron, Simon Johnson, and James Robinson. 'Institutions as the Fundamental Cause of Long-Run Growth,' May 2004. https://doi.org/10.3386/w10481.

8.   Kapur, Devesh, Pratap Bhanu Mehta, and Milan Vaishnav, eds. *Rethinking Public Institutions in India*. Oxford University Press, 2017, 18–19.

9.   Acemoglu, Daron, Simon H. Johnson, and James A. Robinson. 'The Colonial Origins of Comparative Development: An Empirical Investigation.' *SSRN Electronic Journal*, 2000. https://doi.org/10.2139/ssrn.244582.

10. Rigobon, Roberto, and Dani Rodrik. 'Rule of Law, Democracy, Openness, and Income.' *Economics of Transition 13*, no. 3 (July 2005): 533–64. https://doi.org/10.1111/j.1468-0351.2005.00226.x.

11. Subramanian, Arvind. 'The Evolution of Institutions in India and Its Relationship with Economic Growth.' *Oxford Review of Economic Policy 23*, no. 2 (1 June 2007): 196–220. https://doi.org/10.1093/oxrep/grm014.

12. Pritchett, Lant. 'Is India a Flailing State? : Detours on the Four Lane Highway to Modernization.' *SSRN Electronic Journal*, 2009, 31–33.

13. Kapur, Devesh, Pratap Bhanu Mehta, and Milan Vaishnav, eds. *Rethinking Public Institutions in India*. Oxford University Press, 2017, 193–195.

14. Agarwal, O.P & T. Somanathan. *Public Policy Making in India: Issues and Remedies*. (2005).

15. Kapur, Devesh, Pratap Bhanu Mehta, and Milan Vaishnav, eds. *Rethinking Public Institutions in India*. Oxford University Press, 2017, 193–195.

16. Jessica S. Wallack, 'India's Parliament as a Representative Institution', *India Review* 7, no. 2 (26 May 2008): 91–114, https://doi.org/10.1080/14736480802055422.

17. Ibid.

18. Ibid.

19. Ibid.

20. Ibid.

21. World Bank. (2000). Overview of rural decentralization in India (Vol. 1).

22. Kaliappa Kalirajan and Keijiro Otsuka, 'Fiscal Decentralization and Development Outcomes in India: An Exploratory Analysis', *World Development* 40, no. 8 (August 2012): 1511–21, https://doi.org/10.1016/j.worlddev.2012.04.005.

23. Rao, M. Govinda. 'Fiscal Federalism in India — Trends and Reform.' Decentralization Policies in Asian Development, December 2008, 107–40. https://doi.org/10.1142/9789812818645_0005.

24. Sen, Amartya, and Jean Drèze. *India: Economic Development and Social Opportunity*, Oxford University Press, 1996.

25. Kalirajan, Kaliappa, and Keijiro Otsuka. 'Fiscal Decentralization and Development Outcomes in India: An Exploratory Analysis.' *World Development* 40, no. 8 (August 2012): 1511–21. https://doi.org/10.1016/j.worlddev.2012.04.005.

26. Xavier, Fernanda Andrade de, Aparna P. Lolayekar, and Pranab Mukhopadhyay. 'Decentralization and Its Impact on Growth in India.' *Journal of South Asian Development* 16, no. 1 (April 2021): 130–51. https://doi.org/10.1177/09731741211013210.

27. Bidyut Chakrabarty, 'Localizing Governance in India: Pros and Cons', *International Journal of Urban Sciences* 19, no. 2 (4 May 2015): 192–205, https://doi.org/10.1080/12265934.2014.985699.

28. Nirvikar Singh, 'Fiscal Federalism and Decentralization in India', *SSRN Electronic Journal*, 2007, https://doi.org/10.2139/ssrn.1282267.

29. Kaliappa Kalirajan and Keijiro Otsuka, 'Fiscal Decentralization and Development Outcomes in India: An Exploratory Analysis',

World Development 40, no. 8 (August 2012): 1511–21, https://doi.org/10.1016/j.worlddev.2012.04.005.

30. Reddy, Y. Venugopal, and G. Ram Reddy. *Indian Fiscal Federalism*, Oxford University Press, 2019.

31. Jha, Ajay Narayan, 2021. 'Continuity with Change: Approach of the Fifteenth Finance Commission,' Working Papers 21/342, National Institute of Public Finance and Policy.

32. Ibid.

33. Kapur, Devesh, Pratap Bhanu Mehta, and Milan Vaishnav, eds. *Rethinking Public Institutions in India*. Oxford University Press, 2017.

34. Rai, Vinod. *Rethinking Good Governance*, Rupa Publications, 2019.

35. Linda Y. C. Lim, 'Fifty Years of Development in the Singapore Economy: An Introductory Review', *The Singapore Economic Review* 60, no. 03 (August 2015): 1502002, https://doi.org/10.1142/S0217590815020026.

36. Ibid.

37. Jaime Bueno Miranda, 'How Can Colombia Become More Competitive?', World Economic Forum, 17 June 2016, https://www.weforum.org/agenda/2016/06/how-colombia-has-become-more-competitive/.

38. Government of Peru, 'Consejo Nacional de Competitividad y Formalización', gob.pe, 8 May 2022, https://www.gob.pe/983-consejo-nacional-de-competitividad-y-formalizacion.

39. Department of the Taoiseach, Government of Ireland, 'Department of the Taoiseach Strategy Statement 2021-2023', 26 March 2021.

40. Ibid.

41. Ibid.

42. Subu. V. Subramanian et al., 'Progress on Sustainable Development Goal Indicators in 707 Districts of India: A Quantitative Mid-Line Assessment Using the National Family Health Surveys, 2016 and 2021', *The Lancet Regional Health - Southeast Asia* 13 (June 2023): 100155, https://doi.org/10.1016/j.lansea.2023.100155.

43. NITI Aayog and United Nations, 'Localising SDGs Early Lessons From 2019' (NITI Aayog, 2019).

Chapter 8: The Guiding Forces

1. Majumdar, Dr Rukmi. Deloitte Insights. 'India Economic Outlook, October 2023,' https://www2.deloitte.com/us/en/insights/economy/asia-pacific/india-economic-outlook.html.

2. Press Information Bureau, 'India retains 40th rank in the Global Innovation Index 2023'. NITI Aayog. (2023).

3. Shorrocks, Anthony, Rodrigo Lluberas, James Davies, Daniel Waldenström. *Global Wealth Report.* Credit Suisse and Union Bank of Switzerland, 2023.

4. Kapoor, Amit, and Sanjeet Singh. *Export Preparedness Index 2022.* NITI Aayog and Institute for Competitiveness, 2023.

5. Michael E. Porter, Christian H.M. Ketels, Amit Kapoor, 'Competitiveness Roadmap for India@100.' *Institute for Competitiveness,* 24 August 2022. https://competitiveness.in/wp-content/uploads/2022/08/Report_Competitiveness_Roadmap-25_August_2022_Web_Version.pdf.

6. Oliver Cann, 'What Is Competitiveness?' *World Economic Forum* (2016). https://www.weforum.org/agenda/2016/09/what-is-competitiveness/.

7. Press Information Bureau, 'Global Competitiveness Index'. Ministry of Commerce and Industry, 2019.

8. Schwab, Klaus and Saadia Zahidi. *The Global Competitiveness Report : How Countries are Performing on the Road to recovery.* World Economic Forum, 2020.

9. Press Information Bureau. 'Several landmark initiatives taken up under NEP 2020 for the transformation of Education Sector'. Ministry of Education. 2022.

10. Press Information Bureau. 'Providing Education to all children'. Ministry of Education. 2021.

11. Srivastava, Prachi and Claire Noronha. 'The myth of free and barrier-free access: India's Right to Education Act—private schooling costs and household experiences'. In *Non-State Actors in Education in the Global South*, pp. 71–88, Routledge, 2018.

12. Press Information Bureau. 'Ministry of Education releases All India Survey on Higher Education (AISHE) 2020-2021'. Ministry of Education, 2023.

13.   World Economic Forum. 'India Is Failing 175 Million of Its Young People. Here's the Solution', n.d. https://www.weforum.org/agenda/2019/04/india-is-failing-175-million-of-its-young-people/.

14.   Saini, Vandana. 'Skill Development in India. Needs, Challenges and Ways Forward'. *Abhinav National Refereed Journal for Research in Arts and Education.* Volume 4, Issue 4 (2015).

15.   'National Education Policy 2020'. Ministry of Human Resource Development. 2020.

16.   Press information Bureau. 'Government committed to equip workforce with employable skills and knowledge in mission mode.' Ministry of Finance. 2023.

17.   Soni, Rachal. 'Challenges and issues in New Education Policy 2020.' *International Research Journal of Modernization in Engineering Technology and Science.* Vol.3, Issue 4 (2023): 2026–31.

18.   Athar, Sohaib, Roland White and Harsh Goyal. 'Financing India's urban infrastructure needs: Constraints to commercial financing and prospects for policy action.' World Economic Forum, 2021.

19.   Michael E. Porter, Christian H.M. Ketels, Amit Kapoor, 'Competitiveness Roadmap for India@100.' *Institute for Competitiveness*, 24 August 2022. https://competitiveness.in/wp-content/uploads/2022/08/Report_Competitiveness_Roadmap-25_August_2022_Web_Version.pdf.

20.   Press Information Bureau. 'India is committed to achieve the Net Zero emissions target by 2070 as announced by PM Modi, says Dr. Jitendra Singh'. Ministry of Science and Technology. 2023.

21.   Power Sector at a Glance ALL INDIA | Government of India | Ministry of Power, n.d. https://powermin.gov.in/en/content/power-sector-glance-all-india.

22.   The *Times of India.* 'India Seen Facing Wider Coal Shortages, Worsening Power Outage Risks - Times of India,' n.d. https://timesofindia.indiatimes.com/business/india-business/india-seen-facing-wider-coal-shortages-worsening-power-outage-risks/articleshow/91842445.cms.

23.   Allcott, Hunt, Allan Collard Wexler and Stephen D. O' Connell. 'How do electricity shortages affect industry? Evidence from India.' *American Economic Review.* Vol. 106, No. 03 (2016): 587–624.

24. 'India Needs a Resilient Power Sector: Lessons from the Covid-19 Crisis – Analysis - IEA,' n.d. https://www.iea.org/commentaries/india-needs-a-resilient-power-sector-lessons-from-the-covid-19-crisis.

25. Press Information Bureau. 'Story of India being a developing country is a thing of the past, we are now vying with the best; Story true of infrastructure as well: Union Minister for Power and New & Renewable Energy, Shri R. K. Singh.' Ministry of Power. 2023.

26. World Bank. 'India Transportation', n.d. https://www.worldbank.org/en/news/feature/2011/09/23/india-transportation.

27. Press Information Bureau. 'Capital expenditure outlay for 2022-23 increased sharply by 35.4 % with approximately 67 per cent spent between April - December 2022' Ministry of Finance, 2023.

28. India Development Review. 'Reimagining How India's MSMEs Access Credit | IDR,' 8 August 2023. https://idronline.org/article/ecosystem-development/reimagining-how-indias-msmes-access-credit/.

29. Vishwanathan, N.S. 'Asset Quality of Indian banks: Way forward'. RBI Bulletin, 2016.

30. *Understanding the IBC: Key Jurisprudence and Practical Considerations.* Insolvency and Bankruptcy Board of India, 2016.

31. Ibid.

32. World Bank. 'Scores', n.d. https://archive.doingbusiness.org/en/scores.

33. Forbes, Naushad. 'Doing Business in India: What has liberalization changed'. Paper presented at the Center for Research on Economic Development and Policy Reform Conference on Indian Economic Prospects: Advancing Policy Reform. Stanford Center for International Development, Stanford University, United States of America, 2001.

34. *Economy profile: India. Doing Business Report 2020.* World Bank Group, 2020.

35. Press Information Bureau. 'India Improves Rank by 23 Positions in Ease of Doing Business.' Ministry of Commerce and Industry. 2018.

36. Ray, Gautam. '*Doing Business in India: Opportunities and Challenges*', *Journal of Marketing Development and Competitiveness, 5* (2011).

37. Economic Survey 2022–23. Ministry of Finance, Government of India, 2023.

38. Kilgore, J. Michael, Abraham Joseph and Jeff Metersky. 'The logistical challenges of doing business in India.' *Supply Chain Management Review* 11 (2007).

39. Rapley, John. *Understanding Development: Theory and Practice in the Third World.* Lynne Rynner Publishers, 2007.

40. Bhattacharya, Saugata and Urjit R. Patel. 'Markets, regulatory institutions, competitiveness and reforms'. Paper presented at the Workshop on Understanding Reform Global Development Network, Cairo, Egypt, 16–17 January 2003.

41. Conway, Paul, and Richard Herd. 'How Competitive Is Product Market Regulation in India?' OECD Journal: Economic Studies 2009, no. 1 (15 October 2009): 1–25. https://doi.org/10.1787/eco_studies-v2009-art6-en.

42. Kannan, K.P. *Country report : India. Labor Laws and Growth of Micro and Medium Enterprises.* International Labor Organisation, 2014.

43. Ibid.

44. Kaufmann, Daniel and Ana Belver. 'Transparenting and Transparency: Intial Empirics and Policy Applications'. *SSRN Electronic Journal,* 10.2139, 2005.

45. Goldar, Bishwanath and Etsuro Ishigami. 'Foreign direct investment in Asia'. *Economic and Political Weekly,* Vol. 34, No. 22 (29 May–4 June 1999).

46. Press Information Bureau. 'FTAs'. Ministry of Commerce and Industry. 2022.

47. Press Information Bureau. 'India-UAE Comprehensive Economic Partnership Agreement (CEPA) enters into force'. Ministry of Commerce and Industry. 2022.

48. Press Information Bureau. 'India – Canada to re-launch the Comprehensive Economic Partnership Agreement (CEPA) negotiations to unlock full potential of bilateral trade'. Ministry of Commerce and Industry. 2022.

49. *Annual Report 2022-23.* DPIIT, Ministry of Commerce and Industry. Government of India, 2023.

50. *Business Line.* 'Analysing India's FDI Flows', 12 September 2023. https://www.thehindubusinessline.com/opinion/indias-fdi-boom-raises-questions/article67300099.ece.

51. Press Information Bureau. 'Singapore (27.01%), USA (17.94%), Mauritius (15.98%), Netherland (7.86%) and Switzerland (7.31%) emerge as top 5 countries for FDI equity inflows into India FY 2021-22.' Ministry of Commerce and Industry. 2022.

52. 'Consolidated FDI Policy'. DPIIT, Ministry of Commerce and Industry. Government of India, 2020.

53. Press Information Bureau. 'FTAs'. Ministry of Commerce and Industry. 2022.

54. Shehshadri, V.S., 'India's International Trade: Trends and Perspective'. *Indian Foreign Affairs Journal,* Vol. 12, No. 3 (July–September 2017): pp. 181–201.

55. Ministry of Commerce and Trade. https://dashboard.commerce.gov.in/commercedashboard.aspx.

56. Kapoor, Amit, and Sanjeet Singh. *Export Preparedness Index 2022.* NITI Aayog and Institute for Competitiveness, 2023.

57. Ibid.

58. Kapoor, Amit and Michael Green. *Social Progress Index: States and Districts of India.* Economic Advisory Council to the Prime Minister, 2022.

59. Bhattacharya, Sharanya, John Blomquist and Rinku Murgai. 'Poverty to Vulnerability: Rebalancing Social Protection In India.' In the *Pathways to Reducing Poverty and Shared Prosperity In India,* pp. 4–6. World Bank Group, 2019.

60. Economic Survey 2021–22. Ministry of FInance, Government of India, 2022.

61. Chakraborty, Judhajit and R. Nagaraj, 'Has India Deindustrialised Prematurely? A Disaggregated Analysis'. *Economic and Political Weekly,* Vol. 55, Issue No. 48 (5 December 2020), https://www.epw.in/journal/2020/48/special-articles/has-india-deindustrialised-prematurely.html.

62. Rodrik, Dani. 'Premature Deindustrialization'. John F. Kennedy School of Government, Harvard University, 2015.

63. Murthy, S.V.R. 'Measuring Informal Economy in India : Indian Experience'. Paper presented at the 7th IMF Statistics Forum : Measuring the Informal Economy, Washington D.C., United States of America, 14–15 November 2019.

64. Michael E. Porter, Christian H.M. Ketels, Amit Kapoor, 'Competitiveness Roadmap for India@100.' *Institute for Competitiveness*, 24 August 2022. https://competitiveness.in/wp-content/uploads/2022/08/Report_Competitiveness_Roadmap-25_August_2022_Web_Version.pdf.

65. Stiglitz, Joseph E., Amartya Sen and Jean- Paul Fitoussi. *Report by the Commission on the Measurement of Economic Performance and Social Progress.* CMEPSP, 2009.

66. Stiglitz Joseph E., Jean-Paul Fitoussi and Martine Durand, *Beyond GDP: Measuring What Counts for Economic and Social Performance.* OECD, 2018.

67. Michael E. Porter, Christian H.M. Ketels, Amit Kapoor, 'Competitiveness Roadmap for India@100.' Institute for Competitiveness, 24 August 2022. https://competitiveness.in/wp-content/uploads/2022/08/Report_Competitiveness_Roadmap-25_August_2022_Web_Version.pdf.

68. *India Energy Outlook 2021.* International Energy Agency, 2021.

69. KPMG. 'Immediate and Long-Term Impacts of the Russia-Ukraine War on Supply Chains', n.d. https://kpmg.com/us/en/articles/2022/impacts-russia-ukraine-war-supply-chains.html.

70. *India Development Update: Navigating the Storm.* The World Bank Group, 2022.

71. Michael E. Porter, Christian H.M. Ketels, Amit Kapoor, 'Competitiveness Roadmap for India@100.' *Institute for Competitiveness*, 24 August 2022. https://competitiveness.in/wp-content/uploads/2022/08/Report_Competitiveness_Roadmap-25_August_2022_Web_Version.pdf.

72. World Bank. 'India Better Positioned to Navigate Global Headwinds Than Other Major Emerging Economies: New World Bank Report', n.d. https://www.worldbank.org/en/news/press-release/2022/12/05/india-better-positioned-to-navigate-global-headwinds-than-other-major-emerging-economies-new-world-bank-report.

73. Michael E. Porter, Christian H.M. Ketels, Amit Kapoor, 'Competitiveness Roadmap for India@100.' *Institute for Competitiveness*, 24 August 2022. https://competitiveness.in/wp-content/uploads/2022/08/Report_Competitiveness_Roadmap-25_August_2022_Web_Version.pdf.

74. Ibid.

75. Ibid.

76. Ibid.

77. Ibid.

78. Ibid.

79. Ibid.

80. Ibid.

81. United Nations, 'Taking a Whole-of-Government Approach', in *United Nations E-Government Survey 2012*, by United Nations, United Nations E-Government Survey (UN, 2012), 55–71, https://doi.org/10.18356/abdf024f-en.

82. Tom Christensen and Per Lægreid, 'The Whole-of-Government Approach to Public Sector Reform', *Public Administration Review* 67, no. 6 (2007): 1059–66.

83. United Nations, 'Taking a Whole-of-Government Approach', in *United Nations E-Government Survey 2012*, by United Nations, United Nations E-Government Survey (UN, 2012), 55–71, https://doi.org/10.18356/abdf024f-en.

84. Ibid.

85. Ibid.

Chapter 9: The Road Ahead: India's Odyssey to Prosperity

1. Michael E. Porter, Christian H.M. Ketels, Amit Kapoor, 'Competitiveness Roadmap for India@100.' *Institute for Competitiveness*, 24 August 2022. https://competitiveness.in/wp-content/uploads/2022/08/Report_Competitiveness_Roadmap-25_August_2022_Web_Version.pdf.

2. Ibid.

3. Gurcharan Das, *India Unbound*, (Penguin India, 2000), p. 103.

Acknowledgements

The genesis of this book originated from the lecture series organized by NITI Aayog, 'Transforming India', that set the stage for a crucial meeting in May 2017 between the Hon'ble Prime Minister and Professor Michael E. Porter of Harvard Business School. This encounter laid the foundation for the ambitious 'India Competitiveness Initiative' and set forth a visionary goal for India's growth over the next twenty-five years—'policies to aggressively push the nation towards middle-income and beyond by 2047.' As we reflect on the evolution from that meeting to the completion of this book, our gratitude extends to the multitude of individuals and organizations whose collaborative efforts have shaped its content and purpose.

Very few have impacted the discipline of competitiveness and strategy as profoundly as Professor Michael E. Porter. His pioneering work in these areas has not only reshaped academic discourse but has also become a cornerstone for businesses and policymakers globally. Professor Porter's insightful frameworks have provided invaluable guidance, fostering a paradigm shift in how countries approach competition and strategic planning. It is with great reverence that we dedicate this book to the enduring legacy of his work, which continues to influence and elevate the landscape of economic thought and practice on a global scale. Additionally, we acknowledge Professor Christian H.M. Ketels's work, whose visionary insights refined the ideas presented within this book.

We extend our sincere thanks to the Economic Advisory Council to the Prime Minister (EAC-PM) and all the dedicated members and stakeholders instrumental in crafting the 'Competitiveness Roadmap for India@100.' This foundational work serves as the bedrock for the themes explored in this book. We extend special thanks to Bibek Debroy, Chairman of EAC-PM, whose invaluable contributions have been instrumental in propelling this project forward.

The indispensable contributions of the research team at the Institute for Competitiveness, including Natalia Chakma, Shivani Kowadkar, Navya Kumar, Sheen Zutshi, Subhanshi Negi, Teesta Bose, Nabha Joshi, Kartik, Anshul Sharma, Taneesha Shekhawat, Khushi Joshi, Meenakshi Ajith, and Jessica Duggal, played a crucial role in providing the necessary insights and data that enrich the narrative. We acknowledge the support and contributions of Ranveer Nagaich and Rajeshwari Sahay.

Richard Dasher, Director of the US-Asia Technology Management Center, and co-author Amit Kapoor collaborate on ideas pertaining to economic systems and jointly teach at Stanford University. Discussions with Richard have been instrumental in shaping and enriching the content of this book. In addition, the learnings derived from this book are not confined to its pages alone. They form the basis for a forthcoming course on innovation and competitiveness at Stanford. This extension into academia underscores the practical application of our research and the desire for our work to inspire future generations.

This book, positioned as the first instalment in a comprehensive series, extends beyond a standalone work. It is an intricate tapestry woven through collaborations and dialogues that have unfolded over the last six years. The series will delve deeper into critical aspects such as heterogeneity, India's strategic imperatives and the challenges of inequality.

This work is not only a reflection of our commitment to shaping India's journey towards prosperity and inclusive development but also serves as a testament to the collaborative spirit that defines the pursuit of knowledge and progress. The overarching aspiration for this book series is to serve as a thinking model for economies as we navigate the complexities of the future. We envision its impact extending beyond the immediate context, influencing and guiding economic thought globally.

We express our deepest appreciation to the meticulous editorial team at Penguin, led by Manish Kumar, whose dedication and precision have played a key role in bringing this book to fruition. Finally, heartfelt thanks to our spouses, Neera Kapoor and Ranjeeta Kant, for being constant sources of encouragement throughout this transformative journey.

Scan QR code to access the
Penguin Random House India website